The Java™
Programming Language

Second Edition

W9-BRV-842

The Java™ Series

Lisa Friendly, Series Editor
Tim Lindholm, Technical Editor
Please see our web site (http://www.awl.com /cseng/javaseries) for more information on these titles.

Ken Arnold and James Gosling, *The Java™ Programming Language, Second Edition*
ISBN 0-201-31006-6

Mary Campione and Kathy Walrath, *The Java™ Tutorial, Second Edition: Object-Oriented Programming for the Internet* (Book/CD)
ISBN 0-201-31007-4

Mary Campione, Kathy Walrath, Alison Huml, and the Tutorial Team, *The Java™ Tutorial Continued: The Rest of the JDK™* (Book/CD)
ISBN 0-201-48558-3

Patrick Chan, *The Java™ Developers Almanac 1999*
ISBN 0-201-43298-6

Patrick Chan and Rosanna Lee, *The Java™ Class Libraries, Second Edition, Volume 2: java.applet, java.awt, java.beans*
ISBN 0-201-31003-1

Patrick Chan, Rosanna Lee, and Doug Kramer, *The Java™ Class Libraries, Second Edition, Volume 1: java.io, java.lang, java.math, java.net, java.text, java.util*
ISBN 0-201-31002-3

Patrick Chan, Rosanna Lee, and Doug Kramer, *The Java™ Class Libraries, Second Edition, Volume 1: Supplement for the Java™ 2 Platform, Standard Edition, v1.2*
ISBN 0-201-48552-4

Li Gong, *Inside Java™ 2 Platform Security: Architecture, API Design, and Implementation*
ISBN 0-201-31000-7

James Gosling, Bill Joy, and Guy Steele, *The Java™ Language Specification*
ISBN 0-201-63451-1

James Gosling, Frank Yellin, and The Java Team, *The Java™ Application Programming Interface, Volume 1: Core Packages*
ISBN 0-201-63453-8

James Gosling, Frank Yellin, and The Java Team, *The Java™ Application Programming Interface, Volume 2: Window Toolkit and Applets*
ISBN 0-201-63459-7

Jonni Kanerva, *The Java™ FAQ*
ISBN 0-201-63456-2

Doug Lea, *Concurrent Programming in Java™, Second Edition: Design Principles and Patterns*
ISBN 0-201-31009-0

Sheng Liang, *The Java™ Native Interface: Programmer's Guide and Specification*
ISBN 0-201-32577-2

Tim Lindholm and Frank Yellin, *The Java™ Virtual Machine Specification, Second Edition*
ISBN 0-201-43294-3

Henry Sowizral, Kevin Rushforth, and Michael Deering, *The Java™ 3D API Specification*
ISBN 0-201-32576-4

Kathy Walrath and Mary Campione, *The JFC Swing Tutorial: A Guide to Constructing GUIs*
ISBN 0-201-43321-4

Seth White, Maydene Fisher, Rick Cattell, Graham Hamilton, and Mark Hapner, *JDBC™ API Tutorial and Reference, Second Edition: Universal Data Access for the Java™ 2 Platform*
ISBN 0-201-43328-1

The Java™ Programming Language

Second Edition

Ken Arnold
James Gosling

ADDISON-WESLEY

An imprint of Addison Wesley Longman, Inc.

Reading, Massachusetts • Harlow, England • Menlo Park, California
Berkeley, California • Don Mills, Ontario • Sydney
Bonn • Amsterdam • Tokyo • Mexico City

© 1998 SUN MICROSYSTEMS, INC.
2550 GARCIA AVENUE, MOUNTAIN VIEW, CALIFORNIA 94043-1100 U.S.A.
All rights reserved.

RESTRICTED RIGHTS LEGEND: Use, duplication, or disclosure by the United States Government is subject to the restrictions set forth in DFARS 252.227-7013 (c)(1)(ii) and FAR 52.227-19.

The release described in this book may be protected by one or more U.S. patents, foreign patents, or pending applications.

Sun Microsystems, Inc. (SUN) hereby grants to you a fully-paid, nonexclusive, nontransferable, perpetual, worldwide limited license (without the right to sublicense) under SUN's intellectual property rights that are essential to practice this specification. This license allows and is limited to the creation and distribution of clean room implementations of this specification that: (i) include a complete implementation of the current version of this specification without subsetting or supersetting; (ii) implement all the interfaces and functionality of the standard java.* packages as defined by SUN, without subsetting or supersetting; (iii) do not add any additional packages, classes or methods to the java.* packages; (iv) pass all test suites relating to the most recent published version of this specification that are available from SUN six (6) months prior to any beta release of the clean room implementation or upgrade thereto; (v) do not derive from SUN source code or binary materials; and (vi) do not include any SUN binary materials without an appropriate and separate license from SUN.

Sun, Sun Microsystems, Sun Microsystems Computer Corporation, the Sun logo, the Sun Microsystems Computer Corporation logo, Java, JavaSoft, JavaScript JDBC, JDBC Compliant, JavaOS, JavaBeans and HotJava are trademarks or registered trademarks of Sun Microsystems, Inc. UNIX® is a registered trademark in the United States and other countries, exclusively licensed through X/Open Company, Ltd. Apple and Dylan are trademarks of Apple Computer, Inc. All other product names mentioned herein are the trademarks of their respective owners.

THIS PUBLICATION IS PROVIDED "AS IS" WITHOUT WARRANTY OF ANY KIND, EITHER EXPRESS OR IMPLIED, INCLUDING, BUT NOT LIMITED TO, THE IMPLIED WARRANTIES OF MERCHANT-ABILITY, FITNESS FOR A PARTICULAR PURPOSE, OR NON-INFRINGEMENT.

THIS PUBLICATION COULD INCLUDE TECHNICAL INACCURACIES OR TYPOGRAPHICAL ERRORS. CHANGES ARE PERIODICALLY ADDED TO THE INFORMATION HEREIN; THESE CHANGES WILL BE INCORPORATED IN NEW EDITIONS OF THE PUBLICATION. SUN MICROSYS-TEMS, INC. MAY MAKE IMPROVEMENTS AND/OR CHANGES IN THE PRODUCT(S) AND/OR THE PROGRAM(S) DESCRIBED IN THIS PUBLICATION AT ANY TIME.

Library of Congress Cataloging-in-Publication Data
Arnold, Ken
      The Java programming langauge / Ken Arnold, James Gosling. -- [2nd ed.]
          p.   cm. -- (The Java series)
      Includes index.
      ISBN 0-201-31006-6
      1. Java (Computer program language) I. Gosling, James.
  II. Title. III. Series.
  QA76.73.J38A76 1997
  005.13'3--dc21   97-43181
                                                            CIP

The publisher offers discounts on this book when ordered in quantity for special sales. For more information, please contact: Corporate and Professional Publishing Group; Addison Wesley Longman, Inc.; One Jacob Way; Reading, Massachusetts 01867.

Text printed on recycled and acid-free paper.

ISBN 0201310066

7 8 9 101112 MA   03 02 01 00

7th Printing   February 2000

This book is dedicated to the Java team
From whose hard work and vision
A mighty oak has grown

To Susan—*K.A.*

To Judy and Kate—*J.A.G.*

Contents

1 A Quick Tour of Java **1**

1.1 Getting Started 1
1.2 Variables 3
1.3 Comments in Code 5
1.4 Named Constants 5
    1.4.1 Unicode Characters 6
1.5 Flow of Control 7
1.6 Classes and Objects 9
    1.6.1 Creating Objects 10
    1.6.2 Static or Class Fields 11
    1.6.3 The Garbage Collector 11
1.7 Methods and Parameters 12
    1.7.1 Invoking a Method 12
    1.7.2 The `this` Reference 13
    1.7.3 Static or Class Methods 14
1.8 Arrays 14
1.9 String Objects 16
1.10 Extending a Class 18
    1.10.1 Invoking Methods from the Superclass 19
    1.10.2 The `Object` Class 20
1.11 Interfaces 20
1.12 Exceptions 22
1.13 Packages 24
1.14 The Java Platform 26
1.15 Other Topics Briefly Noted 27

2 Classes and Objects **29**

2.1 A Simple Class 30
2.2 Fields 30
2.3 Access Control and Inheritance 31

2.4   Creating Objects 32
2.5   Constructors 33
2.6   Methods 36
         2.6.1   Parameter Values 38
         2.6.2   Using Methods to Control Access 41
2.7   this 42
2.8   Overloading Methods 44
2.9   Static Members 44
2.10   Initialization Blocks 46
2.11   Garbage Collection and finalize 47
         2.11.1   finalize 48
         2.11.2   Resurrecting Objects during finalize 50
2.12   Nested Classes and Interfaces 50
         2.12.1   Local Inner Classes 53
2.13   main 55
2.14   The toString Method 56
2.15   Native Methods 57

3   Extending Classes 59
3.1   An Extended Class 59
3.2   What protected Really Means 63
3.3   Constructors in Extended Classes 64
         3.3.1   Constructor Order Dependencies 65
3.4   Overriding Methods, Hiding Fields, and Nested Classes 67
         3.4.1   The super Keyword 70
3.5   Marking Methods and Classes final 71
3.6   The Object Class 73
3.7   Anonymous Classes 74
3.8   Abstract Classes and Methods 75
3.9   Cloning Objects 77
3.10   Extending Classes: How and When 82
3.11   Designing a Class to Be Extended 83

4   Interfaces 91
4.1   An Example Interface 91
4.2   Single Inheritance versus Multiple Inheritance 94
4.3   Extending Interfaces 95
         4.3.1   Name Conflicts 96
4.4   Implementing Interfaces 97
4.5   Using an Implementation 99
4.6   Marker Interfaces 100
4.7   When to Use Interfaces 101

5   Tokens, Operators, and Expressions **103**

   5.1   Character Set 103

   5.2   Comments 104

   5.3   Tokens 105

   5.4   Identifiers 106

        5.4.1   Java Keywords 106

   5.5   Primitive Types 107

   5.6   Literals 107

        5.6.1   Object References 108

        5.6.2   Boolean 108

        5.6.3   Integers 108

        5.6.4   Floating-Point Numbers 108

        5.6.5   Characters 109

        5.6.6   Strings 109

        5.6.7   Class Literals 110

   5.7   Declarations of Variables 110

        5.7.1   Using `final` for Variables 111

        5.7.2   The Meanings of Names 112

   5.8   Array Variables 114

        5.8.1   Arrays of Arrays 116

   5.9   Initial Values 117

        5.9.1   Array Initializers 117

   5.10   Operator Precedence and Associativity 118

   5.11   Order of Evaluation 120

   5.12   Expression Type 121

   5.13   Type Conversions 121

        5.13.1   Implicit Conversion 121

        5.13.2   Explicit Casts and `instanceof` 122

        5.13.3   String Conversions 125

   5.14   Member Access 125

   5.15   Arithmetic Operators 128

        5.15.1   Integer Arithmetic 128

        5.15.2   Floating-Point Arithmetic 128

        5.15.3   Java Floating-Point Arithmetic and IEEE-754 130

        5.15.4   String Concatenation 130

   5.16   Increment and Decrement Operators 131

   5.17   Relational, Equality, and Logical Operators 132

   5.18   Bitwise Operators 134

   5.19   The Conditional Operator ?: 135

   5.20   Assignment Operators 136

   5.21   Package Names 136

6   Control Flow **139**
   6.1   Statements and Blocks 139
   6.2   if-else 140
   6.3   switch 142
   6.4   while and do-while 144
   6.5   for 145
   6.6   Labels 146
   6.7   break 147
   6.8   continue 148
   6.9   return 149
   6.10   What, No goto? 149

7   Exceptions **151**
   7.1   Creating Exception Types 152
   7.2   throw 153
   7.3   The throws Clause 153
   7.4   try, catch, and finally 155
      7.4.1   finally 157
   7.5   When to Use Exceptions 159

8   Strings **161**
   8.1   Basic String Operations 161
   8.2   String Comparisons 163
   8.3   Utility Methods 166
   8.4   Making Related Strings 167
   8.5   String Conversions 169
   8.6   Strings and char Arrays 170
   8.7   Strings and byte Arrays 171
   8.8   The StringBuffer Class 172
      8.8.1   Modifying the Buffer 173
      8.8.2   Getting Data Out 175
      8.8.3   Capacity Management 176

9   Threads **179**
   9.1   Creating Threads 181
   9.2   Synchronization 183
      9.2.1   synchronized Methods 183
      9.2.2   synchronized Statements 185
   9.3   wait, notifyAll, and notify 188
   9.4   Details of wait and notify 190
   9.5   Thread Scheduling 191
   9.6   Deadlocks 194
   9.7   Ending Thread Execution 195

9.7.1 The End of a Thread's Life 195
9.7.2 Waiting for a Thread to Complete 197
9.7.3 Don't stop 198
9.7.4 Suspending Threads 199
9.8 Ending Application Execution 200
9.9 Using Runnable 201
9.10 volatile 202
9.11 Thread Security and ThreadGroup 203
9.12 Debugging Threads 207

10 Packages **209**
10.1 Package Naming 210
10.2 Package Access 211
10.3 Package Contents 212

11 Documentation Comments **215**
11.1 Paragraphs 216
11.1.1 @see 216
11.1.2 @param 217
11.1.3 @return 217
11.1.4 @exception 217
11.1.5 @deprecated 217
11.1.6 @author 218
11.1.7 @version 218
11.1.8 @since 219
11.2 An Example 219
11.3 Notes on Usage 223

12 The I/O Package **225**
12.1 Byte Streams 226
12.2 InputStream 227
12.3 OutputStream 229
12.4 Character Streams 231
12.4.1 Character Streams and the Standard Streams 231
12.5 Reader 233
12.6 Writer 235
12.7 Summary of I/O Types 236
12.8 InputStreamReader and OutputStreamWriter 237
12.9 Filter Streams 238
12.10 Print Streams 240
12.11 Buffered Streams 240
12.12 ByteArray Byte Streams 242
12.13 CharArray Character Streams 242

12.14   String Character Streams 244
12.15   File Streams and FileDescriptor 245
12.16   Piped Streams 246
12.17   SequenceInputStream 247
12.18   LineNumberReader 248
12.19   Pushback Streams 249
12.20   StreamTokenizer 250
12.21   Data Byte Streams 255
12.22   The Data Stream Classes 257
12.23   RandomAccessFile 258
12.24   The Object Byte Streams 259
        12.24.1 Making Your Classes Serializable 260
        12.24.2 Serialization and Deserialization Order 262
        12.24.3 Customized Serialization and Externalizable 263
        12.24.4 Object Versioning 265
        12.24.5 The Externalizable Interface 267
12.25   The File Class 267
        12.25.1 FilenameFilter 270
12.26   The IOException Classes 271

13   Standard Utilities **273**
13.1   BitSet 274
13.2   Enumeration 276
13.3   Implementing an Enumeration Interface 276
13.4   Vector 278
13.5   Stack 282
13.6   Dictionary 283
13.7   Hashtable 284
13.8   Properties 286
13.9   Observer/Observable 288
13.10   Random 291
13.11   StringTokenizer 292

14   Programming with Types **295**
14.1   Wrapper Classes: An Overview 296
14.2   Void 297
14.3   Boolean 297
14.4   Character 297
14.5   Number 300
14.6   The Integer Wrapper Classes 301
14.7   The Floating-Point Wrapper Classes 302
14.8   Reflection 303
        14.8.1   Class 304

14.8.2 Examining Classes 306
14.8.3 `Field` 309
14.8.4 `Method` 310
14.8.5 Creating New Objects and `Constructor` 312
14.8.6 Arrays 313
14.9 Loading Classes 315
14.9.1 Loading Related Resources 319

15 System Programming **321**
15.1 Standard I/O Streams 321
15.2 Memory Management 322
15.3 System Properties 323
15.4 Creating Processes 325
15.5 `Runtime` 329
15.6 Miscellaneous 331
15.7 Security 331
15.8 `Math` 332

16 Internationalization and Localization **335**
16.1 Locale 336
16.2 Resource Bundles 338
16.2.1 `ListResourceBundle` 340
16.2.2 `PropertyResourceBundle` 342
16.2.3 Subclassing `ResourceBundle` 343
16.3 Time, Dates, and Calendars 343
16.3.1 Calendars 344
16.3.2 Time Zones 348
16.3.3 `GregorianCalendar` and `SimpleTimeZone` 348
16.4 Formatting and Parsing Dates and Times 350

17 Standard Packages **353**
17.1 `java.text`—Internationalization and Localization for Text 354
17.1.1 Collation 354
17.1.2 Formatting and Parsing 355
17.1.3 Text Boundaries 358
17.2 `java.awt`—The Abstract Window Toolkit 359
17.3 `java.applet`—Applets 361
17.4 `java.rmi`—Remote Method Invocation 362
17.5 `java.beans`—Java Components 367
17.6 `java.net`—The Network 367
17.7 `java.math`—Mathematics 370
17.8 `java.sql`—Relational Database Access 372
17.9 `java.security`—Security Tools 372

Appendix A:
Runtime Exceptions **373**
A.1   `RuntimeException` Classes 374
A.2   `Error` Classes 375

Appendix B:
Useful Tables **377**
Table 1: Keywords 377
Table 2: Operator Precedence 378
Table 3: Unicode Digits 378
Table 4: Unicode Letters and Digits 379
Table 5: Special Characters Using \ 380
Table 6: Documentation Comment Tags 380

Further Reading **381**

Index **385**

Preface

Beautiful buildings are more than scientific. They are true organisms,
spiritually conceived; works of art, using the best technology by inspiration
rather than the idiosyncrasies of mere taste or any averaging by the committee mind.
—Frank Lloyd Wright

THE Java™ programming language (hereafter called simply Java) has been warmly received by the world community of software developers and Internet content providers. Users of the Internet and World Wide Web benefit from access to secure, platform-independent applications that can come from anywhere on the Internet. Software developers who create applications in Java benefit by developing code only once, with no need to "port" their applications to every software and hardware platform.

For many, Java was known first as a tool to create applets for the World Wide Web. *Applet* is the term Java uses for a mini-application that runs inside a Web page. An applet can perform tasks and interact with users on their browser pages without using resources from the Web server after being downloaded. Some applets may, of course, talk with the server to do their job, but that's their business.

Java is indeed valuable for distributed network environments like the Web. However, Java goes well beyond this domain to provide a powerful general-purpose programming language suitable for building a variety of applications that either do not depend on network features, or want them for different reasons. Java's ability to execute downloaded code on remote hosts in a secure manner is a critical requirement for many organizations.

Other groups use Java as a general-purpose programming language for projects in which machine independence is less important. Java's ease of programming and safety features help you quickly produce working code. Some common programming errors never occur because of features like garbage collection and type-safe references. Java's support for multithreading caters to modern network-based and graphical user interface–based applications that must attend to multiple tasks simultaneously, and the mechanisms of exception handling ease the task of dealing with error conditions. While its built-in tools are powerful, Java is a simple language in which programmers can quickly become proficient.

Java is designed for maximum portability with as few implementation dependencies as possible. An `int`, for example, is a 32-bit signed two's-complement integer in all Java implementations, irrespective of the CPU architecture on which the Java program executes. Defining everything possible about the language and its runtime environment enables users to run compiled code anywhere and share code with anyone who has a Java environment.

ABOUT THIS BOOK

This book teaches Java programming to people who are familiar with basic programming concepts. It explains Java without being arduously formal or complete. This book is not an introduction to object-oriented programming, although some issues are covered to establish a common terminology. Other books in this series, and much online documentation, focus on Java applets, databases, components, and other specific kinds of programming tasks. For other references, see "Further Reading" on page 381.

This second edition includes the changes introduced in Java 1.1, such as nested classes (including anonymous classes), threading issues, character-based streams, object serialization, documentation comments, new utility classes, and internationalization/localization. You will also find brief coverage of the other core Java packages. If you have already read the first edition, this edition will give you new information, but since most of the language is unchanged, and almost all core package types are still usable, you will want to pay most attention to the newer areas. The first chapter (the "quick tour") is largely unchanged because it covers the elemental parts of Java, which are mostly unaltered.

Java shares many language features common to most programming languages in use today. Java should look familiar to C and C++ programmers because Java was designed with C and C++ constructs where the languages are similar. That said, this book is neither a comparative analysis nor a "bridge" tutorial—no knowledge of C or C++ is assumed. C++ programmers, especially, may be as hindered by what they must unlearn as they are helped by their knowledge.

Chapter 1—*A Quick Tour of Java*—gives a quick overview of Java. Programmers who are unfamiliar with object-oriented programming notions should read the quick tour, while programmers who are already familiar with object-oriented programming paradigms will find the quick tour a useful introduction to the object-oriented features of Java.

Chapters 2, 3, and 4 cover the object-oriented core features of Java, namely, class declarations that define components of a program, and objects manufactured according to class definitions. Chapter 2—*Classes and Objects*—describes the basis of the Java language: classes. Chapter 3—*Extending Classes*—describes how an existing class can be *extended*, or *subclassed*, to create a new class with additional data and behavior. Chapter 4—*Interfaces*—describes how to declare interface types which are abstract descriptions of behavior that provide maximum flexibility for class designers and implementors.

Chapters 5 and 6 cover standard constructs common to most languages. Chapter 5—*Tokens, Operators, and Expressions*—describes the tokens of the language from which statements are constructed, how the tokens and operators are used to build expressions, and how expressions are evaluated. Chapter 6—*Control Flow*—describes how control statements direct the order of statement execution.

Chapter 7—*Exceptions*—describes Java's powerful error-handling capabilities. Chapter 8—*Strings*—describes the built-in language and runtime support for String objects.

Chapter 9—*Threads*—explains Java's implementation of multithreading. Many applications, such as graphical interface–based software, must attend to multiple tasks simultaneously. These tasks must cooperate to behave correctly, and threads meet the needs of cooperative multitasking.

Chapter 10—*Packages*—describes Java's mechanism for grouping collections of Java classes into separate packages. Chapter 11—*Documentation Comments*—shows how to write reference documentation in comments.

Chapters 12 through 15 cover the core Java packages. Chapter 12—*The I/O Package*—describes the Java input/output system, which is based on *streams*. Chapter 13—*Standard Utilities*—covers Java *utility classes* such as vectors and hashtables. Chapter 14—*Programming with Types*—describes Java's type-related classes: individual objects that describe each class and interface, and classes that wrap primitive data types such as integers and floating-point values into their own object types. Chapter 15—*System Programming*—leads you through the *system classes* that provide access to features of the underlying platform.

Chapter 16—*Internationalization and Localization*—covers some of the tools used to create programs that can run in many linguistic and cultural environments. Chapter 17—*Standard Packages*—briefly explores the packages that are part of the Java platform, giving overviews of those packages not covered in more detail in this book.

Appendix A—*Runtime Exceptions*—lists all the runtime exceptions and errors that the Java system itself can throw.

Appendix B—*Useful Tables*—has tables of information that you may find useful for quick reference.

Finally, *Further Reading* lists works that may be interesting for further reading on Java details, object orientation, programming with threads, software design, and other topics.

EXAMPLES AND DOCUMENTATION

All the code examples in the text have been compiled and run on the latest version of the language available at the time the book was written, which was version 1.1.4. Only Java 1.1.4 features are covered—deprecated types, methods, and fields are ignored except where unavoidable. We have also covered issues beyond writing programs that simply compile. Part of learning a language is to learn to use it well. For this reason, we have tried to show principles of good programming style and design.

In a few places we refer to online documentation. Java development environments provide a way to automatically generate documentation (usually HTML documents) from a compiled class using the documentation comments. This documentation is normally viewed using a Web browser.

ACKNOWLEDGMENTS (FIRST EDITION)

No technical book-writing endeavor is an island unto itself, and ours was more like a continent. Many people contributed technical help, excellent reviews, useful information, and book-writing advice.

Contributing editor Henry McGilton of Trilithon Software played the role of "chief editorial firefighter" to help make this book possible. Series editor Lisa Friendly contributed dogged perseverance and support.

A veritable multitude of reviewers took time out of their otherwise busy lives to read, edit, advise, revise, and delete material, all in the name of making this a better book. Kevin Coyle performed one of the most detailed editorial reviews at all levels. Karen Bennet, Mike Burati, Patricia Giencke, Steve Gilliard, Bill Joy, Rosanna Lee, Jon Madison, Brian O'Neill, Sue Palmer, Stephen Perelgut, R. Anders Schneiderman, Susan Sim, Bob Sproull, Guy Steele, Arthur van Hoff, Jim Waldo, Greg Wilson, and Ann Wollrath provided in-depth review. Geoff Arnold, Tom Cargill, Chris Darke, Pat Finnegan, Mick Jordan, Doug Lea, Randall Murray, Roger Riggs, Jimmy Torres, Arthur van Hoff, and Frank Yellin contributed useful comments and technical information at critical junctures.

Alka Deshpande, Sharon Flank, Nassim Fotouhi, Betsy Halstead, Kee Hinckley, Dr. K. Kalyanasundaram, Patrick Martin, Paul Romagna, Susan Snyder, and Nicole Yankelovich collaborated to make possible the five words of non-ISO-Latin-1 text on pages 106 and 260. Jim Arnold provided research help on the proper spelling, usage, and etymology of "smoog" and "moorge." Ed Mooney helped with the document preparation. Herb and Joy Kaiser were our Croatian language consultants. Cookie Callahan, Robert E. Pierce, and Rita Tavilla provided the support necessary to keep this project going at many moments when it would otherwise have stalled with a sputtering whimper.

Thanks to Kim Polese for supplying us the capsule summary of why Java is important to computer users as well as programmers.

Support and advice were provided at critical moments by Susan Jones, Bob Sproull, Jim Waldo, and Ann Wollrath. And we thank our families, who, besides their loving support, would at times drag us out to play when we should have been working, for which we are deeply grateful.

And thanks to the folks at Peet's Coffee and Tea, who kept us buzzed on the best Java on the planet.

ACKNOWLEDGMENTS (SECOND EDITION)

The cast of characters for this second edition is much like the first.

Series Editor Lisa Friendly continued to be doggedly supportive and attentive. The set of reviewers was smaller, overlapping, and certainly as helpful and thorough. Overall reviews by Steve Byrne, Tom Cargill, Mary Dageforde, Tim Lindholm, and Rob Murray were critical to clarity. Brian Beck, Peter Jones, Doug Lea, Bryan O'Sullivan, Sue Palmer, Rosanna Lee, Lori Park, Mark Reinhold, Roger Riggs, Ann Wollrath, and Ken Zadek contributed focused reviews of important parts. Guy Steele's support was ongoing and warm. Rosemary Simpson's extensive and intensive efforts to make a useful index are deeply appreciated. Carla Carlson and Helen Leary gave logistic support that kept all the wheels on the tracks instead of in the ditch. Gerry Wiener provided the Tibetan word on page 260, and we also had help on this from Craig Preston and Takao Miyatani. All who submitted errata and suggestions from the first edition were helpful.

For some inexplicable reason we left the friendly folks of Addison-Wesley off the original acknowledgments—luckily, most of them were present again for this edition. A merged list for both editions includes Kate Duffy, Rosa Gonzales, Mike Hendrickson, Marina Lang, Shannon Patti, Marty Rabinowitz, Sarah Weaver, and Pamela Yee. Others did much that we are blissfully unaware of, but for which we are nonetheless abidingly grateful.

And Peet's Coffee and Tea continued its supporting role as purveyor to the caffeine-consuming connoisseur.

Any errors or shortcomings that remain in this book—despite the combined efforts of these myriads—are completely the responsibility of the authors.

Results! Why, man, I have gotten a lot of results.
I know several thousand things that won't work.
—Thomas Edison

CHAPTER 1

A Quick Tour of Java

See Europe! Ten Countries in Seventeen Days!
—Sign in a travel agent's window

THIS chapter is a whirlwind tour of the Java programming language that gets you started writing Java code quickly.[1] We briefly cover the main points of the language, without slowing you down with full-blown detail. Subsequent chapters contain detailed discussions of specific Java features.

1.1 Getting Started

Java programs are built from *classes*. From a class definition, you can create any number of *objects* that are known as *instances* of that class. Think of a class as a factory with blueprints and instructions to build gadgets—objects are the gadgets the factory makes.

A class contains *members,* the primary kinds being *fields* and *methods.* Fields are data belonging either to the class itself or to objects of the class; they make up the *state* of the object or class. Methods are collections of *statements* that operate on the fields to manipulate the state.

Long tradition holds that the first sample program for any language prints "Hello, world". Here is the Java version:

```
class HelloWorld {
    public static void main(String[] args) {
        System.out.println("Hello, world");
    }
}
```

---

[1] The Java programming language is referred to simply as Java throughout.

Use your favorite text editor to type this program source code into a file. Then run the Java compiler to compile the source of this program into Java *bytecodes*, the "machine language" for the Java Virtual Machine (more on this later). Details of editing and compiling source vary from system to system—consult your system manuals for specific information. On the system we use most often—the Java Development Kit (JDK) provided free of charge by Sun Microsystems—you put the source for HelloWorld into a file named HelloWorld.java. To compile it you type the command

```
javac HelloWorld.java
```

To run the program you type the command

```
java HelloWorld
```

This executes the main method of HelloWorld. When you run the program, it displays

```
Hello, world
```

Now you have a small Java program that does something, but what does it mean?

The program declares a class called HelloWorld with a single method called main. Class members appear between curly braces { and } following the class name. HelloWorld has only one method and no fields.

The main method's only *parameter* is an array of String objects that are the program's arguments from the command line with which it was invoked. Arrays and strings are covered later, as is the meaning of args for the main method.

The main method is declared void because it doesn't return a value. It is one of a few special method names in Java: the main method of a class, if declared as shown, is executed when you run the class as an application. When run, a main method can create objects, evaluate expressions, invoke other methods, and do anything else needed to define an application's behavior.

In this example, main contains a single statement that invokes a method on the System class's out object. Methods are invoked by supplying an object reference and a method name, separated by a dot (.). HelloWorld uses the out object's println method to print a newline-terminated string on the standard output stream.

Exercise 1.1: Enter, compile, and run HelloWorld on your system.

Exercise 1.2: Try changing parts of HelloWorld and see what errors you get.

1.2   Variables

The next example prints the *Fibonacci sequence,* an infinite sequence whose first few terms are

1
1
2
3
5
8
13
21
34

The Fibonacci sequence starts with the terms 1 and 1, and each successive term is the sum of the previous two terms. A Fibonacci printing program is simple, and it demonstrates how to declare *variables*, write a simple loop, and perform basic arithmetic. Here is the Fibonacci program:

```java
class Fibonacci {
    /** Print out the Fibonacci sequence for values < 50 */
    public static void main(String[] args) {
        int lo = 1;
        int hi = 1;

        System.out.println(lo);
        while (hi < 50) {
            System.out.println(hi);
            hi = lo + hi;       // new hi
            lo = hi - lo;       /* new lo is (sum - old lo)
                                   i.e., the old hi */
        }
    }
}
```

This example declares a `Fibonacci` class that, like `HelloWorld`, has a `main` method. The first two lines of `main` declare two variables: `hi` and `lo`. Every variable must have a *type* that precedes its name when the variable is declared. `hi` and `lo` are of type `int`, 32-bit signed integers with values in the range -2^{31} through $2^{31}-1$.

Java has built-in "primitive" data types to support integer, floating-point, boolean, and character values. These primitive types hold data that Java understands directly, as opposed to object types defined by programmers. The type of every variable must be defined explicitly. The primitive data types of Java are:

`boolean`	either `true` or `false`
`char`	16-bit Unicode 2.0 character
`byte`	8-bit integer (signed)
`short`	16-bit integer (signed)
`int`	32-bit integer (signed)
`long`	64-bit integer (signed)
`float`	32-bit floating-point (IEEE 754-1985)
`double`	64-bit floating-point (IEEE 754-1985)

In the Fibonacci program, we declared `hi` and `lo` with initial values of 1. The starting values are set by initialization expressions, using the = operator, when the variables are declared. The = operator sets the variable named on the left-hand side to the value of the expression on the right-hand side. In this program `hi` is the last term in the series and `lo` is the previous term.

Local variables are *undefined* prior to initialization. If you try to use variables before assigning a value, the Java compiler will usually refuse to compile your program until you fix the problem.

The `while` statement in the example provides one way of looping in Java. The expression inside the `while` is evaluated—if the expression is true, the body of the loop is executed and the expression tested again. The `while` is repeated until the expression becomes false. If it never becomes false, the program will run forever unless something intervenes to break out of the loop, such as a `break` statement or an exception.

The expression that `while` tests is a *boolean* expression that has the value `true` or `false`. The boolean expression `hi < 50` in the previous example tests whether the current high value of the sequence is less than 50. If the high value is less than 50, its value is printed and the next value is calculated. If the high value equals or exceeds 50, control passes to the first line of code following the body of the `while` loop. That is the end of the `main` method in this example, so the program is finished.

Notice that the `println` method accepts an integer argument in the Fibonacci example, whereas it accepted a string argument in the `HelloWorld` example. The `println` method is one of many methods that are *overloaded* so that they can accept arguments of different types.

Exercise 1.3: Add a title to the printed list.

Exercise 1.4: Write a program that generates a different sequence, such as a table of squares (multiplication is done using *, such as i * i).

1.3   Comments in Code

The English text scattered through the code is in *comments*. Java has three styles of comments, all illustrated in the example. Comments enable you to write descriptive text alongside your code, annotating it for programmers who may read your code in the future. That programmer may well be *you* months or years later. You save yourself effort by commenting your own code. Also, you often find bugs when you write comments, because explaining what the code is supposed to do forces you to think about it.

Text following // up to the end of the line is ignored by the compiler, as is text between /* and the next */.

The third kind of comment appears at the very top, between /** and */. A comment starting with two asterisks is a *documentation comment* ("doc comment" for short). Documentation comments are intended to describe declarations that follow them. The comment in the previous example is for the main method. These comments can be extracted by a tool that uses them to generate reference documentation for your classes.

1.4   Named Constants

Constants are values like 12, 17.9, and "Strings Like This". Constants are the way you specify values that are not computed and recomputed but remain, well, constant for the life of a program.

Programmers prefer *named constants* for two reasons. One reason is that the name of the constant is a form of documentation. The name can (and should) describe what the particular value is used for.

Another reason is that you define a named constant in a single place in a program. When the constant needs to be changed or corrected, it can be changed in only one place, easing program maintenance. Named constants in Java are created by declaring a variable as static and final and providing its value in the declaration:

```
class CircleStuff {
        static final double π = 3.1416;
}
```

The value of π can be changed in just one place when we discover that five significant digits of precision are not enough. We declared π as double—a double-precision 64-bit floating-point number. Now we could easily change π to a more precise value, such as 3.14159265358979323846.

You can group related constants within a class. For example, a card game might use these constants:

```
class Suit {
    final static int CLUBS    = 1;
    final static int DIAMONDS = 2;
    final static int HEARTS   = 3;
    final static int SPADES   = 4;
}
```

With this declaration, suits in a program would be accessed as Suit.HEARTS, Suit.SPADES, and so on, thus grouping all the suit names within the single name Suit.

1.4.1   Unicode Characters

We take a minor diversion to note the π symbol as the name of a constant in the previous example. In most programming languages, identifiers are limited to the letters and digits available in the ASCII character set.

Java moves you toward the world of internationalized software: you write Java code in *Unicode,* an international character set standard. Unicode characters are 16 bits and provide a character range large enough to write the major languages used in the world, and that is why we can use π for the name of the constant in the example. π is a valid letter from the Greek section of Unicode and is therefore valid in Java source. Most existing Java code is typed in ASCII, a 7-bit character standard, or ISO Latin-1, an 8-bit character standard commonly called Latin-1. But these characters are translated into Unicode before processing, so the Java character set is always Unicode.

Exercise 1.5: Change the HelloWorld application to use a named string constant as the string to print.

Exercise 1.6: Change the Fibonacci application to use a named constant in its loop instead of a literal constant.

1.5   Flow of Control

"Flow of control" is the term for deciding which statements in a program are executed and in what order. The while loop in the Fibonacci program is one control
flow statement. Other control flow statements include if–else, for, switch, do–
while, and *blocks*—multiple statements grouped within { and }. We change the
Fibonacci sequence program by numbering the elements of the sequence and
marking even numbers with an asterisk:

```java
class ImprovedFibonacci {
    /** Print out the first few Fibonacci
     * numbers, marking evens with a '*' */
    static final int MAX_INDEX = 10;

    public static void main(String[] args) {
        int lo = 1;
        int hi = 1;
        String mark;

        System.out.println("1: " + lo);
        for (int i = 2; i < MAX_INDEX; i++) {
            if (hi % 2 == 0)
                mark = " *";
            else
                mark = "";
            System.out.println(i + ": " + hi + mark);
            hi = lo + hi;          // new hi
            /* new lo is (sum - old lo) i.e., the old hi */
            lo = hi - lo;
        }
    }
}
```

Here is the new output:

```
1: 1
2: 1
3: 2 *
4: 3
5: 5
6: 8 *
```

```
7:  13
8:  21
9:  34  *
```

To number the elements of the sequence, we used a `for` loop instead of a `while` loop. A `for` loop is shorthand for a `while` loop, with an initialization and increment phase added. The `for` loop in `ImprovedFibonaci` is equivalent to this `while` loop:

```
int i = 2;
while (i < MAX_INDEX) {
    // …generate the next Fibonacci number and print it…
    i++;
}
```

The ++ operator in this code fragment may be unfamiliar if you're new to C-derived programming languages. The plus-plus operator increments by one the value of any variable it abuts—the contents of variable `i` in this case. The ++ operator is a *prefix* operator when it comes before its operand, and *postfix* when it comes after. Similarly, minus-minus decrements by one the value of any variable it abuts and can also be prefix or postfix. In the context of the previous example, a statement like

```
i++;
```

is equivalent to

```
i = i + 1;
```

Beyond simple assignment, Java supports other assignment operators that apply an arithmetic operation to the value on the left-hand side of the operator. For example, another way to write `i++` in the `for` loop is to write

```
i += 1;
```

which adds the value on the right-hand side of the += operator (namely 1) to the variable on the left-hand side (namely `i`). Most of the binary operators in Java (operators that take two operands) can be joined with = in a similar way.

Inside the `for` loop we use an `if/else` to see whether the current `hi` value is even. The `if` statement tests the expression between the parentheses. If the expression is `true`, the first statement or block in the body of the `if` is executed. If the expression is `false`, the statement or block following the `else` clause is executed. The `else` part is optional: if the `else` is not present, nothing is done when the expression is `false`. After figuring out which (if any) clause to execute, control passes to the code following the body of the `if` statement.

The example tests whether `hi` is even using the %, or *remainder,* operator. It produces the remainder after dividing the value on the left side by the value on the right. If the left-side value is even, the remainder is 0, and the ensuing statement assigns a string containing the even-number indicator to `mark`. The `else` clause is executed for odd numbers, setting `mark` to an empty string.

The `println` invocation is more complex, using the + operator to concatenate strings representing `i`, a separator, a string representing `hi`, and the marker string. The + operator is a concatenation operator when used with strings; when used in an arithmetic expression it is an addition operator.

Exercise 1.7: Change the loop so that `i` counts backward instead of forward.

1.6   Classes and Objects

Java, like any object-oriented programming language, provides a tool to solve programming problems using the notions of classes and objects. Every object in Java has a class that defines its data and behavior. Each class has three kinds of members:

◆ Fields are data variables associated with a class and its objects. Fields store results of computations performed by the class's methods.

◆ Methods contain the executable code of a class. Methods are built from statements. The way in which methods are *invoked*, and the statements contained within those methods, is what ultimately directs program execution.

◆ Classes and interfaces can be members of other classes or interfaces (you will learn about interfaces soon).

Here is the declaration of a simple class that might represent a point on a two-dimensional plane:

```
class Point {
    public double x, y;
}
```

This `Point` class has two fields representing the *x* and *y* coordinates of a point and has (as yet) no methods. A class declaration like this one is, conceptually, a plan that defines what objects manufactured from that class look like, plus sets of instructions that define the behavior of those objects.

Members of a class can have various levels of visibility. The `public` declaration of `x` and `y` in the `Point` class means that any code with access to a `Point` object can read or modify those values. Other levels of visibility limit member access to code in the class itself or to other related classes.

1.6.1   Creating Objects

Objects are created using an expression containing the new keyword. Creating an object from a class definition is also known as *instantiation*; thus, objects are often called *instances.*

In Java, newly created objects are allocated within an area of system memory known as the *heap.* All objects in Java are accessed via *object references*—any variable that may appear to hold an object actually contains a reference to that object. Object references are null when they do not reference any object.

Most of the time, you can be imprecise in the distinction between actual objects and references to objects. You can say, "Pass the object to the method" when you really mean "Pass an object reference to the method." We are careful about this distinction only when it makes a difference. Most of the time, you can use "object" and "object reference" interchangeably.

In the Point class, suppose you are building a graphics application in which you need to track lots of points. You represent each point by its own concrete Point object. Here is how you might create and initialize Point objects:

```
Point lowerLeft = new Point();
Point upperRight = new Point();
Point middlePoint = new Point();

lowerLeft.x = 0.0;
lowerLeft.y = 0.0;

upperRight.x = 1280.0;
upperRight.y = 1024.0;

middlePoint.x = 640.0;
middlePoint.y = 512.0;
```

Each Point object is unique and has its own copy of the x and y fields. Changing x in the object lowerLeft, for example, does not affect the value of x in the object upperRight. The fields in objects are known as *instance variables*, because there is a unique copy of the field in each object (instance) of the class.

1.6.2   Static or Class Fields

Per-object fields are usually what you need. You usually want a field in one object to be distinct from the field of the same name in every other object instantiated from that class.

Sometimes, though, you want fields that are shared among all objects of that class. These shared variables are known as *class variables*—variables specific to the class as opposed to objects of the class.

Why would you want to use class variables? Consider the Sony Walkman factory. Each Walkman has a unique serial number. In object terms, each Walkman object has its own unique serial number field. However, the factory needs to keep a record of the next serial number to be assigned. You don't want to keep that number with every Walkman object. You'd keep only one copy of that number in the factory, or, in object terms, as a class variable.

In Java, you obtain class-specific fields by declaring them `static`, and they are therefore commonly called *static fields*. For example, a `Point` object to represent the origin might be common enough that you should provide it as a `static` field in the `Point` class:

```
public static Point origin = new Point();
```

If this declaration appears inside the declaration of the `Point` class, there will be exactly one piece of data called `Point.origin` that always refers to an object at (0,0). This `static` field is there no matter how many `Point` objects are created, even if none is created. The values of `x` and `y` are zero because that is the default for numeric fields that are not explicitly initialized to a different value.

You saw one `static` object in your first program. The `System` class is a standard Java class that has a `static` field named `out` for printing output to the standard output stream.

When you see *field* in this book, it generally means a per-object field, although the term *non-static field* is sometimes used for clarity.

1.6.3   The Garbage Collector

After creating an object using `new`, how do you get rid of the object when you no longer want it? The answer is simple—stop referring to it. Unreferenced Java objects are automatically reclaimed by a *garbage collector,* which runs in the background and tracks object references. When an object is no longer referenced, the garbage collector can remove it from the storage allocation heap, although it may defer actually doing so until a propitious time.

1.7   Methods and Parameters

Objects of the previously defined Point class are exposed to manipulation by any
code that has a reference to a Point object, because its fields are declared public.
The Point class is an example of the simplest kind of class. Indeed, some classes
are this simple. They are designed to fit purely internal needs for a package or
when simple data containers are all you need.

The real benefits of object orientation, however, come from hiding the implementation of a class behind operations performed on its internal data. In Java,
operations of a class are declared via its methods—instructions that operate on an
object's data to obtain results. Methods access internal implementation details that
are otherwise hidden from other objects. Hiding data behind methods so that it is
inaccessible to other objects is the fundamental basis of data encapsulation.

Methods have zero or more parameters. A method can return a value, or it can
be declared void to indicate that it does not return any value. A method's statements appear in a block of code between curly braces { and } that follow the
method's *signature*—the name of the method and the number and types of its
parameters. If we enhance the Point class with a simple clear method, it might
look like this:

```
public void clear() {
    x = 0;
    y = 0;
}
```

The clear method has no parameters, hence the empty (and) after its name;
clear is declared void because it does not return any value. Inside a method,
fields and other methods of the class can be named directly—we can simply say x
and y without an explicit object reference.

1.7.1   Invoking a Method

Objects in general do not operate directly on the data of other objects, although, as
you saw in the Point class, a class can make its fields publicly accessible. Well-
designed classes usually hide their data so that it can be changed only by methods
of that class. To *invoke* a method, you provide an object reference and the method
name, separated by a dot (.). *Parameters* are passed to the method as a comma-
separated list of values enclosed in parentheses. Methods that take no parameters
still require the parentheses, with nothing between them. The object on which the
method is invoked (the object receiving the method invocation) is often known as
the *receiving object*, or the *receiver*.

A method can return a single value as a result. To return more than one value from a method, you must create an object whose purpose is to hold return values in a single unit and then return that object.

Here is a method called `distance` that's part of the `Point` class shown in previous examples. The `distance` method accepts another `Point` object as a parameter, computes the Euclidean distance between itself and the other point, and returns a double-precision floating-point result:

```
public double distance(Point that) {
    double xdiff = x - that.x;
    double ydiff = y - that.y;
    return Math.sqrt(xdiff * xdiff + ydiff * ydiff);
}
```

Based on the `lowerLeft` and `upperRight` objects created previously, you could invoke `distance` this way:

```
double d = lowerLeft.distance(upperRight);
```

After this statement executes, the variable d contains the Euclidean distance between `lowerLeft` and `upperRight`.

1.7.2 The `this` Reference

Occasionally, the receiving object needs to know its own reference. For example, the receiving object might want to add itself to a list of objects somewhere. An implicit reference named `this` is available to methods, and `this` is a reference to the current (receiving) object. The following definition of `clear` is equivalent to the one just presented:

```
public void clear() {
    this.x = 0;
    this.y = 0;
}
```

You usually use `this` as a parameter to other methods that need an object reference. The `this` reference can also be used to explicitly name the members of the current object. Here's another method of `Point` named `move`, which sets the x and y fields to specified values:

```
public void move(double x, double y) {
    this.x = x;
    this.y = y;
}
```

This move method uses `this` to clarify which x and y are being referred to. Naming the parameters of move x and y is reasonable, because you pass *x* and *y* coordinates to the method. But then those parameters have the same names as `Point`'s fields, and therefore the parameter names are said to *hide* the field names. If we simply wrote x = x we would assign the value of the x parameter to itself, not to the x field as required. The expression `this.x` refers to the object's x field, not the x parameter of move.

1.7.3   Static or Class Methods

Just as you can have per-class static fields, you can also have per-class static methods, often known as *class methods*. Class methods are usually intended to do class-like operations specific to the class itself, usually on static fields and not on specific instances of that class. Class methods are declared using the `static` keyword and are therefore also known as *static methods*.

As with the term *field,* when you see *method,* it generally means a per-object method, although the term *non-static method* is sometimes used for clarity.

Why would you need static methods? Consider the Sony Walkman factory again. The record of the next serial number to be assigned is held in the factory, not in every Walkman. A method that returned the factory's copy of the next available serial number would be a static method, not a method to operate on specific Walkman objects.

The implementation of `distance` in the previous example uses the static method `Math.sqrt` to calculate a square root. The `Math` class supports many methods that are useful for general mathematical manipulation. These methods are declared as static methods because they do not act on any particular object but instead group a related set of functionality in the class itself.

A static method cannot directly access non-static members. When a static method is invoked, there's no specific object for the method to operate on. You could work around this by passing an explicit object reference as a parameter to the static method. In general, however, static methods perform class-related tasks and non-static methods perform object-related tasks. Asking a static method to work on object fields is like asking the Walkman factory to change the serial number of a Walkman hanging on the belt of a jogger in Golden Gate Park.

1.8   Arrays

Simple variables that hold one value are useful but are not sufficient for many applications. A program that plays a game of cards would want a number of `Card` objects it could manipulate as a whole. To meet this need, Java provides *arrays*.

An array is a collection of variables all of the same type. The components of an array are accessed by simple integer indexes. In a card game, a Deck object might look like this:

```java
class Deck {
    final int DECK_SIZE = 52;

    Card[] cards = new Card[DECK_SIZE];

    public void print() {
        for (int i = 0; i < cards.length; i++)
            System.out.println(cards[i]);
    }
    // ...
}
```

First we declare a constant called DECK_SIZE to define the number of cards in a deck. We declare a cards field as an array of type Card by following the type name in the declaration with brackets [and]. We initialize cards to a new array with DECK_SIZE Card variables, initialized to null. An array's length is fixed when it is created and can never change.

The println method invocation shows how array components are accessed by enclosing the index of the desired element within brackets [and] following the array name.

You can probably tell from reading the code that array objects have a length field that says how many elements the array contains. The *bounds* of an array are integers between 0 and length-1. An IndexOutOfBoundsException is thrown if you use an index outside the bounds of the array.

The example also introduces a new variable declaration mechanism: declaring the control variable of a for statement in its initialization clause. Declaring variables in the initialization section of a for loop is a concise and convenient way to declare simple loop variables. This construct is allowed only in the initialization of for statements; you cannot declare variables in the test clause of an if or while statement.

The loop variable i is available only within the code of the for statement. A loop variable declared in this manner disappears when the loop terminates, which means you can reuse that variable name in subsequent for statements.

Exercise 1.8: Modify the Fibonacci application to store the sequence into an array and print the list of values at the end.

Exercise 1.9: Modify the `ImprovedFibonacci` application to store its sequence in an array. Do this by creating a new class to hold both the value and a `boolean` value that says whether the value is even, and then having an array of object references to objects of that class.

1.9   String Objects

Java provides a `String` object type to deal specifically with sequences of character data and provides language-level support for initializing them. The Java `String` class provides a variety of methods to operate on `String` objects.

You've already seen `String` literals in examples like the `HelloWorld` program. When you write a statement such as

```
System.out.println("Hello, world");
```

the Java compiler actually creates a `String` object initialized to the value of the specified string literal and passes that `String` object as the parameter to the `println` method.

You don't need to specify the length of a `String` object when you create it. You can create a new `String` object and initialize it all in one statement, as shown in this example:

```
class StringsDemo {
    static public void main(String args[]) {
        String   myName = "Petronius";

        myName = myName + " Arbiter";
        System.out.println("Name = " + myName);
    }
}
```

Here we create a `String` object reference called `myName` and initialize it with a `String` literal. Following initialization, we use the `String` concatenation + operator to make a new `String` object with a new value. Finally, we print the value of `myName` on the standard output stream. The output when you run this program is

```
Name = Petronius Arbiter
```

In addition to the + sign as a concatenation operator, you can use the += operator as a shorthand for placing the variable name on the right-hand side of the assignment. Here's an upgraded program:

```
class BetterStringsDemo {
    static public void main(String args[]) {
        String myName = "Petronius";
        String occupation = "Reorganization Specialist";

        myName = myName + " Arbiter";
        myName += " ";
        myName += "(" + occupation + ")";
        System.out.println("Name = " + myName);
    }
}
```

Now when you run the program, you get this output:

```
Name = Petronius Arbiter (Reorganization Specialist)
```

`String` objects have a `length` method that returns the number of characters in the `String`. Characters are indexed from 0 through `length()` - 1.

`String` objects are *read-only,* or *immutable:* the contents of a `String` never change. When you see statements like

```
str = "redwood";
// ... do something with str ..
str = "oak";
```

the second assignment gives a new value to the *object reference* `str`, not to the *contents* of the string. Every time you perform operations that seem to modify a `String` object, such as the `+=` in `BetterStringsDemo`, you instead get a new read-only `String` object, while the original `String` object remains unchanged. The `StringBuffer` class provides for mutable strings and is described in Chapter 8, where `String` is also described in detail.

The `equals` method is the simplest way to compare two `String` objects to see whether they have the same contents:

```
if (oneStr.equals(twoStr))
    foundDuplicate(oneStr, twoStr);
```

Other methods for comparing a subpart of the strings or ignoring case differences are also covered in Chapter 8. If you use `==` to compare the string objects, you are actually comparing `oneStr` and `twoStr` to see if they refer to the same object, not testing if the strings have the same contents.

Exercise 1.10: Modify the `StringsDemo` application to use different strings.

Exercise 1.11: Modify `ImprovedFibonacci` to store the `String` objects it creates into an array instead of invoking `println` with them directly.

1.10 Extending a Class

One of the major benefits of object orientation is the ability to *extend*, or *subclass*, the behavior of an existing class and continue to use code written for the original class, which is known as the *superclass*. When you extend a class to create a new class, the new extended class *inherits* all the fields and methods of the superclass.

If the subclass does not specifically *override* the behavior of the superclass, the subclass also inherits all the behavior of its superclass because, as we said, the extended class inherits the fields and methods of its superclass.

The Walkman example can be extended in this way. Later models incorporated two sets of jacks so two people could listen to the same tape. In the object-oriented world, the two-jack model extends, or is a subclass of, the basic model. The two-jack model inherits the characteristics and behavior of the basic model and adds new behavior of its own.

Customers told Sony they wanted to talk to each other while sharing a tape in the two-jack model. Sony enhanced the two-jack model to include two-way communications so people could chat while listening to music. The two-way communications model is a subclass of the two-jack model, inherits all of *its* behavior, and adds new behavior.

Sony created many other Walkman models. Later models extend the capabilities of the basic model—they subclass the basic model and inherit features and behavior from it.

Let's look at an example of extending a Java class. Here we extend our former `Point` class to represent a pixel that might be shown on a screen. The new `Pixel` class requires a color in addition to *x* and *y* coordinates:

```
class Pixel extends Point {
    Color color;

    public void clear() {
        super.clear();
        color = null;
    }
}
```

`Pixel` extends both *data* and *behavior* of its `Point` superclass. `Pixel` extends the data by adding a field named `color`. `Pixel` also extends the behavior of `Point` by overriding `Point`'s `clear` method.

`Pixel` objects can be used by any code designed to work with `Point` objects. If a method expects a parameter of type `Point`, you can hand it a `Pixel` object and it just works. All the `Point` code can be used by anyone with a `Pixel` in hand. This feature is known as *polymorphism*—a single object like `Pixel` can have many (*poly-*) forms (*-morph*) and can be used as both a `Pixel` object and a `Point` object.

`Pixel`'s behavior extends `Point`'s behavior. Extended behavior could be entirely new (adding color in this example) or can be a restriction on old behavior that follows all the original requirements. An example of restricted behavior might be `Pixel` objects that live inside some kind of `Screen` object, restricting x and y to the dimensions of the screen. If the original `Point` class did not forbid restrictions for coordinates, a class with restricted range would not violate the original class's behavior.

An extended class often *overrides* the behavior of its superclass by providing new implementations of one or more of the inherited methods. In the `Pixel` example, we override `clear` to obtain proper behavior that `Pixel` requires. The `clear` that `Pixel` inherited from `Point` knows only about `Point`'s fields but obviously can't know about the new `color` field declared in the `Pixel` subclass.

1.10.1 Invoking Methods from the Superclass

To make `Pixel` do the correct "clear" behavior, we provide a new implementation of `clear` that first invokes its superclass's `clear` using the `super` reference. The `super` reference is a lot like the `this` reference described previously except that `super` references things from the superclass, whereas `this` references things from the current object.

The invocation `super.clear()` looks to the superclass to execute `clear` as it would for an object of the superclass—namely, `Point`. After invoking `super.clear()` to clear out the `Point` part of the object, we add new functionality to set `color` to a reasonable empty value. We choose `null`, a reference to no object.

What would happen had we not invoked `super.clear()` in the previous example? `Pixel`'s `clear` method would set `color` to its `null` value, but the x and y variables that `Pixel` inherited from `Point` would not be set to any "cleared" values. Not clearing all the values of a `Pixel` object, including its `Point` parts, is probably a bug.

When you invoke `super.`*method*`()`, the object runtime system looks back up the inheritance hierarchy to the first superclass that contains the required *method*`()`. If `Point` didn't have a `clear` method, for example, the object runtime would look at `Point`'s superclass for such a method and invoke that, and so on.

For all other references, invoking a method uses the actual class of the *object*, not the type of the object *reference*. Here is an example:

```
Point point = new Pixel();
point.clear();  // uses Pixel's clear()
```

In this example, `Pixel`'s version of `clear` is invoked even though the variable that holds the `Pixel` is declared as a `Point` reference. But if we invoke `super.clear()` inside one of `Pixel`'s methods, that invocation will use the `Point` class's implementation of the `clear` method.

1.10.2 The `Object` Class

Classes that do not explicitly extend any other class implicitly extend the `Object` class. All objects are polymorphically of class `Object`, so `Object` is the generic type for references that can refer to objects of any class:

```
Object oref = new Pixel();
oref = "Some String";
```

In this example, `oref` is legally assigned references to `Pixel` and `String` objects even though those classes have no relationship except that both have `Object` as a superclass. The `Object` class also defines several important methods that are discussed in Chapter 3.

Exercise 1.12: Sketch out a set of classes that reflects the class structure of the Sony Walkman product family we have described. Use methods to hide the data, making all the data `private` and the methods `public`. What methods would belong in the base `Walkman` class? Which methods would be added for which extended classes?

1.11 Interfaces

Sometimes you need only *declare* methods an object must support but not supply the *implementation* of those methods. As long as their behavior meets specific criteria, implementation details of the methods are irrelevant. For example, to ask whether a particular value is contained in a set of values, details of how those values are stored are irrelevant. You want the methods to work equally well with a linked list of values, a hashtable of values, or any other data structure.

Java enables you to define an *interface*, which is like a class but has only declarations of its methods. The designer of the interface declares methods that are supported by classes that *implement* the interface and declares what those methods should do. Here is a Lookup interface:

```
interface Lookup {
    /** Return the value associated with the name, or
     *  null if there is no such value */
    Object find(String name);
}
```

The Lookup interface declares one method, find, that takes a String and returns the value associated with that name, or null if there is no associated value. In the interface no implementation can be given for the method—the class that implements the interface is responsible for providing a specific implementation. Code that uses references of type Lookup (references to objects that implement the Lookup interface) can invoke the find method and get the expected results, no matter what the actual type of the object is:

```
void processValues(String[] names, Lookup table) {
    for (int i = 0; i < names.length; i++) {
        Object value = table.find(names[i]);
        if (value != null)
            processValue(names[i], value);
    }
}
```

A class can implement as many interfaces as you choose. This example implements Lookup using a simple array (methods to set or remove values are left out for simplicity):

```
class SimpleLookup implements Lookup {
    private String[] Names;
    private Object[] Values;

    public Object find(String name) {
        for (int i = 0; i < Names.length; i++) {
            if (Names[i].equals(name))
                return Values[i];
        }
        return null;     // not found
    }

    // ...
}
```

Interfaces can be extended using the extends keyword. An interface can extend one or more other interfaces, adding new constants and new methods that must be implemented by any class that implements the extended interface.

A class's *supertypes* are the class it extends and the interfaces it implements, including all the supertypes of those classes and interfaces. So the class of an object is not only its class but also any of its supertypes, including interfaces. An object can be used polymorphically with both its superclass and any superinterfaces, including any of their supertypes.

Exercise 1.13: Write an extended interface of Lookup that has add and remove methods. Implement the extended interface in a new class.

1.12 Exceptions

What do you do when an error occurs in a program? In many languages, error conditions are signaled by unusual return values like –1. Programmers often don't check for exceptional values because they may assume that errors "can't happen." On the other hand, adding error detection and recovery to what should be a straightforward flow of logic can obscure that logic to the point where the normal flow is completely obscured. An ostensibly simple task such as reading a file into memory might require about seven lines of code. Error checking and reporting expands this to 40 or more lines. Making normal operation the needle in your code haystack is undesirable.

Java uses *checked exceptions* to manage error handling. Checked exceptions force you to consider what to do with errors where they may occur in the code. If a checked exception is not handled, this is noticed at compile time, not at run time when problems have compounded because of the unchecked error.

A method that detects an unusual error condition *throws* an exception. Exceptions can be *caught* by code farther back on the calling stack—this invoking code can handle the exception as needed and then continue executing. Uncaught exceptions are handled by a default handler in the Java implementation, which may report the exception and terminate the thread of execution.

An exception in Java is an object, with type, methods, and data. Representing exceptions as objects is useful, because an exception object can include data, methods, or both to report on or recover from specific kinds of exceptions. Exception objects are generally derived from the Exception class, which provides a string field to describe the error. Java requires all exceptions to be subclasses of the class Throwable, which is the superclass of Exception.

The paradigm for using exceptions in Java is the *try–catch–finally* sequence: you *try* something; if that something throws an exception, you *catch* the exception; and *finally* you clean up from either the normal code path or the exception code path, whichever actually happened.

Here is a dataSet method that returns a set of data read from a file. If the file for the data set cannot be found or if any other I/O exception occurs, this method throws an exception describing the error. First, we define a new exception type BadDataSetException to describe such an error. Then we declare that the method getDataSet throws that exception using a throws clause:

```java
class BadDataSetException extends Exception {
}

class MyUtilities {
    public double[] getDataSet(String setName)
        throws BadDataSetException
    {
        String file = setName + ".dset";
        InputStream in = null;
        try {
            in = new FileInputStream(file);
            return readDataSet(in);
        } catch (IOException e) {
            throw new BadDataSetException();
        } finally {
            try {
                if (in != null)
                    in.close();
            } catch (IOException e) {
                ; // oh, well -- we tried
            }
        }
    }
}
```

First we turn the data set name into a file name. Then we try to open the file and read the data using the method readDataSet. If all goes well, readDataSet will return an array of doubles, which we will return to the invoking code. If opening or reading the file causes an I/O exception, the catch clause is executed. The catch clause creates a new BadDataSetException object and throws it, in effect translating the I/O exception into an exception specific to the getDataSet method. Methods that invoke dataSet can catch the new exception and react to it appropriately. In either case—returning successfully with the data set or catching and then throwing an exception—the code in the finally clause is executed to close the file if it was opened successfully (we skip any errors on the `close` because we have done our best at that point). You will use `finally` clauses for cleanup code that must always be executed. You can even have a `try-finally` statement with no `catch` clauses to ensure that cleanup code will be executed.

If execution of a method can result in checked exceptions, it must declare the types of these exceptions in a `throws` clause, as shown for `dataSet`. Other than exceptions of type `RuntimeException` and `Error`, or subclasses of these exception types, which can be thrown anywhere, a method can throw only those exceptions it declares. It may throw those exceptions directly with `throw` or indirectly by invoking a method that throws exceptions.

Declaring the exceptions that a method throws means the compiler can ensure that the method throws only those exceptions it declared and no others. This check prevents errors in cases when your method should handle another method's exceptions but does not. In addition, the method that invokes your method is assured that your method will not result in unexpected exceptions. This is why the exceptions you must declare in a `throws` clause are called *checked exceptions*. Exceptions that are extensions of `RuntimeException` and `Error` need not be declared and are not checked; they are called *unchecked exceptions*.

Exercise 1.14: Add fields to `BadDataSetException` to hold the set name and the I/O exception that signaled the problem so that whoever catches the exception will know details about the error.

1.13 Packages

Name conflicts are a major problem when you're developing reusable code. No matter how carefully you pick names for classes and methods, someone else is likely to use that name for a different purpose. If you use simple, descriptive names, the problem gets worse since such names are more likely to be used by someone else who was also trying to use simple, descriptive names. Words like "set," "get," "clear," and so on are used often and are almost certain to clash with other people's uses.

The standard solution for name collision in many programming languages is to use a *package prefix* at the front of every class, type, global function, and so on. Prefix conventions create *naming contexts* to ensure that names in one context do not conflict with names in other contexts. These prefixes are usually a few characters long and are usually an abbreviation of the product name, such as `Xt` for the X-Windows Toolkit or `WIN32` for the 32-bit Windows API.

When code uses only a few packages, the likelihood of prefix conflict is small. However, since prefixes are abbreviations, the probability of a name conflict increases with the number of packages used.

Java has adopted a more formal notion of package that has a set of types and subpackages as members. Packages are named and can be imported. Package names are hierarchical, with components separated by dots. When you use part of a package, either you use its fully qualified name, or you *import* all or part of the package. Hierarchical package names enable longer package names. Package names also give you control over name conflicts. If two packages contain classes with the same name, you can use a package-qualified form of the class name— sometimes called the *fully qualified class name*—for one or both of them.

Here is an example of a method that uses fully qualified names to print the current day and time using Java's utility class `Date` (documented in Chapter 16):

```
class Date1 {
    public static void main(String[] args) {
        java.util.Date now = new java.util.Date();
        System.out.println(now);
    }
}
```

And here is a version that uses `import` to declare the type `Date`:

```
import java.util.Date;

class Date2 {
    public static void main(String[] args) {
        Date now = new Date();
        System.out.println(now);
    }
}
```

The name collision problem is not completely solved by the Java package mechanism. Two projects can still give their packages the same name. This problem can be solved only by convention. The standard convention is to use the reversed Internet domain name of the organization to prefix the package name. For example, if the Acme Corporation had the Internet domain `acme.com`, it would use package names of the form `COM.acme.package`.

Having dots separate package components may occasionally cause confusion, because the dot is also used to invoke methods and access fields in object references. This syntax may lead to confusion as to what can be imported. Java novices often try to import `System.out` so they don't have to type it in front of every `println`. This does not work because `System` is a class in which `out` is a static field whose type supports the `println` method.

On the other hand, `java.util` is a package, so you can import `java.util.Date` (or `java.util.*` if you want everything from the package). If you are having problems importing something, check to make sure that you are importing a type.

Java classes are always in a package. A package is named by providing a package declaration at the top of the source file:

```
package COM.sun.games;

class Card {
    // ...
}
```

If a name is not provided via a `package` declaration, the class is made part of an *unnamed package*. An unnamed package is adequate for an application (or applet) that is not loaded with any other code. Classes destined for a library should be written in named packages.

1.14 The Java Platform

Java is designed to maximize portability. Many details about Java are specifically defined for all implementations. For example, a `double` is a 64-bit IEEE 754-1985 floating-point number. Many languages leave precise definitions to particular implementations, making only general guarantees such as minimum range, or they provide a way to ask the system what the range is on the current platform.

Java makes these definitions specific all the way down to the machine language into which Java code is translated. Java source code is compiled into Java *bytecodes*, which are designed to be run on a Java *Virtual Machine*. Bytecodes are a machine language for an abstract machine, executed by the virtual machine on each system that supports Java.[2] Other languages can also be compiled into Java bytecodes.

The virtual machine provides a *runtime*, which provides access to the virtual machine itself (for example, a way to start the garbage collector) and to the outside world (such as the output stream `System.out`). The runtime checks security-sensitive operations with a *security manager*, which can be installed at most once

---

[2] A system can, of course, implement the Java Virtual Machine in silicon—that is, using a special-purpose chip. This does not affect the portability of the bytecodes; it is just another virtual machine implementation.

for a runtime. The security manager could, for example, forbid the application to read or write the local disk, or could allow network connections only to particular machines.

When classes are loaded into a virtual machine, they will first be checked by a *verifier* that ensures the bytecodes are properly formed and meet security and safety guarantees (for example, that the bytecodes never attempt to use an integer as a reference to gain access to parts of memory).

These features combined give Java code complete platform independence to provide a security model suitable for executing code downloaded across the network at varying levels of trust. Java source code compiled into Java bytecodes can be run on any machine that has a Java Virtual Machine. The code can be executed with an appropriate level of protection to prevent careless or malicious class writers from harming the system. The level of trust can be adjusted depending on the source of the bytecodes—bytecodes on the local disk or protected network can be trusted more than bytecodes fetched from arbitrary machines elsewhere in the world.

1.15 Other Topics Briefly Noted

Java has several other features that we mention briefly here and cover later in more detail:

- ◆ *Threads:* Java has built-in thread support for creating multithreaded applications. It uses per-object and per-class monitor-style locks to synchronize concurrent access to object and class data. See Chapter 9 for more details.

- ◆ *I/O:* Java provides a `java.io` package for many different kinds of input and output operations. See Chapter 12 for specifics of the I/O capabilities.

- ◆ *Type classes:* Java has classes to represent most of the primitive types (such as `Integer`, `Double`, and `Boolean`) and a reflection mechanism to allow browsing class types and their members. See Chapter 14 for more information about programming with types.

- ◆ *Utility interfaces and classes:* Java provides a `java.util` package that has many useful classes, such as `BitSet`, `Vector`, `Stack`, and `Date`. See Chapter 13 for more information about utility classes.

Careful—we don't want to learn from this!
—Calvin and Hobbes

CHAPTER 2

Classes and Objects

First things first, but not necessarily in that order.
—Dr. Who, *Meglos*

THE fundamental unit of programming in Java is the *class*. Classes contain methods: collections of executable code that are the focus of computation. Classes also provide the structure for *objects,* as well as the mechanisms to manufacture objects from the class definitions. You can compute with only primitive types—integer, floating-point, and so on—but almost any interesting Java program will create and manipulate objects.

Object-oriented programming strictly separates the notion of *what* is to be done from *how* it is done. "What" is described as a set of methods (and sometimes publicly available data) and their associated semantics. This combination—methods, data, and semantics—is often described as a *contract* between the designer of the class and the programmer who uses it, because it says what happens when certain methods are invoked on an object.

A common assumption is that the methods declared in a class are its entire contract. The semantics of those operations are also part of the contract, even though they may be described only in documentation. Two methods may have the same name and parameters, but they are not equivalent if they have different semantics. For example, not every method called print can be assumed to print a copy of the object. Someone might define a print method with the semantics "process interval" or "prioritize nonterminals." The contract of the method, both signature and semantics together, defines what it means.

The "how" of an object is defined by its class, which defines the implementation of the methods the object supports. Each object is an *instance* of a class. When a method is invoked on an object, the class is examined to find the code to be run. An object can use other objects to do its job, but we start with simple classes that implement all their own methods directly.

2.1   A Simple Class

The basics of a class are its fields (data) and its methods (code to manipulate the data). Here is a simple class called Body that could be used to store data about celestial bodies such as comets, asteroids, planets, and stars:

```
class Body {
    public long idNum;
    public String nameFor;
    public Body orbits;

    public static long nextID = 0;
}
```

First we declare the name of the class. A class declaration creates a *type name* in Java, so references to objects of that type can be declared with a simple

```
Body mercury;
```

This declaration states that mercury is a reference to an object of type Body. The declaration does *not* create an object—it declares only a *reference* that is allowed to refer a Body object. During its existence, the reference mercury may refer to any number of Body objects. These objects must be explicitly created. In this respect, Java is different from languages in which objects are created when you declare variables.

This first version of Body is poorly designed. This is intentional: we will demonstrate the value of certain language features as we improve the class in this chapter.

Exercise 2.1: Write a simple Vehicle class that has fields for (at least) current speed, current direction in degrees, and owner name.

Exercise 2.2: Write a LinkedList class that has a field of type Object and a reference to the next LinkedList element in the list.

2.2   Fields

A class's variables are called *fields;* the Body class's nameFor and orbits are examples. Every Body object has its own specific instances of these fields: a long that uniquely identifies the body from all others, a String that is its name, and a reference to another Body around which it orbits.

Giving each separate object a different instance of the fields means that each object has its own unique state. Changing the `orbits` field in one `Body` object does not affect the `orbits` field in any other `Body` object.

Sometimes, though, you want only one instance of a field shared by all objects of a class. You obtain such fields by declaring them `static`, so they are called *static fields* or *class variables.* When you declare a `static` field in a class, all objects created from that class share a single copy of that field.

In our case, `Body` has one `static` field, `nextID`, which contains the next body identifier to use. The `nextID` field is initialized to zero when the class is initialized after it is loaded and linked. You will see that each newly created `Body` object will be assigned the current value of `nextID` as its identifier.

In this book when we use the term *field* or *method,* we usually mean the non-static kind. When the context makes it ambiguous, we will use the term *non-static field* or *non-static method* to be clear.

Exercise 2.3: Add a static field to your `Vehicle` class for a vehicle identification number, and a non-static field to the `Vehicle` class to hold each car's ID number.

2.3   Access Control and Inheritance

All fields and methods of a class are always available to code in the class itself. To control access from other classes and to control inheritance by subclasses, class members have four possible access control modifiers:

- ◆ *Private:* Members declared `private` are accessible only in the class itself.

- ◆ *Package:* Members declared with no access modifier are accessible in the class itself and are accessible to, and inheritable by, code in the same package. Packages are discussed in Chapter 10.

- ◆ *Protected:* Members declared `protected` are accessible in the class itself, and are accessible to, and inheritable by, code in the same package and code in subclasses. Extending objects is covered in Chapter 3.

- ◆ *Public:* Members declared `public` are accessible anywhere the class is accessible, and they are inherited by all subclasses.

We declared the `Body` class's fields `public` because programmers need access to them to do the work the class is designed for. In a later version of the `Body` class, you will see that such a design is not usually a good idea.

2.4 Creating Objects

In this first version of Body, objects that represent particular celestial bodies are created and initialized like this:

```
Body sun = new Body();
sun.idNum = Body.nextID++;
sun.nameFor = "Sol";
sun.orbits = null; // in solar system, sun is middle

Body earth = new Body();
earth.idNum = Body.nextID++;
earth.nameFor = "Earth";
earth.orbits = sun;
```

First we declare a reference (sun) that can refer to objects of type Body. As mentioned before, such a declaration does *not* create an object; it only defines a variable that *references* objects. The object it refers to must be created explicitly.

We create the sun using new. The new construct is by far the most common way to create objects (we cover the other ways later). When you create an object with new, you specify the type of object you want to create and any parameters to its construction. The Java runtime system allocates enough space to store the fields of the object and initializes it in ways you will soon see. When initialization is complete, the runtime system returns a reference to the new object.

If the system cannot find enough free space to create the object, it may have to run the garbage collector to try to reclaim space. If the system still cannot find enough free space, new throws an OutOfMemoryError exception.

Having created a new Body object, we initialize its variables. Each Body object needs a unique identifier, which it gets from the static nextID field of Body. The code must increment nextID so that the next Body object created will get a unique identifier.

We then make an earth object in a similar fashion. This example builds a solar system model. In this model, the Sun is in the center, and sun's orbits field is null because it doesn't orbit anything. When we create and initialize earth, we set its orbits field to sun. A moon object would have its orbits field set to earth. In a model of the galaxy, the sun would orbit around the black hole presumed to be at the middle of the Milky Way.

Exercise 2.4: Write a main method for your Vehicle class that creates a few vehicles and prints their field values.

Exercise 2.5: Write a `main` method for your `LinkedList` class that creates a few objects of type `Vehicle` and places them into successive nodes in the list.

2.5 Constructors

A newly created object is given an initial state. Fields can be initialized with a value when they are declared, which is sometimes sufficient to ensure a correct initial state.[1] But often you need more than simple data initialization to create the initial state; the creating code may need to supply initial data or perform operations that cannot be expressed as simple assignment.

For purposes other than simple initialization, classes can have *constructors*. Constructors have the same name as the class they initialize. Like methods, they take zero or more parameters, but constructors are not methods and thus have no return type. Parameters, if any, are provided between the parentheses that follow the type name when the object is created with new. Constructors are invoked after the instance variables of a newly created object of the class have been assigned their default initial values and after their explicit initializers are executed.

This improved version of the Body class uses both constructors and initializers to set up each new object's initial state:

```
class Body {
    public long idNum;
    public String name = "<unnamed>";
    public Body orbits = null;

    private static long nextID = 0;

    Body() {
        idNum = nextID++;
    }
}
```

The constructor for Body takes no arguments, but it performs an important function—assigning a proper idNum to the newly created object. In the original code, a simple programmer error—forgetting to assign the idNum or not incrementing nextID after use—could result in different Body objects with the same idNum.

---

[1] Data initialization is covered in detail in "Initial Values" on page 117, but is a simple assignment of an initial value. If no value is assigned to a field it will be zero, '\u0000', false, or null, depending on its type.

That would create bugs in code that relies on the part of the contract that says "All idNum values are different."

By moving responsibility for idNum generation inside the Body class, we have prevented errors of this kind. The Body constructor is now the only entity that assigns idNum and is therefore the only entity that needs access to nextID. We can and should make nextID private so that only the Body class can access it. By doing so, we remove a source of error for programmers using the Body class.

We also are now free to change the way idNum values are assigned to Body objects. A future implementation of this class might, for example, look up the name in a database of known astronomical entities and assign a new idNum only if an idNum had not previously been assigned. This change would not affect any existing code, because existing code is not involved at all in the mechanism for idNum allocation.

The data initializations for name and orbits set them to reasonable values. Therefore, when the constructor returns from the following invocations, all data fields in the new Body object have been set to some reasonable initial state. You can then set state in the object to the values you want:

```
Body sun = new Body();    // idNum is 0
sun.name = "Sol";

Body earth = new Body(); // idNum is 1
earth.name = "Earth";
earth.orbits = sun;
```

The Body constructor is invoked when new creates the object but *after* name and orbits have been set to their initial values. Initializing orbits to null means that sun.orbits doesn't need to be set in our code.

The case shown here—in which you create a body knowing its name and what it orbits—is likely to be fairly common. You can provide another constructor that takes both the name and the orbited body:

```
Body(String bodyName, Body orbitsAround) {
    this();
    name = bodyName;
    orbits = orbitsAround;
}
```

As shown here, one constructor can invoke another constructor from the same class using the this() invocation as its first executable statement. This is called an explicit constructor invocation. If the constructor you want to invoke has parameters, they can be passed to the constructor invocation. Here we use it to invoke the constructor that has no arguments in order to set up the idNum. Now the allocation code is much simpler:

```
Body sun = new Body("Sol", null);
Body earth = new Body("Earth", sun);
```

You could also provide a one-argument constructor for constructing a Body object that doesn't orbit anything. This constructor would be used instead of invoking the two-argument Body constructor with a second argument of null.

Some classes always require that the creator supply certain kinds of data. For example, your application might require that all Body objects have a name. To ensure that all statements creating Body objects supply a name, you would define all Body constructors with a name parameter.

Here are some common reasons for providing specialized constructors:

◆ Some classes have no reasonable initial state without parameters.

◆ Providing an initial state is convenient and reasonable when you're constructing some kinds of objects (the two-argument constructor of Body is an example).

◆ Constructing an object can be a potentially expensive operation, so you want objects to have a correct initial state when they're created. For example, if each object of a class had a table, a constructor to specify the initial size would enable the object to create the table with the right size from the beginning.

◆ A constructor that isn't public restricts who can create objects using it. You could, for example, prevent programmers using your package from extending a class by making all its constructors accessible only inside the package. You can also mark as protected constructors that make sense only for subclasses.

Constructors without arguments are so common that there is a term for them: they are called *no-arg* (for "no arguments") constructors.

If you don't provide any constructors of any kind in a class, the language provides a default no-arg constructor that does nothing. This constructor—called the *default constructor*—is provided automatically only if no other constructors exist because there are classes for which a no-arg constructor would be incorrect (like the Attr class you will see in the next chapter).

If you want both a no-arg constructor and one or more constructors with arguments, you must explicitly provide a no-arg constructor. The default constructor for a class that has no superclass is equivalent to the following (you will see one for an extended class in Chapter 3):

```
public class SimpleClass {
    /** Same as default constructor */
    public SimpleClass() {
    }
}
```

The default constructor is as accessible as the class itself, so here the equivalent of the default constructor is `public` because the class is `public`.

Exercise 2.6: Add two constructors to `Vehicle`: a no-arg constructor and one that takes an initial owner's name. Modify the `main` program so that it generates the same output it did before.

Exercise 2.7: What constructors should you add to `LinkedList`?

2.6   Methods

A class's *methods* typically contain the code that understands and manipulates an object's state. Some classes have `public` fields for programmers to manipulate directly, but in most cases this isn't a very good idea (see "Designing a Class to Be Extended" on page 83). Many objects have tasks that cannot be represented as a simple value to be read or modified but require computation.

   Methods are *invoked* as operations on objects via references using the . operator:

```
reference.method(parameters)
```

Each method takes a specific number of parameters. Java does not include methods that can accept a variable number of parameters. Each parameter has a specified type: either a primitive type or a reference type. Methods also have a return type, which is declared before the method name. For example, here is a method of the Body class to create a `String` that describes a particular Body object:

```
public String toString() {
    String desc = idNum + " (" + name + ")";
    if (orbits != null)
        desc += " orbits " + orbits.toString();
    return desc;
}
```

This method uses + and += to concatenate `String` objects. It first builds a string that describes the identifier and name. If the body orbits another body, we append the string that describes *that* body by invoking its `toString` method. This recursion builds a string of bodies orbiting other bodies until the chain ends with an object that doesn't orbit anything.

The `toString` method is special. If an object has a method named `toString` that takes no parameters and returns a `String`, it is invoked to get a `String` when that object is used in a string concatenation using the + operator. Consider these expressions:

```
System.out.println("Body " + sun);
System.out.println("Body " + earth);
```

The `toString` methods of `sun` and `earth` are invoked implicitly and produce the following output:

```
Body 0 (Sol)
Body 1 (Earth) orbits 0 (Sol)
```

Methods can return more than one result in several ways: return references to objects that store the results as fields, take one or more parameters that reference objects in which to store the results, or return an array that contains the results. Suppose, for instance, that you want to write a method to return what a particular person can do with a given bank account. Multiple actions are possible (deposit, withdraw, and so on), so you must return multiple permissions. You could create a `Permissions` class whose objects store boolean values to say whether a particular action is allowed:

```
public class Permissions {
    public boolean canDeposit,
                   canWithdraw,
                   canClose;
}
```

Here is a method that fills in the fields to return multiple values:

```
public class BankAccount {
    private long number;        // account number
    private long balance;       // current balance

    public Permissions permissionsFor(Person who) {
        Permissions perm = new Permissions();
        perm.canDeposit = canDeposit(who);
        perm.canWithdraw = canWithdraw(who);
```

```
            perm.canClose = canClose(who);
            return perm;
        }


        // ... define canDeposit et al ...
    }
```

If a method does not return any value, the place where a return type would go is filled with a `void`. In methods that return a value, every path through the method must return a value that is assignable to a variable of the declared return type. The `getPermissions` method could not return, say, a `String`, because you cannot assign a `String` object to a variable of type `Permissions`. But you could declare the return type of `getPermissions` as `Object` without changing the `return` statement, because you can assign a `Permissions` object reference to a variable of type `Object`.

2.6.1 Parameter Values

All parameters to Java methods are "pass by value." In other words, values of parameter variables in a method are copies of the values the invoker specified as arguments. If you pass a `boolean` to a method, its parameter is a copy of whatever value was being passed as an argument, and the method can change its parameter's value without affecting values in the code that invoked the method. For example:

```
class PassByValue {
    public static void main(String[] args) {
        double one = 1.0;

        System.out.println("before: one = " + one);
        halveIt(one);
        System.out.println("after:  one = " + one);
    }

    public static void halveIt(double arg) {
        arg /= 2.0;        // divide arg by two
        System.out.println("halved: arg = " + arg);
    }
}
```

The following output illustrates that the value of `arg` inside `halveIt` is divided by two without affecting the value of the variable `one` in `main`:

```
before: one = 1.0
halved: arg = 0.5
after:  one = 1.0
```

You should note that when the parameter is an object reference, the object *reference*—not the object itself—is what is passed "by value." Thus, you can change which object a parameter refers to inside the method without affecting the reference that was passed. But if you change any fields of the object or invoke methods that change the object's state, the object is changed for every part of the program that holds a reference to it. Here is an example to show this distinction:

```java
class PassRef {
    public static void main(String[] args) {
        Body sirius = new Body("Sirius", null);

        System.out.println("before: " + sirius);
        commonName(sirius);
        System.out.println("after:  " + sirius);
    }

    public static void commonName(Body bodyRef) {
        bodyRef.name = "Dog Star";
        bodyRef = null;
    }
}
```

This program produces the following output:

```
before: 0 (Sirius)
after:  0 (Dog Star)
```

Notice that the contents of the object have been modified with a name change, while the reference `bodyRef` still refers to the `Body` object even though the method `commonName` changed the value of its `bodyRef` parameter to `null`. This requires some explanation.

The following diagram shows the state of the references just after `main` invokes `commonName`:

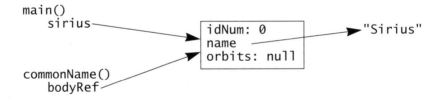

At this point, the two references `sirius` (in `main`) and `bodyRef` (in `commonName`) both refer to the same underlying object. When `commonName` changes the field `bodyRef.name`, the name is changed in the underlying object that the two references share. When `commonName` changes the value of `bodyRef` to `null`, only the value of the `bodyRef` reference is changed; the value of `sirius` remains unchanged because the parameter `bodyRef` is a pass-by-value copy of `sirius`. Inside the method `commonName`, all you are changing is the value in the parameter variable `bodyRef`, just as all you changed in `halveIt` was the value in the parameter variable `arg`. If changing `bodyRef` affected the value of `sirius` in `main`, the "after" line would say "`null`". However, the variable `bodyRef` in `commonName` and the variable `sirius` in `main` both refer to the same underlying object, so the change made inside `commonName` is visible through the reference `sirius`.

Some people will say incorrectly that objects in Java are "pass by reference." The term *pass by reference* properly means that when an argument is passed to a function, the invoked function gets a reference to the original value, not a copy of its value. If the function modifies its parameter, the value in the calling code will be changed because the argument and parameter use the same slot in memory. If Java had pass-by-reference parameters, there would be a way to declare `halveIt` so that the preceding code would modify the value of `one`, or so that `commonName` could change the variable `sirius` to `null`. This is not possible. Java does not pass objects by reference; it passes object references by value. Because two copies of the same reference refer to the same actual object, changes made through one reference are visible through the other. There is exactly one parameter passing mode in Java—pass by value—and that helps keep things simple.

You can declare method parameters to be `final`, meaning that the value of the parameter will not change while the method is running. Had `bodyRef` been declared `final`, the compiler would not have allowed you to change its value to `null`. When you do not intend to change a parameter's value, declare it `final` so the compiler can enforce this expectation. The declaration also helps the compiler or virtual machine optimize some expressions using the parameter, because it is known to remain the same. A `final` modifier of a parameter is an implementation detail that affects only the method's code, not the invoking code, so you can change whether a parameter is final without affecting any invoking code.

2.6.2 Using Methods to Control Access

The Body class with its various constructors is considerably easier to use than its simple data-only form, and we have ensured that the idNum is set both automatically and correctly. But a programmer could still mess up the object by setting its idNum field after construction, because the idNum field is public and therefore exposed to change. The idNum should be read-only data. Read-only data in objects is common, but there is no keyword to apply to a field that allows read-only access outside the class while letting the class itself modify the field.

To enforce read-only access, you must hide the field or make it final, which makes it read-only for the lifetime of the object. You hide the field by making the idNum field private and providing a new method so that code outside the class can read its value using that method:

```
class Body {
    private long idNum; // now "private"

    public String name = "<unnamed>";
    public Body orbits = null;

    private static long nextID = 0;

    Body() {
        idNum = nextID++;
    }

    public long getID() {
        return idNum;
    }

    //...
}
```

Now programmers who want to use the body's identifier will invoke the getID method, which returns the value. There is no longer any way for programmers to modify the identifier—it has effectively become a read-only value outside the class. It can be modified only by the internal methods of the Body class.

Methods that regulate access to internal data are sometimes called *accessor methods*. You could also use accessor methods to protect the `name` and `orbits` fields, and you probably should.

Even if an application doesn't require fields to be read-only, making fields private and adding methods to set and fetch them enables you to add actions that may be needed in the future. If programmers can access a class's fields directly, you have no control over the values they will use or what happens when values are changed. For these reasons, you will see very few `public` fields in subsequent examples in this book.

Methods to get or set a value in an object's state are sometimes said to define a *property* of that object. For example, the `Body` class's `getID` can be said to define an `ID` property for `Body` objects that is retrieved by the `getID` method. Some automatic systems, including JavaBeans, use these conventions to provide automatic property manipulation systems; see "`java.beans`—Java Components" on page 367.

Marking the field as `final` is sometimes an alternative that prevents unwanted modifications to a field, but it has a serious cost. This alternative is discussed along with other aspects of final variables in "Using `final` for Variables" on page 111.

Exercise 2.8: Make the fields in your `Vehicle` class `private`, and add accessor methods for the fields. Which fields should have methods to change them, and which should not?

Exercise 2.9: Make the fields in your `LinkedList` class `private`, and add accessor methods for the fields. Which fields should have methods to change them, and which should not?

Exercise 2.10: Add a `changeSpeed` method that changes the current speed of the vehicle to a passed-in value and add a `stop` method that sets the speed to zero.

Exercise 2.11: Add a method to `LinkedList` to count the number of elements in a list.

2.7   `this`

You have already seen (on page 34) how you can use an explicit constructor invocation to invoke another one of your class's constructors at the beginning of a constructor. You can also use the special object reference `this` inside a non-static method, where it refers to the current object on which the method was invoked.

The this reference is most commonly used as a way to pass a reference to the current object as a parameter to other methods. Suppose a method requires adding the object to a list of objects awaiting some service. It might look something like this:

```
Service.add(this);
```

An implicit this is added to the beginning of any field or method reference inside a method if it is not provided by the programmer. For example, the assignment to str in this class:

```
class Name {
    public String str;

    Name() {
        str = "<unnamed>";
    }
}
```

is equivalent to the following:

```
this.str = "<unnamed>";
```

Conventionally, you use this only when it is needed: when the name of the field you need to access is hidden by a variable or parameter declaration. For example:

```
class Moose {
    String hairdresser;

    Moose(String hairdresser) {
        this.hairdresser = hairdresser;
    }
}
```

The hairdresser field is hidden inside the constructor by the parameter of the same name. To access the hairdresser field instead of the hairdresser parameter, we prefix it with this to specify that the field is the one belonging to "this" object. Deliberately hiding identifiers in this manner is considered good programming practice only in this idiomatic use in constructors and accessor methods.

In addition to this, you can use the keyword super to access hidden fields and invoke overridden methods of the superclass. The super keyword is covered in more detail in "Overriding Methods, Hiding Fields, and Nested Classes" on page 67.

2.8   Overloading Methods

In Java, each method has a *signature*, which is its name together with the number
and types of its parameters. Two methods can have the same name if they have
different numbers or types of parameters and thus different signatures. This feature is called *overloading*, because the simple name of the method has an overloaded (more than one) meaning. When you invoke a method, the compiler
compares the number and type of parameters to find the method that best matches
the available signatures. Here are some orbitsAround methods for our Body
class:

```java
public boolean orbitsAround(Body other) {
    return (orbits == other);
}

public boolean orbitsAround(long id) {
    return (orbits != null && orbits.idNum == idNum);
}
```

Both methods take one parameter, but the type of the parameter differs. If the
method orbitsAround is invoked with a Body reference, the method that compares that reference to the body's own reference is used. If orbitsAround is
invoked with a long body ID, the method compares against that ID. If the invocation matches neither of these signatures, the code will not compile.

The signature does not include the return type or the list of thrown exceptions,
and you cannot overload methods based on these factors. A full discussion of how
the language chooses which available overloaded method to invoke for a given
invocation can be found in "Member Access" on page 125.

Exercise 2.12: Add two turn methods to Vehicle: one that takes a number of
degrees to turn, and one that takes either of the constants Vehicle.TURN_LEFT or
Vehicle.TURN_RIGHT.

2.9   Static Members

A class has three kinds of members: fields, methods, and types (classes and interfaces). Each member specifies how it may be accessed and how it may be inherited (private, protected, public, or package). Each member can also be made
static if so desired. You will learn about class and interface members in "Nested
Classes and Interfaces" on page 50; for now we will concentrate on fields and
methods.

A *static* member is a member that is only one per class, rather than one in every object created from that class. For static fields (class variables), there is exactly one variable, no matter how many objects (even zero) there are of the class. The nextID field in our Body class is an example.

The static fields of a class are initialized before any static field in that class is used and before any method of that class is run. In the following example, the unset method can assume that the UNSET variable has been initialized to the value Double.NaN before the unset method wants to use it:

```
class Value {
    public static double UNSET = Double.NaN;

    private double V;

    public void unset() {
        V = UNSET;
    }

    // ...
}
```

Initializers for static fields cannot invoke methods declared to throw checked exceptions: initializers are run when the class is loaded, and that can occur at an arbitrary time during program execution when nothing is prepared to handle the exceptions.

A static method is invoked on behalf of an entire class, not on a specific object instantiated from that class. Such methods are also known as *class methods*. A static method might perform a general task for all objects of the class, such as returning the next available serial number or something of that nature.

A static method can access only static variables and static methods of the class. There is no this reference because there is no specific object being operated on.

Outside a class, a static member is usually accessed by using the class name rather than through an object reference:

```
prime = Primes.nextPrime();
knownCnt = Primes.knownPrimes.length;
```

Exercise 2.13: Add a static method to Vehicle that returns the highest identification number used thus far.

2.10 Initialization Blocks

A class can have *initialization blocks* to set up fields or other necessary states. Typically, these blocks are `static`. An initialization block is most useful when simple initialization clauses on the field declaration aren't up to the task of initialization. For example, creating a static array and initializing its elements sometimes must be done with executable statements. Here is example code to initialize a small array of primes:

```
class Primes {
    protected static int[] knownPrimes = new int[4];

    static {
        knownPrimes[0] = 2;
        for (int i = 1; i < knownPrimes.length; i++)
                knownPrimes[i] = nextPrime();
    }

}
```

The order of initialization within a class is first-to-last—each field initializer or initialization block is run before the next one, in order from the beginning of the source to the end. The static initializers are run when the class is loaded; the non-static initializers are executed when each object is created, before its constructor is run. With this guarantee, our static block in the example is assured that the `knownPrimes` array is already created before the initialization code block executes.

What if a static initializer in class X invokes a method in Y, but Y's static initializers invoke a method in X to set up *its* static values? This cyclic static initialization cannot be reliably detected during compilation because the code for Y may not be written when X is compiled. If cycles happen, X's static initializers will have been executed only to the point where Y's method was invoked. When Y, in turn, invokes the X method, that method runs with the rest of the static initializers yet to be executed. Any static fields in X that haven't had their initializers executed will still have their default values (`false`, `'\u0000'`, zero, or `null` depending on their type).

Although an initializer for a static field cannot throw a checked exception, a static initialization block can invoke methods that throw exceptions, but only if it is prepared to catch all of them.

You can have non-static initialization blocks, which look just like static blocks without the `static`. Initialization code usually belongs in field initializers and constructors, but occasionally you will find it inconvenient to have a shared constructor to execute common initialization code. This code can be placed in a non-static initialization block, which will be executed when each new object of the class is created. The order for non-static initialization is the same as for static: initializers are executed first-to-last.

2.11 Garbage Collection and `finalize`

Java performs garbage collection for you and eliminates the need to free objects explicitly.

In simple terms, when an object is no longer reachable from any executable code, the space it occupies can be reclaimed. You do not have to do anything to make this happen—in fact, there is nothing you *can* do. An object is "no longer reachable" when no reference to the object exists in any variable of any currently executing method, nor can you find a reference to the object by starting such variables and then following each field or array element, and so on. You create objects using new, but there is no corresponding `delete`. When you are finished with an object, you simply stop referring to it—change your reference to refer to another object or to `null`, or return from a method so its local variables no longer exist and hence refer to nothing. When an object has no references to it anywhere, except in other objects that are also unreferenced, it can be collected. We use the phrase "can be" because space is reclaimed at the garbage collector's discretion, usually only if more space is needed or if the collector wants to avoid running out of memory. A program may exit without running out of space or even coming close, and so may never need to perform garbage collection.

Garbage collection means never having to worry about *dangling references*. In systems where you directly control when objects are deleted, you can delete an object to which some other object still has a reference. That other reference is now dangling, meaning it refers to space that the system considers free. Space that is thought to be free might be allocated to a new object, and the dangling reference would then reference something completely different from what the object thought it referenced. This situation would cause all manner of havoc when the program uses the values in that space as if they were part of something they are not. Java solves the dangling reference problem for you, because an object that's still referenced somewhere will never be garbage-collected and so will never be considered free.

Garbage is collected without your intervention, but collecting garbage still takes work. Creating and collecting large numbers of objects can interfere with time-critical applications. You should design systems to be judicious in the number of objects they create to reduce the amount of garbage to be collected.

Garbage collection is not a guarantee that memory will always be available for new objects. You could create objects indefinitely, place them in lists, and continue doing so until there is no more space and no unreferenced objects to reclaim. You could create a memory leak by, for example, allowing a list of objects to refer to objects you no longer need. Garbage collection solves many, but not all, memory allocation problems.

2.11.1 finalize

You won't normally notice when an orphaned object's space is reclaimed—"it just works." But a class can implement a finalize method that is executed before an object's space is reclaimed. Such a finalize method gives you a chance to use the state contained in the object to reclaim other non-Java resources. It is declared like this:

```
protected void finalize() throws Throwable {
    // ...
}
```

Using finalize methods is important when you're dealing with non-Java resources that are not reclaimed by garbage collection, which collects only memory. For example, open files (usually a limited resource) cannot wait until the finalize phase of garbage collection to be reclaimed. There is no guarantee that the object holding the open file will be collected before all the open file resources are used up. Still, objects that allocate external resources should provide a finalize method that cleans them up so the class doesn't itself create a resource leak. You will also need to provide a mechanism for programmers to explicitly reclaim those resources. For example, a class that opens a file to do its work should have some form of close method to close the file, enabling programmers using that class to manage the number-of-open-files resource explicitly.

Sometimes close may not be invoked even though a client is finished with an object. Some programmers may not have run into problems that require them to do so. You can delay the consequences of this "open file" leak by adding a finalize method that invokes close, thereby ensuring that, whatever the quality of the other programmer's code, it never leaks open files. Here is what that might look like:

```
public class ProcessFile {
    private Stream file;

    public ProcessFile(String path) {
        file = new Stream(path);
```

```
        }

        // ...

        public void close() {
            if (file != null) {
                file.close();
                file = null;
            }
        }

        protected void finalize() throws Throwable {
            try {
                close();
            } finally {
                super.finalize();
            }
        }
    }
```

Note that `close` is carefully written to be correct if it is invoked more than once. Otherwise, if someone invoked `close`, finalizing the object would cause another close on the file, which might not be allowed.

Note also that in this example, `finalize` invokes `super.finalize` in a `finally` clause. Train yourself so that you always do so in any `finalize` method you write. If you don't invoke `super.finalize`, you may correctly finalize your own part of the object, but the superclass's part will not get finalized. Invoking `super.finalize` is one of those good habits you should adopt even when your class doesn't extend any other class. In addition to being good training, invoking `super.finalize` in such a case means that you can always add a superclass to a class like `ProcessFile` without remembering to examine its `finalize` method for correctness. Invoking the superclass's `finalize` method in a `finally` clause ensures that the superclass's cleanup will happen even if your cleanup causes an exception.

The body of a `finalize` method can use `try-catch` to handle exceptions in methods it invokes. If an exception is thrown by a `finalize` method invoked by the garbage collector, that exception will be ignored. Exceptions are covered in detail in Chapter 7.

The garbage collector may reclaim objects in any order or never reclaim them. Memory resources are reclaimed when the garbage collector thinks the time is appropriate. Not being bound to an ordering guarantee, the garbage collector can operate in whatever manner is most efficient, and that helps minimize the over-head of garbage collection. You can, if necessary, invoke the garbage collector to try to force earlier collection—see "Memory Management" on page 322.

When an application exits, no further garbage collection is performed, so any objects that have not yet been collected will not have their finalize methods invoked. In many cases this will not be a problem. For example, on most systems when the virtual machine exits, the underlying system automatically closes all open files and sockets. However, for non-system resources, such as temporary files that should be removed, you will have to invent other solutions.

2.11.2 Resurrecting Objects during finalize

A finalize method can "resurrect" an object by making it referenced again—for example, by adding it to a static list of objects. Resurrection is discouraged, but there is nothing Java can do to stop you.

However, Java invokes finalize exactly once on any object, even if that object is collected more than once because a previous finalize resurrected it. If resurrecting objects is important to your design, the object would be resurrected only once—probably not the behavior you wanted.

If you think you need to resurrect objects, you should review your design carefully—you may uncover a flaw. If your design review convinces you that you need something like resurrection, the best solution is to clone the object or create a new object, not to resurrect it. The finalize method can insert a reference to a new object that will continue the state of the dying object rather than a reference to the dying object itself. Being new, the cloned object's finalize method will be invoked in the future (if needed), enabling it to insert yet another copy of itself in yet another list, ensuring the survival, if not of itself, at least of its progeny.

2.12 Nested Classes and Interfaces

Classes and interfaces can be members of another class or interface. These *nested classes* and *nested interfaces* are part of the contract or implementation of their *enclosing type*, and they have the same accessibility choices as other members.

The simplest form of nested class is the static nested class. A static nested class acts just like any top-level class except that its name and accessibility are defined by its *enclosing class*, the one in which it is declared. For example, on page 37 we showed a Permissions class that bears information about a BankAccount object. Because the Permissions class is part of the contract of the

BankAccount class—it is how a BankAccount object communicates a set of permissions—it is a good candidate to be a nested class:

```
public class BankAccount {
    private long number;        // account number
    private long balance;       // current balance

    public static class Permissions {
        public boolean canDeposit,
                       canWithdraw,
                       canClose;
    }
    // ...
}
```

The Permissions class is defined inside the BankAccount class, making it a member of that class. When getPermissions returns a Permissions object, it can call the class simply Permissions in the same way it can refer to balance without qualification: Permissions is a member of the class. The full name of the class is BankAccount.Permissions. This is a clear indication that this class exists as part of the BankAccount class, not as a stand-alone tool. If BankAccount were in a package named bank, the full name of the class would be bank.BankAccount.Permissions. Outside the class, the usual name of the class is BankAccount.Permissions. BankAccount is a class, not a package, and it is usually BankAccount that is the imported class name. You could import the class BankAccount.Permissions and then use the name Permissions, but you would lose the important information about the subsidiary nature of the class. Importing bank.* imports only the top-level classes of the package bank so you can use BankAccount as a short name but not BankAccount.Permissions.

Nested classes are class members, and you can declare them to be accessible in any way you like. You can, for example, declare a class that is an implementation detail to be private. We declare Permissions to be public because programmers using BankAccount need to use the class.

You often need to closely tie a nested class to a particular object of the enclosing class. Consider, for example, a method for the BankAccount class that lets you see the last action performed on the account, such as a deposit or withdrawal:

```
public class BankAccount {
    private long number;        // account number
    private long balance;       // current balance
    private Action lastAct;     // last action performed
```

```java
    public class Action {
        private String act;
        private long amount;
        Action(String act, long amount) {
            this.act = act;
            this.amount = amount;
        }
        public String toString() {
            return number + ": " + act + " " + amount;
        }
    }

    public void deposit(long amount) {
        balance += amount;
        lastAct = new Action("deposit", amount);
    }

    public void withdraw(long amount) {
        balance -= amount;
        lastAct = new Action("withdraw", amount);
    }
    // ...
}
```

The class `Action` records a single action on the account. It is not declared `static`, and that means it exists relative to an object of the class, not relative to the entire class. This relationship is defined when the `Action` object is created, as shown in the `deposit` and `withdraw` methods. When an object is created from a non-static nested class such as `Action`, an *enclosing object* is associated with the object as a sort of "outer `this`" reference. As is common in Java, the default object is `this` if none is specified. The creation code in `deposit` is the same as the more explicit

```java
lastAct = this.new Action("deposit", amount);
```

Any `BankAccount` object could be substituted for `this`. Non-static nested classes are called *inner classes.*[2]

The `toString` method of `Action` uses the `number` field of the `BankAccount` class directly. A nested class can use other members of its enclosing class—

---

[2]   Static nested classes are formally called *top-level nested classes.* Although useful in formal contexts, the term is also oxymoronic and hence confusing so we do not use it in this book.

including private fields—without qualification because it is part of the enclosing class's implementation. An inner class can simply name the members of its enclosing object to use them; a static nested class can directly access only static members of the enclosing class. When `deposit` creates an `Action` object, a reference to the enclosing `BankAccount` object is automatically stored in the new `Action` object. Using this saved reference, the `Action` object can always refer to the enclosing `BankAccount` object's `number` field by the simple name `number`, as shown in `toString`.

The name of the reference to the enclosing object is `this` preceded by the enclosing class name. For example, `toString` could reference the `number` field of the enclosing `BankAccount` object explicitly:

```
return BankAccount.this.number + ": " + act + " " + amount;
```

The `this` nomenclature reinforces the idea that the enclosing object and the inner object are tightly bound as part of the same implementation of the enclosing class.

Nested interfaces are always static because an enclosing object reference is inherently part of an implementation and interfaces have no implementation.

A nested class can have its own nested classes and interfaces. References to enclosing objects can be obtained for any level of nesting in the same way: the name of the class and `this`. If class X encloses class Y which encloses class Z, code in Z can explicitly access fields of X by using X.`this`.

Inner classes cannot have static members.

The language does not prevent you from deeply nesting classes, but good taste should. A doubly-nested class such as Z has three naming contexts: itself, its immediate enclosing class Y, and outermost class X. Someone reading the code for Z must understand each class thoroughly to know in which context an identifier is bound and which enclosing object was bound to which nested object. We recommend nesting only one level under most circumstances. Nesting more than two levels invites a readability disaster and should probably never be attempted.

Exercise 2.14: Create a version of `BankAccount` that records the last ten actions on the account. Add a `history` method that returns a `History` object that will return `Action` objects one at a time via a `next` method, returning `null` at the end of the list. Should `History` be a nested class? If so, should it be static or not?

2.12.1 Local Inner Classes

You can create inner classes and interfaces in code blocks, such as a method body. Inner classes in code—called *local inner classes*—are not members of the class of which the code is a part. Therefore, they cannot be private, protected, public, static, or final, because these modifiers apply only to class members. Just like local variables declared in a code block, local inner classes are part of the code block in which they are defined. They have access to the final variables in the code block as well as to the other members of the class, both static and non-static.

Consider the standard interface Enumeration defined in the `java.util` package. This interface defines a way to iterate through a group of objects. It is commonly used to provide a sequence of elements in a container object but can be used for any generic iteration:

```
package java.util;

public interface Enumeration {
    boolean hasMoreElements();
    Object nextElement() throws NoSuchElementException;
}
```

The hasMoreElements method returns `true` if there are more elements to return via nextElement. The exception NoSuchElementException—also part of the `java.util` package—is thrown if nextElement is invoked when there are no more elements. See "Enumeration" on page 276 for more details.

Here is a simple method that returns an Enumeration iterator to walk through an array of objects:

```
public static Enumeration walkThrough(final Object[] objs) {
    class Enum implements Enumeration {
        private int pos = 0;
        public boolean hasMoreElements() {
            return (pos < objs.length);
        }
        public Object nextElement()
            throws NoSuchElementException
        {
            if (pos >= objs.length)
                throw new NoSuchElementException();
            return objs[pos++];
        }
    }

    return new Enum();
}
```

The Enum class is local to the walkThrough method; it is not a member of the enclosing class. Because Enum is local to the method, it has access to all the final variables of the method. It needs a pos field to keep track of where it is in the objs array, and it uses the objs array from the parameter. (The code assumes that Enumeration and NoSuchElementException are imported from java.util in the source that contains walkThrough.)

Only final variables are accessible from local inner classes because this keeps the values consistent. Without this restriction, a different local inner object in walkThrough could modify the value of objs after walkThrough returned. That object would be interfering with the operation of our Enum object. Because objs is final, its value cannot change and it can be reliable for both objects.

2.13 main

Details of invoking a Java application vary from system to system, but whatever the details, you must always provide the name of a Java class that drives the application. When you run a Java program, the system locates and runs the main method for that class. The main method must be public, static, and void (it returns nothing), and it must accept a single argument of type String[]. Here is an example that prints its parameters:

```java
class Echo {
    public static void main(String[] args) {
        for (int i = 0; i < args.length; i++)
            System.out.print(args[i] + " ");
        System.out.println();
    }
}
```

The arguments in the string array passed to main are the *program arguments.* They are usually typed by users when they run the program. For example, on a command-line system such as UNIX or a DOS shell, you might invoke the Echo application this way:

```
java Echo in here
```

In this command, java is the Java bytecode interpreter, Echo is the name of the class, and the rest of the parameters are the program arguments. The java command finds the compiled bytecodes for the class Echo, loads them into a Java Virtual Machine, and invokes Echo.main with the program arguments contained in strings in the String array. The result is the following output:

```
in here
```

The name of the class is not included in the strings passed to main. You already know the name because it is the name of the enclosing class.

An application can have any number of `main` methods because each class can have one. Only one `main` is used any given time you run a program. The `main` that's actually used is specified when the program is run, as `Echo` was. The ability to have multiple `main` methods has one salutary effect: each class can have a `main` that tests its own code, providing an excellent hook for unit-testing a class. This is something we recommend as a coding technique.[3]

Exercise 2.15: Change `Vehicle.main` to create cars with owners whose names are specified on the command line, and then print them.

2.14 The `toString` Method

If an object supports a public `toString` method that takes no parameters and returns a `String` object, that method is invoked whenever a + or += expression has an object of that type where a `String` is expected. Here, for instance, is code that would print an array of celestial bodies:

```
static void displayBodies(Body[] bodies) {
    for (int i = 0; i < bodies.length; i++)
        System.out.println(i + ": " + bodies[i]);
}
```

If you examine the `println` invocation, you will see two implicit string conversions: the first for the index `i` and the second for the Body objects, with a separating string between them. All primitive types are implicitly converted to `String` objects when used in `String` expressions, but not at other times.

There is no universal `String`-to-object mechanism in Java. You can, of course, provide your own class decoding function. This method will typically either be some kind of `fromString` method that replaces an existing object's state or a constructor that takes a `String` parameter that sets up the object's initial state.

Exercise 2.16: Add a `toString` method to `Vehicle`.

Exercise 2.17: Add a `toString` method to `LinkedList`.

---

[3] Many of the example classes in this book have `main` methods. Space does not allow us to show the `main` method for every example, but it is how we usually write our own classes for non-trivial applications and libraries.

2.15 Native Methods

If you need to write a Java program that will use some existing code that isn't written in Java, or if you need to manipulate some hardware directly, you can write *native methods*. A native method lets you implement a method that can be invoked from Java but is written in a "native" language, usually C or C++.

If you use a native method, all portability and safety of the code are lost. You cannot, for instance, use a native method in almost any code you expect to download and run from across a network connection (an applet, for example). The downloading system may or may not be of the same architecture, and even if it is, it might not trust your system well enough to run arbitrary compiled C code. The advantages of writing pure Java code are lost.

Native methods are implemented using an API provided by the people who wrote the virtual machine on which the code executes. The standard one for C programmers is called JNI—Java Native Interface. Others are being defined for other native languages. A description of these APIs is beyond the scope of this book.

> *The significant problems we face cannot be solved*
> *by the same level of thinking that created them.*
> —Albert Einstein

CHAPTER 3

Extending Classes

You will understand this when I tell you that I can trace
my ancestry back to a protoplasmal primordial atomic globule.
—Gilbert and Sullivan, *The Mikado*

THE quick tour (Chapter 1) described briefly how a class can be *extended*, or *subclassed*, and how an extended class can be used wherever the original class was legal. The term for this capability is *polymorphism*, meaning that an object of a given class can have multiple forms, either as its own class or as any superclass it extends. The extended class is a *subclass* or *extended class* of the class it extends; the class that is extended is its *superclass*.

The collection of methods and fields that are accessible from outside a class, together with the description of how those members are expected to behave, is often referred to as the class's *contract*. The contract is what the class designer has promised that the class will do. Whenever you extend a class to add new functionality, you create a new class with an expanded contract. You do not, however, change the part of the contract you *inherit* from the class you extended. Changing the way that the superclass's contract is implemented is reasonable, but you should never change the implementation in a way that violates the superclass's contract.

3.1 An Extended Class

Every class you have seen so far is an extended class, whether or not it is declared with an `extends` clause. A class such as `Body` that does not explicitly extend another class implicitly extends Java's `Object` class. In other words, `Object` is at the root of the Java class hierarchy. The `Object` class declares methods that are implemented by all objects. Variables of type `Object` can refer to any object, whether it is a class instance or an array.

For example, if you make a list class whose elements can be any type of object, you can declare it to have a field of type `Object`. The list still would not be able to hold primitive types (`int`, `boolean`, and so on), but you can make objects of these types if you need to, using the *wrapper classes* (`Integer`, `Boolean`, and so on) described in Chapter 14. The `Object` class itself is described in more detail on page 72.

To demonstrate subclassing, we start with a basic attribute class designed to store name–value pairs. Attribute names are human-readable strings, such as "color" or "location." Attributes can have any type of value, so the value is stored in a variable of type `Object`:

```java
class Attr {
    private String name;
    private Object value = null;

    public Attr(String name) {
        this.name = name;
    }

    public Attr(String name, Object value) {
        this.name = name;
        this.value = value;
    }

    public String getName() {
        return name;
    }

    public Object getValue() {
        return value;
    }

    public Object setValue(Object newValue) {
        Object oldVal = value;
        value = newValue;
        return oldVal;
    }

    public String toString() {
```

```
        return name + "='" + value + "'";
    }
}
```

An attribute must have a name, so the `Attr` constructors require name parameters. The name must be read-only, because it may be used, for example, as a key into a hashtable or sorted list. In such a case, if the name field were modified from outside the class, the attribute object would become "lost" because it would be filed under the old name, not the modified one. The value, however, can be changed at any time.

The next class extends the notion of attribute to store color attributes, which might be strings that name or describe colors. Color descriptions might be color names like "red" or "ecru" that must be looked up in a table, or numeric values that can be decoded to produce a standard, more efficient color representation we call `ScreenColor` (assumed to be defined elsewhere). Decoding a description into a `ScreenColor` object is expensive enough that you would like to do it only once. So we extend the `Attr` class to create a `ColorAttr` class to support a method to retrieve a decoded `ScreenColor` object. We implement it so the decoding is done only once:

```
class ColorAttr extends Attr {
    private ScreenColor myColor; // the decoded color

    public ColorAttr(String name, Object value) {
        super(name, value);
        decodeColor();
    }

    public ColorAttr(String name) {
        this(name, "transparent");
    }

    public ColorAttr(String name, ScreenColor value) {
        super(name, value.toString());
        myColor = value;
    }

    public Object setValue(Object newValue) {
        // do the superclass's setValue work first
        Object retval = super.setValue(newValue);
        decodeColor();
        return retval;
```

```
        }

        /** Set value to ScreenColor, not description */
        public ScreenColor setValue(ScreenColor newValue) {
            // do the superclass's setValue work first
            super.setValue(newValue.toString());
            ScreenColor oldValue = myColor;
            myColor = newValue;
            return oldValue;
        }

        /** Return decoded ScreenColor object */
        public ScreenColor getColor() {
            return myColor;
        }

        /** set ScreenColor from description in getValue */
        protected void decodeColor() {
            if (getValue() == null)
                myColor = null;
            else
                myColor = new ScreenColor(getValue());
        }
    }
```

First we create a new `ColorAttr` class that `extends` the `Attr` class. The `ColorAttr` class does everything the `Attr` class does and adds new behavior. Therefore, the `Attr` class is the superclass of `ColorAttr`, and `ColorAttr` is a subclass of `Attr`. The *class hierarchy* for these classes looks like this, going top-down from superclass to subclass:

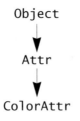

The extended `ColorAttr` class does three primary things:

◆ It provides three constructors: two to mirror its superclass and one to directly provide a `ScreenColor` object.

◆ It both overloads and overrides the setValue method of its base class so that it can set the color object when the value is changed.

◆ It provides a new getColor method to return a value that is the color description decoded into a ScreenColor object.

Exercise 3.1: Starting with the Vehicle class from Chapter 2, create an extended class called PassengerVehicle to add a capability for counting the number of seats available in the car and the number currently occupied. Provide a new main method in PassengerVehicle to create a few of these objects and print them out.

3.2   What protected Really Means

We noted briefly that making a class member protected means it can be accessed by classes that extend that class, but that is loose language. More precisely, beyond being accessible within the class itself and to code within the same package, a protected member can also be accessed from a class through object references that are of at least the same type as the class—that is, references of the class's type or one its subtypes. An example will make this easier to understand. Assume the following class hierarchy:

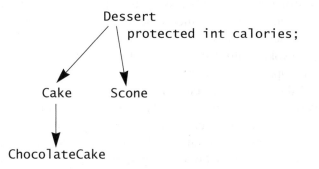

The calories field in the Dessert class is protected. Each class that extends Dessert inherits its calories field. However, code in the Cake class can access the calories field *only* through a reference of type Cake or a subclass of Cake, including, for example, references of type ChocolateCake. Code in the Cake class could not access the calories field through a reference of type Scone. This restriction ensures that the protected fields of a class are not accessed outside the part of the class hierarchy of the accessing class. If your Cake code had a reference of the more generic Dessert type, you couldn't use it to access calories, but you could cast it to a `Cake` reference and use the result—assuming, of course, that the object being referenced really was (at least) a `Cake`.

A `protected` method, class, or interface is treated in the same way: you can access it only using a reference to a type that is at least the type of the class code using the reference.

Protected static fields, methods, and classes and interfaces can be accessed in any extended class. If `calories` were a static field, any method (static or not) in `Cake`, `ChocolateCake`, and `Scone` could access it.

Members declared `protected` are also available to any code within the class itself or within the package. If all these `Dessert` classes are in the same package, they can access one another's `calories` fields, as can any unrelated type in that package. In the list "private, package, protected, public," each access level adds to the kinds of code to which a member is accessible.

3.3 Constructors in Extended Classes

When you extend a class, the new class must choose one of its superclass's constructors to invoke. The part of the object controlled by the superclass must be constructed properly, in addition to ensuring a correct initial state for your subclass's added fields.

In a constructor in the subclass, you can directly invoke one of the superclass's constructors using another kind of explicit constructor invocation, the `super()` construct. This is shown in the first constructor of the `ColorAttr` class. If you do not invoke a superclass constructor as your constructor's first executable statement, the superclass's no-arg constructor is automatically invoked before any statements of the new constructor are executed. If the superclass doesn't have a no-arg constructor, you must explicitly invoke one of the superclass's constructors, or you can invoke another of your own constructors using the `this()` construct. If you use `super()`, it must be the first statement of the new constructor.

The first constructor of `ColorAttr` shows how to invoke a superclass constructor. It passes the name and value up to its superclass's two-argument constructor. Then it invokes its own `decodeColor` method to make `myColor` hold a reference to the correct color object.

You can defer the choice of which superclass constructor to use by invoking one of your class's own constructors using `this()` instead of `super()`. The second constructor of `ColorAttr` does precisely this. We chose to ensure that every color attribute has a color. If a color value is not supplied, we provide a default of "transparent."

The third constructor of `ColorAttr` enables the programmer creating a new `ColorAttr` object to specify the `ScreenColor` object itself. The first two constructors must convert their parameters to ScreenColor objects using the decodeColor method, and that presumably has some overhead. When the programmer already has a ScreenColor object to provide as a value, we want to avoid the overhead of that conversion. This is an example of providing a constructor that adds efficiency, not capability.

In this example, ColorAttr has constructors with the same signatures as its superclass's constructors. This arrangement is by no means required. Sometimes part of an extended class's benefit is to provide useful parameters to the superclass constructors based on few or no parameters of its own. It is common to have an extended class that has no constructor signatures in common with its superclass.

The language provides a default no-arg constructor for you. The default constructor for an extended class starts by invoking the superclass's no-arg constructor. However, if the superclass does not have a no-arg constructor, the new extended class must provide at least one constructor. The default constructor for an extended class is equivalent to

```java
public class ExtendedClass extends SimpleClass {
    public ExtendedClass() {
        super();
    }
}
```

Remember that a default constructor is as public as its class. ExtendedClass is public, so the default constructor is also public.

3.3.1 Constructor Order Dependencies

When an object is created, all its fields are set to default initial values for their respective types (zero for all numeric types, false for boolean, \u0000 for char, and null for object references). Then the constructor is invoked. Each constructor has three phases:

1. Invoke a superclass's constructor.
2. Initialize the fields using their initializers and any initialization blocks.
3. Execute the body of the constructor.

Here is an example we can trace:

```java
class X {
    protected int xMask = 0x00ff;
    protected int fullMask;
```

```
    public X() {
        fullMask = xMask;
    }

    public int mask(int orig) {
        return (orig & fullMask);
    }
}

class Y extends X {
    protected int yMask = 0xff00;

    public Y() {
        fullMask |= yMask;
    }
}
```

If you create an object of type Y and follow the construction step by step, here are the values of the fields after each step:

Step	What Happens	xMask	yMask	fullMask
0	Fields set to default values	0	0	0
1	Y constructor invoked	0	0	0
2	X constructor invoked	0	0	0
3	X field initialization	0x00ff	0	0
4	X constructor executed	0x00ff	0	0x00ff
5	Y field initialization	0x00ff	0xff00	0x00ff
6	Y constructor executed	0x00ff	0xff00	0xffff

Understanding this ordering is important when you invoke methods during construction. When you invoke a method, you always get the implementation of that method for the actual type of the object. If the method uses fields of the actual type, they may not have been initialized yet. During step 4, if the constructor X invokes mask, it would use a fullMask value of 0x00ff, not 0xffff. This is true even though a later invocation of mask—after the object was completely constructed—uses 0xffff.

Also, imagine that class Y overrides mask with an implementation that explicitly uses the yMask field in its calculations. When the constructor X uses the mask method, it would actually invoke Y's mask method, and at that point yMask would be 0 instead of the expected 0xff00.

Methods you invoke during the construction phase of an object must be designed with these factors in mind. Your constructors should avoid invoking overridable methods—methods that are neither private, static, nor final. If you do invoke such methods, clearly list them in your documentation to alert anyone wanting to override these methods of their potential unusual use.

Exercise 3.2: Type in the classes X and Y as shown previously, and add print statements to trace the values of the masks. Add a `main` method and run it to see the results. Add an override of `mask` to Y and run the test again.

Exercise 3.3: If it were critical to set up these masks properly during construction, how could you work around these problems?

3.4   Overriding Methods, Hiding Fields, and Nested Classes

In our new `ColorAttr` class we have both *overridden* and *overloaded* the method `setValue`:

- *Overloading* a method is what we have already discussed: providing more than one method with the same name but with different signatures to distinguish them.

- *Overriding* a method means replacing the superclass's implementation of a method with one of your own. The signatures must be identical. Note that only accessible non-static methods can be overridden.

In the `ColorAttr` class, we overrode `Attr.setValue(Object)` by providing a new `ColorAttr.setValue(Object)` method that uses the `super` keyword to invoke the superclass's implementation and then invokes `decodeColor`. The `super` reference can be used in method invocations to access methods from the superclass that are overridden in this class. We discuss `super` in detail later.

When you're overriding methods, both the signature and return type must be the same as the superclass. A subclass can change whether a parameter in an overridden method is `final`; a `final` modifier for a parameter is not part of the method signature—it is an implementation detail. Also, the overriding method's `throws` clause can be different from that of the superclass method's as long as every exception type listed in the overriding method is the same or a subtype of the exceptions listed in the superclass's method. That is, each type in the overriding method's `throws` clause must be polymorphically compatible with at least one of the types listed in the `throws` clause of the supertype's method. This means that the `throws` clause of an overriding method can have fewer types listed than the method in the superclass, or more specific types, or both. The overriding method can even have no `throws` clause, which means that it results in no checked exceptions.

Overriding methods have their own access specifiers. An extended class can change the access of a superclass's methods, but only if it provides more access. A method declared `protected` in the superclass can be redeclared `protected` (the usual thing to do) or declared `public`, but it cannot be declared `private`. Making a method less accessible than it was in a superclass would actually be a meaningless access restriction because the increased restriction could be foiled by simply referring to an object via a reference to a supertype that gives wider access to the method.

Fields cannot be overridden; they can only be *hidden*. If you declare a field in your class with the same name as one in your superclass, that other field still exists, but it can no longer be accessed directly by its simple name. You must use `super` or another reference of your superclass's type to access it. You will usually use the name of the superclass to access a hidden static field.

When you invoke a method on an object, the *actual class* of the *object* governs which implementation is used. When you access a field, the *declared type* of the *reference* is used. The following example will help to explain:

```
class SuperShow {
    public String str = "SuperStr";

    public void show() {
        System.out.println("Super.show: " + str);
    }
}

class ExtendShow extends SuperShow {
    public String str = "ExtendStr";

    public void show() {
        System.out.println("Extend.show: " + str);
    }

    public static void main(String[] args) {
        ExtendShow ext = new ExtendShow();
        SuperShow sup = ext;
        sup.show();
        ext.show();
```

```
        System.out.println("sup.str = " + sup.str);
        System.out.println("ext.str = " + ext.str);
    }
}
```

There is only one object, but we have two references to it: one reference as its actual class and the other as its superclass. Here is the output of the example when run:

```
Extend.show: ExtendStr
Extend.show: ExtendStr
sup.str = SuperStr
ext.str = ExtendStr
```

For the show method, the behavior is as you expect: the actual class of the object, not the type of the reference, governs which version of the method is called. When we have an ExtendShow object, invoking show always calls ExtendShow's show even if we access it via a reference declared with the type SuperShow.

For the str field, the declared type of the *reference*, not the actual class of the *object*, determines which class's field is accessed. In fact, each ExtendShow object has *two* String variables, both called str, one of which is inherited and hidden by ExtendShow's own, different field called str:

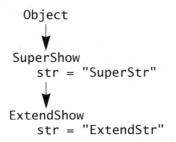

You've already seen that method overriding enables you to extend existing code by reusing it with objects of expanded, specialized functionality not foreseen by the inventor of the original code. But where fields are concerned, it is hard to think of cases in which hiding them is a useful feature.

If an existing method had a parameter of type SuperShow and accessed str with that object's reference, it would always get SuperShow.str even if the method were actually handed an object of type ExtendShow. If the classes were designed to use a method instead of a field to access the string, the overridden method would be invoked in such a case and the ExtendShow.str could be returned. This hiding behavior is often another reason to prefer defining classes with private data accessed only by methods, which are overridden, not hidden.

Hiding fields is allowed in Java because implementors of existing super-classes must be free to add new `public` or `protected` fields without breaking subclasses. If Java forbade using the same field name in a superclass and a sub-class, adding a new field to an existing superclass could potentially break any sub-classes already using those names.

If adding new fields to existing superclasses would break some unknown number of subclasses, you'd be effectively immobilized, unable to add `public` or `protected` fields to a superclass. Purists might well argue that classes should have only `private` data, but Java lets you decide on your style.

Nested classes and interfaces can also be hidden in subclasses. If a subclass has a nested class and its superclass has a nested class with the same name, the subclass's nested class will hide the superclass's nested class. You can explicitly name the superclass's nested class to access it or its members.

3.4.1   The super Keyword

The `super` keyword is available in all non-static methods of a class. In field access and method invocation, `super` acts as a reference to the current object as an instance of its superclass. Using `super` is the only case where the type of the ref-erence governs selection of the method implementation to be used. An invocation of `super.`*method* always uses the superclass's implementation of *method*. It does not use any overridden implementation of that method farther down the class hier-archy.

Method invocation using `super` is different in this way from all other invoca-tions, which choose the method implementation based on the class of the object, not on the type of the reference. Here is an example that shows `super` in action:

```
class That {
    /** return the class name */
    protected String nm() {
        return "That";
    }
}

class More extends That {
    protected String nm() {
        return "More";
    }

    protected void printNM() {
        That sref = (That)this;
```

```
            System.out.println("this.nm()  = " + this.nm());
            System.out.println("sref.nm()  = " + sref.nm());
            System.out.println("super.nm() = " + super.nm());
        }
    }
```

Although sref and super both refer to the same object using the type That, only super will ignore the real class of the object to use the superclass's implementation of nm. The reference sref will act the same way this acts, selecting an implementation of nm based on the actual class of the object. Here is the output of printNM:

```
    this.nm()  = More
    sref.nm()  = More
    super.nm() = That
```

3.5   Marking Methods and Classes final

Marking a method final means that no extended class can override the method to change its behavior. In other words, this is the *final* version of that method. Entire classes can also be marked final:

```
    final class NoExtending {
        // ...
    }
```

A class marked final cannot be extended by any other class, and all the methods of a final class are themselves implicitly final.

There are two major ramifications of marking a method as final. The first is security: anyone who uses the class can be sure that the behavior will not change, no matter what actual type of object is given to them.

Final classes and methods can improve security. If a class is final, nobody can declare a class that extends it, and therefore nobody can violate its contract. If a method is final, you can rely on its implementation details (unless it invokes non-final methods, of course). You could use final, for example, on a validatePassword method to ensure that it does what it is advertised to do instead of being overridden to always return true. Or you can mark the class that contains the method as final so that it can never be extended to confuse the implementation of validatePassword.

Marking a method or class final is a serious restriction on the use of the class. If you make a method final, you should really intend that its behavior be completely fixed. You restrict the flexibility of your class for other programmers who might want to use it as a basis to add functionality to their code. Marking an entire class `final` prevents anyone else from extending your class, limiting its usefulness to others. If you make anything `final`, be sure that you want to create these restrictions.

In many cases, you can achieve the security of marking a whole class `final` by leaving the class extensible and instead marking each method in the class as `final`. In this way, you can rely on the behavior of those methods while still allowing extensions that can add functionality without overriding methods. Of course, fields that the `final` methods rely on should be `final` or `private`, or else an extended class could change behavior by changing those fields.

A second ramification is that `final` simplifies optimizations. When a non-`final` method is invoked, the Java runtime system determines the actual class of the object, binds the method invocation to the correct implementation of the method for that type, and then invokes that implementation. But if the `getName` method was `final` in the `Attr` class, for example, and you have a reference to an object of type `Attr` or any extended type, it may be possible to simplify the steps needed to invoke the method. In the simplest case, such as `getName`, an invocation can be replaced with the actual body of the method. This mechanism is known as *inlining*. The inlined method makes the following two statements perform equivalently:

```
System.out.println("id = " + rose.name);
System.out.println("id = " + rose.getName());
```

Although the two statements are equally efficient, a `getName` method allows the name field to be read-only and gives you the benefits of abstraction, allowing you to change the implementation.

For the kinds of optimization discussed here, `private` and `static` methods are equivalent to `final` methods because they cannot be overridden.

Some type checks become faster with `final` classes. In fact, many type checks become compile-time checks, and errors can be caught earlier. If the Java compiler encounters a reference to a `final` class, it knows that the object referred to is exactly that type. The entire class hierarchy for that class is known, so the compiler can check whether any use is valid or invalid. With a non-`final` reference, some checks can happen only at run time.

Exercise 3.4: Which methods (if any) of `Vehicle` and `PassengerVehicle` might reasonably be made `final`?

3.6   The `Object` Class

All classes extend the `Object` class, directly or indirectly, and therefore inherit `Object`'s methods. These methods fall into two categories: general utility methods and methods that support threads. Thread support is covered in Chapter 9. This section describes `Object`'s utility methods and how they affect classes. The utility methods are:

public boolean **equals(Object obj)**
> Compares the receiving object and the object referenced by `obj` for equality, returning `true` if they have the same value and `false` if they don't. If you want to determine whether two references refer to the same object, you can compare them using `==` and `!=`. The `equals` method is concerned with value equality. The default implementation of `equals` in `Object` assumes that an object is equal only to itself.

public int **hashCode()**
> Returns a hash code for this object. Each object has a hash code for use in hashtables. The default implementation returns a value that is usually unique for different objects. It is used when storing objects in `Hashtable` objects, described in "Hashtable" on page 284.

protected Object **clone()** throws CloneNotSupportedException
> Returns a clone of this object. A *clone* is a new object that is a copy of the object on which `clone` was invoked. Cloning is discussed in greater detail in "Cloning Objects" on page 77.

public final Class **getClass()**
> Returns the particular object of type `Class` that represents the class of this object. Java has run-time representation for classes—an object of class `Class`—which the method `getClass` returns. The `Class` class is described in "Class" on page 304.

protected void **finalize()** throws Throwable
> Finalizes the object during garbage collection. This method was discussed in detail in "finalize" on page 48.

Both the `hashCode` and `equals` methods should be overridden if you want to provide a notion of equality different from the default implementation provided in the `Object` class. The default is that any two different objects are not `equal` and their hash codes are usually distinct.

If your class has a notion of equality in which two different objects can be `equal`, those two objects should return the same value from `hashCode`. This is because the `Hashtable` mechanism relies on `equals` returning `true` when it finds a key of the same value in the table. For example, the `String` class overrides equals to return true if the two String objects have the same contents. It also overrides hashCode to return a hash based on the contents of the String so that two strings with the same contents have the same hashCode.

The term *identity* is used for reference equality: if two references are identical, then == between the two will be true. The term *equivalence* is used to describe value equality—objects that may or may not be identical, but for which equals will return true. So one can say that the default implementation of equals is that equivalence is the same as identity. A class that defines a broader notion of equality can have objects that are not identical be equivalent by overriding equals to return true based on the state of the objects instead of their identities.

Some hashtables are concerned with identity of objects, not equivalence. If you need to write such a hashtable, you want hash codes that are different for different objects. The method System.identityHashCode returns the same value that Object.hashCode would return for an object if it were not overridden. If you simply use hashCode on the objects you are storing, you might get a hash code based on equivalence, not on identity, which could be far less efficient.

Exercise 3.5: Override equals and hashCode for Vehicle.

3.7 Anonymous Classes

When the weight of a full class seems too much for your needs, you can declare *anonymous classes* that extend a class or implement an interface. These classes are defined at the same time they are created with new. For example, consider the method walkThrough defined on page 54. The class Enum is fairly lightweight and is not needed outside the method. The name Enum doesn't add much value to the code—what is important is that it is an Enumeration object. The method walkThrough could use an anonymous class instead:

```
public static Enumeration walkThrough(final Object[] objs) {
    return new Enumeration() {
        private int pos = 0;
        public boolean hasMoreElements() {
            return (pos < objs.length);
        }
        public Object nextElement()
            throws NoSuchElementException
        {
            if (pos >= objs.length)
                throw new NoSuchElementException();
```

```
            return objs[pos++];
        }
    };
}
```

Anonymous classes are defined in the new expression itself. The type specified to the new is the supertype of the anonymous class. Because Enumeration is
an interface, the anonymous class in walkThrough implicitly extends Object. If
the supertype is a class, you invoke one of its constructors as usual in the new. The
following anonymous subclass of Attr (see page 60) would print the new value of
the attribute any time it was changed:

```
Attr name = new Attr("Name") {
    public Object setValue(Object nv) {
        System.out.println("Name set to " + nv);
        return super.setValue(nv);
    }
};
```

This statement creates an anonymous subclass of Attr that invokes the Attr
class's one-argument constructor. Anonymous classes cannot have their own constructors because constructors always have the same name as their class and anonymous classes have no names.

Anonymous classes are simple and direct but can easily become very hard to
read. The further they nest, the harder they are to understand. The nesting of the
anonymous class code that will execute in the future inside the method code that is
executing now adds to the potential for confusion. You should probably avoid
anonymous classes that are longer than about six lines, and use them in only the
simplest of expressions. We stretch this rule in the walkThrough example because
the sole purpose of the method is to return that object, but when a method does
more, anonymous classes must be kept quite small to keep the code legible. When
anonymous classes are used properly, they are a good tool for keeping simple
classes simple. When misused, they create impenetrable inscrutability.

3.8 Abstract Classes and Methods

An extremely useful feature of object-oriented programming is the concept of the
abstract class. Using abstract classes, you can declare classes that define only part
of an implementation, leaving extended classes to provide specific implementation of some or all of the methods. The opposite of *abstract* is *concrete*—a class

that has only concrete methods, including implementations of any abstract methods inherited from superclasses, is a concrete class.

Abstract classes are helpful when some of the behavior is defined for most or all objects of a given type, but some behavior makes sense only for particular classes and not a general superclass. In Java, such a class is declared `abstract`, and each method not implemented in the class is also marked `abstract`. (If you need to define some methods, but you don't need to provide any implementation, you probably want to use interfaces instead, which are described in Chapter 4.)

For example, suppose you want to create a benchmarking harness to provide an infrastructure for writing benchmarked code. The class implementation could understand how to drive and measure a benchmark, but it couldn't know in advance which benchmark would be run. Most `abstract` classes fit a pattern in which a class's particular area of expertise requires someone else to provide a missing piece. In this benchmarking example, the missing piece is code that needs to be benchmarked. Here is what such a class might look like:

```java
abstract class Benchmark {
    abstract void benchmark();

    public long repeat(int count) {
        long start = System.currentTimeMillis();
        for (int i = 0; i < count; i++)
            benchmark();
        return (System.currentTimeMillis() - start);
    }
}
```

Any class with any `abstract` methods must be declared `abstract`. This redundancy helps the reader quickly see that the class is `abstract` without scanning to see whether any method in the class is declared `abstract`.

The `repeat` method provides the benchmarking expertise. It knows how to time a run of `count` repetitions of the benchmark. If the timing needs become more complex (perhaps measuring the time of each run and computing statistics about the variations), this method can be enhanced without affecting any extended class's implementation of its specialized benchmark code.

The `abstract` method `benchmark` must be implemented by each subclass that is not `abstract` itself. This is why it has no implementation in this class, just a declaration. Here is an example of a simple Benchmark extension:

```java
class MethodBenchmark extends Benchmark {
    /** Do nothing, just return. */
    void benchmark() {
```

```
        }

        public static void main(String[] args) {
            int count = Integer.parseInt(args[0]);
            long time = new MethodBenchmark().repeat(count);
            System.out.println(count + " methods in " +
                                time + " milliseconds");
        }
    }
```

This class times how long it takes to invoke an empty method `benchmark`. You can now time method invocations by running the application `MethodBenchmark` with the number of times to repeat the test. The count is taken from the program arguments and decoded using the `Integer` class's `parseInt` method on the argument string, as described in "String Conversions" on page 169.

You cannot create an object of an `abstract` class because there would be no implementation for some methods that might well be invoked.

Any class can override methods from its superclass to declare them `abstract`, turning a concrete method into an `abstract` one at that point in the type tree. This technique is useful, for example, when a class's default implementation is invalid for a part of the class hierarchy.

Exercise 3.6: Write a new extended class that benchmarks something else, such as how long it takes to run a loop from 0 to some passed-in parameter.

Exercise 3.7: Change `Vehicle` so that it has an `EnergySource` object reference, which is associated with the `Vehicle` in its constructor. `EnergySource` must be an `abstract` class, because a `GasTank` object's measure of fullness will differ from that of a `Battery` object. Put an `abstract` empty method in `EnergySource` and implement it in `GasTank` and `Battery` classes. Add a `start` method to `Vehicle` that ensures that the energy source isn't `empty`.

3.9 Cloning Objects

The `Object.clone` method helps you write *clone* methods for your own classes. A clone method returns a new object whose initial state is a copy of the current state of the object on which `clone` was invoked. Subsequent changes to the new clone object should not affect the state of the original object.

There are three major considerations in writing a `clone` method:

◆ The empty `Cloneable` interface, which you must implement to provide a `clone` method that can be used to clone an object.[1]

◆ The `Object.clone` method, which performs a simple clone by copying all fields of the original object to the new object. This method works for many classes but may need to be supplemented by an overriding method.

◆ The `CloneNotSupportedException`, which can be used to signal that a class's `clone` method shouldn't have been invoked.

A given class can have one of four different attitudes toward `clone`:

◆ Support `clone`. Such a class implements `Cloneable` and declares its `clone` method to throw no exceptions.

◆ Conditionally support `clone`. Such a class might be a collection class that can be cloned in principle but cannot successfully be cloned unless its contents can be cloned. This kind of class will implement `Cloneable`, but will let its `clone` method pass through any `CloneNotSupportedException` it may receive from other objects it tries to clone. Or a class may have the ability to be cloned itself but not require that all subclasses also have the ability to be cloned.

◆ Allow subclasses to support `clone` but don't publicly support it. Such a class doesn't implement `Cloneable`, but if the default implementation of `clone` isn't correct, the class provides a protected `clone` implementation that clones its fields correctly.

◆ Forbid `clone`. Such a class does not implement `Cloneable` and provides a `clone` method that always throws `CloneNotSupportedException`.

`Object.clone` checks whether the object on which it was invoked implements the `Cloneable` interface and throws `CloneNotSupportedException` if it does not. Otherwise, `Object.clone` creates a new object of exactly the same type as the original object on which `clone` is invoked and initializes the fields of the new, cloned object to have the same values as the fields of the original object. When `Object.clone` is finished, it returns a reference to the new object.

---

[1] `Cloneable` should have been spelled `Clonable`, and the current, incorrect spelling may be deprecated in a future release.

The simplest way to make a class that can be cloned is to declare that it implements the Cloneable interface, and redeclare the clone method to be public:

```
public class MyClass extends HerClass implements Cloneable {
    public Object clone() throws CloneNotSupportedException {
        return super.clone();
    }
    // ...
}
```

Now, any other code can make a clone of a MyClass object. In this simple case, all fields of MyClass will be assigned by Object.clone into the new object that is returned.

Object.clone has the throws CloneNotSupportedException declaration. This means a class can declare that it can be cloned, but a subclass can decide that it can't be cloned. Such a subclass would implement the Cloneable interface because it extends a class that does so, but the subclass could not, in fact, be cloned. The extended class would make this known by overriding clone to always throw CloneNotSupportedException and documenting that it does so. Be careful—this means that you cannot determine whether a class can be cloned by a run-time check to see whether the class implements Cloneable. Some classes that can't be cloned will be forced to signal this condition by throwing an exception.

Most classes can be cloned in principle. Even if your class does not support the Cloneable interface, you must ensure that its clone method is correct. In many classes, the default implementation of clone will be wrong because it duplicates a reference to an object that shouldn't be shared. In such cases, clone should be overridden to behave correctly. The default implementation assigns each field from the source to the same field in the destination object.

If, for example, your objects have a reference to an array, a clone of one of your objects will refer to the same array. If the array holds read-only data, such a shared reference is probably fine. But if it is a list of objects that should be distinct for each of your objects, you probably don't want the clone's manipulation of its own list to affect the list of the original source object, or vice versa.

Here is an example of the problem. Suppose you have a simple integer stack class:

```
public class IntegerStack implements Cloneable {
    private int[] buffer;
    private int top;

    public IntegerStack(int maxContents) {
```

```
        buffer = new int[maxContents];
        top = -1;
    }

    public void push(int val) {
        buffer[++top] = val;
    }

    public int pop() {
        return buffer[top--];
    }
}
```

Now let's look at some code that creates an `IntegerStack` object, puts some data onto the stack, and then clones it:

```
IntegerStack first = new IntegerStack(2);
first.push(2);
first.push(9);
IntegerStack second = (IntegerStack)first.clone();
```

With the default `clone` method, the data in memory will look something like this:

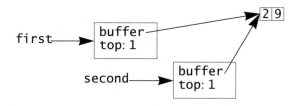

Now consider what happens when future code invokes `first.pop()`, followed by `first.push(17)`. The top element in the stack `first` will change from 9 to 17, which is expected. The programmer will probably be surprised, however, to see that the top element of `second` will *also* change to 17 because there is only one array that is shared by the two stacks.

The solution is to override `clone` to make a copy of the array:

```
public Object clone() {
    try {
        IntegerStack nObj = (IntegerStack)super.clone();
        nObj.buffer = (int[])buffer.clone();
        return nObj;
    } catch (CloneNotSupportedException e) {
```

```
                // Cannot happen -- we support
                // clone, and so do arrays
                throw new InternalError(e.toString());
        }
    }
```

First the `clone` method invokes `super.clone`. This invocation is very important because the superclass may be working around its own problem of shared objects. If you do not invoke the superclass's method, you solve your own cloning problem but may create another one. Furthermore, `super.clone` will eventually invoke the method `Object.clone`, which creates an object of the correct type. If the method `IntegerStack.clone` used `new` to create an `IntegerStack` object, it would be incorrect for any object that extended `IntegerStack`. The extended class's invocation of `super.clone` would give it an `IntegerStack` object, not an object of the correct, extended type.

The return value of `super.clone` is then cast to an `IntegerStack` reference. Casting, described in "Type Conversions" on page 121, changes a reference of one type (in this case, `Object` as the return value of `clone`) to a reference of another type (in this case, `IntegerStack`). A cast succeeds only if the referenced object is actually of the type to which the reference is being cast.

`Object.clone` initializes each field in the new clone object by assigning it the value from the same field of the object being cloned. You then need write special code only to deal with fields for which copying the value is incorrect. `IntegerStack.clone` doesn't need to copy the `top` field, because it is already correct from the "copy values" default.

With the specialized `clone` method in place, the example code now creates memory that looks like this:

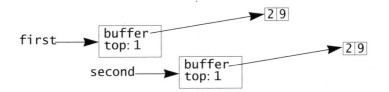

Sometimes making `clone` work correctly is not worth the trouble, and some classes should not support `clone`. In such cases, you should define a `clone` method that throws `CloneNotSupportedException` so that objects with bad state will never be created by an unsuspecting subclass that uses `clone`.

You can declare that all subclasses of a class must support `clone` properly by overriding your `clone` method with one that drops the declaration of

`CloneNotSupportedException`. Subclasses implementing the `clone` method cannot throw `CloneNotSupportedException`, because methods in the subclass cannot add an exception to a method. In the same way, if your class makes its `clone` method `public`, all extended classes must also have `public clone` methods, because a subclass cannot make a method less visible than it was in its superclass.

The object serialization mechanism allows you to write entire object graphs to a stream of bytes and, using that generated stream of bytes, create an equivalent copy of the original object graphs. Serialization can provide a way to make deeper copies than those provided by `clone`. See "The `Object` Byte Streams" on page 259.

Exercise 3.8: Make `Vehicle` and `PassengerVehicle` into `Cloneable` types. Which of the four described attitudes should each class take toward cloning? Is the simple copying done by `Object.clone` correct for the clone methods of these classes?

Exercise 3.9: Write a `Garage` class whose objects can hold up to some number of `Vehicle` objects in an array. Make `Garage` a `Cloneable` type, and write a proper `clone` method for it. Write a `Garage.main` method to test it.

Exercise 3.10: Make your `LinkedList` class `Cloneable`, with `clone` returning a new list that refers to the same values as the original list, not clones of the values. In other words, changes to one list should not affect the other list, but changes to the objects referenced by the list would be visible in both lists.

3.10 Extending Classes: How and When

The ability to write extended classes is a large part of the benefits of object-oriented programming. When you extend a class to add new functionality, you create what is commonly termed an *IsA* relationship—the extension creates a new kind of object that "is a" kind of the original class. The IsA relationship is quite different from a *HasA* relationship, in which one object uses another object to store state or do work—it "has a" reference to that other object.

Let's look at an example. Consider a `Point` class that represents a point in two-dimensional space by an (*x*, *y*) pair. You might extend `Point` to create, say, a `Pixel` class to represent a colored point on a screen. A `Pixel` IsA `Point`: anything that is true of a simple `Point` would also be true of a `Pixel`. The `Pixel` class might add mechanisms to represent the color of the pixel or a reference to an object that represents the screen on which the pixel is drawn. As a point in a two-dimensional space (the plane of a display) with an extension to the contract (it has color and a screen), a `Pixel` IsA `Point`.

On the other hand, a circle is not a point. Although a circle can be described by a point and a radius, it has properties that no point would have. For example, if you had a method to place the center of a rectangle at a particular point, would it really make sense to pass in a circle? A circle HasA center that IsA point, but a circle Is*Not*A point with a radius, and therefore should not be a subclass of `Point`.

There are times when the correct choice is not obvious and for which different choices will be correct depending on the application. In the end, applications must run and make sense.

Getting IsA versus HasA relationships correct is both subtle and potentially critical. For example, one obvious and common way to design an employee database using object-oriented tools is to use an `Employee` class that has the data all persons share (such as name and employee number) and extend it to classes for particular kinds of employees, such as `Manager`, `Engineer`, and `FileClerk`.

This design fails in real-world situations, in which one person operates simultaneously in more than one role. For example, an engineer might be an acting manager in a group and must now appear in two guises. As another example, a teaching assistant is often both a student and a staff member at a university.

A more flexible design would create a `Role` class and extend it to create classes for roles such as `Manager`. Then you would change the design of the `Employee` class to have a set of `Role` objects. Now a person could be associated with an ever-changing set of roles in the organization. We have changed from saying that a manager IsAn employee to saying that manager IsA role, and that an employee can HaveA manager's role as well as other roles.

If the wrong initial choice is made, changing deployed systems will be hard, because changes could require major alterations in code. For example, methods in the first employee database design would no doubt rely on the fact that a `Manager` object could be used as an `Employee`. This would no longer be true if we had to change to the role-based design, and all the original code would break.

3.11 Designing a Class to Be Extended

Now we can justify the complexity of the `Attr` class defined on page 60. Why weren't `name` and `value` simply public variables? That would avoid the need for three methods, because the fields could be accessed and modified directly.

The answer is that the `Attr` class is designed to be extended. If we store our data in public fields, it will have two bad effects:

◆ The name field could be modified at any time by the programmer—a bad move because the Attr object represents the (mutable) value of a particular (immutable) name. For example, changing the name after inserting the attribute into a list sorted by name would result in an out-of-order list.

◆ There would be no way to add functionality. By providing accessor methods, you can override them to enhance functionality, as we did in ColorAttr to pre-decode a new value into an actual ScreenColor object. If value were a public field, the programmer could change it at any time, and we would have to provide a different way to get the ScreenColor object that remembered the last value and compared it to the current one to see whether it needed to do some new decoding. The resulting code would be more complex and probably less efficient.

A non-final class has two interfaces. The *public* interface is for programmers *using* your class. The *protected* interface is for programmers *extending* your class. Both interfaces are real contracts, and both should be designed carefully.

For example, suppose you want to provide a benchmarking harness for comparing varieties of sorting algorithms. Some things can be said of all sorting algorithm benchmarks: they all have data on which they must operate; that data must support an ordering mechanism; and the number of comparisons and swaps they require to do their work is an important factor in the benchmark.

You can write an abstract class that helps you with these features, but you cannot write a generic sort method—the actual operations of sorting are determined by each extended class. Here is a SortDouble class that sorts arrays of double values, tracking the number of swaps, comparisons, and tests required in a SortMetrics class we will define later:

```
abstract class SortDouble {
    private double[] values;
    private SortMetrics curMetrics = new SortMetrics();

    /** Invoked to do the full sort */
    public final SortMetrics sort(double[] data) {
        values = data;
        curMetrics.init();
        doSort();
        return getMetrics();
    }

    public final SortMetrics getMetrics() {
        return (SortMetrics)curMetrics.clone();
```

```java
    }

    protected final int getDataLength() {
        return values.length;
    }

    /** For derived classes to probe elements */
    protected final double probe(int i) {
        curMetrics.probeCnt++;
        return values[i];
    }

    /** For derived classes to compare elements */
    protected final int compare(int i, int j) {
        curMetrics.compareCnt++;
        double d1 = values[i];
        double d2 = values[j];
        if (d1 == d2)
            return 0;
        else
            return (d1 < d2 ? -1 : 1);
    }

    /** For derived classes to swap elements */
    protected final void swap(int i, int j) {
        curMetrics.swapCnt++;
        double tmp = values[i];
        values[i] = values[j];
        values[j] = tmp;
    }

    /** Derived classes implement this -- used by sort */
    protected abstract void doSort();
}
```

This class defines fields to hold the array being sorted (values) and a reference to a metrics object (curMetrics) to track the measured operations. To ensure that these counts are correct, SortDouble provides routines to be used by extended sorting classes when they need to examine data or perform comparisons and swaps.

When you design a class, you can decide whether to trust its extended classes. The SortDouble class is designed not to trust them, and that is generally the best way to design classes for others to extend. A guarded design not only prevents malicious use, it also prevents bugs.

SortDouble carefully restricts access to each member to the appropriate level. It uses final on all its non-abstract methods. These factors are all part of the contract of the SortDouble class, which includes protecting the measurement of the sort algorithm from tampering. Making the methods final also ensures that no derived class overrides these methods to change behavior, and also allows the compiler and runtime to make them as efficient as possible.

SortMetrics objects describe the cost of a particular sorting run. The class has three public fields. Its only task is to communicate data, so there is no need to hide that data behind accessor methods. SortDouble.metrics returns a copy of the data so that it doesn't give out a reference to its internal data. This prevents both the code that creates SortDouble objects and the code in the extended classes from changing the data. Here is the SortMetrics class:

```
final class SortMetrics implements Cloneable {
    public long probeCnt,          // simple data probes
                compareCnt,        // comparing two elements
                swapCnt;           // swapping two elements

    public void init() {
        probeCnt = swapCnt = compareCnt = 0;
    }

    public String toString() {
        return probeCnt + " probes " +
                compareCnt + " compares " +
                swapCnt + " swaps";
    }

    /** This class supports clone */
    public Object clone() {
        try {
            return super.clone(); // default mechanism works
        } catch (CloneNotSupportedException e) {
            // can't happen: this and Object both clone
            throw new InternalError(e.toString());
```

```
            }
        }
    }
```

The following class extends SortDouble. The SimpleSortDouble class implements doSort with a very slow but simple sort algorithm whose primary advantage is that it is easy to code and easy to understand:

```
class SimpleSortDouble extends SortDouble {
    protected void doSort() {
        for (int i = 0; i < getDataLength(); i++) {
            for (int j = i + 1; j < getDataLength(); j++) {
                if (compare(i, j) > 0)
                    swap(i, j);
            }
        }
    }
}
```

Now we can write a test harness for sort algorithms that must be changed only slightly to test a new sort algorithm. Here it is shown as a driver for testing the class SimpleSortDouble:

```
public class TestSort {
    static double[] testData = {
                        0.3, 1.3e-2, 7.9, 3.17,
                    };

    static public void main(String[] args) {
        SortDouble bsort = new SimpleSortDouble();
        SortMetrics metrics = bsort.sort(testData);
        System.out.println("Metrics: " + metrics);
        for (int i = 0; i < testData.length; i++)
            System.out.println("\t" + testData[i]);
    }
}
```

The main method shows how code that drives a test works: it creates an object of a class extended from SortDouble, provides it with the data to be sorted, and invokes sort. The sort method initializes the metrics and then invokes the abstract method doSort. Each extended class implements doSort to do its sorting, invoking dataLength, compare, and swap when it needs to. When doSort returns, the counts reflect the number of each operation performed. To test a different algorithm, you can simply change the class name after the new. Here is what one run of TestSort looks like:

```
Metrics: 0 probes 6 compares 2 swaps
        0.013
        0.3
        3.17
        7.9
```

Now let us return to the issue of designing a class to be extended, with these classes as examples. We carefully designed the protected interface of SortDouble to allow extended classes more intimate access to the data in the object but only to things we *want* them to manipulate. The access for each part of the class design has been carefully chosen:

- *Public:* The public part of the class is designed for use by the code that tests how expensive the sorting algorithm is. An example of testing code is in TestSort.main. This code provides the data to be sorted and gets the results of the test. For the test code, the metrics are read-only. The public sort method we provide for the test code ensures that the metrics are initialized before they are used.

    Making the actual doSort method protected forces the test code to invoke it indirectly via the public sort method; thus, we guarantee that the metrics are always initialized and avoid another possible error.

    To the test code, the only available functionality of the class is to drive a test of a particular sorting algorithm and provide the results. We used methods and access protection to hide the rest of the class, which should not be exposed to the testing code.

- *Protected:* The protected part of the class is designed for use by the sorting code to produce a properly metered sort. The protected contract lets the sorting algorithm examine and modify the data to produce a sorted list by whatever means the sort desires. It also gives the sorting algorithm a context in which it will be properly driven so it can be measured. This home is the doSort method.

    The extended class is not considered trustworthy, and that is why it can access the data only indirectly, through methods that have access to the data. For example, to hide a comparison by avoiding compare, the sort would have to use probe to find out what is in the array. Because calls to probe are also metered, this would, in the end, hide nothing.

In addition, `getMetrics` returns a clone of the actual metrics, so a sorting implementation cannot modify the values.

◆ *Private:* The class keeps private to itself data that should be hidden from the outside—namely, the data being sorted and the metrics. Outside code cannot access these fields, directly or indirectly.

As we said earlier, in order to prevent intentional cheating and accidental misuse, `SortDouble` is designed not to trust its extended classes. For example, if `SortDouble.values` (the array being sorted) were `protected` instead of `private`, we could eliminate the `probe` method, because sort algorithms normally count only comparisons and swaps. But if we had, the programmer writing an extended class could avoid using `swap` to swap data. The results would be invalid in ways that might be hard to notice. Counting probes and declaring the array `private` preclude some bugs as well as intentionally devious programming.

If a class is not designed to be extended, it often will be misused by subclasses. If your class will have subclasses, you should design its `protected` parts carefully. The end result may be to have no protected members if extended classes need no special access. If you do not design the `protected` part of your class, the class should have no `protected` members, making subclasses rely on its public contract.

Exercise 3.11: Find at least one security hole in `SortDouble` that would let a sorting algorithm cheat on its metrics without getting caught. Fix the security hole. Assume that the sorting algorithm author doesn't get to write `main`.

Exercise 3.12: Write a generic `SortHarness` class that can sort any object type. How would you provide a way to represent ordering for the objects in a generic way, given that you cannot use < to compare them?

> *Insanity is hereditary. You can catch it from your kids.*
> —Erma Bombeck

CHAPTER 4

Interfaces

*"Conducting" is when you draw "designs" in the nowhere—with your stick,
or with your hands—which are interpreted as "instructional messages"
by guys wearing bow ties who wish they were fishing.*
—Frank Zappa

THE fundamental units of *design* in Java are the `public` methods that can be invoked on objects. *Interfaces* are a way to declare a type consisting only of abstract methods and related constants, classes, and interfaces, enabling any implementation to be written for those methods. An interface is an expression of pure design, whereas a class is a mix of design and implementation.

A class can implement the methods of an interface in any way that the designer of the class chooses. An interface thus has many more possible implementations than a class has.

4.1 An Example Interface

The previous chapter introduced the `Attr` class and showed how to extend it to make specialized types of attribute objects. Now all you need is the ability to associate attributes with objects. There are two ways to do this: one is *composition;* the other is *inheritance.* An object could, if you chose, contain a set of attributes and allow programmers access to that set. Or you could say that being able to store attributes on an object is a part of its type and so should be part of the class hierarchy. Both positions are legitimate. We believe that representing the ability to hold attributes in the class hierarchy is most useful. We will create an `Attributed` type to be used for objects that can be attributed by attaching `Attr` objects to them.

However, Java has *single inheritance* of *implementation*, which means that you can extend only one class. If you create an `Attributed` class for programmers to extend, then either `Attributed` must be at the base of all classes—that is, be part of the `Object` class—or programmers must decide whether to inherit from `Attributed` or from some other useful class. Every time you created a useful feature like `Attributed`, you would end up wanting to add its capabilities to the root `Object` class, which would grow quickly to unmanageable proportions.

Java has *multiple interface inheritance*, so instead of adding the capabilities of `Attributed` to `Object`, we can make `Attributed` into an interface. To make an attributed version of our celestial body class, for example, its declaration might look like this:

```
class AttributedBody extends Body
    implements Attributed
```

To do this, we need an `Attributed` interface:

```
public interface Attributed {
    void add(Attr newAttr);
    Attr find(String attrName);
    Attr remove(String attrName);
    java.util.Enumeration attrs();
}
```

This interface declares four methods: one for adding a new attribute to an `Attributed` object; one for finding whether an attribute of a given name has been added to that object; one for removing an attribute from an object; and one for returning a list of the attributes currently attached to the object. This list is returned using the `Enumeration` interface defined for Java's collection classes. `java.util.Enumeration` is covered in detail in Chapter 13.

All methods in an interface are implicitly `abstract`; because an interface cannot provide an implementation of its declared methods, an interface doesn't need to declare its methods `abstract`. Each class that implements the interface must implement all its methods, or, if the class implements only some of the methods in an interface, that class is (and must be declared) `abstract`.

Methods in an interface are always public. Interface methods may not be `static` because `static` methods are class-specific, never `abstract`, and an interface can have only `abstract` methods.

Fields in an interface, on the other hand, are always `static` and `final`. They are a way to define constants used when invoking methods. An interface that had differing levels of verbosity in its contract might have the following:

```
interface Verbose {
    int SILENT  = 0;
    int TERSE   = 1;
```

```
      int NORMAL   = 2;
      int VERBOSE = 3;

      void setVerbosity(int level);
      int getVerbosity();
  }
```

SILENT, TERSE, NORMAL, and VERBOSE can be passed to the setVerbosity method, giving names to constant values that represent specific meanings. These values must be constant, so all fields in an interface are implicitly static and final.

You declare nested classes and interfaces in an interface for the same reason that you declare nested classes and interfaces in a class: nested classes and interfaces allow you to associate types that are strongly related to an interface inside that interface. For example, a class that was used only to return multiple values from an interface's method could be represented as a nested class in that interface:

```
interface Changeable {
    class Record {
        public Object changer;
        public String changeDesc;
    }

    Record getLastChange();
    // ...
}
```

The method getLastChange returns a Changeable.Record object that contains which object made the change and a string describing the change. This class has meaning relative only to the Changeable interface, so making a top-level class not only is unnecessary, but would also separate it from the context of its use. As a nested class it is tightly bound to its origin and context.

Any class or interface nested inside an interface is public. Any classes nested inside an interface are also static.

Any interface nested inside a class can be public, protected, package-accessible, or private. As with package-accessible top-level interfaces, the accessibility of the interface does not affect the accessibility of the interface's members, all of which are public.

4.2   Single Inheritance versus Multiple Inheritance

In Java, a new class can extend exactly one superclass, a model known as *single inheritance*. Extending a class means that the new class inherits not only its superclass's contract but also its superclass's implementation. Some object-oriented languages employ *multiple inheritance,* in which a new class can have two or more superclasses.

Multiple inheritance is useful when a new class wants to add new behavior and keep most or all of the old behavior. But when there is more than one superclass, problems arise when a superclass's behavior is inherited in two ways. Assume, for a moment, the following type tree:

This is commonly called *diamond inheritance,* and there is nothing wrong with it. Many legitimate designs show this structure. The problems exist in the inheritance of implementation, when W's implementation stores some state. If class W had, for example, a public field named goggin, and if you had a reference to an object of type Z called zref, what would zref.goggin refer to? It might refer to X's copy of goggin, or it might refer to Y's copy, or X and Y might share a single copy of goggin because Z is really only a W once even though it is both an X and a Y. To avoid such issues, Java uses the single-inheritance model of object-oriented programming.

Single inheritance precludes some useful and correct designs. The problems of multiple inheritance arise from multiple inheritance of implementation, so Java provides a way to inherit a contract without inheriting implementation. The way is to declare an interface type instead of a class type.

Interfaces in the class hierarchy, therefore, add multiple inheritance to Java.

In a given class, the classes that are extended and the interfaces that are implemented are collectively called the *supertypes,* and from the viewpoint of the supertypes, the new class is a *subtype.* The full type of the new class includes all its supertypes, so a reference to an object of its type can be used polymorphically— that is, anywhere a reference to an object of any of its supertypes (class or interface) is required. Interface definitions create type names just as class definitions do; you can use the name of an interface as a type name of a variable, and any object that implements that interface can be assigned to that variable.

4.3 Extending Interfaces

Interfaces can be extended, too, using the `extends` keyword. Interfaces, unlike classes, can extend more than one interface:

```
interface Shimmer extends FloorWax, DessertTopping {
    double amazingPrice();
}
```

The `Shimmer` interface extends both `FloorWax` and a `DessertTopping`, which means that all methods and constants defined by `FloorWax` and `DessertTopping` are part of the `Shimmer` contract, as is its added `amazingPrice` method.

If you want a class to implement an interface and extend another class, you need multiple inheritance. In other words, you will have a new class that can be used in the places allowed both by its superclass and by its superinterface types. Consider the following declaration:

```
interface W { }
interface X extends W { }
class Y implements W { }
class Z extends Y implements X { }
```

These types create something that looks like diamond inheritance, but there is no question about whether it uses X's fields or Y's fields—X has no per-object fields because it is an interface, so only Y's per-object fields are available. The diamond looks like this, with interfaces circled:

We could instead construct the diamond with W, X, and Y all being interfaces and Z a class. Here is what this would look like:

```
interface W { }
interface X extends W { }
interface Y extends W { }
class Z implements X, Y { }
```

Now Z is the only actual class in the hierarchy.

Interfaces, unlike classes, do not have a single root interface akin to the `Object` class. Even so, you can assign an expression of any interface type to a reference of type `Object`, because that object must be of *some* class, and all classes are subclasses of `Object`. For example, given the preceding example, the following assignment to `obj` is legal:

```
protected void twiddle(W wRef) {
    Object obj = wRef;
    // ...
}
```

4.3.1   Name Conflicts

The last two examples demonstrated that a class or interface can be a subtype of more than one interface. This raises a question: what happens when a method of the same name appears in more than one interface? If methods in interfaces X and Y have the same name but different numbers or types of parameters, the answer is simple: the Z interface will have two overloaded methods that have the same name but different signatures. If the two methods have exactly the same signature, the answer is also simple: Z will have one method with that signature. If they differ only in return type, you cannot implement both interfaces.

If the two methods differ only in the types of exceptions they throw, your class must satisfy two method declarations that have the same signature (name and parameters) but throw different exceptions. But methods in a class cannot differ only in the exceptions they throw, so there must be only one implementation that satisfies both `throws` clauses. This example illustrates the situation:

```
interface X {
    void setup() throws SomeException;
}

interface Y {
    void setup();
}

class Z implements X, Y {
    public void setup() {
        // ...
    }
}
```

In this case, class Z can provide a single implementation that satisfies both X.setup and Y.setup. A method can throw fewer exceptions than its supertype declares, so Z.setup doesn't have to declare that it throws the SomeException type that X.setup says it is allowed to. Of course, this makes sense only if one implementation can also serve the declared contracts for both methods—if the two methods *mean* different things, you probably cannot write a single implementation that does what is expected for both meanings.

If two methods disagree in their list of exceptions in such a way that you cannot find an implementation signature that satisfies both interface signatures for the method, an interface cannot extend the two interfaces, nor can a class implement the two interfaces.

Even if you can write a method signature that the Java compiler will accept, you must think about whether you can provide a single implementation that satisfies the contracts of both methods. This requirement may be much harder or even impossible.

Interface *constants* are simpler. If two interfaces have constants of the same name you can always join them in an inheritance tree, but you must use the full name for those constants. For example, the interfaces PokerDeck and TarotDeck might both have DECK_SIZE constants of different values, and a MultiDeck interface or class could implement both interfaces. But inside MultiDeck and its subtypes you would use the constants' qualifed names PokerDeck.DECK_SIZE and TarotDeck.DECK_SIZE because the simple name DECK_SIZE would be ambiguous.

4.4   Implementing Interfaces

Interfaces describe contracts in a pure, abstract form, but an interface is interesting only if a class implements it.

Some interfaces are purely abstract—they do not have any useful general implementation but must be implemented afresh for each new class. Most interfaces, however, may have several useful implementations. In the case of our Attributed interface, we can imagine several possible implementations that use various strategies to store a set of attributes.

One strategy might be simple and fast when only a few attributes are in a set; another one might be optimized for attribute sets that are queried more often than they are changed; yet another design might be optimized for sets that change frequently. If there were a package of various implementations for the Attributed interface, a class might choose to implement the Attributed interface through any one of them or through its own implementation.

As an example, here is a simple implementation of `Attributed` that uses the utility `java.util.Hashtable` class. The class `AttributedImpl` declares that it implements the interface `Attributed`, so the class must implement all the interface's methods. `AttributedImpl` implements the methods using a `Hashtable`, described on page 284. Later, this implementation is used to implement the `Attributed` interface for a specific set of objects to which you would want to add attributes. First, here is the `AttributedImpl` class:

```
import java.util.*;

class AttributedImpl implements Attributed {
    protected Hashtable attrTable = new Hashtable();

    public void add(Attr newAttr) {
        attrTable.put(newAttr.getName(), newAttr);
    }

    public Attr find(String name) {
        return (Attr)attrTable.get(name);
    }

    public Attr remove(String name) {
        return (Attr)attrTable.remove(name);
    }

    public Enumeration attrs() {
        return attrTable.elements();
    }
}
```

The initializer for `attrTable` creates a `Hashtable` object to hold attributes. This `Hashtable` object does most of the actual work. The `Hashtable` class uses the object's `hashCode` method to hash any object it is given as a key. No explicit hash method is needed since `String` already provides a good `hashCode` implementation.

When a new attribute is added, the `Attr` object is stored in the hashtable under its name, and then you can easily use the hashtable to find and remove attributes by name.

The `attrs` method returns an `Enumeration` that lists all the attributes in the set. `Enumeration` is an interface defined in `java.util` for *collection classes* like `Hashtable` to use when returning lists (see "Enumeration" on page 276). The same type is used here because it is a standard way for Java classes to represent a list. In effect, the `Attributed` interface defines a collection type, so we use the normal mechanism for returning the contents of a collection, namely, the `Enumeration` class. Using `Enumeration` has another benefit: it is easy to implement `Attributed` using a standard collection class that uses `Enumeration`, such as `Hashtable`, because the standard collection's methods return `Enumeration` objects.

4.5   Using an Implementation

You can use an implementing class like `AttributedImpl` by simply extending the class. This is the simplest tool when it is available because all the methods and their implementations are inherited. But if you need to support more than one interface or extend a different class, you must use a different approach. The most common approach is to create an object of an implementing class and *forward* all the methods of the interface to that object, returning any values.

In forwarding, each method in the class that is inherited from the interface invokes the implementation from another object and returns the result. Here is an implementation of the `Attributed` interface that uses an `AttributedImpl` object to build an attributed version of our previously-defined celestial body class Body (see page 41):

```
import java.util.Enumeration;

class AttributedBody extends Body
    implements Attributed
{
    AttributedImpl attrImpl = new AttributedImpl();

    AttributedBody() {
        super();
    }

    AttributedBody(String name, Body orbits) {
        super(name, orbits);
    }

    // Forward all Attributed methods to the attrImpl object

    public void add(Attr newAttr)
        { attrImpl.add(newAttr); }
```

```
public Attr find(String name)
    { return attrImpl.find(name); }
public Attr remove(String name)
    { return attrImpl.remove(name); }
public Enumeration attrs()
    { return attrImpl.attrs(); }
}
```

The declaration that AttributedBody extends Body and implements Attributed defines the contract of AttributedBody. The implementations of all Body's methods are inherited from the Body class itself. Each method of Attributed is implemented by forwarding the invocation to the AttributedImpl object's equivalent method, returning its value (if any). This also means that you must add a field of type AttributedImpl to use in the forwarding methods and initialize that field to refer to an AttributedImpl object.

Forwarding is both straightforward and much less work than implementing Attributed from scratch. Forwarding also enables you to quickly change the implementation you use, should a better implementation of Attributed become available at some future date.

4.6   Marker Interfaces

Some interfaces do not declare any methods but simply mark a class as having some general property. The Cloneable interface is such a *marker* interface—it has neither methods nor fields, but marks a class as partaking in the cloning mechanism (see "Cloning Objects" on page 77).

Marker interfaces are the degenerate case of "contract" because they define no language-level behavior. All their contract is in the documentation that describes the expectations you must satisfy if your class implements that interface. The interfaces Serializable and Externalizable (described in "The Object Byte Streams" on page 259) are marker interfaces, as are both Remote ("java.rmi—Remote Method Invocation" on page 362) and EventListener ("java.awt—The Abstract Window Toolkit" on page 359).

Marker interfaces can have a profound impact on the behavior of the classes that implement them. Do not be fooled into thinking that they are unimportant merely because they have no methods.

4.7   When to Use Interfaces

There are two important differences between interfaces and abstract classes:

- ◆ Interfaces provide a form of multiple inheritance, because you can implement multiple interfaces. A class can extend only one other class, even if that class has only `abstract` methods.

- ◆ An `abstract` class can have a partial implementation, `protected` parts, `static` methods, and so on, whereas interfaces are limited to `public` constants and methods with no implementation.

These differences usually direct the choice of which tool is best to use in a particular implementation. If multiple inheritance is important or even useful, interfaces are used. However, an abstract class enables you to provide some or all of the implementation so that it can be inherited easily, rather than by explicit forwarding. Forwarding is tedious to implement and error-prone, so using an abstract class should not be dismissed lightly.

However, any major class you expect to be extended, whether abstract or not, should be an implementation of an interface. Although this approach requires a little more work on your part, it enables a whole category of use that is otherwise precluded. For example, suppose we had created an `Attributed` class instead of an `Attributed` interface with an `AttributedImpl` implementation class. In that case, programmers who wanted to create new classes that extended other existing classes could never use `Attributed`, since you can extend only one class—the class `AttributedBody` could never have been created. Because `Attributed` is an interface, programmers have a choice: they can extend `AttributedImpl` directly and avoid the forwarding, or, if they cannot extend, they can at least use forwarding to implement the interface. And if the general implementation provided is incorrect, they can write their own implementation. You can even provide multiple possible implementations of the interface to prospective users. Whatever implementation strategy programmers prefer, the objects they create are `Attributed`.

Exercise 4.1: Rewrite your solution to Exercise 3.7 on page 77 using an interface if you didn't write it that way in the first place.

Exercise 4.2: Rewrite your solution to Exercise 3.12 on page 89 using an interface if you didn't write it that way in the first place.

Exercise 4.3: Should the `LinkedList` class from previous exercises be an interface? Rewrite it that way with an implementation class before you decide.

Exercise 4.4: Design a collection class hierarchy using only interfaces.

Exercise 4.5: Think about whether the following types should be represented as interfaces, abstract classes, or concrete classes: (a) `TreeNode` to represent nodes in an N-ary tree; (b) `TreeWalker` to walk the tree in a particular order (such as depth-first or breadth-first); (c) `Drawable` for objects that can be drawn by a graphics system; (d) `Application` for programs that can be run from a graphical desktop.

Exercise 4.6: What changes in your assumptions about each of the problems in Exercise 4.5 would make you change your answers?

There are two ways of constructing a software design:
one way is to make it so simple that there are obviously no deficiencies;
the other is to make it so complicated that there are no obvious deficiencies.
—C.A.R. Hoare

CHAPTER 5

Tokens, Operators, and Expressions

There's nothing remarkable about it.
All one has to do is hit the right keys at the right time
and the instrument plays itself.
—Johann Sebastian Bach

THIS chapter discusses the fundamental building blocks of Java—namely, its tokens, operators, and expressions. You have already seen a lot of Java code and have gained familiarity with its components. This chapter describes the basic elements in detail.

5.1 Character Set

Most programmers are familiar with source code that is prepared using one of two major families of character representations: ASCII and its variants (including Latin-1) and EBCDIC. Both character sets contain characters used in English and several other Western European languages.

Java, on the other hand, is written in *Unicode*, a 16-bit character set. The first 256 characters of Unicode are the Latin-1 character set, and most of the first 128 characters of Latin-1 are equivalent to the 7-bit ASCII character set. Current Java environments read ASCII or Latin-1 files, converting them to Unicode on the fly.[1]

Few existing text editors support Unicode characters, so Java recognizes the *escape sequence* \u*dddd* to encode Unicode characters, where each *d* is a hexadecimal digit (0–9, and a–f or A–F to represent decimal values 10–15). This

---

[1] Java uses Unicode 2.0 with bug fixes. See "Further Reading" on page 381 for reference information.

sequence can appear anywhere in code—not only in character and string constants but also in identifiers. More than one u may appear at the beginning; thus, the character ஃ can be written as either \u0b87 or \uuu0b87.[2]

5.2   Comments

There are three kinds of comments in Java:

`// comment`	Characters from // to the end of the line are ignored.
`/* comment */`	Characters between /* and the next */ are ignored, including line terminators \r, \n, and \r\n.
`/** comment */`	Characters between /** and the next */ are ignored, including line terminators. These documentation comments come immediately before identifier declarations and are included in automatically generated documentation. These comments are described in Chapter 11.

Java comments can include any valid Unicode character, such as yin-yang (\u262f), asterism (\u2042), interrobang (\u203d), won (\u20a9), scruple (\u2108), or a snowman (\u2603).[3]

Java comments do not nest. This following tempting code does not compile:

```
/* Comment this out for now: not implemented
   /* Do some really neat stuff */
   universe.neatStuff();
*/
```

The first /* starts a comment; the very next */ ends it, leaving the code that follows to be parsed; and the invalid, stand-alone */ is a syntax error. The best way

---

[2] There is a good reason to allow multiple u's. When translating a Unicode file into an ASCII file, you must translate Unicode characters that are outside the ASCII range into an escape sequence. Thus, you would translate ஃ into \u0b87. When translating back, you make the reverse substitution. But what if the original Unicode source had not contained ஃ but had used \u0b87 instead? Then the reverse translation would not result in the original source (to the parser, it would be equivalent, but possibly not to the reader of the code). The solution is to have the translator add an extra u when it encounters an existing \u*dddd,* and have the reverse translator remove a u and, if there aren't any left, replace the escape sequence with its equivalent Unicode character.

[3] These characters are ☯, ⁂, ‽, ₩, ⸘, and ☃, respectively.

to remove blocks of code from programs is either to put a // at the beginning of each line or use if (false) like this:

```
if (false) {
    // invoke this method when it works
    dwim();
}
```

Of course, this code assumes that the dwim method is defined somewhere.

5.3 Tokens

The *tokens* of a language are its basic words. A parser breaks source code into tokens and then tries to figure out which statements, identifiers, and so forth make up the code. In Java, white space (spaces, tabs, newlines, and form feeds) is not significant except to separate tokens or as the contents of character or string literals. You can take any valid Java code and replace any amount of intertoken white space (white space outside strings and characters) with a different amount of white space (but not none) without changing the meaning of the program.

White space must be used to separate tokens that would otherwise constitute a single token. For example, in the statement

```
return 0;
```

you cannot drop the space between return and 0 because that would create

```
return0;
```

consisting of the single identifier return0. Use extra white space appropriately to make your code human-readable, even though the parser ignores it. Note that the parser treats comments as white space.

The tokenizer for Java is a "greedy" tokenizer. It grabs as many characters as it can to build up the next token, not caring if this creates an invalid sequence of tokens. So because ++ is longer than +, the expression

```
j = i+++++i;    // INVALID
```

is interpreted as the invalid expression

```
j = i++ ++ +i;  // INVALID
```

instead of the valid

```
j = i++ + ++i;
```

5.4   Identifiers

Java *identifiers*, used for names of declared entities such as variables, constants and labels, must start with a letter—including any currency symbol (such as $, ¥, and £) or connecting punctuation (such as _)—followed by letters, digits, or both. Because Java source code is written in Unicode, the definitions of letter and digit are much broader than in most programming languages. Java "letters" can include glyphs from Armenian, Korean, Gurmukhi, Georgian, Devanagari, and almost any other script written in the world today. Thus, not only is kitty a valid identifier, but mаčka, кошка, پیشی, பூனைக்குட்டி, and 猫 are, too.[4] The terms *letter* and *digit* are pretty broad in Unicode: if something is considered a letter or digit in a language, it probably is in Java, too. For a complete definition, see the tables "Unicode Digits" on page 378 and "Unicode Letters and Digits" on page 379.

Any difference in characters within an identifier makes that identifier unique. Case is significant: A, a, á, À, Å, and so on, are different identifiers. Characters that look the same, or nearly the same, can be confused. For example, the Latin capital letter n "N" and the Greek capital ν "N" look alike but are different characters (\u004e and \u039d, respectively). The only way to avoid confusion is to write each identifier in one language—and thus in one known set of characters—so that programmers trying to type the identifier will know whether you meant E or Е.[5]

Java identifiers can be as long as you like, but use some taste. Identifiers that are too long are hard to use correctly and actually obscure your code.

5.4.1   Java Keywords

Java language keywords cannot be used as identifiers. The following table lists Java's keywords (keywords marked with a [†] are reserved but currently unused):

abstract	default	if	private	throw
boolean	do	implements	protected	throws
break	double	import	public	transient
byte	else	instanceof	return	try
case	extends	int	short	void
catch	final	interface	static	volatile
char	finally	long	super	while
class	float	native	switch	
const[†]	for	new	synchronized	
continue	goto[†]	package	this	

---

[4]   These are the word "cat" or "kitty" in English, Serbo-Croatian, Russian, Persian, Tamil, and Japanese, respectively.

[5]   One is a Cyrillic letter, the other is ASCII. Determine which is which and win a prize.

Although they appear to be keywords, `null`, `true`, and `false` are formally literals, just like the number 12, so they do not appear in the above table. However, you cannot use `null`, `true`, or `false` as identifiers, just as you cannot use 12 as an identifier. These words can be used as part of identifiers, as in `annulled`, `construe`, and `falsehood`.

5.5 Primitive Types

The primitive data types of Java are:

`boolean`	either `true` or `false`
`char`	16-bit Unicode 2.0 character
`byte`	8-bit signed two's-complement integer
`short`	16-bit signed two's-complement integer
`int`	32-bit signed two's-complement integer
`long`	64-bit signed two's-complement integer
`float`	32-bit IEEE 754-1985 floating-point number
`double`	64-bit IEEE 754-1985 floating-point number

Each primitive Java language type has a corresponding class in the `java.lang` package. These *wrapper classes*—`Boolean`, `Character`, `Byte`, `Short`, `Integer`, `Long`, `Float`, and `Double`—also define useful constants and methods. For example, most of these types declare constants `MIN_VALUE` and `MAX_VALUE` in their corresponding language classes.

The `Float` and `Double` classes also have `Nan`, `NEGATIVE_INFINITY`, and `POSITIVE_INFINITY` constants. Both also provide an `isNaN` method that tests whether a floating-point value is "Not a Number"—that is, whether it is the result of a floating-point expression that has no valid result, such as dividing zero by zero. The NaN value can be used to indicate an invalid floating-point value; this is similar to the use of `null` for object references that do not refer to anything. The wrapper classes are covered in more detail in Chapter 14.

5.6 Literals

Each type in Java has *literals*, which are the way that constant values of that type are written. The next few subsections describe how literal (unnamed) constants for each type are specified.

5.6.1   Object References

The only literal object reference is `null`. It can be used anywhere a reference is expected. `null` conventionally represents an invalid or uncreated object. `null` is not of any type, not even `Object`.

5.6.2   Boolean

The boolean literals are `true` and `false`.

5.6.3   Integers

Integer constants are strings of octal, decimal, or hexadecimal digits. The start of the constant declares the base of the number: a leading `0` (zero) denotes an octal number (base 8); a leading `0x` or `0X` denotes a hexadecimal number (base 16); any other set of digits is assumed to be a decimal number (base 10). All the following numbers have the same value:

```
29 035 0x1D 0X1d
```

Integer constants are `long` if they end in L or l, such as `29L`; L is preferred over l because l (lowercase L) can easily be confused with 1 (the digit one). Otherwise, integer constants are assumed to be of type `int`. If an `int` literal is directly assigned to a `short`, and its value is within the valid range for a `short`, the integer literal is treated as if it were a `short` literal. A similar allowance is made for integer literals assigned to `byte` variables. In all other cases you must explicitly cast when assigning an `int` to a `short` or `byte`.

5.6.4   Floating-Point Numbers

Floating-point numbers are expressed as decimal numbers with an optional decimal point, optionally followed by an exponent. At least one digit must be present. The number can be followed by f or F to denote a single-precision constant, or by d or D to denote a double-precision constant. All these literals denote the same floating-point number:

```
18. 1.8e1 .18E2
```

Floating-point constants are of type `double` unless they are specified with a trailing f or F, which makes them `float` constants, such as `18.0f`. A trailing d or D specifies a `double` constant. Zero can be positive `0.0` or negative `-0.0`. Positive and negative zero are considered equal when you use `==` but produce different results when used in some calculations. For example, the expression 1d/0d is +∞, whereas 1d/-0d is -∞.

A double constant cannot be assigned directly to a float variable, even if the value of the double is within the valid float range. The only constants you may directly assign to float variables and fields are float constants.

5.6.5 Characters

Character literals appear between single quotes: 'Q'. Any valid Unicode character can appear between the quotes. You can use \u*dddd* for Unicode characters inside character literals just as you can elsewhere. Certain special characters can be represented by an *escape sequence*. These are:

\n	newline (\u000A)
\t	tab (\u0009)
\b	backspace (\u0008)
\r	return (\u000D)
\f	form feed (\u000C)
\\	backslash itself (\u005C)
\'	single quote (\u0027)
\"	double quote (\u0022)
ddd	a char by octal value, where each *d* is one of 0–7

Octal character constants can have three or fewer digits and cannot exceed \377 (\u00ff). Hexadecimal characters must always have four digits.

5.6.6 Strings

String literals appear between double quotes: "along". Any character can be included in string literals. A string literal references an object of type String. To learn more about strings, see Chapter 8.

Newlines are not allowed in the middle of strings. If you want to embed a newline character in the string, use the escape sequence \n.

Characters in strings can be specified using the octal digit mechanism, but all three octal digits should be used to prevent accidents when an octal value is specified next to a valid octal digit in the string. For example, the string "\0116" is equivalent to "\t6", whereas the string "\116" is equivalent to "N".

5.6.7 Class Literals

For every Java type there is an associated `Class` object. You can name the `Class` object for a type directly by following the type name with ".class", as in

```
String.class
java.lang.String.class
java.util.Enumeration.class
boolean.class
```

The first two of these class literals refer to the same `Class` object because `String` and `java.lang.String` are two different names for the same class. The third class literal is a reference to the `Class` object for the `Enumeration` interface discussed on page 54. The last is a `Class` object that represents the primitive type `boolean`. For more on `Class` objects, see Chapter 14.

5.7 Declarations of Variables

A *declaration* states the type, access, and other attributes of an identifier. A declaration is broken into three parts: *modifiers*, followed by a *type*, followed by a list of *identifiers*.

The type part of a declaration specifies which kinds of values and behavior are supported by the declared entities.

There is no difference between variables declared in one declaration or in multiple declarations of the same type. For example:

```
float[] x, y;
```

is the same as

```
float[] x;
float[] y;
```

Declarations can appear at any point in the source code. They need not be at the beginning of a class, method, or block of code. In general, identifiers are available any time after their declaration inside the block in which they are declared (see "Statements and Blocks" on page 139), with the proviso that non-static fields and methods are not available to static initializers or methods.

Modifiers are optional in a variable declaration. The `static` modifier declares that a field is one-per-class, not one-per-object. The `transient` modifier declares that the field will not, by default, be serialized; see "The `Object` Byte Streams" on page 259 for a discussion about serialization.

A declaration can be preceded by any of several modifiers. Modifiers are allowed in any order, but we recommend that you adopt a consistent order. Here is the order we use throughout the book: first are any access modifiers (`public`, `private`, or `protected`), followed by (in order, if present) `static`, `transient`, `synchronized`, and `final`. Using a consistent order improves readability of code.

5.7.1   Using `final` for Variables

The `final` modifier declares that the value of the variable is set exactly once and will thereafter always have the same value. Any variable—fields, local variables, and parameters—can be declared `final`. Variables that are `final` must be initialized before they are used. Typically this is done directly in the declaration:

```
final int id = nextID++;
```

You can set the value later on in the code if the compiler can verify that the variable will not be used before it is set. Such a final variable is called a *blank final*. Blank final fields are useful when the value of the field will be set in a constructor:

```
class NamedObj {
    final String name;

    NamedObj(String name) {
        this.name = name;
    }
}
```

Blank finals are also useful when you must calculate the value in something more than an initializer expression:

```
static final int[] numbers = numberList();
static final int maxNumber; // max value in numbers

static {
    int max = numbers[0];
    for (int i = 1; i < numbers.length; i++)
        if (numbers[i] > max)
            max = numbers[i];
    maxNumber = max;
}
```

Blank finals give you an alternative to accessor methods for values that are set only once during construction. For example, the version of the Body class shown on page 41 made idNum private to prevent it being changed. You could solve the same problem using final instead:

```
class Body {
    public final long idNum;       // now a blank final

    public String name = "<unnamed>";
    public Body orbits = null;

    private static long nextID = 0;

    Body() {
        idNum = nextID++;          // initialize blank final
    }

    //...
}
```

Because the field idNum is final, making it public does not create the danger of the programmer setting the value to something improper. Using blank finals for read-only values that are set only on construction can be useful, but it prevents some future modifications of the class. For example, suppose you wanted to change Body to defer setting idNum until it is first requested. You could not make that change with idNum as a blank final because you would not be able to detect the first access. Even if you could detect it, you could not defer initializing the blank final—you must initialize it during construction. A final field must be initialized at its declaration, set in all constructors, or initialized in exactly one initialization block.

As discussed on page 40, method parameters that are final are initialized to a value when the method is invoked with arguments. A final parameter will not change during each invocation of the method but may be different on separate invocations, depending on the arguments provided.

5.7.2   The Meanings of Names

When an identifier is created, it lives in a particular *namespace*. Identifiers in the same namespace must have names that are unique. When you use an identifier to name a variable, class, or method, the meaning of the name is determined by searching as follows:

1. Local variables declared in a code block, `for` loop, or as parameters to the `catch` clause of a `try` statement. A code block is one or more statements enclosed within braces. Variables can be declared in a `for` loop's initialization statement.
2. If the code is in a method or constructor, the parameters to the method or constructor.
3. A member of the class or interface. These are the fields and methods of the type, including any inherited members.
4. If the type is a nested type, the enclosing block or class. If the type is a static nested type, only static members of an enclosing block or class are searched. Reapply this search rule to any blocks and classes enclosing the enclosing type recursively.
5. Explicitly named imported types.
6. Other types declared in the same package.
7. Implicitly named imported types.
8. Packages available on the host system.

Each new nested block or `for` statement can declare new names. To avoid confusion, you cannot use this nesting to redeclare an identifier that is in an outer code block, in a `for` statement, or used for a parameter. Once there is a local identifier or parameter called, say, über, you cannot create a new, different identifier with the name über in a nested block.

These namespaces are further subdivided by the type of identifier involved. A variable can have the same name as a package, type, method, field, or statement label. A pathological case of this is something like the following:

```
class Reuse {
    Reuse Reuse(Reuse Reuse) {
      Reuse:
        for (;;) {
            if (Reuse.Reuse(Reuse) == Reuse)
                break Reuse;
        }
        return Reuse;
    }
}
```

The order of lookup means that identifiers declared inside a method can hide identifiers outside it. Hiding is generally bad style because a human reading the code must check all levels of the hierarchy to determine which variable is being used.

The nesting of scope gives variables a meaning in a region of the code corresponding to their intended use. For example, a variable declared in the initializer clause of a `for` statement is unavailable outside the scope of the `for`. This arrangement is appropriate when code outside the `for` loop should not discover where the iteration ended.

Nesting is needed to make local code robust. If hiding outer variables were not allowed, adding a new field to a class or interface could break existing code that used variables of the same name. Scoping is meant as protection for the system as a whole rather than support for reusing identifier names.

5.8   Array Variables

Java *arrays* provide ordered collections of elements. Components of an array can be primitive types or references to objects, including references to other arrays. The declaration

```
int[] ia = new int[3];
```

declares an array named `ia` that initially refers to an array of three `int` values.

Array dimensions are omitted in the declaration of any array variable. The number of components in an array is determined when it is *created* using `new`, not when it is declared. An array object's length is fixed at its creation and cannot be changed. Note that it is the length of the array *object* that is fixed. In the example, a new array of a different size could be assigned to the array reference `ia` at any time.

The first element of the array `ia` has index 0 (zero), and the last element has index *length*–1. In our example, the last element of the array is `ia[2]`. Every subscript use is checked to ensure that it is within the proper range. An out-of-range array access throws an `IndexOutOfBoundsException`.

The length of an array is available via the `length` field. In our example, the following code would loop over the array, printing each value:

```
for (int i = 0; i < ia.length; i++)
    System.out.println(i + ": " + ia[i]);
```

Arrays are implicit extensions of `Object`. Given a class X, classes Y and Z that extend X, and arrays of each, the class hierarchy looks something like this:

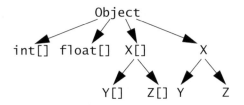

This class relationship allows polymorphism for arrays. You can assign an array to a variable of type `Object` and cast it back. An array of objects of type Y is usable wherever an array of objects of its base type X is required. This seems natural but can require a run-time check that is sometimes unexpected. An array of X can contain either Y or Z references, but an array of Y cannot contain references to X or Z objects. The following code would generate an `ArrayStoreException` on either of its final two lines, which violate this rule:

```
Y[] yArray = new Y[3];      // a Y array
X[] xArray = yArray;        // valid: Y is assignable to X
xArray[0] = new Y();
xArray[2] = new X();        // INVALID: can't store X in Y[]
xArray[1] = new Z();        // INVALID: can't store Z in Y[]
```

If xArray were a reference to a real X[] object, it would be valid to store both an X and a Z object into it. But xArray actually refers to a Y[] object so it is not valid to store either an X reference or a Z reference in it. Such assignments are checked at run time if needed to ensure that no improper reference is stored into an array.

Like any other object, arrays are created and are subject to normal garbage collection mechanisms.

The major limitation on the "object-ness" of arrays is that they cannot be extended to add new methods. The following construct is not valid:

```
class ScaleVector extends double[] { // INVALID
    // ...
}
```

When you declare an array of an object type, you are really declaring an array of variables of that type. Consider the following code:

```
Attr[] attrs = new Attr[12];

for (int i = 0; i < attrs.length; i++)
    attrs[i] = new Attr(names[i], values[i]);
```

After the initial new of the array, `attrs` has a reference to an array of 12 variables that are initialized to `null`. The `Attr` objects are created only when the loop is executed.

If you prefer, Java allows the array brackets to come after the variable instead of the type:

```
int ia[] = new int[3];
```

This code is equivalent to the original definition of `ia`. However, the first style is preferable because it places the type declaration entirely in one place.

5.8.1 Arrays of Arrays

Java supports arrays of arrays. The code to declare and print a two-dimensional matrix, for example, might look like this:

```
float[][] mat = new float[4][4];
setupMatrix(mat);
for (int y = 0; y < mat.length; y++) {
    for (int x = 0; x < mat[y].length; x++)
        System.out.print(mat[y][x] + " ");
    System.out.println();
}
```

The first (leftmost) dimension of an array must be specified when the array is created. Other dimensions can be left unspecified, to be filled in later. Specifying more than the first dimension is a shorthand for a nested set of new statements. Our new creation could have been written more explicitly as:

```
float[][] mat = new float[4][];
for (int y = 0; y < mat.length; y++)
    mat[y] = new float[4];
```

One advantage of arrays of arrays is that each nested array can have a different size. You can emulate a 4×4 array, but you can also create an array of four `int` arrays, each of which has a different length necessary to hold its own data.

Exercise 5.1: Write a program that calculates Pascal's triangle to a depth of 12, storing each row of the triangle in an array of the appropriate length and putting each of the row arrays into an array of 12 `int` arrays. Design your solution so that the results are printed by a method that prints the array of arrays using the lengths of each array, not a constant 12. Now change the code to use a constant other than 12 without modifying your printing method.

5.9 Initial Values

A variable can be initialized in its declaration. The initial value for the variable can be given by following the variable name with an = and an expression:

```
final double π = 3.14159265358979323846;
float radius = 1.0f;  // start with unit circle
```

Java assigns a default initial value to all elements of a newly created array, and to fields if no initial value is specified. The default value depends on the type:

Type	Initial Value
boolean	false
char	'\u0000'
byte, short, int, long	0
float	+0.0f
double	+0.0
object reference	null

Java does not assign any default initial value to local variables in a method, constructor, or static initializer, because failure to provide an initial value for a local variable is usually a bug. You must initialize local variables before using them.

A variable's scope determines when it is initialized. Local variables are initialized each time their declaration is executed. Object fields and members of arrays are initialized when the object or array is created with new—see "Constructor Order Dependencies" on page 65 for precise details. A class's static variables are initialized before any code for that class is run.

Field initializers cannot throw checked exceptions, nor invoke methods that throw checked exceptions, because there is no way to catch them. You can work around this rule for non-static fields by placing the assignment inside a constructor or a non-static initialization block, because the constructor or block can handle the exception. For static fields, the work-around is to set the initial value inside a static initializer that handles the exception.

5.9.1 Array Initializers

Arrays can be initialized by providing values inside braces following their declaration. The following array declaration creates and initializes an array object:

```
String[] dangers = { "Lions", "Tigers", "Bears" };
```

The following code gives the same result:

```
String[] dangers = new String[3];

dangers[0] = "Lions";
dangers[1] = "Tigers";
dangers[2] = "Bears" ;
```

Arrays of arrays can be initialized by nesting array initializers. Here is a declaration that initializes an array to the top few rows of Pascal's triangle, with each row represented by its own array:

```
int[][] pascalsTriangle = {
            { 1 },
            { 1, 1 },
            { 1, 2, 1 },
            { 1, 3, 3, 1 },
            { 1, 4, 6, 4, 1 },
       };
```

Indexes in an array of arrays work from the outermost inward. For example, in the preceding array, `pascalsTriangle[0]` refers to the `int` array that has one element, `pascalsTriangle[1]` refers to the `int` array that has two elements, and so on.

You can initialize any array upon creation. For example, you could create an array on an assignment line:

```
Object[] things = new String[] { "one", "two", "many" };
```

The array created with the new is called an *anonymous array*. The new expression creates the array and initializes its elements to the values given in the initialization list. Anonymous arrays derive their dimensions from the contents of the initializer; you never specify an array dimension when you create an anonymous array.

5.10 Operator Precedence and Associativity

Operator precedence is the "stickiness" of operators relative to each other. Operators have different precedences. For example, relational operators have a higher precedence than boolean operators, so you can say

```
if (i >= min && i <= max)
    process(i);
```

without any confusion. Because * (multiply) has a higher precedence than - (minus), the expression

```
5 * 3 - 3
```

has the value 12, not zero. Precedence can be overridden using parentheses; if zero were the desired value, for example, the following would do the trick:

```
5 * (3 - 3)
```

When two operators with the same precedence appear next to each other, the associativity of the operators determines which are evaluated first. Because + (add) is left-associative, the expression

```
a + b + c
```

is equivalent to

```
(a + b) + c
```

The following table lists all the operators in order of precedence from highest to lowest. All the operators are binary except those shown as unary with *expr*, the creation and cast operators (which are also unary), and the conditional operator (which is ternary). Operators with the same precedence appear on the same line of the table:

postfix operators	`[]` . (*params*) *expr*++ *expr*--
unary operators	++*expr* --*expr* +*expr* -*expr* ~ !
creation or cast	new (*type*)*expr*
multiplicative	* / %
additive	+ -
shift	<< >> >>>
relational	< > >= <= instanceof
equality	== !=
bitwise AND	&
bitwise exclusive XOR	^
bitwise inclusive OR	|
logical AND	&&
logical OR	||
conditional	?:
assignment	= += -= *= /= %= >>= <<= >>>= &= ^= |=

All binary operators except assignment operators are *left-associative*. Assignment is *right-associative*. In other words, a=b=c is equivalent to a=(b=c).

Parentheses are often needed in expressions in which assignment is embedded in a boolean expression, or in which bitwise operations are used. For an example of the former, examine the following code:

```
while ((v = stream.next()) != null)
    processValue(v);
```

Assignment operators have lower precedence than equality operators; without the parentheses, it would be equivalent to

```
while (v = (stream.next() != null)) // INVALID
    processValue(v);
```

and probably not what you want. It is also likely to be invalid code since it would be valid only in the unusual case in which v is boolean.

Many people find the precedence of the bitwise operators &, ∧, and | hard to remember. Binary bitwise operators in complex expressions should be parenthesized for readability and to ensure correct precedence.

Our use of parentheses is sparse—we use them only when code seems otherwise unclear. Operator precedence is part of the language and should be generally understood. Others inject parentheses liberally. Try not to use parentheses everywhere—code becomes illegible, looking like LISP with none of LISP's saving graces.

5.11 Order of Evaluation

Java guarantees that operands to operators will be evaluated left-to-right. For example, given x+y+z, the compiler evaluates x, evaluates y, adds the values together, evaluates z, and adds that to the previous result. The compiler does not evaluate, say, y before x, or z before either y or x.

Order of evaluation matters if x, y, or z has side effects of any kind. If they are, for instance, invocations of methods that affect the state of the object or print something, you would notice if they were evaluated in any other order. The language guarantees that this will not happen.

Except for the operators &&, ||, and ?: (described later), every operand of an operator will be evaluated before the operation is performed. This is true even for operations that raise exceptions. For example, an integer division by zero results in an ArithmeticException, but it will do so only after both operands have been fully evaluated.

5.12 Expression Type

Every expression has a type. The type of an expression is determined by the types of its component parts and the semantics of operators. If an arithmetic or bitwise operator is applied to integer values, the result of the expression is of type `int` unless one or both sides are `long`, in which case the result is `long`. All integer operations are performed in either `int` or `long` precision, so the smaller `byte` and `short` integer types are always promoted to `int` before evaluation.

If either operand of an arithmetic operator is floating-point, the operation is performed in floating-point arithmetic. Such operations are done in `float` unless at least one operand is a `double`, in which case `double` is used for the calculation and result.

A + operator is a `String` concatenation when either operand to + is of type `String` or if the left-hand side of a += is a `String`.

When used in an expression, a `char` value is converted to an `int` by setting the top 16 bits to zero. For example, the Unicode character \uffff would be treated as equivalent to the integer `0x0000ffff`. This treatment is different from the way a `short` with the value `0xffff` would be treated—sign extension makes the `short` equivalent to `-1`, and its `int` equivalent would be `0xffffffff`.

5.13 Type Conversions

Java is a *strongly typed* language, which means that it checks for type compatibility at compile time in almost all cases. Java prevents incompatible assignments by forbidding anything questionable. It also provides cast operations for when the compatibility of a type can be determined only at run time, or when you want to explicitly force a type conversion for primitive types that would otherwise lose range, such as assigning a `double` to a `float`. We discuss these conversions in terms of assignment, but what we say also applies to conversions within expressions and when using values as method parameters.

5.13.1 Implicit Conversion

Some kinds of conversions happen automatically, without any work on your part. There are two kinds of *implicit* conversions.

The first kind of implicit conversion applies to primitive values. Any numeric value can be assigned to any numeric variable whose type supports a larger range of values. A `char` can be used wherever an `int` is valid. A floating-point value can be assigned to any floating-point variable of equal or greater precision.

Java also allows implicit conversion of integer types to floating-point, but not vice versa. There is no loss of range going from integer to floating-point, because the range of any floating-point type is larger than the range of any integer.

Preserving magnitude is not the same as preserving the precision of a value. You can lose precision in some implicit conversions. Consider, for example, assigning a long to a float. The float has 32 bits of data and the long has 64 bits of data. A float stores fewer significant digits than a long, even though a float stores numbers of a larger range. You can lose data in an assignment of a long to a float. Consider the following:

```java
long orig = 0x7effffffffffffffL;
float fval = orig;
long lose = (long)fval;

System.out.println("orig = " + orig);
System.out.println("fval = " + fval);
System.out.println("lose = " + lose);
```

The first two statements create a long value and assign it to a float value. To show that this loses precision, we explicitly cast fval to a long and assign it to another variable (explicit casts are covered later). If you examine the output, you can see that the float value lost some precision: the long variable orig that was assigned to the float variable fval has a different value from the one generated by the explicit cast back into the long variable lose:

```
orig = 9151314442816847871
fval = 9.1513144E18
lose = 9151314442816847872
```

The second type of implicit conversion is reference conversion. An object that is an instance of a class includes an instance of each of its supertypes. You can use an object reference of one type wherever a reference of any supertype is required.

The null object reference is assignable to any object reference type, including array references.

5.13.2 Explicit Casts and `instanceof`

When one type cannot be assigned to another type with implicit conversion, often it can be explicitly *cast* to the other type. A cast requests a new value of a new type that is the best available representation of the old value in the old type. Some casts are not allowed—for example, a `boolean` cannot be cast to an `int`—but explicit casting can be used to assign a `double` to a `long`, as in this code:

```
double d = 7.99;
long l = (long)d;
```

When a floating-point value is cast to an integer, the fractional part is lost by rounding toward zero; for instance, `(int)-72.3` is `-72`. Methods are available in the `Math` class that round floating-point values to integers in other ways. See "`Math`" on page 332 for details.

A `double` can also be explicitly cast to a `float`, or an integer type can be explicitly cast to a smaller integer type. When casting from a `double` to a `float`, three things can happen: you can lose precision, you can get a zero, or you can get an infinity where you originally had a finite value outside the range of a `float`.

Integer types are converted by chopping off the upper bits. If the value in the larger integer fits in the smaller type to which it is cast, no harm is done. But if the larger integer has a value outside the range of the smaller type, dropping the upper bits changes the value, including possibly changing sign. The code

```
short s = -134;
byte b = (byte)s;

System.out.println("s = " + s + ", b = " + b);
```

produces the following output because the upper bits of s are lost when storing the value in b:

```
s = -134, b = 122
```

A `char` can be cast to any integer type and vice versa. When an integer is cast to a `char`, only the bottom 16 bits of data are used; the rest are discarded. When a `char` is cast to an integer type, any additional upper bits are filled with zeros. Once those bits are assigned, they are treated as they would be in any other value. Here is some code that casts the highest Unicode character to both an `int` (implicitly) and a `short` (explicitly). The `int` is a positive value equal to `0x0000ffff`, because the upper bits of the character were set to zero. But the same bits in the `short` are a negative value, because the top bit of the `short` is the sign bit:

```
class CharCast {
    public static void main(String[] args) {
        int i = '\uffff';
        short s = (short)'\uffff';

        System.out.println("i = " + i);
```

```
        System.out.println("s = " + s);
    }
}
```

And here is the program's output:

```
i = 65535
s = -1
```

Explicit casts can also be used with object types. Although an object of an extended type can be used where a supertype is needed, the converse is not generally true. Suppose you had the following class hierarchy:

```
                Tool
               /    \
              ↓      ↓
          Wrench   Hammer
```

A reference of type Tool does not necessarily refer to an object of type Wrench; the object might be of type Hammer. So you cannot, for example, pass the Tool reference when an object of type Wrench is expected. Such casting is called *narrowing* or *downcasting* (casting down the class hierarchy). It is also called *unsafe casting* because it is not always valid. Going from a more-extended to a less-extended type is called *widening* or *upcasting* (casting up the class hierarchy); it is also sometimes called *safe casting* because it is always valid.

But sometimes you know that the Tool object is actually an instance of Wrench. In such a case, you can cast down the type tree using an explicit cast:

```
Wrench turner = (Wrench)wonder;
```

If this is valid—that is, if wonder really refers to a Wrench object—turner will refer to the same object wonder does, but turner can be used to access the functionality that Wrench adds. If the cast is not valid, a ClassCastException is thrown. If the cast isn't even potentially correct (for example, if Wrench were not an extended class of the declared type for wonder), this code would not compile, preventing an error in which the code assumes an incorrect class hierarchy.

Sometimes a method does not require an object of a more extended type, but if it *has* an extended object, the method can use the extended functionality. You could simply do the cast and handle the exception, but exception handling may be slow and is usually poor style. Use instanceof to test an object's type:

```
public void use(Tool wonder) {
    // ...
    if (wonder instanceof Wrench) {
```

```
            Wrench turner = (Wrench)wonder;
            // ... use Wrench's functionality
        }
    }
```

The `null` reference is not an instance of any object type at all, so

```
    null instanceof Type
```

is always `false`, for any *Type,* even `Object`.

5.13.3 String Conversions

The `String` class is special: it is used implicitly in the + string concatenation operator, and literal strings refer to `String` objects. You've already seen examples of output code: wherever a `String` object is needed when concatenating strings, Java tries to convert the non-`String` side (if any) into a `String`. Such conversions are defined for all primitive types and are accomplished for any object by invoking its `toString` method (see "The `toString` Method" on page 56).

When a null reference is converted to a `String`, the result is the string `"null"`. If no `toString` method is defined for a class, it inherits the one from `Object`, which returns a string representation of the object type.

5.14 Member Access

You access members of objects using the `.` operator, as in `ref.method()`. You can also use `.` to access static members, using either a class name or an object reference. If you use an object reference for a static member, the declared type of the reference, not the actual type of the object, determines which class's static members to use. Elements of arrays are accessed using brackets, as in `array[i]`.

You will get a a `NullPointerException` if you use `.` or [] on a reference with the value `null` (unless you are using `.` to invoke a static method). You will get an `IndexOutOfBoundsException` if an index is outside an array's bounds.[6]

For an invocation of a method to be correct, arguments of the proper number and type must be provided so that exactly one matching method can be found in the class. If a method is not overloaded, determining the correct method is simple, because only one parameter count is associated with the method name. Matching

---

[6] The range check can often be optimized away when, for example, it can be proven that a loop index variable is always within range, but it is guaranteed that an index will never be used if it is out of range.

is also simple if only one method is declared with the name and number of arguments provided.

If two or more methods of the same name have the same number of parameters, choosing the correct method is more complex. The compiler uses a "most specific" algorithm to do the match:

1. Find all the methods that could possibly apply to the invocation—namely, all the overloaded methods that have the correct name and whose parameters are of types that can be assigned the values of all the arguments. If one method matches exactly for all arguments, invoke that method.

2. If any method in the set has parameter types that are all assignable to any other method in the set, the other method is removed from the set because it is less specific. Repeat until no eliminations can be made.

3. If exactly one method remains, that method is the most specific and will be invoked. If more than one method remains, the invocation is ambiguous because there is no most specific method, so the invoking code is invalid.

For instance, suppose you had an expanded version of the dessert types shown on page 63:

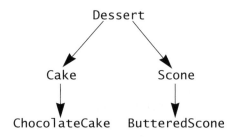

Also suppose you had several overloaded methods that took particular combinations of Dessert parameters:

```
void moorge(Dessert d, Scone s)       { /* first form  */ }
void moorge(Cake c, Dessert d)        { /* second form */ }
void moorge(ChocolateCake cc, Scone s) { /* third form  */ }
```

Now consider the following invocations of moorge:

```
moorge(dessertRef, sconeRef);
moorge(chocolateCakeRef, dessertRef);
moorge(chocolateCakeRef, butteredSconeRef);
moorge(cakeRef, sconeRef);       // INVALID
```

The first invocation uses the first form of `moorge` because the parameter and argument types match exactly. The second invocation uses the second form because it is the only form for which the provided arguments can be assigned to the parameter types. In both cases, the method to invoke is clear after step 1 in the method-matching algorithm.

The third invocation requires more thought. The list of potential overloads includes all three forms, because a `ChocolateCakeRef` is assignable to any of the first parameter types, a `ButteredScone` reference is assignable to either of the second parameter types, and none of the signatures matches exactly. So after step 1, you have a set of three candidate methods.

Step 2 requires you to eliminate less specific methods from the set. In this case, the first form is removed from the set because the third form is more specific—a `ChocolateCake` reference can be assigned to the first form's `Dessert` parameter and a `Scone` reference can be assigned to the first form's `Scone` parameter, so the first form is less specific. The second form is removed from the set in a similar manner. After this, the set of possible methods has been reduced to one—the third form of `moorge`—and that method form will be invoked.

The final invocation is invalid. After step 1, the set of possible matches includes the first and second forms. Because neither form's parameters are assignable to the other, neither form can be removed from the set in step 2. Therefore, you have an ambiguous invocation that cannot be resolved by the compiler, and so it is an invalid invocation of `moorge`.

These rules also apply to the primitive types. An `int`, for example, can be assigned to a `float`, and resolving an overloaded invocation will take that into account just as it considered that a `ButteredScone` reference was assignable to a `Scone` reference.

Methods may not differ only in return type or in the list of exceptions they throw, because there are too many ambiguities to determine which overloaded method is wanted. If, for example, there were two `doppelgänger` methods that differed only in that one returned an `int` and the other returned a `short`, both methods would make equal sense in the following statement:

```
double d = doppelgänger();
```

A similar problem exists with exceptions, because you can catch any, all, or none of the exceptions a method might throw in the code where you invoke the overloaded method. There would be no way to determine which of two methods to use when they differed only in thrown exceptions.

5.15 Arithmetic Operators

Java supports several binary arithmetic operators that operate on any numerical type:

+	addition
–	subtraction
*	multiplication
/	division
%	remainder

Java also supports unary - for negation. The sign of a number can be inverted with code like this:

```
val = -val;
```

There is also a unary +, as in +3. Unary plus is included for symmetry—without it, you could not write constants such as +2.0.

5.15.1 Integer Arithmetic

Integer arithmetic is modular two's-complement arithmetic—that is, if a value exceeds the range of its type (int or long), it is reduced modulo the range. So integer arithmetic never overflows or underflows but only wraps.

Integer division truncates toward zero (7/2 is 3, and -7/2 is -3). For integer types, division and remainder obey the rule

```
(x/y)*y + x%y == x
```

So 7%2 is 1, and -7%2 is -1. Dividing by zero or remainder by zero is invalid for integer arithmetic and throws ArithmeticException.

Character arithmetic is integer arithmetic after the char is implicitly converted to int.

5.15.2 Floating-Point Arithmetic

Java uses the IEEE 754-1985 standard on floating-point, both for representation and arithmetic, with default modes. Under this standard, arithmetic can overflow to infinity (become too large for the double or float) or underflow to zero (become too small for the double or float). The result of an invalid expression, such as dividing infinity by infinity, is a NaN value—for "Not a Number."

Arithmetic with finite operands performs as expected, within the limits of precision of `double` or `float`. Signs of floating-point arithmetic results are also as expected. Multiplying two numbers having the same sign results in a positive value; multiplying two numbers having opposite signs results in a negative value.

Adding two infinities results in the same infinity if their signs are the same, and NaN if their signs differ. Subtracting infinities of the same sign produces NaN; subtracting infinities of opposite signs produces an infinity of the same sign as the left operand. For example, $(\infty - (-\infty))$ is ∞. Arithmetic operations involving any value that is NaN have a result that is also NaN. Overflows result in a value that is an infinity of the proper sign. Underflows result in a zero of the proper sign. Java floating-point arithmetic has a negative zero `-0.0`, which compares equal to `+0.0`. Although they compare equal, the two zeros can produce different results. For example, the expression `1f/0f` yields positive infinity and `1f/-0f` yields negative infinity.

If the result of an underflow is `-0.0` and if `-0.0 == 0.0`, how do you test for a negative zero? You must use the zero in an expression where sign matters and then test the result. For example, if `x` has a zero value, the expression `1/x` will yield negative infinity if `x` is negative zero, or positive infinity if `x` is positive zero.

The rules for operations on infinities match normal mathematical expectations. Adding or subtracting any number to or from either infinity results in that infinity. For example, $(-\infty + x)$ is $-\infty$ for any finite number x.

You can get an infinity value from the constants `POSITIVE_INFINITY` and `NEGATIVE_INFINITY` in the wrapper classes `Float` and `Double`. For example, `Double.NEGATIVE_INFINITY` is the `double` value of minus infinity.

Multiplying infinity by zero yields NaN. Multiplying infinity by a non-zero finite number produces an infinity of the appropriate sign.

Floating-point division and remainder can produce infinities or NaN but never raise an exception. This table shows the results of the various combinations:

x	y	x/y	x%y
Finite	±0.0	±∞	NaN
Finite	±∞	±0.0	x
±0.0	±0.0	NaN	NaN
±∞	Finite	±∞	NaN
±∞	±∞	NaN	NaN

Otherwise, floating-point remainder (%) acts analogously to integer remainder as described earlier. See the `Math.IEEERemainder` method in "Math" on page 332 for a different remainder calculation.

5.15.3 Java Floating-Point Arithmetic and IEEE-754

Java floating-point arithmetic is a subset of the IEEE-754-1985 standard. If you need a complete understanding of these issues, you should consult *The Java Language Specification.* Here is a summary of the key differences:

◆ *Nonstop arithmetic:* The Java system will not throw exceptions, trap, or otherwise signal the IEEE exceptional conditions of invalid operation, division by zero, overflow, underflow, or inexact. Java arithmetic has no signaling NaN value.

◆ *Rounding:* Java arithmetic is *round toward nearest*—it rounds inexact results to the nearest representable value, with ties going to the value with a zero least-significant bit. This is the IEEE default mode. But Java arithmetic rounds toward zero when converting a floating value to an integer. Java does not provide user-selectable rounding modes for floating-point computations.

◆ *Relational set:* Except for !=, Java arithmetic has no relational predicates that include the unordered condition. However, all cases except one can be constructed by the programmer using existing relations and logical inversion. The exception is "ordered but unequal," which can be obtained by an expression such as x < y || x > y.

◆ *Extended formats:* Java arithmetic does not support any extended formats except that double will serve as single-extended. Other extended formats are not a requirement of the standard.

5.15.4 String Concatenation

You can use + to concatenate two strings. Here is an example:

```
String boo = "boo";
String cry = boo + "hoo";
cry += "!";
System.out.println(cry);
```

And here is its output:

```
boohoo!
```

You can also use + to concatenate a String with a string representation of any primitive type or of an object. For example, the following method brackets a string with the guillemet characters used for quotation marks in many European languages:

```
public static String guillemete(String quote) {
    return '«' + quote + '»';
}
```

This implicit conversion of primitive types and objects to strings happens only when you're using + or += in expressions involving strings. It does not happen anywhere else. A method, for example, that takes a String parameter must be passed a String. You cannot pass it an object or float and have it converted implicitly.

5.16 Increment and Decrement Operators

The ++ and -- operators are the increment and decrement operators, respectively. The expression i++ is equivalent to i = i + 1 except that i is evaluated only once. For example, the statement

```
++arr[where()];
```

invokes where only once and uses the result as an index into the array only once. On the other hand, in the statement

```
arr[where()] = arr[where()] + 1;
```

the where method is called twice: once to determine the index on the right-hand side, and a second time to determine the index on the left-hand side. If where returns a different value each time it is invoked, the results will be quite different from those of the ++ expression.

The increment and decrement operators can be either *prefix* or *postfix* operators—they can appear either before or after what they operate on. If the operator comes before (prefix), the operation is applied before the value of the expression is returned. If the operator comes after (postfix), the operation is applied after the original value is used. For example:

```
class IncOrder {
    public static void main(String[] args) {
        int i = 16;
        System.out.println(++i + " " + i++ + " " + i);
    }
}
```

The output is

```
17 17 18
```

The first value printed is i preincremented to 17; the second value is i after that increment but before it is postincremented to 18; finally, i is printed after its post-increment from the middle term.

The increment and decrement operators ++ and -- can also be applied to char variables to get to the next or previous Unicode character.

5.17   Relational, Equality, and Logical Operators

Java supports a standard set of relational and equality operators, all of which yield boolean valaues:

>	greater than
>=	greater than or equal to
<	less than
<=	less than or equal to
==	equal to
!=	not equal to

The unary operator ! inverts a boolean; hence !true is the same as false. Boolean values are normally tested directly—if x and y are booleans, the code

```
if (x || !y) {
    // ...
}
```

is considered cleaner than the equivalent, but more verbose

```
if (x == true || y == false) {
    // ...
}
```

Results of boolean expressions can be joined with && and ||, which mean "conditional AND" and "conditional OR," respectively. These operators avoid evaluating their second operand if possible. For example:

```
if (w && x) {        // outer "if"
    if (y || z) {    // inner "if"
        // ...        inner "if" body
    }
}
```

The inner `if` is executed only if both w *and* x are `true`. If w is `false`, Java does not evaluate x. The body of the inner `if` is executed if either y or z is `true`. If y is `true`, Java does not evaluate z.

Much Java code relies on this rule for program correctness or efficiency. For example, the evaluation shortcuts make the following code safe:

```
if (ix >= 0 && ix < array.length && array[ix] != 0) {
    // ...
}
```

The range checks are done first. Only if `ix` is within bounds will it be used to access an `array` element.

Only the equality operators `==` and `!=` are allowed to operate on boolean values, because the question of whether `true` is greater than or less than `false` is meaningless. These operators can be used to create a "logical XOR" test. The following code invokes `sameSign` only if both x and y have the same sign (or zero); otherwise it invokes `differentSign`:

```
if (x < 0 == y < 0)
    sameSign();
else
    differentSign();
```

Floating-point values follow normal ordering (`-1.0` is less than `0.0` is less than positive infinity) except that NaN is an anomaly. All relational and equality operators that test a number against NaN return `false`, except `!=`, which always returns `true`. This is true even if both values are NaN. For example,

```
Double.NaN == Double.NaN
```

is always `false`. To test whether a value is NaN, use the type-specific NaN testers: the static methods `Float.isNaN(float)` and `Double.isNaN(Double)`.

Two object references can be tested for equality. The expression `ref1==ref2` is `true` if the two references refer to the same object or if both are `null`, even if the two references are of different declared types. Otherwise, it is `false`.

Using equality operators on `String` objects does not work as expected. Given `String` objects `str1` and `str2`, `str1==str2` tests whether `str1` and `str2` refer to the same `String` object. It does *not* test whether they have the same contents. Content equality is tested using `String.equals`, described in Chapter 8.

5.18   Bitwise Operators

The binary bitwise operators are:

    &   bitwise AND
    | bitwise inclusive OR
    ^   bitwise exclusive or (XOR)

There is also a unary bitwise complement operator ~, which toggles each bit in its operand. An `int` with value `0x00003333` has a complemented value of `0xffffcccc`.

The other bitwise operators shift bits within an integer value:

    `<<`   Shift bits left, filling with zero bits on the right-hand side
    `>>`   Shift bits right, filling with the highest (sign) bit on the left-hand side
    `>>>`   Shift bits right, filling with zero bits on the left-hand side

The left-hand side of a shift expression is what is shifted, and the right-hand side is how much to shift. For example, `var >>> 2` will shift the bits in `var` two places to the right, dropping the bottom two bits from the end and filling the top two bits with zero.

Shift operators have a slightly different type rule from most other binary integer operations. For shift operators, the resulting type is the type of the left-hand operand—that is, the value that is shifted. If the left-hand side of the shift is an `int`, the result of the shift is an `int`, even if the shift count is provided as a `long`.

If the shift count is larger than the number of bits in the word, or if it is negative, the actual count will be different from the provided count. The actual count used in a shift is the count you provide, masked by the size of the type minus one. For a 32-bit `int`, for example, the mask used is `0x1f` (31), so both `(n << 35)` and `(n << -29)` are equivalent to `(n << 3)`.

Bitwise operators can also be used on `boolean` values. & and | return the same value as their logical counterparts && and ||, with one important difference: the bitwise operators always evaluate both operands, whereas the logical operators evaluate both operands only if necessary.

The bitwise ^ is `true` if the booleans are not the same: one or the other is `true`, but not both. Using ^ is another way to create "logical XOR":

```
if ((x < 0) ^ (y < 0))
    differentSign();
else
    sameSign();
```

Bitwise operators can be used only on integer types and booleans, not on floating-point or reference values. Shift operators can be used only on integer types. In the rare circumstance when you actually need to manipulate the bits in a floating-point value, you can use the conversion methods on the classes `Float` and `Double`, discussed in "The Floating-Point Wrapper Classes" on page 302.

5.19 The Conditional Operator ?:

The *conditional operator* provides a single expression that yields one of two values based on a boolean expression. The following:

```
value = (userSetIt ? usersValue : defaultValue);
```

is equivalent to

```
if (userSetIt)
    value = usersValue;
else
    value = defaultValue;
```

The primary difference between the `if` statement and the `?:` operator is that the latter has a value. The conditional operator results in a more compact expression, but programmers disagree about whether it is more clear. We use whichever seems clearer at the time. When to use parentheses around a conditional operator expression is a matter of personal style, and practice varies widely. Parentheses are not required by the language.

The result expressions (the second and third ones) must have assignment-compatible types. The type of one result expression must be assignable to the type of the other one without an explicit cast, no matter which one is assignable to the other. The type of the result of the conditional operator is the more general of the two types. For example, in

```
double scale = (halveIt ? 1 : 0.5);
```

the two sides are `int` (1) and `double` (0.5). An `int` is assignable to a `double`, so the `1` is cast to `1.0` and the result of the conditional operator is `double`. This rule also holds for reference types—if one type is assignable to the other, the least-extended type is the type of the operation. If neither type is assignable to the other, the operation is invalid.

This operator is also called the *question/colon operator* because of its form, and the *ternary operator* because it is the only ternary (three-operand) operator in the Java language.

5.20   Assignment Operators

The simple = is the most basic form of assignment operator. Java supports many other assignment forms. Any arithmetic or binary bitwise operator can be concatenated with = to form another assignment operator. For example,

```
arr[where()] += 12;
```

is the same as

```
arr[where()] = arr[where()] + 12;
```

except that the expression on the left-hand side of the assignment is evaluated only once. In the example, `arr[where()]` is evaluated only once in the first expression.

Given the variable `var` of type `Type`, the value `expr`, and the binary operator `op`, the expression

```
var op= expr
```

is equivalent to

```
var = (Type)((var) op (expr))
```

except that `var` is evaluated only once. This means that `op=` is valid only if `op` is valid for the types involved. You cannot, for example, use `<<=` on a `double` variable because you cannot use `<<` on a `double` variable.

Note the parentheses used in the expanded form you just saw. The expression

```
a *= b + 1
```

is analogous to

```
a = a * (b + 1)
```

and not to

```
a = a * b + 1
```

Although `a += 1` is the same as `++a`, `++` is considered idiomatic and is preferred.

5.21   Package Names

Package names consist of a sequence of identifiers separated by dots (`.`). Unicode-capable editors will be rare for some time, so it makes sense to use only Latin-1 characters in package names if the package is expected to be widely distributed. See Chapter 10 to learn about packages and their uses.

Exercise 5.2: Using what you've learned in this chapter but without writing Java code, figure out which of the following expressions are invalid and what the type and values are of the valid expressions:

```
3 << 2L - 1
(3L << 2) - 1
10 < 12 == 6 > 17
10 << 12 == 6 >> 17
13.5e-1 % Float.POSITIVE_INFINITY
Float.POSITIVE_INFINITY + Double.NEGATIVE_INFINITY
Double.POSITIVE_INFINITY - Float.NEGATIVE_INFINITY
0.0 / -0.0 == -0.0 / 0.0
Integer.MAX_VALUE + Integer.MIN_VALUE;
Long.MAX_VALUE + 5;
(short)5 * (byte)10
(i < 15 ? 1.72e3f : 0)
i++ + i++ + --i      // i = 3 at start
```

> *Math was always my bad subject.*
> *I couldn't convince my teachers that many of my answers were meant ironically.*
> —Calvin Trillin

CHAPTER 6

Control Flow

> *"Would you tell me, please, which way I ought to go from here?"*
> *"That depends a good deal on where you want to get to."*
> —Lewis Carroll, *Alice in Wonderland*

A program consisting only of a list of consecutive statements is immediately useful because the statements are executed in the order in which they're written. But the ability to control the order in which statements are executed—that is, to test conditions and execute different statements based on the results of the tests—adds enormous value to our programming toolkit. This chapter covers almost all the *control flow statements* that direct the order of execution. Exceptions are covered separately in Chapter 7.

6.1 Statements and Blocks

The two basic statements are *expression statements* and *declaration statements*, of which you've seen a plethora. Expression statements, such as i++ or method invocations, are expressions that have a semicolon at the end. The semicolon terminates the statement.[1] Not all expressions can become statements, since it would be almost always meaningless to have, for example, an expression such as x <= y stand alone as a statement. Only the following types of expressions can be made into statements by adding a terminating semicolon:

◆ Assignment expressions—those that contain = or one of the *op=* operators

---

[1] There is a distinction between *terminator* and *separator*. The comma between identifiers in declarations is a separator because it comes between elements in the list. The semicolon is a terminator because it ends each statement. If the semicolon were a statement separator, the last semicolon in a code block would be unnecessary and (depending on the choice of the language designer) possibly invalid.

◆ Prefix or postfix forms of ++ and --

◆ Method calls (whether or not they return a value)

◆ Object creation expressions—those that use new to create an object

Declaration statements (formally called *local variable declaration statements*) declare a variable and initialize it to a value. They can appear anywhere inside a block, not just at the beginning. Local variables exist only as long as the block containing their declaration is executing. Local variables must be initialized before use, either by initialization when declared or by assignment. If any local variable is used before it is initialized, the code will not compile.

In addition to the expression statements listed, several other kinds of statements, such as if and for statements, affect flow of control through the program. This chapter covers each type of statement in detail.

Braces ({ and }) group zero or more statements into a *block*. A block can be used where any single statement is allowed because a block *is* a statement, albeit a compound one.

6.2   if–else

The most basic form of conditional control flow is the if statement, which chooses whether to execute statements that follow it. Its syntax is:

```
if (boolean-expression)
    statement1
else
    statement2
```

First, the boolean expression is evaluated. If its value is true, then statement1 is executed; otherwise, if there is an else clause, statement2 is executed. The else clause is optional.

A series of tests can be built by joining another if to the else clause of a previous if. Here is a method that maps a string—expected to be one of a particular set of words—into an action to be performed with a value:

```
public void setProperty(String keyword, double value)
    throws UnknownProperty
{
    if (keyword.equals("charm"))
        charm(value);
    else if (keyword.equals("strange"))
        strange(value);
```

```
    else
        throw new UnknownProperty(keyword);
}
```

What happens if there is more than one preceding `if` without an `else`? For example:

```
public double sumPositive(double[] values) {
    double sum = 0.0;

    if (values.length > 1)
        for (int i = 0; i < values.length; i++)
            if (values[i] > 0)
                sum += values[i];
    else     // oops!
        sum = values[0];
    return sum;
}
```

The `else` clause *looks* as if it is bound to the array length check, but that is a mirage of indentation and Java ignores indentation. Instead, an `else` clause is bound to the most recent `if` that does not have one. Thus, the previous block of code is equivalent to

```
public double sumPositive(double[] values) {
    double sum = 0.0;

    if (values.length > 1)
        for (int i = 0; i < values.length; i++)
            if (values[i] > 0)
                sum += values[i];
            else     // oops!
                sum = values[0];
    return sum;
}
```

This is probably not what was intended. To bind the `else` clause to the first `if`, you can use braces to create blocks:

```
public double sumPositive(double[] values) {
    double sum = 0.0;

    if (values.length > 1) {
        for (int i = 0; i < values.length; i++)
```

```
            if (values[i] > 0)
                sum += values[i];
        } else {
            sum = values[0];
        }
        return sum;
    }
```

Exercise 6.1: Using if-else in a loop, write a method that takes a string parameter and returns a string with all the special characters in the original string replaced by their Java equivalents. For example, a string with a " in the middle of it should create a return value with that " replaced by \".

6.3   switch

A switch statement evaluates an integer expression whose value is used to find an appropriate case label among those listed inside the following block. If a matching case label is found, control is transferred to the first statement following it. If a matching case label is not found, control is transferred to the first statement following a default label. If there is no default label, the entire switch statement is skipped.

This example dumps the state of an object, adding new output at greater verbosity levels and then printing the output of the next lower level of verbosity:

```
public static final int TERSE = 0,
                        NORMAL = 1,
                        BLATHERING = 2;

// ...

public int Verbosity = TERSE;

public void dumpState()
    throws UnexpectedStateException
{
    switch (Verbosity) {
      case BLATHERING:
        System.out.println(stateDetails);
        // FALLTHROUGH
```

```
    case NORMAL:
      System.out.println(basicState);
      // FALLTHROUGH

    case TERSE:
      System.out.println(summaryState);
      break;

    default:
      throw new UnexpectedStateException(Verbosity);
  }
}
```

The class defines symbolic constants to represent the verbosity states. When the time arrives to dump the object's state, it is done at the requested verbosity level.

The FALLTHROUGH comments document where control *falls through* the next case label to the code below. Thus, if verbosity is BLATHERING, all three output parts are printed; if verbosity is NORMAL, two parts are printed; and if verbosity is TERSE, only one part is printed.

A case or default label does *not* force a break out of the switch. Nor does it imply an end to execution of statements. This is why we have a break statement after the TERSE output is finished. Without the break, execution would continue through into the code for the default label and throw the exception every time.

Falling through to the next case can be useful in some circumstances. But in most cases a break should come after the code that a case label selects. Good coding style suggests that you always use some form of FALLTHROUGH comment to document an intentional fall-through.

Fall-through is most often used so that you can have multiple case labels for the same code. This example uses fall-through to translate a hexadecimal digit into an int:

```java
public int hexValue(char ch) throws NonHexDigitException {
    switch (ch) {
      case '0': case '1': case '2': case '3': case '4':
      case '5': case '6': case '7': case '8': case '9':
        return (ch - '0');

      case 'a': case 'b': case 'c':
      case 'd': case 'e': case 'f':
        return (ch - 'a') + 10;

      case 'A': case 'B': case 'C':
```

```
    case 'D': case 'E': case 'F':
      return (ch - 'A') + 10;

    default:
      throw new NonHexDigitException(ch);
  }
}
```

There are no `break` statements because the `return` statements exit the code blocks before they can fall through.

You should terminate the last group of statements in a switch with a `break`, `return`, or `throw`, as you would a group of statements in an earlier case. Doing so reduces the likelihood of accidentally falling through the bottom of what *used* to be the last part of the switch when a new `case` is added.

All `case` labels must be constant expressions; the expressions must contain only literals or named constants initialized with constant expressions. In any single `switch` statement, each `case` value must be unique, and there can be at most one `default` label.

Exercise 6.2: Rewrite your method from Exercise 6.1 to use a `switch`.

6.4   while and do-while

The `while` loop looks like this:

```
while (boolean-expression)
    statement
```

The boolean expression is evaluated and, if it is `true`, the statement (which can, of course, be a block) is executed repeatedly until the boolean expression evaluates to `false`.

A `while` loop executes zero or more times since the boolean expression might be `false` the first time it is evaluated. Sometimes you want to execute a loop body at least once, which is why Java also has a do–while loop:

```
do
    statement
while (boolean-expression);
```

Here, the boolean expression is evaluated *after* the statement is executed. While the expression is `true`, the statement is executed repeatedly. The statement in a do–while loop is almost always a block.

6.5 for

The for statement is used to loop over a range of values from beginning to end. It looks like this:

```
for (init-expr; boolean-expr; incr-expr)
    statement
```

This is equivalent to

```
{
    init-expr;
    while (boolean-expr) {
        statement
        incr-expr;
    }
}
```

with the proviso that incr-expr is always executed if a continue is encountered (see "continue" on page 148).

Typically, the for loop is used to iterate a variable over a range of values until some logical end to that range is reached.

The initialization and iteration statements of a for loop can be a comma-separated list of expressions. The expressions separated by the commas are, like most operators, evaluated left-to-right. For example, to march two indexes through an array in opposite directions, the following code would be appropriate:

```
for (i = 0, j = arr.length - 1; j >= 0; i++, j--) {
    // ...
}
```

You can define what an iteration range is. A for loop is often used, for example, to iterate through the elements of a linked list or to follow a mathematical sequence of values. This capability makes the for construct more powerful than equivalent constructs in many other languages, which restrict for-style constructs to incrementing a variable over a range of values.

Here is an example of such a loop, designed to calculate the smallest power of 10 that is greater than or equal to a value:

```
public static int tenPower(int value) {
    int exp, v;
    for (exp = 0, v = value - 1; v > 0; exp++, v /= 10)
```

```
        continue;
    return exp;
}
```

In this case, two variables move synchronously through the value range: the exponent (exp) and the value of 10^{exp} (v). Both the test value and the exponent are looped over. In such cases, a comma-separated list of expressions is a good technique to ensure that they are always in lockstep.

The body of this loop is simply a `continue` statement, which starts the next iteration of the loop. The body of the loop has nothing to do—all the work of the loop is in the test and iteration clauses of the `for` statement itself. The `continue` style shown here is one way to show an empty loop body; another way is to put a simple semicolon on a line by itself or to use an empty block with braces. Simply putting a semicolon at the end of the `for` line is dangerous—if the semicolon is accidentally deleted or forgotten, the statement that follows the `for` can silently become the body of the `for`.

All the expressions in the `for` construct are optional. If either *init-expr* or *incr-expr* is left out, its part in the loop is simply omitted. If *boolean-expr* is left out, it is assumed to be `true`. Thus, the idiomatic way to write an infinite loop is as a "for ever" loop:

```
for (;;)
    statement
```

Presumably, the loop is terminated by some other means, such as a `break` statement (described later) or by throwing an exception.

Conventionally, the `for` loop is used only when you are looping through a range of related values. It is bad style to violate this convention by using initialization or increment expressions that are unrelated to the boolean loop test.

Exercise 6.3: Write a method that takes two `char` parameters and prints the characters between those two values, including the end points.

6.6   Labels

Statements can be labeled. Labels are typically used on blocks and loops. A label precedes a statement:

```
label: statement
```

Labeled blocks are useful with `break` and `continue`.

6.7   break

A break statement can be used to exit from any block, not just from a switch. A break is most often used to break out of a loop, but can be used to immediately exit any block. In this example, we are looking for the first empty slot in an array of references to Contained objects:

```
class Container {
    private Contained[] Objs;

    // ...

    public void addIn(Contained obj)
        throws NoEmptySlotException
    {
        int i;
        for (i = 0; i < Objs.length; i++)
            if (Objs[i] == null)
                break;
        if (i >= Objs.length)
            throw new NoEmptySlotException();
        Objs[i] = obj;      // put it inside me
        obj.inside(this); // let it know it's inside me
    }
}
```

An unlabeled break terminates the innermost switch, for, while, or do. To terminate an outer statement, label the outer statement and use its label name in the break statement:

```
private float[][] Matrix;

public boolean workOnFlag(float flag) {
    int y, x;
    boolean found = false;

  search:
    for (y = 0; y < Matrix.length; y++) {
        for (x = 0; x < Matrix[y].length; x++) {
            if (Matrix[y][x] == flag) {
                found = true;
                break search;
```

```
            }
        }
    }
    if (!found)
        return false;

    // do some stuff with flagged value at Matrix[y][x]
    return true;
}
```

Whether to always use labels is a matter of individual preference. It is a good defensive measure against a later maintainer of the code enclosing your code with a switch statement or a loop.

Note that a labeled break is not a goto. The goto statement would enable indiscriminate jumping around in code, obfuscating the flow of control. A break or continue that references a label, on the other hand, exits from or repeats only that specific labeled block, and the flow of control is obvious by inspection.

6.8   continue

A continue statement skips to the end of a loop's body and evaluates the boolean expression that controls the loop. A continue is often used to skip over an element of a loop range that can be ignored or treated with trivial code. For example, a token stream that included a simple "skip" token might be handled this way:

```
while (!stream.eof()) {
    token = stream.next();
    if (token.equals("skip"))
        continue;
    // ... process token ...
}
```

A continue statement has meaning only inside loops: while, do-while, and for. A continue statement can specify a label of an enclosing loop, which applies the continue to the named loop instead of the innermost loop. A labeled continue will break out of any inner loops on its way to the next iteration of the named loop. No label is required on the continue in the preceding example since there is only one enclosing loop.

6.9 return

A `return` statement terminates execution of a method and returns to the invoker. If the method returns no value, a simple return statement will do:

```
return;
```

If the method has a return type, the `return` must include an expression of a type that could be assigned to the return type. For example, if a method returns `double`, a `return` could have an expression that was a `double`, `float`, or integer:

```
protected double nonNegative(double val) {
    if (val < 0)
        return 0;    // an int constant
    else
        return val; // a double
}
```

A `return` can also be used to exit constructors and static initializer code. Neither construct has a return value, so `return` is used without specifying a return value. Constructors are invoked as part of the new process that in the end returns a reference to an object, but each constructor plays only a part of that role; no constructor "returns" the final reference.

6.10 What, No goto?

Java has no `goto` construct to transfer control to an arbitrary statement in a method, although `goto` is common in languages to which Java is related. The primary uses for `goto` in these other languages are:

- ◆ Controlling outer loops from within nested loops. Java provides labeled `break` and `continue` statements to meet this need.
- ◆ Skipping the rest of a block of code that is not in a loop when an answer or error is found. Use a labeled `break`.
- ◆ Executing cleanup code before a method or block of code exits. Use either a labeled break or, more cleanly, the `finally` construct of the `try` statement covered in the next chapter.

Labeled `break` and `continue` have the advantage that they transfer control to a strictly limited place. A `finally` block is even stricter as to where it transfers control, and it works in all circumstances, including exceptions. With these constructs you can write clean Java code without a goto.

Furious activity is no substitute for understanding.
—H.H. Williams

CHAPTER 7

Exceptions

A slipping gear could let your M203 grenade launcher fire when you least expect it.
That would make you quite unpopular in what's left of your unit.
—The U.S. Army's *PS* magazine, August 1993

DURING execution, applications can run into many kinds of errors of varying degrees of severity. When methods are invoked on an object, the object can discover internal state problems (inconsistent values of variables), detect errors with objects or data it manipulates (such as a file or network address), determine that it is violating its basic contract (such as reading data from an already closed stream), and so on.

Many programmers do not test for all possible error conditions, and for good reason: code becomes unintelligible if each method invocation checks for all possible errors before the next statement is executed. This trade-off creates a tension between correctness (checking for all errors) and clarity (not cluttering the basic flow of code with many error checks).

Exceptions provide a clean way to check for errors without cluttering code. Exceptions also provide a mechanism to signal errors directly rather than use flags or side effects such as fields that must be checked. Exceptions make the error conditions that a method can signal an explicit part of the method's contract. The list of exceptions can be seen by the programmer, checked by the compiler, and preserved by extended classes that override the method.

An exception is *thrown* when an unexpected error condition is encountered. The exception is then *caught* by an encompassing clause further up the method invocation stack. If the exception is not caught, a default exception handler takes effect, usually printing useful information about where the exception was thrown (such as a call stack).

7.1   Creating Exception Types

Exceptions in Java are objects. All exception types—that is, any class designed
for throwable objects—must extend the Java language class `Throwable` or one of
its subclasses. The `Throwable` class contains a string that can be used to describe
the exception. By convention, new exception types extend `Exception`, a subclass
of `Throwable`.

Java exceptions are primarily *checked exceptions,* meaning that the compiler
checks that your methods throw only exceptions they have declared themselves to
throw. The standard runtime exceptions and errors extend the classes
`RuntimeException` and `Error`, making them *unchecked exceptions*. All exceptions
you create should extend `Exception`, making them checked exceptions.

Sometimes it is useful to have more data to describe the exceptional condition
than just the string that `Exception` provides. In such cases, `Exception` can be
extended to create a class that contains the added data (usually set in the constructor).

For example, suppose a `replaceValue` method is added to the `Attributed`
interface discussed in Chapter 4. This method replaces the current value of a
named attribute with a new value. If the named attribute doesn't exist, an exception
should be thrown, because it is reasonable to assume that one should replace
only existing attributes. That exception should contain the name of the attribute.
To represent the exception, create the `NoSuchAttributeException` class:

```
public class NoSuchAttributeException extends Exception {
    public String attrName;

    NoSuchAttributeException(String name) {
        super("No attribute named \"" + name + "\" found");
        attrName = name;
    }
}
```

`NoSuchAttributeException` extends `Exception` to add a constructor that takes
the name of the attribute; it also adds public fields to store the data. The constructor
invokes the superclass's constructor with a string description of what happened.
This exception type is useful to code that catches the exception, because it
holds both a human-usable description of the error and the data that created the
error. Adding useful data is one reason to create a new exception type.

Another reason to create a new exception type is that the type of the exception
is an important part of the exception data, because exceptions are caught according
to their type. For this reason, you would invent `NoSuchAttributeException`
even if you did not want to add data. In this way, a programmer who cared only

about such an exception could catch it exclusive of other exceptions that might be generated either by the methods of the `Attributed` interface, or by other methods used on other objects in the same area of code.

In general, new exception types should be created when programmers will want to handle one kind of error and not another kind. Programmers can then use the exception type to execute the correct code rather than examine the contents of the exception to determine whether they really care about the exception, or catch an irrelevant exception by accident.

7.2   throw

Exceptions are thrown using the `throw` statement, which takes an object as its parameter. For example, here is an addition to `AttributedImpl` from Chapter 4 that implements `replaceValue`:

```
public void replaceValue(String name, Object newValue)
    throws NoSuchAttributeException
{
    Attr attr = find(name);          // look up the attr
    if (attr == null)                // it isn't found
        throw new NoSuchAttributeException(name);
    attr.setValue(newValue);
}
```

The `replaceValue` method first looks up the current `Attr` object for the name. If there isn't one, it throws a new object of type `NoSuchAttributeException`, providing the constructor with the attribute name. Exceptions are objects, so they must be created before being thrown. If the attribute does exist, its value is replaced with the new value.

An exception can also be generated by invoking a method that itself throws an exception.

7.3   The throws Clause

The definition of the `replaceValue` method declares which checked exceptions it throws. Java requires such a declaration because programmers invoking a method need to know the exceptions it can throw just as much as they need to know its normal behavior. The checked exceptions that a method throws are as important as the type of value it returns. Both must be declared.

The checked exceptions a method can throw are declared with a `throws` clause, which takes a comma-separated list of exception types.

You can throw exceptions that are extensions of the type of exception in the `throws` clause because you can use a class polymorphically anywhere its superclass is expected. A method can throw several different classes of exceptions—all of them extensions of a particular exception class—and declare only the superclass in the `throws` clause. By doing so, however, you hide potentially useful information from programmers invoking the method, because they don't know which of the possible extended exception types could be thrown. For documentation purposes, the `throws` clause should be as complete and specific as possible.

The contract defined by the `throws` clause is strictly enforced—you can throw only a type of exception that has been declared in the `throws` clause. Throwing any other type of exception is invalid, whether you use `throw` directly or use it indirectly by invoking another method. If a method has no `throws` clause, it does not mean that *any* exceptions can be thrown: it means *no* (checked) exceptions can be thrown.

All the standard runtime exceptions (such as `ClassCastException` and `ArithmeticException`) are extensions of the `RuntimeException` class. The more serious errors are signaled by exceptions that are extensions of `Error`, and these exceptions can occur at any time in any code. `RuntimeException` and `Error` are the only exceptions you do not need to list in your `throws` clauses. They are ubiquitous, and every method can potentially throw them. This is why they are unchecked by the compiler. The complete list of standard unchecked exception classes is in Appendix A.

Initializers and static initialization code blocks cannot throw checked exceptions, either directly or by invoking a method that throws such an exception. There is nothing to catch and handle exceptions during object construction. When you are initializing fields, the solution is to initialize them inside a constructor, which can throw or catch the exceptions. For static initializers, the solution is to put the initialization inside a static block that catches and handles the exception. Static blocks cannot throw exceptions, but they can catch them.

Java is strict about enforcing checked exception handling because doing so helps avoid bugs that come from not dealing with errors. Experience has shown that programmers forget to handle errors or defer handling them until some future time that never arrives. The `throws` clause states clearly which exceptions are being thrown by methods and makes sure they are dealt with in some way by the invoker.

If you invoke a method that lists a checked exception in its `throws` clause, you have three choices:

◆ Catch the exception and handle it.

♦ Catch the exception and map it into one of your exceptions by throwing an exception of a type declared in your own `throws` clause.

♦ Declare the exception in your `throws` clause and let the exception pass through your method (although you might have a `finally` clause that cleans up first; see the next section for details).

To do any of these things, you need to catch exceptions thrown by other methods, and that is the subject of the next section.

Exercise 7.1: Create an `ObjectNotFoundException` class for the `LinkedList` class we've built in previous exercises. Add a `find` method that looks for an object in the list and either returns the `LinkedList` object that contains the desired object or throws the exception if the object isn't found in the list. Why is this preferable to returning `null` if the object isn't found? What additional data if any should `ObjectNotFoundException` contain?

7.4   try, catch, and finally

Exceptions are caught by enclosing code in `try` blocks. The basic syntax for a `try` block is:

```
try {
    statements
} catch (exception_type1 identifier1) {
    statements
} catch (exception_type2 identifier2) {
    statements

. . . . .
} finally {
    statments
}
```

The body of the `try` statement is executed until either an exception is thrown or it finishes successfully. If an exception is thrown, each `catch` clause is examined in turn, from first to last, to see whether the type of the exception object is assignable to the type declared in the `catch`. When an assignable `catch` clause is found, its block is executed with its identifier set to reference the exception object. No other `catch` clause will be executed. Any number of `catch` clauses can be associated with a particular `try`, including zero, as long as each clause catches a different type of exception. If no appropriate `catch` is found, the exception percolates out of the `try` statement into any outer `try` that might handle it.

If a `finally` clause is present in a `try`, its code is executed after all other processing in the `try` is complete. This happens no matter how the completion was achieved, whether normally, through an exception, or through a control flow statement such as `return` or `break`.

This example code is prepared to handle one of the exceptions `replaceValue` threw:

```
Object value = new Integer(8);
try {
    attributedObj.replaceValue("Age", value);
} catch (NoSuchAttributeException e) {
    // shouldn't happen, but recover if it does
    Attr attr = new Attr(e.attrName, value);
    attributedObj.add(attr);
}
```

The `try` sets up a statement (which must be a block) that does something that is normally expected to succeed. If everything succeeds, the block is finished. If any exception is thrown during execution of the code in the `try` block, either directly via a `throw` or indirectly by a method invoked inside it, execution of the code inside the `try` stops, and the attached `catch` clause is examined to see whether it wants to catch the exception that was thrown.

A `catch` clause is somewhat like an embedded method that has one parameter—namely, the exception to be caught. Inside a `catch` clause, you can attempt to recover from the exception, or you can clean up and rethrow the exception so that any code calling yours also has a chance to catch it. Or a `catch` can do what it needs to and then fall out the bottom, in which case control flows to the statement after the `try` statement (after executing the `finally` clause, if there is one).

A general `catch` clause—one that catches exceptions of type `Exception`, for example—is usually a poor implementation choice since it will catch *any* exception, not just the specific one we are interested in. Had we used such a clause in our code, it could have ended up handling, for example, a `ClassCastException` as if it were a missing attribute problem.

You cannot put a superclass `catch` clause before a `catch` of one of its subclasses. The `catch` clauses are examined in order, so a `catch` that picked up one exception type before a `catch` for an extended type of exception would be a mistake. The first clause would always catch the exception, and the second clause would never be reached. The compiler will not accept the following code:

```
class SuperException extends Exception { }
class SubException extends SuperException { }

class BadCatch {
    public void goodTry() {
        /* This is an INVALID catch ordering */
        try {
            throw new SubException();
        } catch (SuperException superRef) {
            // Catches both SuperException and SubException
        } catch (SubException subRef) {
            // This would never be reached
        }
    }
}
```

Only one exception is handled by any single encounter with a `try` clause. If a `catch` or `finally` clause throws another exception, the `catch` clauses of the `try` are not reexamined. The `catch` and `finally` clauses are outside the protection of the `try` clause itself. Such exceptions can, of course, be handled by any encompassing `try` block in which the inner `catch` or `finally` clauses were nested.

7.4.1 `finally`

The `finally` clause of a `try` statement provides a mechanism for executing a section of code whether or not an exception is thrown. Usually the `finally` clause is used to clean up internal state or to release non-object resources, such as open files stored in local variables. Here is a method that closes a file when its work is done, even if an error occurs:

```
public boolean searchFor(String file, String word)
    throws StreamException
{
    Stream input = null;

    try {
        input = new Stream(file);
        while (!input.eof())
            if (input.next() == word)
```

```
            return true;
        return false;          // not found
    } finally {
        if (input != null)
            input.close();
    }
}
```

If the new fails, `input` will never be changed from its initial `null` value. If the new succeeds, `input` will reference the object that represents the open file. When the `finally` clause is executed, the `input` stream is closed only if it has been open. Whether or not the operations on the stream generate an exception, the contents of the `finally` clause ensure that the file is closed, thus conserving the limited resource of simultaneous open files. The `searchFor` method declares that it throws `StreamException` so that any exceptions generated are passed through to the invoking code after cleanup.

A `finally` clause can also be used to clean up for `break`, `continue`, and `return`, which is one reason you will sometimes see a `try` clause with no `catch` clauses. When any control transfer statement is executed, all relevant `finally` clauses are executed. There is no way to leave a `try` block without executing its `finally` clause.

The preceding example relies on `finally` in this way to clean up even with a normal `return`. One of the most common reasons `goto` is used in other languages is to ensure that certain things are cleaned up when a block of code is complete, whether or not it was successful. In our example, the `finally` clause ensures that the file is closed when either `return` statement is executed or if the stream throws an exception.

A `finally` clause is always entered with a reason. That reason may be that the `try` code finished normally, that it executed a control flow statement such as `return`, or that an exception was thrown in code executed in the `try` block. The reason is remembered when the `finally` clause exits by falling out the bottom. However, if the `finally` block creates its own reason to leave by executing a control flow statement (such as `break` or `return`) or by throwing an exception, that reason supersedes the original one, and the original reason is forgotten. For example, consider the following code:

```
try {
    // ... do something ...
    return 1;
} finally {
    return 2;
}
```

When the `try` block executes its return, the `finally` block is entered with the "reason" of returning the value 1. However, inside the `finally` block the value 2 is returned, so the initial intention is forgotten. In fact, if any of the other code in the `try` block had thrown an exception, the result would still be to return 2. If the `finally` block did not return a value but simply fell out the bottom, the "return the value 1" reason would be remembered and implemented.

7.5   When to Use Exceptions

We used the phrase "unexpected error condition" at the beginning of this chapter when describing when to throw exceptions. Exceptions are not meant for simple, expected situations. For example, reaching the end of a stream of input is expected, so the method that returns the next input from the stream has "hit the end" as part of its expected behavior. A return code indicating end-of-input is reasonable, as it is for callers to check the return value, and such a convention is also easier to understand. Consider the following typical loop using a return flag:

```
while ((token = stream.next()) != Stream.END)
    process(token);
stream.close();
```

Compare that to this loop, which relies on an exception to signal the end of input:

```
try {
    for (;;) {
        process(stream.next());
    }
} catch (StreamEndException e) {
    stream.close();
}
```

In the first case, the flow of control is direct and clear. The code loops until it reaches the end of the stream, and then it closes the stream. In the second case, the code seems to loop forever. Unless you know that end of input is signaled with a `StreamEndException`, you don't know the loop's natural range. Even when you know about `StreamEndException`, this construction can be confusing since it moves the loop termination from inside the `for` loop into the surrounding `try` block.

In some situations no reasonable flag value exists. For example, a class for a stream of `double` values can contain any valid `double`, and there is no possible end-of-stream marker. The most reasonable design is to add an explicit `eof` test method that should be called before any read from the stream:

```
while (!stream.eof())
    process(stream.nextDouble());
stream.close();
```

On the other hand, continuing to read *past* an end-of-file is not expected. It means that the program didn't notice the end and is trying to do something it should never attempt. This is an excellent case for a `ReadPastEndException`. Such behavior is outside the expected use of your stream class, and throwing an exception is the right way to handle it.

Deciding which situations are expected and which are not is a fuzzy area. The point is not to abuse exceptions as a way to report expected situations.

Exercise 7.2: Decide which way the following conditions should be communicated to the programmer:

- ◆ Someone tries to set the capacity of a `PassengerVehicle` object to a negative value.
- ◆ A syntax error is found in a configuration file that an object uses to set its initial state.
- ◆ A method that searches for a programmer-specified word in a string array cannot find any occurrence of the word.
- ◆ A file provided to an "open" method does not exist.
- ◆ A file provided to an "open" method exists, but security prevents the user from using it.
- ◆ During an attempt to open a network connection to a remote server process, the remote machine cannot be contacted.
- ◆ In the middle of a conversation with a remote server process, the network connection stops operating.

There is something to be said for every error;
but whatever may be said for it,
the most important thing to be said about it is that it is erroneous.
—G.K. Chesterton

CHAPTER 8

Strings

What's the use of a good quotation if you can't change it?
—Dr. Who, *The Two Doctors*

JAVA strings are standard objects with built-in language support. You have already seen many examples of using quotes to create string objects. You've also seen the + and += operators that concatenate strings to create new strings. The `String` class, however, has much more functionality to offer. `String` objects are read-only, so Java also provides a `StringBuffer` class for mutable strings. This chapter describes the `String` and `StringBuffer` classes, including conversion of strings to other types such as integers and booleans.

8.1   Basic `String` Operations

The `String` class provides read-only strings and supports operations on them. Strings can be created implicitly either by using a quoted string (such as `"Größe"`) or by using + or += on two `String` objects to create a new one.

You can also construct `String` objects explicitly using the new mechanism. The `String` class supports the following constructors:

public **String()**
> Constructs a new `String` with the value `""`.

public **String(String value)**
> Constructs a new `String` that is a copy of the specified `String` object value.

The two basic methods of `String` objects are `length` and `charAt`. The `length` method returns the number of characters in the string, and `charAt` returns the `char` at the specified position. This loop counts the number of each kind of character in a string:

```
for (int i = 0; i < str.length(); i++)
    counts[str.charAt(i)]++;
```

In any `String` method, using a string position less than zero or greater than `length() - 1` throws an `IndexOutOfBoundsException`.

There are also simple methods to find the first or last occurrence of a particular character or substring in a string. The following method returns the number of characters between the first and last occurrences of a given character in a string:

```
static int countBetween(String str, char ch) {
    int begPos = str.indexOf(ch);
    if (begPos < 0)            // not there
        return -1;
    int endPos = str.lastIndexOf(ch);
    return endPos - begPos - 1;
}
```

The `countBetween` method finds the first and last positions of the character `ch` in the string `str`. If the character does not occur twice in the string, the method returns -1. The difference between the two character positions is one more than the number of characters in between (if the two positions were 2 and 3, the number of characters in between is 0).

Several overloads of the method `indexOf` search forward in a string, and several overloads `lastIndexOf` search backward. Each method returns the index of what it found, or returns -1 if the search was unsuccessful:

Method	**Returns Index Of...**
`indexOf(char ch)`	first position of `ch`
`indexOf(char ch, int start)`	first position of `ch` $\geq$ `start`
`indexOf(String str)`	first position of `str`
`indexOf(String str, int start)`	first position of `str` $\geq$ `start`
`lastIndexOf(char ch)`	last position of `ch`
`lastIndexOf(char ch, int start)`	last position of `ch` $\leq$ `start`
`lastIndexOf(String str)`	last position of `str`
`lastIndexOf(String str, int start)`	last position of `str` $\leq$ `start`

Exercise 8.1: Write a method that counts the number of occurrences of a given character in a string.

Exercise 8.2: Write a method that counts the number of occurrences of a particular string in another string.

8.2 String Comparisons

The `String` class supports several methods to compare strings and parts of strings. Before we describe the methods, though, we must explain that internationalization and localization issues of full Unicode strings are not addressed with these methods. For example, when you're comparing two strings to determine which is "greater," characters in strings are compared numerically by their Unicode values, not by their localized notion of order. To a French speaker, c and ç are the same letter differing only by a small diacritical mark. Sorting a set of strings in French should ignore the difference between them, placing `"açb"` before `"acz"` because b comes before z. But the Unicode characters are different—c (\u0063) comes before ç (\u00e7) in the Unicode character set—so these strings will actually sort the other way around.

The first compare operation is `equals`, which returns `true` if it is passed a reference to a `String` object having the same contents—that is, the two strings have the same length and exactly the same Unicode characters. If the other object isn't a `String` or if the contents are different, `String.equals` returns `false`.

To compare strings while ignoring case, use the `equalsIgnoreCase` method. By "ignore case," we mean that Ë and ë are considered the same but are different from E and e. Characters with no case distinctions, such as punctuation, compare equal only to themselves. Unicode has many interesting case issues, including a notion of "titlecase." Case issues in the `String` class are handled in terms of the case-related methods of the `Character` class, described in "Character" on page 297.

To sort strings, you need a way to compare them. The `compareTo` method returns an `int` that is less than, equal to, or greater than zero when the string on which it is invoked is less than, equal to, or greater than the other string. The ordering used is Unicode character ordering.

The `compareTo` method is useful for creating an internal canonical ordering of strings. A binary search, for example, requires a sorted list of elements, but it is unimportant that the sorted order be local language order. Here is a binary search lookup method for a class that has a sorted array of strings:

```
private String[] table;

public int position(String key) {
    int lo = 0;
```

```
        int hi = table.length - 1;
        while (lo <= hi) {
            int mid = lo + (hi - lo) / 2;
            int cmp = key.compareTo(table[mid]);
            if (cmp == 0)        // found it!
                return mid;
            else if (cmp < 0)    // search the lower part
                hi = mid - 1;
            else                 // search the upper part
                lo = mid + 1;
        }
        return -1;               // not found
    }
```

This is the basic binary search algorithm. It first checks the midpoint of the search range to determine whether the key is greater than, equal to, or less than the element at that position. If they are the same, the element has been found and the search is over. If the key is less than the element at the position, the lower half of the range is searched; otherwise, the upper half is searched. Eventually, either the element is found or the lower end of the range becomes greater than the higher end, in which case the key is not in the list.

In addition to entire strings, regions of strings can also be compared for equality. The method for this is regionMatches, and it has two forms:

public boolean **regionMatches(int start, String other, int ostart, int len)**

> Returns true if the given region of this String has the same Unicode characters as the given region of the string other. Checking starts in this string at the position start, and in the other string at position ostart. Only the first len characters are compared.

public boolean **regionMatches(boolean ignoreCase, int start, String other, int ostart, int len)**

> This version of regionMatches behaves exactly like the previous one, but the boolean ignoreCase controls whether case is significant.

For example:

```
class RegionMatch {
    public static void main(String[] args) {
        String str = "Look, look!";
        boolean b1, b2, b3;

        b1 = str.regionMatches(6, "Look", 0, 4);
```

```
        b2 = str.regionMatches(true, 6, "Look", 0, 4);
        b3 = str.regionMatches(true, 6, "Look", 0, 5);

        System.out.println("b1 = " + b1);
        System.out.println("b2 = " + b2);
        System.out.println("b3 = " + b3);
    }
}
```

Here is its output:

```
    b1 = false
    b2 = true
    b3 = false
```

The first comparison yields `false` because the character at position 6 of the main string is `'l'`, and the character at position 0 of the other string is `'L'`. The second comparison yields `true` because case is not significant. The third comparison yields `false` because the comparison length is now 5, and the two strings are not the same over five characters, even ignoring case.

You can do simple tests for the beginnings and ends of strings using `startsWith` and `endsWith`:

`public boolean` **`startsWith(String prefix, int toffset)`**
    Returns `true` if this `String` starts (at `toffset`) with the given `prefix`.

`public boolean` **`startsWith(String prefix)`**
    Equivalent to `startsWith(prefix, 0)`.

`public boolean` **`endsWith(String suffix)`**
    Returns `true` if this `String` ends with the given `suffix`.

In general, using `==` to compare strings will give you the wrong results. Consider the following code:

```
    if (str == "¿Peña?")
        answer(str);
```

This does not compare the contents of the two strings. It compares one object reference (`str`) to another (the string object representing the literal `"¿Peña?"`). Even if `str` contains the string `"¿Peña?"` this `==` expression will almost always yield `false` because the two strings will be held in different objects. Using `==` on objects only tests whether the two references are to the same object, not whether they are equivalent objects.

However, any two string literals with the same contents will refer to the same String object. For example, == probably works correctly in the following code:

```
String str = "¿Peña?";
// ...
if (str == "¿Peña?")
    answer(str);
```

Because str is initially set to a string literal, comparing against another string literal is equivalent to comparing the strings for equal contents. But be careful—this trick works only if you are sure that all string references involved are references to string literals. If str is changed to refer to a manufactured String object, such as the result of a user typing some input, the == operator will return false even if the user types ¿Peña? as the string.

8.3   Utility Methods

The String class provides two methods that are useful in special applications. One is hashCode, which returns a hash based on the contents of the string. Any two strings with the same contents will have the same hash code, although two different strings might also have the same hash. Hash codes are useful for hashtables, such as the Hashtable class in java.util.

The other utility method is intern, which returns a String that has the same contents as the one it is invoked on. However, any two strings with the same contents return the same String object from intern, which enables you to compare string *references* to test equality, instead of the slower test of string *contents*. For example:

```
int putIn(String key) {
    String unique = key.intern();
    int i;
    // see if it's in the table already
    for (i = 0; i < tableSize; i++)
        if (table[i] == unique)
            return i;
    // it's not there--add it in
    table[i] = unique;
    tableSize++;
    return i;
}
```

All the strings stored in the `table` array are the result of an `intern` invocation. The table is searched for a string that was the result of an `intern` invocation on another string that had the same contents as the `key`. If this string is found, the search is finished. If not, we add the unique representative of the `key` at the end. Dealing with the results of `intern` makes comparing object references equivalent to comparing string contents, but much faster.

8.4   Making Related Strings

Several `String` methods return new strings that are like the old one but with a specified modification. New strings are returned because `String` objects are read-only. You could extract quoted substrings from another string using a method like this one:

```
public static String quotedString(
    String from, char start, char end)
{
    int startPos = from.indexOf(start);
    int endPos = from.lastIndexOf(end);
    if (startPos > endPos)     // start after end
        return null;
    else if (startPos == -1)  // no start found
        return null;
    else if (endPos == -1)    // no end found
        return from.substring(startPos);
    else                        // both start and end found
        return from.substring(startPos, endPos + 1);
}
```

The method `quotedString` returns a new `String` object containing the quoted string inside `from` that starts with the character `start` and ends with `end`. If `start` is found but not `end`, the method returns a new `String` object containing everything from the start position to the end of the string. `quotedString` works by using the two overloaded forms of `substring`. The first form takes only an initial start position and returns a new string containing everything in the original string from that point on. The second form takes both a start and an end position and returns a new string that contains all the characters in the original string from the start to the endpoint, including the character at the start but not the one at the end. This "up to but not including the end" behavior is the reason that the method adds one to endPos to include the quotes in the returned string. For example, the string returned by

```
quotedString("Il a dit «Bonjour!»", '«', '»');
```

is

```
«Bonjour!»
```

Here are the rest of the "related string" methods:

```
public String replace(char oldChar, char newChar)
```
Returns a new String with all instances of oldChar replaced with the character newChar.

```
public String trim()
```
Returns a new String with any leading and trailing white space removed.

Case issues are *locale sensitive*—that is, they vary from place to place and from culture to culture. The Java platform allows users to specify a locale, which includes language and character case issues. Locales are represented by Locale objects, which are discussed in more detail in Chapter 16. The methods toLowerCase and toUpperCase use the current default locale, or you can pass a specific locale as an argument:

```
public String toLowerCase()
```
Returns a new String with each character converted to its lowercase equivalent if it has one according to the default locale.

```
public String toUpperCase()
```
Returns a new String with each character converted to its uppercase equivalent if it has one according to the default locale.

```
public String toLowerCase(Locale loc)
```
Returns a new String with each character converted to its lowercase equivalent if it has one according to the specified locale.

```
public String toUpperCase(Locale loc)
```
Returns a new String with each character converted to its uppercase equivalent if it has one according to the specified locale.

The concat method returns a new string that is equivalent to the string returned when you use + on two strings. The following two statements are equivalent:

```
newStr = oldStr.concat(" (not)");
newStr = oldStr + " (not)";
```

Exercise 8.3: As shown, the quotedString method assumes only one quoted string per input string. Write a version that will pull out all the quoted strings and return an array.

8.5   String Conversions

You often need to convert strings to and from something else, such as integers or booleans. In Java conversion, the convention is that the type being converted *to* has the method that does the conversion. For example, converting from a String to an integer requires a static method in class Integer. This table shows all the types that Java will convert, and how to convert each to and from a String:

Type	To String	From String
boolean	String.valueOf(boolean)	new Boolean(String).booleanValue()
byte	String.valueOf(int)	Byte.parseByte(String, int base)
short	String.valueOf(int)	Short.parseShort(String, int base)
int	String.valueOf(int)	Integer.parseInt(String, int base)
long	String.valueOf(long)	Long.parseLong(String, int base)
float	String.valueOf(float)	new Float(String).floatValue()
double	String.valueOf(double)	new Double(String).doubleValue()

For boolean and the floating-point values, the technique shown actually creates a Boolean, Float, or Double object and then asks for its value. For these types there is no equivalent for parseInt that directly parses a value. For the integer conversions you can provide a base ranging between 2 and 32. If you omit the base, the method will use base ten.

There is no method that converts characters of the recognizable Java language forms (\b, \u*dddd*, and so on) into char variables or vice versa. You can invoke String.valueOf with a single char to obtain a String containing that one character.

Neither are there ways to create number strings in the Java language format, with a leading 0 meaning an octal number or a leading 0x meaning a hexadecimal number. The classes Integer, Short, and Byte do support decode methods that decode strings into the appropriate types, understanding a leading 0x to mean a hexadecimal number and a leading 0 to mean an octal number. No equivalent method exists for Long.

Your classes can support string encoding and decoding by having a toString method and a constructor that creates a new object given the string description. Classes with a toString method can be used with valueOf. The method String.valueOf(Object obj) is defined to return either "null" or the result of `obj.toString`. The `String` class provides enough overloads of `valueOf` that you can convert any object to a `String` by invoking `valueOf`.

8.6   Strings and char Arrays

A `String` maps to an array of `char` and vice versa. You often want to build a string in a `char` array and then create a `String` object from the contents. Assuming that the writable `StringBuffer` class (described later) isn't adequate, several `String` methods and constructors help convert a `String` to an array of `char`, or convert an array of `char` to a `String`.

For example, the following simple algorithm squeezes out all occurrences of a character from a string:

```
public static String squeezeOut(String from, char toss) {
    char[] chars = from.toCharArray();
    int len = chars.length;
    for (int i = 0; i < len; i++) {
        if (chars[i] == toss) {
            --len;
            System.arraycopy(chars, i + 1,
                             chars, i, len - i);
            --i;    // re-examine this spot
        }
    }
    return new String(chars, 0, len);
}
```

The method `squeezeOut` first converts its input string `from` into a character array using the method `toCharArray`. It then loops, searching for `toss` characters. When an occurrence of `toss` is found, the length of the returned string is reduced by one, and all the characters in the array are shifted down. We then decrement i so that the new character at position i is examined to see whether it should be tossed out. When the method is finished looping over the array, it returns a new `String` object that contains the squeezed string. The `String` constructor used takes the source array, the starting position within the array, and the number of characters as arguments.

There is also a `String` constructor that takes only the character array as a parameter and uses all of it. Both of these constructors make copies of the array, so you can change the array contents after you have created a `String` from it without affecting the contents of the `String`.

You can use the two static `String.copyValueOf` methods instead of the constructors if you prefer. For instance, `squeezeOut` could have been ended with

```
return String.copyValueOf(chars, 0, len);
```

There is also a single-argument form of `copyValueOf` that copies the entire array. For completeness, two static `valueOf` methods are also equivalent to the two `String` constructors.

The `toCharArray` method is simple and sufficient for most needs. When more control is required over copying pieces of a string into a character array, you can use the `getChars` methods:

public void **getChars(int srcBegin, int srcEnd, char[] dst,**
   int dstBegin)

> Copies characters from this `String` into the specified array. The characters of the specified substring are copied into the character array, starting at `dst[dstBegin]`. The specified substring is the part of the string starting at `srcBegin`, up to but not including `srcEnd`. Any access outside the bounds of either `String` or `char` array throws an `IndexOutOfBoundsException`.

8.7 Strings and byte Arrays

There are methods to convert arrays of 8-bit characters to and from 16-bit Unicode `String` objects. This conversion must be done under some encoding, which will be different depending on the source of the 8-bit characters. For example, an array of ASCII or Latin-1 bytes would be converted to characters simply by setting the high bits to zero, but that would not work for other 8-bit encodings, such as those for Hebrew. In the following constructors and methods, you can name an encoding or use the user or platform's default encoding:

public **String(byte bytes[], int offset, int length)**

> Creates a new string from the specified subarray of `bytes`, which are converted to characters using the default encoding for the default locale. If the range specified by `offset` and `length` is not entirely within the byte array, you will get an `IndexOutOfBoundsException`.

public **String(byte bytes[])**

> Equivalent to `String(bytes, 0, bytes.length)`.

public byte[] **getBytes()**

> Returns a byte array that encodes the contents of the string using the default encoding for the default locale.

```
public String(byte bytes[], int offset, int length, String enc)
    throws UnsupportedEncodingException
```
Creates a new string from the specified part of bytes converted to characters using the encoding named in enc.

```
public String(byte, bytes[], String enc)
    throws UnsupportedEncodingException
```
Equivalent to String(bytes, 0, bytes.length, enc).

```
public byte[] getBytes(String enc)
    throws UnsupportedEncodingException
```
Returns a byte array that encodes the contents of the string using the encoding named in enc.

Encodings are named using their standard and common names. The local platform defines which character encodings are understood. You can always use "UTF8" and "ISO-Latin-1" (also known as "ISO-8859-1"). To test whether an encoding is supported, create a string from an empty byte array with the encoding name and see whether it generates an UnsupportedEncodingException.

The String constructors for building from byte arrays make copies of the data, so further modifications to the arrays will not affect the contents of the String.

8.8   The StringBuffer Class

If read-only strings were the only kind available, you would have to create a new String object for each intermediate result in a sequence of String manipulations. Consider, for example, how the compiler would evaluate the following expression:

```
public static String guillemete(String quote) {
    return '«' + quote + '»';
}
```

If the compiler were restricted to String expressions, it would have to do the following:

```
quoted = String.valueOf('«').concat(quote)
            .concat(String.valueOf('»'));
```

Each valueOf and concat invocation creates another String object, so this operation would construct four String objects, of which only one would be used afterward. The others strings would have incurred overhead to create, to set to proper values, and to garbage collect.

The compiler is more efficient than this. It uses a `StringBuffer` object to build strings from expressions, creating the final `String` only when necessary. `StringBuffer` objects can be modified, so new objects are not needed to hold intermediate results. Using `StringBuffer`, the previous string expression would be represented as:

```
quoted = new StringBuffer().append('«')
            .append(quote).append('»').toString();
```

This code creates just one `StringBuffer` object to hold the construction, appends stuff to it, and then uses `toString` to create a `String` from the result.

To build and modify a string, you probably want to use the `StringBuffer` class. `StringBuffer` provides the following constructors:

public **StringBuffer()**
> Constructs a `StringBuffer` with an initial value of "".

public **StringBuffer(String str)**
> Constructs a `StringBuffer` with an initial value the same as `str`.

`StringBuffer` is similar to `String`, and it supports methods that have the same names and contracts as some `String` methods. However, `StringBuffer` does not extend `String` or vice versa. They are independent classes—both of them extend `Object`.

8.8.1   Modifying the Buffer

There are several ways to modify the buffer of a `StringBuffer` object, including appending to the end and inserting in the middle. The simplest method is `setCharAt`, which changes the character at a specific position. The following `replace` method does what `String.replace` does, except that it uses a `StringBuffer` object. The `replace` method doesn't need to create a new object to hold the results, so successive `replace` calls can operate on one buffer:

```
public static void
    replace(StringBuffer str, char from, char to)
{
    for (int i = 0; i < str.length(); i++)
        if (str.charAt(i) == from)
            str.setCharAt(i, to);
}
```

The `setLength` method truncates or extends the string in the buffer. If you invoke `setLength` with a length smaller than the length of the current string, the string is truncated to the specified length. If the length is longer than the current string, the string is extended by filling with null characters (\u0000).

There are also `append` and `insert` methods to convert any data type to a `String` and then append the result to the end or insert the result at a specified position. The `insert` methods shift characters over to make room for inserted characters as needed. The following types are converted by these `append` and `insert` methods:

```
Object          String          char[]
boolean         char            int
long            float           double
```

There are also `append` and `insert` methods that take part of a `char` array as an argument. For example, to create a `StringBuffer` that describes the square root of an integer, you could write

```
String sqrtInt(int i) {
    StringBuffer buf = new StringBuffer();

    buf.append("sqrt(").append(i).append(')');
    buf.append(" = ").append(Math.sqrt(i));
    return buf.toString();
}
```

The `append` and `insert` methods return the `StringBuffer` object itself, enabling us to append to the result of a previous append.

The `insert` methods take two parameters. The first is the index at which to insert characters into the `StringBuffer`. The second is the value to insert, after conversion to a `String` if necessary. Here is a method to put the current date at the beginning of a buffer:

```
public static StringBuffer addDate(StringBuffer buf) {
    String now = new java.util.Date().toString();
    buf.insert(0, now).insert(now.length(), ": ");
    return buf;
}
```

The `addDate` method first creates a string with the current time using `java.util.Date`, whose default constructor creates an object that represents the time it was created. Then it inserts the string that represents the current date, followed by a simple separator string. Finally, it returns the buffer it was passed so that invoking code can use the same kind of method concatenation that proved useful in `StringBuffer`'s own methods.

The reverse method reverses the order of characters in the StringBuffer. For example, if the contents of the buffer are "good", the contents after invoking reverse are "doog".

8.8.2 Getting Data Out

To get a String object from a StringBuffer object, you simply invoke the toString method.

There are no StringBuffer methods to remove a part of a buffer—you must create a character array from the buffer and build a new buffer with the remaining contents. This is the most likely use for the getChars method, which is analogous to String.getChars.

public void **getChars(int srcBegin, int srcEnd, char[] dst, int dstBegin)**

> Copies the characters of the specified part of the buffer (determined by srcBegin and srcEnd) into the array dst, starting at dst[dstBegin]. Copying starts at the position srcBegin and goes up to, *but does not include,* the position at srcEnd. srcBegin must be a legal index in the buffer, and srcEnd can be no greater than the current string buffer length (which is one beyond the legal last index). If either index is invalid, or if the subarray of dst cannot hold all the data, an IndexOutOfBoundsException is thrown.

Here is a method that uses getChars to remove part of a buffer:

```
public static StringBuffer
    remove(StringBuffer buf, int pos, int cnt)
{
    if (pos < 0 || cnt < 0 || pos + cnt > buf.length())
        throw new IndexOutOfBoundsException();

    int leftover = buf.length() - (pos + cnt);
    if (leftover == 0) {      // a simple truncation
        buf.setLength(pos);
        return buf;
    }

    char[] chrs = new char[leftover];
    buf.getChars(pos + cnt, buf.length(), chrs, 0);
    buf.setLength(pos);
    buf.append(chrs);
    return buf;
}
```

First, `remove` ensures that the array references will stay in bounds. You could handle the actual exception later, but checking now gives you more control. Then `remove` calculates how many bytes follow the removed portion. If there are none, it truncates and returns. Otherwise, `remove` retrieves them using `getChars` and then truncates the buffer and appends the leftover characters before returning.

8.8.3   Capacity Management

The buffer of a `StringBuffer` object has a capacity, which is the length of the string it can store before it must allocate more space. The buffer grows automatically as characters are added, but it is more efficient to specify the size of the buffer only once.

The initial size of a `StringBuffer` object can be set by using the constructor that takes a single `int`:

public **StringBuffer(int capacity)**
> Constructs a `StringBuffer` with the given initial `capacity` and an initial value of `""`.

public synchronized void **ensureCapacity(int minimum)**
> Ensures that the capacity of the buffer is at least the specified `minimum`.

public int **capacity()**
> Returns the current capacity of the buffer.

You can use these methods to avoid repeatedly growing the buffer. Here, for example, is a rewrite of the `sqrtInt` method from page 174 that ensures you allocate new space for the buffer at most once:

```
String sqrtIntFaster(int i) {
    StringBuffer buf = new StringBuffer(50);
    buf.append("sqrt(").append(i).append(')');
    buf.append(" = ").append(Math.sqrt(i));
    return buf.toString();
}
```

The only change is to use a constructor that creates a `StringBuffer` object large enough to contain the result string. The value 50 is somewhat larger than required; therefore, the buffer will never have to grow.

Exercise 8.4: Write a method to convert strings containing decimal numbers into comma-punctuated numbers, with a comma every third digit from the right. For example, given the string `"1543729"`, the method should return the string `"1,543,729"`.

***Exercise** 8.5:* Modify the method to accept parameters specifying the separator character to use and the number of digits between separator characters.

When ideas fail, words come in very handy.
—Johann Wolfgang von Goethe

CHAPTER 9

Threads

How can you be in two places at once when you're not anywhere at all?
—Firesign Theater

WE usually write programs that operate one step at a time, in a sequence. In the following picture, the value of a bank balance is fetched, it is increased by the value of the deposit, and then it is copied back into the account record:

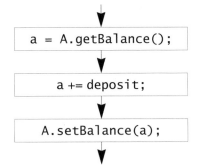

Real bank tellers and computer programs go through similar sequences. In a computer, a sequence of steps executed one at a time is called a *thread*. This *single-threaded* programming model is the one most programmers use.

In a real bank, more than one thing happens at a time:

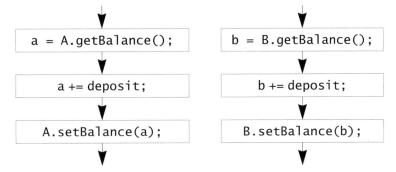

Inside a computer, the analogue to having multiple real-world bank tellers is called *multithreading*. A thread, like a bank teller, can perform a task independent of other threads. And just as two bank tellers can use the same filing cabinets, threads can share access to objects.

This shared access is simultaneously one of the most useful features of multi-threading and one of its greatest pitfalls. This kind of get–modify–set sequence has what is known as a *race hazard* or *race condition*. A race hazard exists when two threads can potentially modify the same piece of data in an interleaved way that can corrupt data. In the bank example, imagine that someone walks up to a bank teller to deposit money into an account. At almost the same time, a second customer asks another teller to handle a deposit into the same account. Each teller

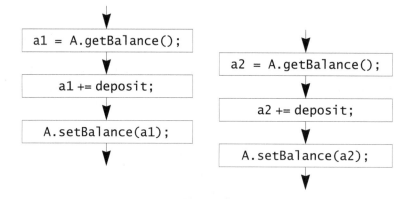

goes to the filing cabinet to get the current account balance (assuming this is an old-fashioned bank that still uses paper files) and gets the same information. Then the tellers go back to their stations, add in the deposit, and return to the filing cabinet to record their separately calculated results. Using this procedure, only the last deposit recorded actually affects the balance. The first modification is lost.

In a real bank this problem can be handled by having the first teller put a note into the file that says, "I'm working on this one, wait until I'm finished." Essentially the same thing is done inside the computer: a *lock* is associated with an object to tell when the object is or is not being used.

Many real-world software problems can best be solved by using multiple threads of control. For example, an interactive program that displays data graphically often needs to let users change display parameters in real time. Interactive programs often obtain their best dynamic behavior using threads. Single-threaded systems usually provide an illusion of multiple threads either by using interrupts or by *polling*. Polling mixes the display and user input parts of an application. In particular, the display code must be written so it will poll often enough to respond to user input in fractions of a second. Display code either must ensure that display operations take minimal time or must interrupt its own operations to poll. The resulting mixture of two unrelated functional aspects of a program leads to complex and often unmaintainable code.

These kinds of problems are more easily solved in a multithreaded system. One thread of control updates the display with current data, and another thread responds to user input. If user input is complex—for example, filling out a form—display code can run independently until it receives new data. In a polling model, either display updates must pause for complex input or complicated handshaking must be used so that display updates can continue while the user types data into the form. Such a model of shared control within a process can be directly supported in a multithreaded system instead of being handcrafted for each new polling case.

9.1 Creating Threads

Threads are defined by a class in the standard Java libraries. To create a thread of control, you start by creating a `Thread` object:

```
Thread worker = new Thread();
```

After a `Thread` object is created, you can configure it and then run it. Configuring a thread involves setting its initial priority, name, and so on. When the thread is ready to run, you invoke its `start` method. The `start` method spawns a new thread of control based on the data in the `Thread` object, then returns. Now the virtual machine invokes the new thread's `run` method, making the thread active.

When a thread's `run` method returns, the thread has exited. You can request that a thread cease running by invoking its `interrupt` method, forcibly stop it by invoking `stop`, freeze it with `suspend`, or manipulate it in many other ways, as you shall soon see.

The standard implementation of `Thread.run` does nothing. To get a thread that does something you must either extend `Thread` to provide a new `run` method or create a `Runnable` object and pass it to the thread's constructor. We first discuss how to create new kinds of threads by extending `Thread`. We describe how to use `Runnable` later (see "Using `Runnable`" on page 201).

Here is a simple two-threaded program that prints the words "ping" and "PONG" at different rates:

```
public class PingPong extends Thread {
    private String word;  // what word to print
    private int delay;    // how long to pause

    public PingPong(String whatToSay, int delayTime) {
```

```
        word = whatToSay;
        delay = delayTime;
    }

    public void run() {
        try {
            for (;;) {
                System.out.print(word + " ");
                sleep(delay);    // wait until next time
            }
        } catch (InterruptedException e) {
            return;                 // end this thread
        }
    }
    public static void main(String[] args) {
        new PingPong("ping",  33).start(); // 1/30 second
        new PingPong("PONG", 100).start(); // 1/10 second
    }
}
```

We define a type of thread called PingPong. Its run method loops forever, printing its word field and sleeping for delay microseconds. PingPong.run cannot throw exceptions because Thread.run, which it overrides, doesn't throw any exceptions. Accordingly, we must catch the InterruptedException that sleep can throw (more on InterruptedException later).

Now we can create some working threads, and PingPong.main does just that. It creates two PingPong objects, each with its own word and delay cycle, and invokes each thread object's start method. Now the threads are off and running. Here is some example output:

```
ping PONG ping PONG ping ping PONG ping ping ping
PONG ping ping ping PONG ping ping PONG ping ping
ping PONG ping ping PONG ping ping ping PONG ping
ping PONG ping ping ping PONG ping ping PONG ping
ping ping PONG ping ping PONG ping ping ping PONG
ping ping PONG ping ping ping PONG ping ping PONG ...
```

You can give a thread a name, either as a String parameter to the constructor or as the parameter of a setName invocation. You can get the current name of a thread by invoking getName. Thread names are strictly for programmer convenience; they are not used by the runtime environment.

You can obtain the `Thread` object for the currently running thread by invoking the static method `Thread.currentThread`.

9.2 Synchronization

Recall the bank teller example from the beginning of this chapter. When two tellers (threads) need to use the same file (object), there is a possibility of interleaved operations that can corrupt the data. In the bank, tellers *synchronize* their access by putting notes in the files. The equivalent action in multithreading is to put a *lock* on an object. When an object is locked by a thread, the lock advises other users that they should not use the object in certain ways until the lock is released.

9.2.1 synchronized Methods

To make a class usable in a multithreaded environment, appropriate methods are usually declared `synchronized` ("appropriate" is defined later). If one thread invokes a `synchronized` method on an object, that object is *locked*. Another thread invoking a `synchronized` method on that same object will block until the lock is released:

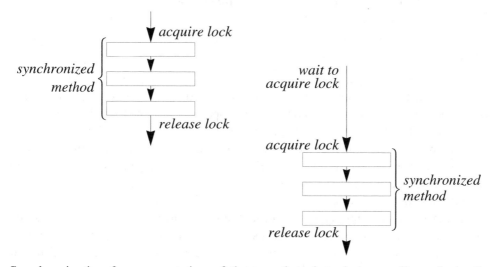

Synchronization forces execution of the two threads to be *mutually exclusive* in time. Unsynchronized access does not wait for any locks but proceeds regardless of locks that may be held on the object.

Locks are *per thread,* so invoking a synchronized method from within another method synchronized on the same object will proceed without blocking, releasing the lock only when the outermost synchronized method returns. The per-thread behavior prevents a thread from blocking on a lock it already has. You should exercise some caution here—the synchronized code you invoke may assume that the object's fields are in a consistent state that the invoking synchronized code is in the middle of changing.

Synchronization makes the interleaved execution example work: if the code sequence is a synchronized method, then when the second thread attempts to access the object while the first thread is using it, the second thread is blocked until the first one finishes.

For example, if the Account class were written to live in a multithreaded environment, it would look like this:

```
class Account {
    private double balance;

    public Account(double initialDeposit) {
        balance = initialDeposit;
    }
    public synchronized double getBalance() {
        return balance;
    }
    public synchronized void deposit(double amount) {
        balance += amount;
    }
}
```

Now we can explain what is "appropriate" in synchronizing methods.

The constructor does not need to be synchronized because it is executed only when creating an object, and that can happen in only one thread for any given new object. The balance field is protected from unsynchronized change by the synchronized accessor methods. This is yet another reason to prefer accessor methods to public or protected fields: using methods, you can synchronize access to the data, but you have no way to do so if the fields can be accessed directly outside your class.

If the value of a field can change, its value should never be read at the same time another thread is writing it. Access to the field must be synchronized. If one thread were reading the value while another was setting it, the read might return an invalid partial value. With the synchronized declaration, two or more running threads are guaranteed not to interfere with each other. However, there is no guarantee as to the order of operations. If the read starts first, it will finish before the write starts, and vice versa. If you want actions to happen in a guaranteed order, threads must coordinate their activities in some application-specific way.

Static methods can also be synchronized, which uses a class-wide lock for that class. Two threads cannot execute synchronized static methods on the same class at the same time. The per-class lock for a static method has no effect on any objects of that class—you can still invoke synchronized methods on an object while another thread has the class locked in a synchronized static method. Only other synchronized static methods are blocked.

When an extended class overrides a synchronized method, the new method can be synchronized or not. The superclass's method will still be synchronized when it is invoked, so an unsynchronized method in an extended class will not remove the synchronized behavior of the superclass's implementation. If the unsynchronized method uses super.*method()* to invoke the superclass's *method*, the object will become locked at that time, and will become unlocked when the superclass's *method* returns.

9.2.2 synchronized Statements

The synchronized statement enables you to execute synchronized code that locks an object without requiring you to invoke a synchronized method in that object. The synchronized statement has two parts: an object to be locked and a statement to execute when the lock is obtained. The general form of the synchronized statement is:

```
synchronized (expr) {
    statements
}
```

The parenthesized expression *expr* must produce an object to lock—usually, an object reference. When the lock is obtained, the *statements* in the block are executed as if the block were a synchronized method on that object. Here is a method to replace each element in an array with its absolute value, relying on a synchronized statement to control access to the array:

```
/** make all elements in the array non-negative */
public static void abs(int[] values) {
    synchronized (values) {
        for (int i = 0; i < values.length; i++) {
            if (values[i] < 0)
                values[i] = -values[i];
        }
    }
}
```

The `values` array contains the elements to be modified. We synchronize `values` by naming it as the object of the `synchronized` statement. Now the loop can proceed, guaranteed that the array is not changed during execution by any other code that is similarly synchronized on the `values` array.

The term *synchronized code* describes any code that is inside `synchronized` methods or `synchronized` statements.

There is no requirement that the object of a `synchronized` statement actually be used in the body of the statement. Sometimes the object's sole function is to act as a lock object for a larger collection of objects. In such a case, the representative object may have little or no direct function—it may literally be just an `Object`— but it will be used as the object of all `synchronized` statements that want to manipulate some or all of those other objects.

Another design alternative in such cases is to design the representative class with several `synchronized` methods to operate on the other objects. Not only is this approach a clean encapsulation of the operations, it also eliminates a source of error—namely, programmers forgetting to put accesses inside `synchronized` statements. In some cases, too many operations need to be performed on the objects being protected to encapsulate them all as methods in a class, and you must rely on the `synchronized` statement to protect multithreaded access.

Sometimes a designer hasn't considered a multithreaded environment when designing a class, and none of its methods are `synchronized`. To use such a class in a multithreaded environment, you have two choices:

- Create an extended class to override the appropriate methods, declare them `synchronized`, and forward method calls through the `super` reference.

- Use a `synchronized` statement to access the object in a thread-safe manner.

The extended class is a better general solution. It eliminates the errors of a programmer forgetting to put accesses within a `synchronized` statement. However, if only one or two places in the code require synchronized access, a `synchronized` statement may be simpler.

One common use of the `synchronized` statement is for an inner object to synchronize on its enclosing object:

```
public class Outer {
    private int data;
    // ...

    private class Inner {
        void setOuterData() {
            synchronized (Outer.this) {
```

```
                        data = 12;
                }
            }
        }
    }
```

Like any other object, an inner object is independently synchronized—locking an inner object has no effect on its enclosing object's lock, nor does locking an enclosing object affect any enclosed inner objects. An inner class that needs to synchronize with its enclosing object must do so explicitly.

The class-wide lock for static methods is a lock on the `Class` object for the class. If you need a `synchronized` statement to use the same lock used by static methods, you can use the class literal for your class:

```
public class Mapping {
    public static String getMapped(String name) {
        if (inCache(name))                  // in cache?
            return cachedMap(name);         // return cached
        synchronized (Mapping.class) {  // static lock
            // ... calculate mapping and add to cache ...
            return mappedTo;                // return mapping
        }
    }
}
```

In this class, the check for values in a static cache can be unsynchronized. We need to synchronize on the shared cache only if the mapping for `name` is not already cached. The `synchronized` statement in the `getMapped` method locks the `Class` object for `Mapping` in the same way a `synchronized` static method of the class would. (`Class` objects are discussed in detail in Chapter 14.)

Exercise 9.1: Write a class whose objects hold a current value and have a method that will add to that value, printing the new value. Write a program that creates such an object, creates multiple threads, and invokes the adding method repeatedly from each thread. Write the class so that no addition can be lost.

Exercise 9.2: Modify your code from Exercise 9.1 to use a synchronized static method instead of an object.

Exercise 9.3: Modify your code from Exercise 9.2 so that one thread safely decrements the value without using a synchronized static method.

9.3   `wait`, `notifyAll`, and `notify`

The `synchronized` locking mechanism suffices for keeping threads from interfering with each other, but you also need a way to communicate between threads.
For this purpose, the `wait` method lets one thread wait until some condition
occurs, and the notification methods `notifyAll` and `notify` tell waiting threads
that something has occurred that might satisfy that condition. The `wait` and notification methods are defined in class `Object` and are inherited by all classes. They
apply to particular objects, just as locks do.

There is a standard pattern that it is important to use with `wait` and notification. The thread waiting for a condition should do something like this:

```
synchronized void doWhenCondition() {
    while (!condition)
        wait();
    … Do what must be done when the condition is true …
}
```

A number of things are going on here:

◆ Everything is executed within `synchronized` code. If it were not, the state
  of the object would not be stable. For example, if the method were not `syn-
  chronized`, then after the `while` statement, there would be no guarantee
  that the condition remained `true` because another thread may have changed
  the situation that the condition tests.

◆ One of the important aspects of the definition of `wait` is that when it pauses
  the thread, it *atomically* releases the lock on the object. Saying that the
  thread suspension and lock release are atomic means that they happen
  together, indivisibly. Otherwise, there would be a race hazard: a notification
  could happen after the lock is released but before the thread is suspended.
  The notification would have no effect on the thread, effectively getting lost.
  When a thread is restarted after being notified, the lock is atomically reac-
  quired.

◆ The condition test should *always* be in a loop. Never assume that being
  awakened means that the condition has been satisfied. In other words, don't
  change the `while` to an `if`.

On the other side, the notification methods are invoked by synchronized code
that changes one or more conditions on which some other thread may be waiting.
Notification code typically looks something like this:

```
synchronized void changeCondition() {
    ... change some value used in a condition test ...
    notifyAll();
}
```

Multiple threads may be waiting on the same object. Using `notify` picks one of the waiting threads (if any) and wakes it up. Because you cannot predict which thread will be awakened, you should almost always use `notifyAll` to wake up waiting threads instead of using `notify`, which will wake up only one thread. Otherwise, you may wake up a thread that is waiting on the object but for a different condition from the one you satisfied. That thread will discover that its condition has not been satisfied and go back to waiting, while some thread waiting on the condition you *did* satisfy will never get awakened.

The following example class implements a queue. The class has methods to insert and remove elements from the queue.

```
class Queue {
        // The first and last elements in the queue
    Element head, tail;

    public synchronized void append(Element p) {
        if (tail == null)
            head = p;
        else
            tail.next = p;
        p.next = null;
        tail = p;
        notifyAll();  // Let waiters know something arrived
    }

    public synchronized Element get() {
        try {
            while (head == null)
                wait();     // Wait for an element
        } catch (InterruptedException e) {
            return null;
        }

        Element p = head;  // Remember first element
        head = head.next;  // Remove it from the queue
        if (head == null)  // Check for an empty queue
            tail = null;
```

```
            return p;
        }
    }
```

This implementation of a queue looks very much like a queue used in single-threaded systems. It differs in a few aspects: the methods are `synchronized`; when an element is appended to the queue, waiters are notified; and instead of returning `null` when the queue is empty, the `get` method waits for some other thread to insert something so that `get` will block until an element is available. Many threads (not just one) may be appending elements to the queue, and many threads (again, not just one) may be getting elements from the queue.

9.4   Details of `wait` and `notify`

There are three forms of `wait` and two forms of `notify`. All of them are methods in the `Object` class and operate on the current thread:

`public final void` **`wait(long timeout)`** `throws InterruptedException`
> The current thread waits until it is notified or the specified `timeout` expires. `timeout` is in milliseconds. If `timeout` is zero, the `wait` will not time out but will continue until notification.

`public final void` **`wait(long timeout, int nanos)`**
`throws InterruptedException`
> A finer-grained `wait`, with the timeout interval as the sum of the two parameters: `timeout` in milliseconds and `nanos` in nanoseconds, in the range 0–999999).

`public final void` **`wait()`** `throws InterruptedException`
> Equivalent to `wait(0)`.

`public final void` **`notify()`**
> Notifies *at most one* thread waiting for a condition to change. You cannot choose which thread will be notified, so use this form of `notify` only when you are sure you know which threads are waiting for what at which times. If you are not sure of any of these factors, you should use `notifyAll`.

`public final void` **`notifyAll()`**
> Notifies *all* the threads waiting for a condition to change.

If no threads are waiting when either `notifyAll` or `notify` is invoked, the notification is not remembered. If a thread subsequently decides to `wait`, an earlier notification will have no effect on it. Only notifications that occur after the `wait` commences will affect a waiting thread.

These methods can be invoked only from within synchronized code, using the lock for the object on which they are invoked. The invocation can be directly made from the synchronized code, or can be made indirectly from a method invoked in such code. You will get an IllegalMonitorStateException if you attempt to invoke these methods on objects from outside the synchronized code that acquired the lock.

Exercise 9.4: Write a program that prints out each second elapsed from the start of execution with a thread that prints a message every fifteen seconds. Have the message-printing thread be notified by the time-printing thread. Add another thread that prints a different message every seven seconds without modifying the time-printing thread.

9.5   Thread Scheduling

Java can run on both single- and multiprocessor machines and you can run with multiple threads or a single thread, so the threading guarantees are general. On a system with N available processors, you will usually see N of the highest-priority runnable threads executing. Lower-priority threads are guaranteed to run only when higher-priority threads are blocked (not runnable). Lower-priority threads might, in fact, run at other times to prevent starvation, but you cannot rely on it.

A thread is blocked if it is waiting or executing any other system or thread function that is blocked. When a thread blocks, Java picks the highest-priority runnable thread (or one of those with the highest priority if there is more than one thread at that priority) and lets it run.

The Java runtime can reschedule even the highest-priority thread to let another thread at the same priority run. This means that all threads with the top priority will eventually run. This is a weak guarantee, however, because "eventually" could be too late. Use priority only to affect scheduling policy for efficiency purposes. Do not rely on thread priority for algorithm correctness.

A thread's priority is initially the same as the priority of the thread that created it. The priority can be changed using setPriority with a value between Thread's constants MIN_PRIORITY and MAX_PRIORITY. The standard priority for the default thread is NORM_PRIORITY. The priority of a running thread can be changed at any time. If you assign a thread a priority lower than its current one, the system may let another thread run, because the original thread may no longer be among those with the highest priority. The getPriority method returns the priority of a thread.

Generally, the continuously running part of your application should run in a lower-priority thread than the thread dealing with rarer events such as user input.

When users push a "Cancel" button, for example, they expect the application to cancel what it's doing. If display update and user input are at the same priority and the display is updating, considerable time may pass before the user input thread reacts to the button. If you put the display thread at a lower priority, it will still run most of the time because the user interface thread will be blocked waiting for user input. When user input is available, the user interface thread will preempt the display thread to act on the user's request. For this reason, a thread that does continual updates is often set to MIN_PRIORITY to avoid hogging all available cycles.

Several static methods of the Thread class control the current thread:

`public static void `**`sleep(long millis)`**` throws InterruptedException`

> Puts the currently executing thread to sleep for at least the specified number of milliseconds. "At least" means there is no guarantee the thread will wake up in exactly the specified time. Other thread scheduling can interfere, as can the granularity and accuracy of the system clock, among other factors.

`public static void `**`sleep(long millis, int nanos)`**
`  throws InterruptedException`

> Puts the currently executing thread to sleep for at least the specified number of milliseconds and nanoseconds. Nanoseconds are in the range 0–999999.

`public static void `**`yield()`**

> Causes the currently executing thread to yield so that any other runnable threads can run. The thread scheduler chooses a thread to run from the runnable threads. The thread that is picked can be the one that yielded, because it may be the highest-priority runnable thread.

The following program shows how yield works. The application takes a list of words and creates a thread that is responsible for printing each word. The first parameter to the application says whether each thread will yield after each println; the second parameter is the number of times each thread should repeat its word. The remaining parameters are the words to be repeated:

```
class Babble extends Thread {
    static boolean doYield; // yield to other threads?
    static int howOften;    // how many times to print

    private String word;    // my word

    Babble(String whatToSay) {
        word = whatToSay;
    }

    public void run() {
```

```
            for (int i = 0; i < howOften; i++) {
                System.out.println(word);
                if (doYield)
                    yield();    // give another thread a chance
            }
        }

    public static void main(String[] args) {
        howOften = Integer.parseInt(args[1]);
        doYield = new Boolean(args[0]).booleanValue();

        // create a thread for each word at max priority
        Thread cur = currentThread();
        cur.setPriority(Thread.MAX_PRIORITY);
        for (int i = 2; i < args.length; i++)
            new Babble(args[i]).start();
    }
}
```

When the threads do not yield, each thread gets large chunks of time, usually enough to finish all the prints without any other thread getting cycles. For example, suppose the program is run with doYield set to false in the following way:

```
Babble false 2 Did DidNot
```

The output is likely to look like this:

```
Did
Did
DidNot
DidNot
```

If each thread yields after each println, other printing threads will have a chance to run. Suppose we set doYield to true with an invocation such as this:

```
Babble true 2 Did DidNot
```

The yields give the other threads a chance to run, and the other threads will yield in turn, producing an output more like this:

```
Did
DidNot
Did
DidNot
```

The output shown is only approximate. A different thread implementation could give different results, or the same implementation might give different results on different runs of the application. But under all implementations, invoking `yield` can give other threads a more equitable chance at getting cycles.

Exercise 9.5: Modify `Babble` so that each thread yields after printing its word. Run it multiple times and examine the output: is it always the same? If possible, run it on different Java systems and compare.

9.6   Deadlocks

Whenever you have two threads and two objects with locks, you can have a *dead-lock*, in which each thread has a lock on one of the objects and is waiting for a lock on the other object. If object *X* has a `synchronized` method that invokes a `synchronized` method on object *Y*, which in turn has a `synchronized` method invoking a `synchronized` method on object *X*, two threads may wait for each other to complete in order to get a lock, and neither thread will be able to run. This situation is also called a *deadly embrace*. Consider this scenario, in which `jareth` and `cory` are objects of some class `Friendly`:

1. Thread number 1 invokes `synchronized` method `jareth.hug`. Thread number 1 now has the lock on `jareth`.

2. Thread number 2 invokes `synchronized` method `cory.hug`. Thread number 2 now has the lock on `cory`.

3. Now `jareth.hug` invokes `synchronized` method `cory.hugBack`. Thread number 1 is now blocked waiting for the lock on `cory` (currently held by thread number 2) to become available.

4. Finally, `cory.hug` invokes `synchronized` method `jareth.hugBack`. Thread number 2 is now blocked waiting for the lock on `jareth` (currently held by thread number 1) to become available.

We have now achieved deadlock: `cory` won't proceed until the lock on `jareth` is released and vice versa, so the two threads are stuck in a permanent purgatory.

You could get lucky, of course, and have one thread complete the entire `hug` without the other one starting. If steps 2 and 3 happened to occur in the opposite order, `jareth` would complete both `hug` and `hugBack` before `cory` needed the lock on `jareth`. But a future run of the same application might deadlock because of a different choice of the thread scheduler. Several design changes would fix this problem. The simplest would be to make `hug` and `hugBack` not `synchronized` but have both methods synchronize on a single object shared by all `Friendly` objects. This technique would mean that only one hug could happen at a time in all the threads of a single runtime, but it would eliminate the possibility of deadlock. Other, more complicated techniques would enable multiple simultaneous hugs without deadlock.

You are responsible for avoiding deadlock. Java neither detects nor prevents deadlocks. It can be frustrating to debug deadlock problems, so you should solve them by avoiding the possibility in your design. You can read *Concurrent Programming in Java,* a book in this series, to get advice on how to create well-designed multithreaded programs. "Further Reading" on page 381 has other useful references to give you a background in thread and lock design.

Exercise 9.6: Write a program that uses `hug` and `hugBack` to create the described potential deadlock. How often does the deadlock actually happen on your system? If you add `yield` calls, can you change the likelihood of deadlock? If you can, try this exercise on more than one kind of system.

9.7   Ending Thread Execution

9.7.1   The End of a Thread's Life

A thread is finished executing when its `run` method returns. Having `run` return is the normal way to end a thread's life, but you can also get a thread to halt in other ways. Returning from `run` is the cleanest, but it requires some work on the programmer's part. This is usually done by *interrupting* the thread. For example:

Thread 1	*Thread 2*

```
       Thread 1                              Thread 2
    thread2.interrupt();               while (!isInterrupted()) {
                                          // do a little work
                                       }
```

Interrupting the thread advises it that you want it to pay attention, usually to get it to halt execution. An interrupt does *not* force the thread to halt, although it will interrupt the slumber of a sleeping thread.

Interruption is also useful when you want to give the running thread some control over when it will handle an event. For example, a display update loop might need to access some database information using a transaction and would prefer to handle a user's "cancel" after waiting until a transaction completes normally. The user interface thread might implement a "Cancel" button by interrupting the display thread to give the display thread that control. This approach will work well as long as the display thread is well behaved and checks at the end of every transaction to see whether it has been interrupted, halting if it has.

The methods that relate to interrupting a thread are `interrupt`, which sends an interrupt to a thread; `isInterrupted`, which tests whether a thread has been interrupted; and `interrupted`, a `static` method that tests whether the current thread has been interrupted and then clears the "interrupted" state of the thread. You should use `isInterrupted` to check whether a thread is in an interrupted state. Use `interrupted` only when you intend to release the current thread from being interrupted so that it can proceed as if `interrupt` has not been invoked (until `interrupt` is invoked again to deliver a new interrupt).

Interrupting a thread will normally not affect what it is doing, but a few methods, such as `sleep` and `wait`, throw `InterruptedException`. If your thread is executing one of these methods when it is interrupted, the method will throw the `InterruptedException`. Such a thrown interruption clears the "interrupted" state of the thread, so handling code for `InterruptedException` commonly looks like this:

```
void tick(int count, long pauseTime) {
    try {
        for (int i = 0; i < count; i++) {
            System.out.println('.');
            System.out.flush();
            Thread.sleep(pauseTime);
        }
    } catch (InterruptedException e) {
        Thread.currentThread().interrupt();
    }
}
```

The `tick` method prints a dot every `pauseTime` milliseconds up to a maximum of `count` times. If something interrupts the thread in which `tick` is running, `sleep` will throw `InterruptedException`. The ticking will then cease, and the `catch` clause will re-interrupt the thread. You could instead declare that `tick` itself throws `InterruptedException` and simply let the exception percolate upward, but then every invoker of `tick` would have to handle the same possibility. Reinterrupting the thread allows `tick` to clean up its own behavior and then let other code handle the interrupted exception as it normally would.

9.7.2 Waiting for a Thread to Complete

One thread can wait for another thread to finish using one of the `join` methods. The simple form waits forever for a particular thread to die:

```
class CalcThread extends Thread {
    private double result;

    public void run() {
        result = calculate();
    }

    public double getResult() {
        return result;
    }

    public double calculate() {
        // ... calculate a value for "result"
    }
}

class ShowJoin {
    public static void main(String[] args) {
        CalcThread calc = new CalcThread();
        calc.start();
        doSomethingElse();
        try {
            calc.join();
            System.out.println("result is "
                + calc.getResult());
        } catch (InterruptedException e) {
            System.out.println("No answer: interrupted");
        }
    }

}
```

First, a new thread type, `CalcThread`, is defined to calculate a result. We start a `CalcThread`, do something else for a while, and then `join` that thread. When `join` returns, `CalcThread.run` is guaranteed to have finished, and `result` will be set. If `CalcThread` is already finished when `doSomethingElse` has completed, `join` returns immediately. When a thread dies, its object doesn't go away, so you can still access its state.

Two other forms of `join` take timeout values analogous to `wait`. Here are the three forms of `join`:

`public final synchronized void `**`join(long millis)`**
   `throws InterruptedException`
> Waits for this thread to finish or the specified number of milliseconds to elapse, whichever is first. A timeout of 0 milliseconds means to wait forever.

`public final synchronized void `**`join(long millis, int nanos)`**
   `throws InterruptedException`
> Waits for this thread to finish, with more precise timing. Again, a total time-out of 0 nanoseconds means to wait forever. Nanoseconds are in the range 0–999999.

`public final void `**`join()`** ` throws InterruptedException`
> Equivalent to `join(0)`.

Invoking a thread's `destroy` method is drastic. It kills the thread dead without releasing any locks held on objects in the thread, so using `destroy` could leave other threads blocked forever. Avoid invoking `destroy` if you possibly can.

9.7.3   Don't `stop`

You can force a thread to halt by invoking its `Thread` object's `stop` method, which throws a `ThreadDeath` exception to the target thread. `ThreadDeath` is a subclass of `Error`, not a subclass of `Exception` (see Appendix A for a discussion of why this is so). Programmers should not catch `ThreadDeath`—a `finally` clause can handle any cleanup. A thread can also throw `ThreadDeath` itself to terminate its own execution.

The problem with using `stop` on a thread is that it can shatter the consistency of the objects running in that thread. Suppose, for example, that a class uses a synchronized method to ensure that all values in an array are set to related values:

```
class Store {
    double values[];
    // ...

    synchronized void setArrayValue(double seed) {
        for (int i = 0; i < values.length; i++)
            values[i] = i * seed;
    }
}
```

As long as all access to the array `values` is synchronized, this code will guarantee that no one will see the contents of `value` as anything but a complete sequence. No observer would ever see one value in the array calculated from one `seed` parameter and the next one calculated from a different `seed`. But if a thread executing this code is stopped, the method will terminate without completing the loop. At this point, the array `values` will be left in an inconsistent state—some elements set to `i*value` and others left with an older value—that would not normally be possible. Anyone using the object after the `stop`, presumably from a different thread, will see something they should never see.

You should use `stop` only when you have no other choice, or when you can guarantee that no objects used in the stopped thread will be used from any other code. This usually means that the stopped thread is performing a stand-alone task and is being stopped because that task is no longer relevant or needed. You should try to design your systems to use interruption, in which the thread decides when it is safely interruptible and so can maintain consistency guarantees. Note that any methods of other classes (such as the `String` class's `intern` method) suffer the same problem, so the stand-alone task should not involve *any* outside classes that you do not control.

Another form of the `stop` method can be passed a different exception instead of `ThreadDeath`. There are much better ways to send messages to another thread than throwing an exception, so you should not use this method under normal circumstances.

9.7.4 Suspending Threads

Threads can be *suspended* when you want to ensure that they will run only when you are ready for them to do so. This technique is risky, riskier even than using `stop` on a thread, because the suspended thread might well be holding on to one or more locks on objects. The locks will not be released until the thread resumes execution, so code that uses those locks will also be suspended. Using `suspend`, you can easily create a deadlock that will never be broken.

Consider a user pressing a "Cancel" button during an expensive operation. You might want to suspend processing to confirm whether the user really wants to cancel the computation. That code might look like this:

```
Thread spinner; // the thread doing the processing

public void userHitCancel() {
    spinner.suspend();              // whoa!
    if (askYesNo("Really Cancel?"))
        spinner.interrupt();        // interrupt it
```

```
        else
            spinner.resume();                // giddyap!
    }
```

The userHitCancel method first invokes suspend on the processing thread to freeze the running thread until explicitly resumed. Then the user is asked whether the cancel was intentional. If it was, interrupt asks the thread to halt execution. Otherwise, resume makes it runnable again.

Now consider what happens if the user interface that asks the question "Really Cancel?" also updates the values from the running calculation driven by spinner. If the thread is in the middle of updating the data that is read by the display update, and if that update is done in a synchronized method, then spinner will have a lock on the object. So the display code is trying to ask the user a question while blocked on an operation that cannot complete until the user answers. This is probably a deadlock—the display code is blocked so it cannot get user input, but the lock it needs will not be released until that user input is processed.

For this reason you should probably avoid using suspend and resume to manage your threads. The code could just let the calculation continue, placing the spinner thread at a lower priority so that getting the answer to the question would be a higher priority than continuing the calculation. Or it could invoke a method on the thread to set a variable that is polled occasionally to see whether the calculation should pause.

Suspending a suspended thread or resuming a thread that is not suspended has no effect.

9.8   Ending Application Execution

Each application starts with one thread—the one that executes main. If your application creates no other threads, the application will finish when main returns. But if you create other threads, what happens to them when main returns?

There are two kinds of threads: *user* and *daemon*. The presence of a user thread keeps the application running, whereas a daemon thread is expendable. When the last user thread is finished, any daemon threads are stopped and the application is finished. You use the method setDaemon(true) to mark a thread as a daemon thread, and you use getDaemon to test that flag. By default, daemon status is inherited from the thread that creates the new thread and cannot be changed after a thread is started; an IllegalThreadStateException is thrown if you try.

If your main method spawns a thread, that thread inherits the user-thread status of the original thread. When main finishes, the application will continue to run until the other thread finishes, too. There is nothing special about the original thread—it just happened to be the first one to get started for a particular run of an application, and it is treated just like any other user thread. An application will run until all user threads have completed. For all the runtime knows, the original thread was designed to spawn another thread and die, letting the spawned thread do the real work. If you want your application to exit when the original thread dies, you can mark all the threads you create as daemon threads.

9.9 Using Runnable

The Runnable interface abstracts the concept of something that will execute code while it is active. The Runnable interface declares a single method:

```
public void run();
```

The Thread class implements the Runnable interface because a thread is something that executes code when it is active. You have seen that Thread can be extended to provide specific computation for a thread, but this approach is awkward in many cases. First, class extension is single inheritance—if you extend a class to make it runnable in a thread, you cannot extend any other class, even if you need to. Also, if your class needs only to be runnable, inheriting all the overhead of Thread is more than you need.

Implementing Runnable is easier in many cases. You can execute a Runnable object in its own thread by passing it to a Thread constructor. If a Thread object is constructed with a Runnable object, the implementation of Thread.run will invoke the runnable object's run method.

Here is a Runnable version of the PingPong class from page 181. If you compare the versions, you will see that they look almost identical. The major differences are in the supertype (Runnable versus Thread) and in main.

```
class RunPingPong implements Runnable {
    String word;                  // what word to print
    int delay;                    // how long to pause

    RunPingPong(String whatToSay, int delayTime) {
        word = whatToSay;
        delay = delayTime;
    }

    public void run() {
        try {
            for (;;) {
```

```
                System.out.print(word + " ");
                Thread.sleep(delay); // wait until next time
            }
        } catch (InterruptedException e) {
            return;                  // end this thread
        }
    }

    public static void main(String[] args) {
        Runnable ping = new RunPingPong("ping",  33);
        Runnable pong = new RunPingPong("PONG", 100);
        new Thread(ping).start();
        new Thread(pong).start();
    }
}
```

First, a new class is defined that implements Runnable. Its implementation of the run method is the same as PingPong's. In main, two RunPingPong objects with different timings are created; a new Thread object is then created for each object and is started immediately.

Four Thread constructors enable you to specify a Runnable object:

public **Thread(Runnable target)**
    Constructs a new Thread that uses the run method of the specified target.

public **Thread(Runnable target, String name)**
    Constructs a new Thread with the specified name and uses the run method of the specified target.

public **Thread(ThreadGroup group, Runnable target)**
    Constructs a new Thread in the specified ThreadGroup and uses the run method of the specified target. You will learn about ThreadGroup soon.

public **Thread(ThreadGroup group, Runnable target, String name)**
    Constructs a new Thread in the specified ThreadGroup with the specified name and uses the run method of the specified target.

Exercise 9.7: Rewrite your answer to Exercise 9.5 to use Runnable.

9.10 volatile

The synchronized mechanism works nicely, but if you choose not to use it, multiple threads could potentially modify a field at the same time. If you are doing this on purpose (possibly because you have some other way to synchronize access), you should mark that field volatile. For example, if you had a value that was continuously displayed by a graphics thread and that could be changed by non-synchronized methods, the display code might look something like this:

```
currentValue = 5;
for (;;) {
    display.showValue(currentValue);
    Thread.sleep(1000); // wait 1 second
}
```

If there is no way for showValue to change the value of currentValue, the compiler might assume that it can treat currentValue as unchanged inside the loop and simply use the constant 5 each time it invokes showValue.

But if currentValue is a field that is updated by other threads while the loop is running, the compiler's assumption would be wrong. Declaring the field currentValue to be volatile prevents the compiler from making such assumptions, forcing it to reread the value on every iteration of the loop.

9.11 Thread Security and ThreadGroup

When you're programming multiple threads—some of them created by library classes—it can be useful to place limitations on the threads to protect them from one another.

Threads are split into *thread groups* for security reasons. A thread group can be contained within another thread group, providing a hierarchy. Threads within a thread group can modify the other threads in the group, including any threads farther down the hierarchy. A thread cannot modify threads outside its own group or contained groups.

You can use these restrictions to protect threads from manipulation by other threads. If new threads are placed in a separate thread group inside an existing thread group, the new threads' priorities can be changed from within either the subgroup or the outer group, but threads in the subgroup cannot change the priority of threads in the outer group.

Every thread belongs to a thread group. Each thread group is represented by a ThreadGroup object that describes the limits on threads in that group. You can specify the thread group in the thread constructor; the default is to place each new thread in the same thread group as that of the thread that created it. When a thread dies, the Thread object is removed from its group.

public **Thread(ThreadGroup group, String name)**

> Constructs a new thread in the specified thread group with the given name
> (which can be null). The name need not be unique; it is to help you debug.

The ThreadGroup object associated with a thread cannot be changed after the
thread is created. You can get a thread's group by invoking its getThreadGroup
method. You can also check whether you are allowed to modify a Thread by
invoking its checkAccess method, which throws SecurityException if you
cannot modify the thread and simply returns if you cam (it is a void method).

Thread groups can be *daemon groups.* A daemon ThreadGroup is automatically destroyed when it becomes empty. Setting a ThreadGroup to be a daemon
group does not affect whether any thread or group contained in that group is a daemon. It affects only what happens when the group becomes empty.

Thread groups can also be used to set an upper limit on the priority of the
threads they contain. After you invoke setMaxPriority with a maximum priority, any attempt to set a thread priority higher than the thread group's maximum is silently reduced to that maximum. Existing threads are not affected by
this invocation. To ensure that no other thread in the group will ever have a
higher priority than that of a particular thread, you can set that thread's
priority to MAX_PRIORITY and then set the group's maximum priority to be
less than that. The limit also applies to the thread group itself. Any attempt to
set a new maximum priority for the group that is higher than the current maximum will be silently reduced.

```
static public void maxThread(Thread thr) {
    ThreadGroup grp = thr.getThreadGroup();
    thr.setPriority(Thread.MAX_PRIORITY);
    grp.setMaxPriority(thr.getPriority() - 1);
}
```

This method works by setting the thread's priority to the maximum possible and
then setting the group's maximum allowable priority to less than the thread's priority. The new group maximum is set to one less than the thread's actual priority—not to Thread.MAX_PRIORITY-1—because an existing group maximum
might limit your ability to set the thread to MAX_PRIORITY. You want the thread's
priority to be the highest possible and the group's maximum priority to be less
than the thread's, whatever that may have turned out to be.

ThreadGroup supports the following constructors and methods:

public **ThreadGroup(String name)**

> Creates a new ThreadGroup. Its parent will be the ThreadGroup of the cur-
> rent thread. Like Thread names, the name of a group is not used by the run-
> time system. A NullPointerException is thrown if the name is null.

public **ThreadGroup(ThreadGroup parent, String name)**
> Creates a new ThreadGroup with a specified name in the ThreadGroup parent. As with the other constructor, a name must be provided.

public final String **getName()**
> Returns the name of this ThreadGroup.

public final ThreadGroup **getParent()**
> Returns the parent ThreadGroup, or null if it has none.

public final void **setDaemon(boolean daemon)**
> Sets the daemon status of this thread group.

public final boolean **isDaemon()**
> Returns the daemon status of this thread group.

public final synchronized void **setMaxPriority(int maxPri)**
> Sets the maximum priority of this thread group.

public final int **getMaxPriority()**
> Gets the current maximum priority of this thread group.

public final boolean **parentOf(ThreadGroup g)**
> Checks whether this thread group is a parent of the group g, or is the group g. This might be better thought of as "part of," since a group is part of itself.

public final void **checkAccess()**
> Throws SecurityException if the current thread is not allowed to modify this group. Otherwise, this method simply returns.

public final synchronized void **destroy()**
> Destroys this thread group. The thread group must contain no threads or this method throws IllegalThreadStateException. You cannot use destroy to terminate all threads in the group—that must be done manually using the enumeration methods described later. If the group contains other groups, they must also be empty of threads.

You can examine the contents of a thread group using two parallel sets of methods: one gets the threads contained in the group, and the other gets the thread groups contained in the group. You will see an example of how these methods are used in the safeExit method on page 329.

public synchronized int **activeCount()**
> Returns an estimate of the number of active threads in this group, including threads contained in all subgroups. This is an estimate because by the time you get the number it may be out of date. Threads may have died, or new ones may have been created, during or after the invocation of activeCount.

`public int` **enumerate(Thread[] threadsInGroup, boolean recurse)**

Fills the `threadsInGroup` array with a reference to every active thread in the group, up to the size of the array. If `recurse` is `false`, only threads directly in the group are included; if it is `true`, all threads in the group's hierarchy will be included. `ThreadGroup.enumerate` gives you control over whether you recurse, but `ThreadGroup.activeCount` does not. You can get a reasonable estimate of the size of an array needed to hold the results of a recursive enumeration, but you will overestimate the size needed for a non-recursive `enumerate`.

`public int` **enumerate(Thread[] threadsInGroup)**

Equivalent to `enumerate(threadsInGroup, true)`.

`public synchronized int` **activeGroupCount()**

Like `activeCount`, but counts groups, instead of threads, in all subgroups. "Active" means "existing." There is no concept of an inactive group; the term "active" is used for consistency with `activeCount`.

`public int` **enumerate(ThreadGroup[] groupsInGroup, boolean recurse)**

Like the similar `enumerate` method for threads, but fills an array of `ThreadGroup` references instead of `Thread` references.

`public int` **enumerate(ThreadGroup[] groupsInGroup)**

Equivalent to `enumerate(groupsInGroup, true)`.

You can also use a `ThreadGroup` to manage threads in the group. Invoking `stop`, `suspend`, or `resume` on a thread group invokes the same method on each thread in the group, including threads in all subgroups. However, it is no safer to invoke these methods on a thread group than it is to invoke them on an individual thread; see "Don't `stop`" on page 198 and "Suspending Threads" on page 199 for cautions. These methods are the only way to use a `ThreadGroup` to directly affect threads. There is no `interrupt` method in `ThreadGroup`, so when you need to interrupt all the threads in a group you must use `enumerate` to get a list of threads and interrupt them yourself.

There are also two static methods in the `Thread` class to act on the current thread's group. They are shorthands for invoking `currentThread`, invoking `getThreadGroup` on that thread, and then invoking the method on that group.

`public static int` **activeCount()**

Returns the number of active threads in the current thread's `ThreadGroup`.

`public static int` **enumerate(Thread[] tarray)**

Equivalent to invoking `enumerate(tarray)` on the `ThreadGroup` of the current thread.

The `ThreadGroup` class also supports a method that is invoked when a thread dies because of an uncaught exception:

public void **uncaughtException(Thread thr, Throwable exc)**
>   Invoked when thread `thr` in this group dies because of an uncaught exception `exc`.

You can override this method to handle uncaught exceptions in your own idiom. The default implementation invokes `uncaughtException` on the group's parent group if there is one, or uses the method `Throwable.printStackTrace` if there is no parent group. If you were writing a graphical environment, you might want to display the stack trace in a window rather than simply print it to `System.out`, which is where `printStackTrace` puts its output. You could override `uncaughtException` in your group to create the window you need and redirect the stack trace into the window.

Exercise 9.8: Write a method that invokes `interrupt` on all threads in a group, including subgroups.

Exercise 9.9: Write a method that takes a thread group and starts a thread that periodically print the hierarchy of threads and thread groups within that group. Test it with a program that creates several short-lived threads in various groups.

9.12 Debugging Threads

A few `Thread` methods are designed to help you debug a multithreaded application. These print-style debugging aids can be used to print the state of an application. You can invoke the following methods on a `Thread` object to help you debug your threads:

public String **toString()**
>   Returns a string representation of the thread, including its name, its priority, and the name of its thread group.

public int **countStackFrames()**
>   Returns the number of stack frames in this thread.

public static void **dumpStack()**
>   Prints a stack trace for the current thread on `System.out`.

There are also debugging aids to track the state of a thread group. You can invoke the following methods on `ThreadGroup` objects to print their state:

`public String` **`toString()`**
> Returns a string representation of the `ThreadGroup`, including its name and priority.

`public synchronized void` **`list()`**
> Lists this `ThreadGroup` recursively to `System.out`.

I'll play it first and tell you what it is later.
—Miles Davis

CHAPTER 10

Packages

A library is an arsenal of liberty.
—Unknown

Pᴀᴄᴋᴀɢᴇꜱ have members that are related classes, interfaces, and subpackages. Packages are useful for several reasons:

◆ Packages create a grouping for related interfaces and classes.

◆ Interfaces and classes in a package can use popular public names (such as List and Constants) that make sense in one context but might conflict with the same name in another package.

◆ Packages can have types and members that are available only within the package. Such identifiers are available to the package code but inaccessible to outside code.

Let us look at a package for the attribute classes we discussed in previous chapters. We name the package attr. Each source file whose classes and interfaces belong in the attr package states its residence with its package declaration:

```
package attr;
```

This statement declares that all classes and interfaces defined in this source file are part of the attr package. A package declaration should appear first in your source file, before any class or interface declarations. Only one package declaration can appear in a source file. The package name is implicitly prefixed to each type name contained within the package.

When you write code outside the package that needs types declared within the package you have two options. One is to precede each type name with the package name. This option is reasonable if you use only a few items from a package.

The other way to access types from a package is to *import* part or all of the package. A programmer who wants to use the `attr` package could put the following line near the top of a source file (after any `package` declaration but before anything else):

```
import attr.*;
```

Then the types can be accessed simply by name, such as `Attributed`. An import that uses a * is called an *import on demand* declaration. You can also perform a *single type import:*

```
import attr.Attr;
```

Code in a package imports the rest of its package implicitly, so everything defined in a package is available to all types in the package.

The `package` and `import` mechanisms give programmers control over potentially conflicting names. If a package used for another purpose, such as linguistics, has a class called `Attributed` for language attributes, programmers who want to use both packages in the same source file have several options:

- ◆ Refer to all types by their fully qualified names, such as `attr.Attributed` and `lingua.Attributed`.

- ◆ Import `attr.Attributed` or `attr.*`, use the simple name `Attributed` for `attr.Attributed`, and use the full name of `lingua.Attributed`.

- ◆ Do the converse: import `lingua.Attributed` or `lingua.*`, use the simple name `Attributed` for `lingua.Attributed`, and use the full name of `attr.Attributed`.

- ◆ Import all of both packages—`attr.*` and `lingua.*`—and use the fully qualified names `attr.Attributed` and `lingua.Attributed` in your code. (If a type with the same name exists in two packages imported on demand, you cannot use the simple name of either type.)

10.1 Package Naming

A package name should be unique for classes and interfaces in the package, so choosing a name that's both meaningful and unique is an important aspect of package design. But with programmers around the globe developing Java language packages, there is no way to find out who is using what package names. Choosing unique package names is therefore a problem. If you are certain a package will be used only inside your organization, you can choose a name using an internal arbiter to ensure that no two projects pick clashing names.

But in the world at large, this approach is insufficient. Java package identifiers are simple names. A good way to ensure unique package names is to use an Internet domain name. If you work at a company named Magic, Inc., the attribute package declaration should be

```
package COM.magic.attr;
```

Notice that the components of the domain name are reversed from the normal domain name convention, and that the highest-level domain name (in this case, COM) is spelled in capital letters. The capital letters are used to prevent conflicts with package names chosen by those who are not following the convention. They aren't likely to use all uppercase, but they might give a package the same name as one of the many high-level domain names.

If you use this convention, your package names will not conflict with those of anyone else, except possibly within your organization. If such conflicts arise (likely in a large organization), you can further qualify using a more specific domain. Many large companies have internal subdomains with names such as east and europe. You could further qualify the package name using that subdomain name:

```
package COM.magic.japan.attr;
```

Package names can become quite long under this scheme, but it is relatively safe. No one else using this technique will choose the same package name, and programmers not using the technique are unlikely to pick your names.

Many development environments reflect package names in the file system, often by requiring that all code for a single package be in a particular folder or directory, and that the name of the directory reflect the package name. Consult your development environment's documentation for details.

10.2 Package Access

Top-level classes and interfaces within a package have two accesses: package and public. A public class or interface is accessible to code outside that package. Types that are not public have package scope: they are available to all other code in the same package, but are hidden outside the package and even from code in nested packages. Declare as public only those types needed by programmers using your package, hiding types that are package implementation details. This technique gives you flexibility when you want to change the implementation—programmers cannot rely on implementation types they cannot access, and that leaves you free to change them.

A class member that is not declared `public`, `protected`, or `private` can be used by any code within the package, but is hidden outside the package. In other words, the default access for an identifier is "package" except for members of interfaces, which are public.

Fields or methods not declared `private` in a package are available to all other code in that package. Thus, classes within the same package are considered "friendly" or "trusted." However, subpackages are not trusted relative to enclosing packages. For example, protected and package identifiers in package `dit` are not available to code in package `dit.dat`, and vice versa.

10.3 Package Contents

Packages should be designed carefully so they contain only functionally related classes and interfaces. Classes in a package can freely access each other's non-private members. Protecting class members is intended to prevent misuse by classes that have access to internal details of other classes. Anything not declared `private` is available to all types in the package, so unrelated classes could end up working more intimately than expected with other classes.

Packages should also provide logical groupings for programmers who are looking for useful interfaces and classes. A package of unrelated classes makes the programmer work harder to figure out what is available. Logical grouping of classes helps programmers reuse your code, because they can more easily find what they need. Including only related, coherent sets of types in a package also means that you can use obvious names for types, avoiding name conflicts.

Packages can be nested inside other packages. For example, `java.lang` is a nested package in which `lang` is nested inside the larger `java` package. The `java` package contains only other packages. Nesting allows a hierarchical naming system for related packages.

For example, to create a set of packages for adaptive systems such as neural networks and genetic algorithms, you could create nested packages by naming the packages with dot-separated names:

```
package adaptive.neuralNet;
```

A source file with this declaration lives in the `adaptive.neuralNet` package, which is itself a subpackage of the `adaptive` package. The `adaptive` package might contain classes related to general adaptive algorithms, such as generic problem statement classes or benchmarking. Each package deeper in the hierarchy—such as `adaptive.neuralNet` or `adaptive.genetic`—would contain classes specific to the particular kind of adaptive algorithm.

Package nesting is an organizational tool for related packages, but it provides no special access between packages. Class code in `adaptive.genetic` cannot access package-accessible identifiers of the `adaptive` or `adaptive.neuralNet` packages. Package scope applies only to a particular package. Nesting can group related packages and help programmers find classes in a logical hierarchy, but it confers no other benefits.

If a `package` declaration is not provided in a source file, types declared in that source file go into an *unnamed package.* In any running virtual machine there is only one unnamed package per class loader, so all types without a specific package name that are loaded in the same way are treated as being in the same package. Class loading is covered in Chapter 14.

Let me assure you that at First National, you're not just a number.
You're two numbers, a dash, three more numbers, another dash, and another number.
—James Estes

CHAPTER 11

Documentation Comments

Any member introducing a dog into the Society's premises shall be liable to a fine of £10.
Any animal leading a blind person shall be deemed to be a cat.
—Rule 46, Oxford Union Society

DOCUMENTATION comments, usually called *doc comments,* let you associate reference documentation for programmers directly with your code. The contents of the doc comment can be used to generate reference documentation, typically presented using HTML.

Doc comments start with the three characters /** and continue until the next */. Each doc comment describes the identifier whose declaration immediately follows. Leading * characters are ignored on doc comment lines, as are whitespace characters surrounding a leading *. The first sentence of the comment is the summary for the identifier; "sentence" means all text up to the first period with following white space. Consider the doc comment:

```
/**
 * Do what the invoker intends.  "Intention" is defined by
 * an analysis of past behavior as described in ISO 4074-6.
 */
public void dwim() throws IntentUnknownException;
```

The summary for the method dwim will be "Do what the invoker intends."

Standard HTML tags are often embedded in doc comments as formatting directives and as cross-reference links to other documentation. You can use almost any standard HTML tag except the header tags <h1>, <h2>, and so on, which are reserved for use by the generated documentation tags.

Doc comments are typically designed as fairly terse reference documentation. The reference documentation typically covers the contract of the documented interface, class, constructor, method, or field to the level of detail most programmers need. This approach is distinct from a full specification, which can be too long for reference documentation. A full specification might devote several pages of text to a single method, where the reference documentation might be one or two paragraphs, possibly even short ones. Specifications should be produced separately, although they can be cross-referenced by the doc comment, as you will soon see.

The procedure for generating documentation from the doc comments varies among development environments. One common procedure is to run the `javadoc` command on the packages or types; hence, the generated documentation is often called *javadoc*.

11.1 Paragraphs

Doc comments can contain *tagged paragraphs* that hold particular kinds of information. All these tags start with @, as in `@see` or `@deprecated`. These paragraphs are treated specially in the generated documentation, resulting in marked paragraphs, links to other documentation, and other special treatment.

Except for tagged paragraphs, text in a doc comment is treated as input text for HTML. You can create paragraph breaks in the documentation using the standard <p> tag.

11.1.1 @see

The `@see` tag creates a link to other javadoc documentation. You can name any identifier, although you must qualify it sufficiently. You can, for example, usually name a member of the class with its simple name. However, if the member is an overloaded method, you must specify which overload of the method you mean by listing the types of parameters. You can specify an interface or class that is in your own package by its unqualified name, but you must specify types from other packages with fully qualified names. You can specify members of other types using a # to separate the type name from the member name. The following are all potentially valid @see tags:

```
@see #getName
@see Attr
@see COM.magic.attrs.Attr
@see COM.magic.attrs.Attr#nameOf
@see COM.magic.attrs.Attr#nameOf()
@see COM.magic.attrs.Attr#nameOf(String)
@see COM.magic.attrs.Deck#DECK_SIZE
@see <a href="spec.html#attrs">Specification</a>
```

The first form refers to the method `getName` in the same class or interface; the same syntax can be used for fields. The last form allows you to insert a link to other documentation, such as the full specification, in the "See Also" section of your javadoc.

11.1.2 @param

The `@param` tag documents a single parameter to a method. If you use `@param` tags you should have one for each parameter of the method. The first word of the paragraph is taken as the parameter name, and the rest is its description:

```
@param max    The maximum number of words to read.
```

11.1.3 @return

The `@return` tag documents the return value of a method:

```
@return       The number of words actually read.
```

11.1.4 @exception

The `@exception` tag documents an exception thrown by the method. If you use `@exception` tags you should have one for each type of exception the method throws. This list often includes more than just the checked exceptions that must be declared in the `throws` clause—it is a good idea to declare all exceptions in the `throws` clause, whether or not they are required, and the same is true when you're using `@exception` tags. For example, suppose that your method checks its parameters to ensure that none is `null`, throwing `IllegalArgumentException` if it finds a `null` argument. You should declare `IllegalArgumentException` in your `throws` clause and your `@exception` tags.

```
@exception UnknownName    The name is unknown.
@exception java.io.IOException
                Reading the input stream failed; this exception
                is passed through from the input stream.
@exception IllegalArgumentException
                The name is <code>null</code>.
```

11.1.5 @deprecated

The `@deprecated` tag marks an identifier as being deprecated: unfit for continued use. Code using a deprecated type, constructor, method, or field will generate a warning when compiled. You should ensure that the deprecated entity continues working so that you don't break existing code that hasn't yet been updated. Deprecation helps you encourage users of your code to update to the latest version, but preserves the integrity of existing code. Users can shift to newer mechanisms when they choose to instead of being forced to shift as soon as you release a new version of your types. You should direct users to a replacement for deprecated entities:

```
/**
 * Do what the invoker intends.  "Intention" is defined by
 * an analysis of past behavior as described in ISO 4074-6.
 *
 * @deprecated  You should use dwishm instead
 * @see         #dwishm
 */
public void dwim() throws IntentUnknownException;
```

The @deprecated tag is noticed by the compiler if it is at the beginning of a line of the doc comment. The compiler marks the following identifier as being deprecated with the results described previously. This is the only place in Java where the contents of a comment affect the generated results of the compiler.

11.1.6 @author

The @author tag specifies an author of the code. You can specify as many @author paragraphs as you desire.

```
@author Aristophanes
@author Ursula K. LeGuin
@author Ibid
```

You should use only one author per @author paragraph to get consistent output in all circumstances.

11.1.7 @version

The @version tag lets you specify an arbitrary version specification.

```
@version 1.1β
```

11.1.8 `@since`

The `@since` tag lets you specify an arbitrary version specification that denotes when the tagged entity was added to your system.

```
@since 2.1
```

Tagging the "birth version" can help you track which entities are newer and therefore may need intensified documentation or testing.

11.2   An Example

The following is a doc commented version of the `Attr` class from page 60:

```java
/**
 * An <code>Attr</code> object defines an attribute as a
 * name/value pair, where the name is a <code>String</code>
 * and the value an aribrary <code>Object</code>.
 *
 * @version 1.1
 * @author Plato
 * @since 1.0
 */
class Attr {
    /** The attribute name. */
    private String name;
    /** The attribute value. */
    private Object value = null;

    /**
     * Creates a new attribute with the given name and an
     * initial value of <code>null</code>.
     * @see Attr#Attr(String,Object)
     */
    public Attr(String name) {
        this.name = name;
    }

    /**
     * Creates a new attribute with the given name and
     * initial value.
     * @see Attr#Attr(String)
```

```
    */
    public Attr(String name, Object value) {
        this.name = name;
        this.value = value;
    }

    /** Returns this attribute's name. */
    public String getName() {
        return name;
    }

    /** Returns this attribute's value. */
    public Object getValue() {
        return value;
    }

    /**
     * Sets the value of this attribute.
     * @param newValue  The new value for the attribute.
     * @returns  The original value.
     * @see #getValue()
     */
    public Object setValue(Object newValue) {
        Object oldVal = value;
        value = newValue;
        return oldVal;
    }

    /**
     * Returns a string of the form <code>name=value</code>.
     */
    public String toString() {
        return name + "='" + value + "'";
    }
}
```

For simple methods like nameOf, whose whole description is what it returns, the
@return tag is omitted as overkill. Similarly, the constructors do not use @param
tags because the description is sufficiently complete. Different organizations will
make different choices of when to use each tag. The following two pages show
how the HTML javadoc output might look for this class.

```
                    Netscape: : Class Attr
 File   Edit   View   Go   Communicator                              Help
 Back  Forward  Reload   Home  Search  Guide    Print  Security   Stop      N
    Bookmarks   Location: file:/vob/java_prog/src/out/docCommentAttr
```

Class Attr

```
java.lang.Object
   |
   +----Attr
```

class **Attr**
extends Object

An Attr object defines an attribute as a name/value pair, where the name is a String and the value an aribrary Object.

Version:
   1.1
Author:
   Plato

Constructor Index

• **Attr**(String)
   Creates a new attribute with the given name and an initial value of null.
• **Attr**(String, Object)
   Creates a new attribute with the given name and initial value.

Method Index

• **getName**()
   Returns this attribute's name.
• **getValue**()
   Returns this attribute's value.
• **setValue**(Object)
   Set the value of the attribute
• **toString**()
   Returns a string of the form name=value.

Constructors

• **Attr**

public Attr(String name)

   Creates a new attribute with the given name and an initial value of null.

   See Also:
      Attr

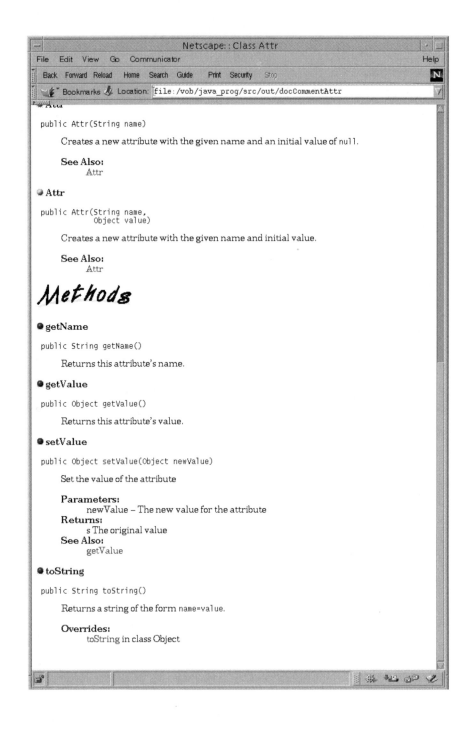

The following text appears within the browser window image:

Netscape:: Class Attr

File   Edit   View   Go   Communicator   Help

Back Forward Reload   Home   Search Guide   Print Security   Stop

Bookmarks   Location: file:/vob/java_prog/src/out/docCommentAttr

public Attr(String name)

> Creates a new attribute with the given name and an initial value of null.
>
> **See Also:**
> > Attr

Attr

public Attr(String name,
            Object value)

> Creates a new attribute with the given name and initial value.
>
> **See Also:**
> > Attr

Methods

getName

public String getName()

> Returns this attribute's name.

getValue

public Object getValue()

> Returns this attribute's value.

setValue

public Object setValue(Object newValue)

> Set the value of the attribute
>
> **Parameters:**
> > newValue – The new value for the attribute
>
> **Returns:**
> > s The original value
>
> **See Also:**
> > getValue

toString

public String toString()

> Returns a string of the form name=value.
>
> **Overrides:**
> > toString in class Object

You should use doc comments to document all members, including private and package-accessible ones. Documentation generators such as `javadoc` let you specify whether you want to generate documentation from these comments, and having organized, readable documentation of your class's internals is quite useful when someone else needs to learn about them.

Exercise 11.1: Add doc comments to your `LinkedList` class from Exercise 2.17. Generate the javadoc and ask a someone else to write a simple program using your class. Repeat, improving your comments if necessary, until someone can do so.

Exercise 11.2: Expand on Exercise 11.1 by including the private members. Generate the full (private members included) javadoc and ask someone else to explain the class to you. Repeat, improving your comments if necessary, until someone can do so.

11.3 Notes on Usage

Tightly coupling the reference documentation to the source code has many advantages, but it does not turn all programmers into good documentation writers. Programmers will continue to vary in their ability and interest in writing good reference documentation. Many organizations have technical writers to produce the reference documentation. Doc comments require write access to the source, and technical writers often do not have permission to modify source code. The use of doc comments will require a change in such organizations.

Another issue is *comment skew,* in which comments become out of date as the source code changes over time. You can reduce this problem by putting only contractual information in your doc comments, and not describing the implementation. When the implementation changes, the doc comment will still be correct as long as the contract remains unmodified. Changing the contract of an existing type, constructor, method, or field is a questionable practice in many cases, so such changes should be rare. Describing only the contract is generally a good practice in any case, because it frees you to change details of the implementation in the future. Implementation details of public methods need to be documented—use regular comments for this purpose.

You can further reduce the problem of comment skew by defining a standard marker for programmers to place in doc comments that need attention. For example, if you add a new method to a class, you could write the first draft of the doc comment, but flag the comment as one that might need review and rework by the documentation team:

```
/**
 * …initial draft…
 * DOCISSUE Review -- programmer's first draft
 */
```

A script run over the source could find these markers and show them to the documentation team, alerting them to work that remains to be done.

The universe is made of stories,
not atoms.
—Muriel Rukeyser

CHAPTER 12

The I/O Package

From a programmer's point of view,
the user is a peripheral that types when you issue a read request.
—Peter Williams

JAVA I/O (input/output) is defined in terms of *streams*. Streams are ordered sequences of data that have a *source* (input streams) or *destination* (output streams). The I/O classes isolate programmers from the specific details of the underlying operating system, while enabling access to system resources through files and other means. Most stream types (such as those dealing with files) support the methods of some basic interfaces and abstract classes, with few (if any) additions. The best way to understand Java I/O is to start with the basic interfaces and abstract classes. You will also see examples of the abstractions in action with specific kinds of streams.

The package `java.io` has two major parts: *byte streams* and *character streams*. Java uses 16-bit Unicode characters, whereas bytes are (as always) eight bits. Streams that work with bytes cannot properly carry characters, and some character-related issues are not meaningful in byte streams. The byte streams are called *input streams* and *output streams,* and the character streams are called *readers* and *writers*. For nearly every input stream there is a corresponding output stream, and for most input or output streams there is a corresponding reader or writer character stream of similar functionality, and vice versa.

Because of these overlaps, this chapter describes the streams in fairly general terms. When we talk simply about streams, we mean any of the streams. When we talk about input streams or output streams, we mean the byte variety. The character streams are referred to as readers and writers. For example, when we talk about the `Buffered` streams we mean the entire family of `BufferedInputStream`, `BufferedOutputStream`, `BufferedReader`, and `BufferedWriter`. When we talk about `Buffered` byte streams we mean both `BufferedInputStream` and

BufferedOutputStream. When we talk about Buffered character streams, we mean BufferedReader and BufferedWriter.

Some classes in java.io fall outside this model. First are the data streams that read and write primitive data types and strings. These are byte streams that support a richer set of methods for dealing with these types, and they are covered in "Data Byte Streams" on page 255. Next are the object streams, which translate objects into a byte stream and reconstitute copies of the original objects from those bytes; see "The Object Byte Streams" on page 259. Finally, utility classes help you access an underlying file system. Coverage of utility classes starts with "The File Class" on page 267.

The java.text classes described in Chapter 16 can be used for some number-formatting purposes, but there is no general set of classes for formatted input and output.

All code presented in this chapter uses the types in java.io, and every example has imported java.io.* even when there is no explicit import statement in the code.

The IOException class is used by many methods in java.io to signal exceptional conditions. Some extended classes of IOException signal specific problems, but most problems are signaled by an IOException object with a descriptive string. Details are provided in "The IOException Classes" on page 271.

12.1 Byte Streams

The java.io package defines abstract classes for basic byte input and output streams. These abstract classes are then extended to provide several useful stream types. Stream types are almost always paired: where there is a FileInputStream, there is usually a FileOutputStream.

In addition, there are classes for handling file names, a read/write stream class named RandomAccessFile, and a tokenizer for breaking an InputStream into tokens, assuming the bytes are Latin-1 eight-bit characters.

Before we discuss specific kinds of input and output byte streams, it is important to understand the basic InputStream and OutputStream abstract classes. The type tree for the byte streams of java.io in Figure 12–1 shows the type hierarchy of the byte streams.

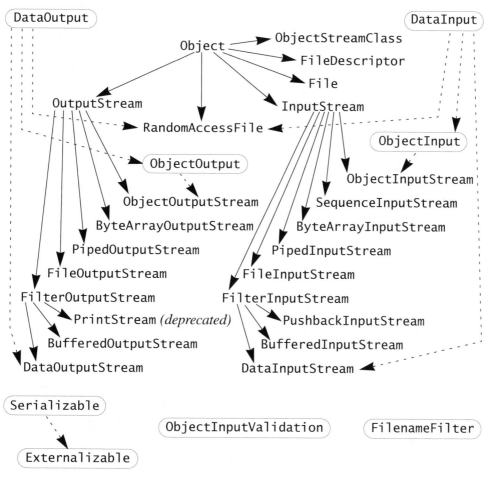

FIGURE 12–1: *Type Tree for Byte Streams in* `java.io`

12.2 InputStream

The abstract class `InputStream` declares methods to read bytes from a particular source. `InputStream` is the base class of most byte input streams in `java.io`, and it supports the following methods:

```
public InputStream()
```
      Constructs an `InputStream` object.

```
public abstract int read() throws IOException
```
Reads a single byte of data and returns the byte that was read, in the range 0 to 255, not –128 to 127. The flag value –1 is returned when the end of the stream is reached. This method blocks until input is available.

```
public int read(byte[] buf) throws IOException
```
Reads into an array of bytes. This method blocks until input is available and then fills buf with as many bytes as were read, up to buf.length bytes. It returns the actual number of bytes read, or –1 when the end of the stream is reached.

```
public int read(byte[] buf, int off, int len) throws IOException
```
Reads into a subarray of a byte array. This method blocks until input is available and then fills the subarray of buf starting with offset off up to len bytes. You will get an IndexOutOfBoundsException if this operation goes outside the bounds of the array.

```
public long skip(long count) throws IOException
```
Skips as many as count bytes of input or until the end of the input stream. Returns the actual number of bytes skipped.

```
public int available() throws IOException
```
Returns the number of bytes that can be read without blocking.

```
public void close() throws IOException
```
Closes the input stream. This method should be invoked to release any resources (such as file descriptors) associated with the stream. If this method is not invoked, associated resources remain in use until the garbage collector gets around to running a stream's finalize method. Once a stream has been closed, further operations on the stream will throw an IOException. Closing a previously closed stream has no effect.

The following program counts the total number of bytes in a file, or from System.in if no file is specified:

```java
import java.io.*;

class CountBytes {
    public static void main(String[] args)
        throws IOException
    {
        InputStream in;
        if (args.length == 0)
            in = System.in;
        else
```

```
        in = new FileInputStream(args[0]);

    int total = 0;
    while (in.read() != -1)
        total++;

    System.out.println(total + " bytes");
    }
}
```

This program either takes a filename from the command line or reads from its standard input stream, System.in. The variable in represents the input stream. If a file name is not provided, the standard input stream is used; if one is provided, a FileInputStream object is created, which is a subclass of InputStream.

The while loop counts the total number of bytes in the file. At the end, the results are printed. Here is the output of the program when used on itself:

```
318 bytes
```

You might be tempted to set total using available, but it won't work on many kinds of streams. The available method returns the number of bytes that can be read *without blocking*. For a file, the number of bytes available is usually its entire contents. If System.in is a stream associated with a keyboard, the answer can be as low as zero: when there is no pending input, the next read will block.

The implementation of InputStream requires only that a subclass provide the single-byte variant of read. However, most streams can improve performance by overriding other methods as well.

12.3 OutputStream

The abstract class OutputStream is analogous to InputStream; it provides an abstraction for writing bytes to a destination. Its methods are:

public **OutputStream()**
> Constructs an OutputStream object.

public abstract void **write(int b)** throws IOException
> Writes b as a byte. The byte is passed as an int because it is often the result of an arithmetic operation on a byte. Expressions involving bytes are type int, so making the parameter an int means that the result can be passed without a cast to byte. Note, however, that only the lowest 8 bits of the inte-

ger are written—the upper 24 bits are lost. This method blocks until the byte is written.

public void **write(byte[] buf)** throws IOException
Writes an array of bytes. This method blocks until the bytes are written.

public void **write(byte[] buf, int offset, int len)**
throws IOException
Writes part of an array of bytes, starting at buf[offset] and writing len bytes. You will get an IndexOutOfBoundsException if this operates outside the bounds of the array.

public void **flush()** throws IOException
Flushes the stream. If the stream has buffered any bytes from the various write methods, flush writes them immediately to their destination. Then, if that destination is another stream, it is also flushed. One flush invocation will flush all the buffers in a chain of streams.

public void **close()** throws IOException
Closes the stream, flushing if necessary. This method releases any resources associated with the stream. Once a stream has been closed, further operations on the stream will throw an IOException. Closing a previously closed stream has no effect.

Here is an application to copy its input to its output, translating one particular byte value to a different one along the way. The TranslateByte application takes two parameters: a from string and a to string. Bytes that match the value in the string from are translated into the value in the string to.

```java
import java.io.*;

class TranslateByte {
    public static void main(String[] args) {
        try {
            byte from = Byte.parseByte(args[0]);
            byte to = Byte.parseByte(args[1]);
            int b;
            while ((b = System.in.read()) != -1)
                System.out.write(b == from ? to : b);
        } catch (IOException e) {
            e.printStackTrace(System.err);
            System.exit(-1);
        }
    }
}
```

The implementation of `OutputStream` requires only that a subclass provide the single-byte variant of `write`. However, most streams can improve performance by overriding other methods as well.

Exercise 12.1: Rewrite the `TranslateByte` program as a method that translates the contents of an `InputStream` onto an `OutputStream`, in which the mapping and the streams are parameters. For each type of `InputStream` and `OutputStream` you read about in this chapter, write a new `main` method that uses the translation method to operate on a stream of that type. If you have paired input and output streams, you can cover both in one `main` method.

12.4 Character Streams

The abstract classes for reading and writing streams of characters are `Reader` and `Writer`. Each supports similar methods to those of its byte stream counterpart—`InputStream` and `OutputStream`, respectively. For example, `InputStream` has a `read` method that returns a `byte` as the lowest eight bits of an `int`, and `Reader` has a `read` method that returns a `char` as the lowest 16 bits of an `int`. And where `OutputStream` has methods that write `byte` arrays, `Writer` has methods that write `char` arrays. The type tree for the character streams of `java.io` appears in Figure 12–2 on page 232.

The character streams have a different synchronization paradigm. The byte streams are synchronized on each stream object. The text streams synchronize on a protected `lock` field. By default, `lock` is a reference to the stream object itself; operations from multiple threads on a single stream are thus prevented from executing at the same time. This arrangement would prevent, say, the characters from one thread's `write` invocation from being intermixed with the characters from another thread's `write`.

Some subclasses override the `lock` field to be a different useful object. For example, the `StringWriter` class that writes its character into a `StringBuffer` object sets its `lock` object to be the `StringBuffer` object. If you are writing a reader or writer, you should set the `lock` field to an appropriate object if `this` is not appropriate.

12.4.1 Character Streams and the Standard Streams

The standard streams `System.in`, `System.out`, and `System.err` existed before the character streams were invented, so these streams are byte streams even though logically they should be character streams. This situation creates some anomalies. It is impossible, for example, to replace `System.in` with a

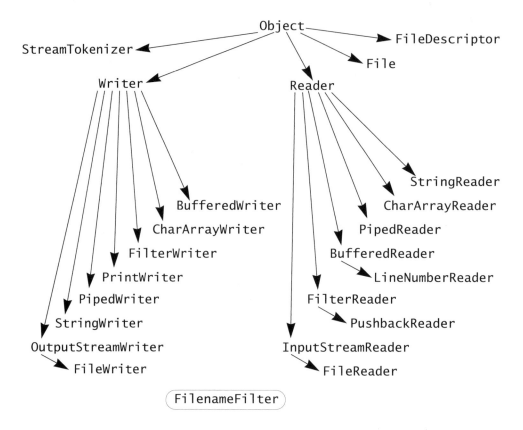

FIGURE 12–2: *Type Tree for Character Streams in* `java.io`

LineNumberReader to keep track of the standard input stream's current line number. Using an `InputStreamReader`—an object that converts a byte input stream to a character input stream—attached to `System.in`, you can create a `LineNumberReader` object to keep track of the current line number (see "LineNumberReader" on page 248). But `System.in` is an `InputStream`, so you cannot replace it with a `LineNumberReader`, which is a type of `Reader`, not an `InputStream`.

This historical fact requires us to discuss a deprecated class—the only time we do so in this book. The type of `System.out` is `PrintStream`. You should not create `PrintStream` objects for your own output, but there is no way to replace `PrintStream` with a character-oriented `PrintWriter` object.

The types `InputStreamReader` and `OutputStreamWriter` convert to and from particular byte encodings of characters and Unicode `char` values. See "InputStreamReader and OutputStreamWriter" on page 237.

12.5 Reader

The abstract class `Reader` provides a character stream analogous to the byte stream `InputStream`. Its methods are:

protected **Reader()**
> Creates a new `Reader` that will synchronize on itself.

protected **Reader(Object lock)**
> Creates a new `Reader` that will synchronize on the given `lock` object.

public int **read()** throws IOException
> Reads a single character, blocking until one is available, an error occurs, or the end of the stream is reached. When the end of the stream is reached, `read` returns -1.

public int **read(char[] cbuf)** throws IOException
> Reads into the array `cbuf`. This method blocks until input is available and then fills `buf` with as many characters as were read, up to `cbuf.length` characters. It returns the actual number read, or –1 when the end of the stream is reached.

public abstract int **read(char[] cbuf, int off, int len)**
  throws IOException
> Reads into a subarray of a `char` array. This method blocks until input is available and then fills the subarray of `cbuf` starting with offset `off` up to `len` bytes. You will get an `IndexOutOfBoundsException` if this operation goes outside the bounds of the array.

public long **skip(long count)** throws IOException
> Skips as many as `count` characters of input or until the end of the input stream. Returns the actual number of characters skipped.

public boolean **ready()** throws IOException
> Returns `true` if the stream is ready to read, that is, if the next invocation of `read` will not block. Note that a return value of `false` does not guarantee that the next invocation of `read` will block.

public abstract void **close()** throws IOException
> Closes the stream, flushing if necessary. This method releases any resources associated with the stream. Once a stream has been closed, further operations on the stream will throw an `IOException`. Closing a previously closed stream has no effect.

As an example, the following program counts the number of whitespace characters in a character stream:

```java
import java.io.*;

class CountSpace {
    public static void main(String[] args)
        throws IOException
    {
        Reader in;
        if (args.length == 0)
            in = new InputStreamReader(System.in);
        else
            in = new FileReader(args[0]);

        int ch;
        int total;
        int spaces = 0;
        for (total = 0; (ch = in.read()) != -1; total++) {
            if (Character.isWhitespace((char)ch))
                spaces++;
        }

        System.out.println(total + " chars, "
            + spaces + " spaces");
    }
}
```

This program either takes a filename from the command line, or reads from its standard input stream, `System.in`. The variable `in` refers to the reader object that will be used. If a filename is is provided, a `FileInputStream` object is created, which is a subclass of `InputStream`.

The `for` loop counts the total number of characters in the file and the number of spaces, using the `Character` class's `isWhitespace` method to test whether a character is white space. At the end, the results are printed. Here is the output of the program when used on itself:

```
452 chars, 110 spaces
```

Subclasses of `Reader` need implement only the `read` that reads into a subarray and the `close` method, but many subclasses can provide better performance if they also override other methods.

12.6 `Writer`

The abstract class `Writer` provides a stream analogous to `OutputStream` but designed for use with characters instead of bytes. Here are its methods:

protected **`Writer()`**
>Creates a new `Writer` that will synchronize on itself.

protected **`Writer(Object lock)`**
>Creates a new `Writer` that will synchronize on the given `lock` object.

public void **`write(int c)`** throws IOException
>Writes `c` as a character using the lowest 16 bits. The higher bits are ignored.

public void **`write(char[] cbuf)`** throws IOException
>Writes the array `cbuf`.

public abstract void **`write(char[] cbuf, int off, int len)`**
 throws IOException
>Writes `len` characters from `cbuf`, starting with `cbuf[off]`. You will get an `IndexOutOfBoundsException` if this operates outside the array bounds.

public void **`write(String str)`** throws IOException
>Writes the string `str`.

public void **`write(String str, int off, int len)`** throws IOException
>Writes `len` characters of the string `str`, starting at position `off`. You will get an `IndexOutOfBoundsException` if this operates past the end of the string.

public abstract void **`flush()`** throws IOException
>Flushes the stream. If the stream has buffered any characters from the various `write` methods, `flush` writes them immediately to their destination. Then, if that destination is another stream, it is also flushed. One `flush` invocation will flush all the buffers in a chain of streams.

public abstract void **`close()`** throws IOException
>Closes the stream, flushing if necessary. This method releases any resources associated with the stream. Once a stream has been closed, further operations on the stream will throw an `IOException`. Closing a previously closed stream has no effect.

Subclasses of `Writer` need implement only the `write` that uses a subarray, the `close` method, and `flush`. All other `Writer` methods are implemented in terms of these three methods. As with `Reader`, many subclasses can provide better performance if they also override other methods.

12.7 Summary of I/O Types

The `java.io` package defines several types of streams. The stream types usually have input/output pairs, and most of them have both byte stream and character stream variants:

- `Piped` streams are designed as a pair to provide a conduit so that bytes written on, say, a `PipedOutputStream` can be read from a `PipedInputStream` (bytes and characters).

- `ByteArray` streams use a `byte` array as a source or destination (bytes only).

- `CharArray` streams use a `char` array as a source or destination (characters only).

- `String` streams use string types as input or output sources for characters (characters only).

- `File` streams tie a stream to a file, adding several methods specific to file behavior (bytes and characters).

- `Filter` streams are abstract classes representing streams with some filtering operation applied as data is read or written. For example, a `FilterReader` object gets input from another `Reader` object, processes (filters) the characters in some manner, and returns the filtered result. You build sequences of filtered streams by chaining various filters into one large filter. Output can be filtered similarly (bytes and characters).

- `Buffered` streams add buffering so that `read` and `write` need not, for example, access the file system for every invocation. The character variants of these streams also add the notion of line-oriented text (bytes and characters).

- `Data` streams are broken into interface and implementation parts. The `DataInput` and `DataOutput` interfaces define methods to read and write representations of built-in types. These interfaces are implemented by the `DataInputStream` and `DataOutputStream` classes (bytes only).

- `Object` streams allow you to read and write entire objects and graphs of objects. The objects must implement the `Serializable` interface, so you need to prepare your classes to be used this way (bytes only).

- `InputStreamReader` and `OutputStreamWriter` allow you to have readers and writers that interact with byte streams (characters only).

The I/O package also has input and output streams that have no output or input counterpart:

◆ SequenceInputStream converts a sequence of InputStream objects into a single InputStream so a list of concatenated input streams can be treated as a single input stream (bytes only).

◆ LineNumberReader extends BufferedReader to track line numbers of the input stream (characters only).

◆ Pushback streams add a pushback buffer you can use to put back data when you have read too far. This is useful for scanning and parsing (bytes and characters).

◆ PrintWriter provides print and println methods for formatting printed data in human-readable text form. As described earlier, the standard streams System.out and System.err are not PrintWriter objects but instead are PrintStream objects for historical reasons.

In addition to these stream types, a few other useful I/O classes are provided:

◆ File (not to be confused with the File stream classes) provides an abstraction of file pathnames on the local file system, including path component separators, the local suffix separator, and useful methods to manipulate file names.

◆ RandomAccessFile provides mechanisms to deal with files as randomly accessed streams of bytes. It implements the DataInput and DataOutput interfaces as well as most input and output methods of InputStream and OutputStream.

◆ The StreamTokenizer class breaks a Reader into a stream of tokens—recognizable "words"— that are often needed when parsing user input (characters only).

These classes can be extended to create new kinds of stream classes for specific applications.

12.8 InputStreamReader and OutputStreamWriter

The conversion streams InputStreamReader and OutputStreamWriter translate between Unicode and byte streams using a specified encoding or the default encoding for the local system. An InputStreamReader object is given a byte input stream as its source and produces the corresponding Unicode characters. An OutputStreamWriter object is given a byte output stream as its destination and produces encoded byte forms of the Unicode characters written on it. For example, the following code would read bytes encoded under ISO 8859-6 for Arabic characters, translating them into the appropriate Unicode characters:

```
public Reader readArabic(String file) throws IOException {
    InputStream fileIn = new FileInputStream(file);
    return new InputStreamReader(fileIn, "iso-8859-6");
}
```

By default, these conversion streams will work in the platform's default encoding, but other encodings can be specified. These classes are the "glue" that lets you use existing eight-bit character encodings for local character sets in a consistent, platform-independent fashion. Encoding values are discussed in "Strings and byte Arrays" on page 171.

The FileReader and FileWriter classes are subclasses of these conversion streams. This helps you read and write local files correctly in a consistent, Unicode-savvy fashion using the local encoding. However, if the default local encoding isn't what you need, you must use an explicit InputStreamReader or OutputStreamWriter object.

There are no ReaderInputStream and WriterOutputStream classes to translate in the other directions.

12.9 Filter Streams

Filter streams enable you to chain streams to produce composite streams of greater power. Filter byte streams add new constructors to the basic ones in the InputStream and OutputStream classes. These constructors accept a stream of the appropriate type (input or output) to which to connect. Many character streams already have constructors that take another character stream, so most Reader and Writer classes can act as filters even if they do not extend FilterReader or FilterWriter.

The following program prints the line number where the first instance of a particular character is found in a file:

```
import java.io.*;

class FindChar {
    public static void main(String[] args)
        throws Exception
    {
        if (args.length != 2)
            throw new Exception("need char and file");
```

```
                   int match = args[0].charAt(0);
                   FileReader fileIn = new FileReader(args[1]);
                   LineNumberReader in = new LineNumberReader(fileIn);
                   int ch;
                   while ((ch = in.read()) != -1) {
                       if (ch == match) {
                           System.out.println("'" + (char)ch +
                               "' at line " + in.getLineNumber());
                           System.exit(0);
                       }
                   }
                   System.out.println((char)ch + " not found");
                   System.exit(1);
               }
           }
```

This program creates a `FileReader` named `fileIn` to read from the named file and then inserts a `LineNumberReader` named `in` before it. `LineNumberReader` objects get their bytes from the reader they are attached to, keeping track of line numbers. When we read characters from `in`, we are really reading characters from `fileIn`, which reads them from the input file. When this program is run on itself looking for the letter `'I'`, its output is

```
'I' at line 10
```

You can tell, if you count carefully, that the line numbers start at zero, not at one.

You can chain any number of `Filter` byte or character streams. The original source of input can be an object that is not a `Filter` stream if the original source isn't reading from another input stream. You can use an `InputStreamReader` to convert a byte input stream to a character input stream.

`Filter` output streams can be chained similarly, so that data written to one stream will filter and write data to the next output stream. All the streams, from the first to the next-to-last, must be `Filter` output stream objects, but the last stream can be any kind of output stream. You can use an `OutputStreamWriter` to convert a byte output stream to a character output stream.

Exercise 12.2: Create a subclass of `FilterReader` that will return one line of input at a time via a method that blocks until a full line of input is available.

Exercise 12.3: Create a subclass of `FilterWriter` that converts each word in the output into uppercase letters.

Exercise 12.4: Create a pair of `Filter` stream classes that compress bytes using any algorithm you choose, with the `CompressInputStream` being able to decompress the bytes that the compressing `CompressOutputStream` class created.

12.10 Print Streams

The `Print` streams format data for human reading. Because printing is clearly character-related output, the `PrintWriter` class is the class you should use. However, for historical reasons `System.out` is a `PrintStream` that assumes all bytes are Latin-1 characters. `System.out` is the only `PrintStream` you should use. Each of the `Print` streams extends the proper `Filter` stream, so you can filter data on its way downstream. The `Print` streams provide `print` and `println` methods for the following types:

```
char      int      float     Object    boolean
char[]    long     double    String
```

A simple `println` with no parameters ends the current line.

PrintWriter supports four constructors. You can provide `PrintWriter` with either a downstream `Writer` or `OutputStream`. Each of these constructors has two variants: one that takes only the downstream object, and a second that takes a `boolean` to control autoflushing. If the autoflush `boolean` is `true`, `println` invokes `flush`. Otherwise, `println` invocations are treated like any other method, and `flush` is not invoked. Autoflush behavior cannot be changed after the stream is constructed.

When you create a `PrintWriter` with an `OutputStream` instead of a `Writer`, the `PrintWriter` will wrap the byte stream in a `BufferedStreamWriter` that uses the default character encoding. If this is wrong for your purposes, you can create your `PrintWriter` with a `Writer` that writes to the byte stream using a character encoding of your choosing.

12.11 Buffered Streams

The `Buffered` stream classes buffer their data to avoid every `read` or `write` going directly to the next stream. These classes are often used in conjunction with `File` streams—accessing a disk file is much slower than using a memory buffer, and buffering helps reduce file accesses.

When a buffered stream is created, its buffer size can be specified explicitly, or it can use a default size. The buffered stream creates an array to hold data on its way through the stream.

When `read` is invoked on an empty `Buffered` byte or character stream, it invokes a `read` on its source stream, fills the buffer with as much data as is available, and returns the requested data from that buffer. Future `read` invocations return data from that buffer until its contents are exhausted, and that causes another `read` on the source stream. This process continues until the source stream is exhausted.

`Buffered` output streams behave similarly. When a `write` fills the buffer, the destination stream's `write` is invoked to empty the buffer. This buffering can turn many small `write` requests on the `Buffered` stream into a single `write` request on the underlying destination.

Here is how to create a buffered output stream to write bytes to a file:

```
OutputStream getBufferedFile(String path)
    throws IOException
{
    OutputStream out = new FileOutputStream(path);
    return new BufferedOutputStream(out);
}
```

You create a `FileOutputStream` with the path, put a `BufferedOutputStream` in front of it, and return the buffered stream object. This scheme enables you to buffer output destined for the file.

You must retain a reference to the `FileOutputStream` object if you want to invoke methods on it later because there is no way to obtain the downstream object from a `Filter` stream. If you keep a reference to a downstream object, you must ensure that the first upstream object is flushed before operating on the downstream object because data written to upper streams may not have yet been written all the way downstream. Closing an upstream object also closes all downstream objects, so a retained reference may cease to be usable.

The `Buffered` character streams also understand lines of text. The `newLine` method of `BufferedOutputStream` writes a line separator to the stream. Each system defines what constitutes a line separator using the system `String` property `line.separator`, which need not be a single character. You should use `newLine` to end lines in text files that may be read by humans on the local system (see "System Properties" on page 323).

The method `readLine` in `BufferedReader` returns a line of text as a `String`. The method `readLine` accepts any of the standard set of line separators: line feed (\n), carriage return (\r), or carriage return followed by line feed. This implies that you should never set `line.separator` to use any other sequence. Otherwise, lines terminated by `newLine` would not be recognized by `readLine`. The string returned by `readLine` does not include the line separator.

12.12 ByteArray Byte Streams

You can use arrays of bytes as the source or destination of byte streams by using `ByteArray` streams. `ByteArray` stream methods are `synchronized` so that they are thread-safe. The `ByteArrayInputStream` class uses a `byte` array as its input source. It has two constructors:

public **ByteArrayInputStream(byte[] buf)**
> Creates a `ByteArrayInputStream` from the specified array of bytes. The input array is used directly, not copied. When the end of `buf` is reached, that is the end of input from the stream.

public **ByteArrayInputStream(byte[] buf, int offset, int length)**
> Creates a `ByteArrayInputStream` from the specified array of bytes using only the subarray of `buf` from `buf[offset]` to `buf[offset+length-1]` or the end of the array, whichever is smaller.

The `ByteArrayOutputStream` class provides a dynamically growing `byte` array to hold output. It adds constructors and methods:

public **ByteArrayOutputStream()**
> Creates a new `ByteArrayOutputStream` with a default size.

public **ByteArrayOutputStream(int size)**
> Creates a new `ByteArrayOutputStream` with the specified initial size.

public synchronized byte[] **toByteArray()**
> This method returns a copy of the data; bytes in the array can be modified without changing the bytes of the output.

public int **size()**
> Returns the current buffer size.

public String **toString(int hiByte)**
> Creates a new `String` object from the contents of the byte stream. The top 8 bits of each 16-bit character in the string are set to the lower 8 bits of `hiByte`. The no-argument form of `toString` is equivalent to `toString(0)`.

When you are finished writing into a `ByteArrayOutputStream` via upstream filter streams, you should flush the upstream objects before using `toByteArray`.

12.13 CharArray Character Streams

The `CharArray` character streams are analogous to the `ByteArray` byte streams—they let you use `char` arrays as a source or destination. You construct `CharArrayReader` objects with an array of `char`:

public **CharArrayReader(char[] cbuf)**
> Creates a CharArrayReader from the specified array of characters. The input array is used directly, not copied. When the end of cbuf is reached, that is the end of input from the stream. Because the array is used directly you should take care not to modify it while it is being used as an input source.

public **CharArrayReader(char[] cbuf, int offset, int length)**
> Creates a CharArrayReader from the specified array of characters using only the subarray of cbuf from offset to (offset+length-1) or the end of the array, whichever is smaller. The input array is used directly, not copied, so the cautions about modifying the array given for the single-argument constructor apply to this constructor as well.

Extended classes can use the protected variables in CharArrayReader that manage the buffer: buf, which is the buffer itself; pos, which is the current position in the buffer; and count, which is one past the index of the last character to be read from the buffer.

CharArrayWriter writes characters into a buffer array that grows as needed. You can then use the resulting array.

public **CharArrayWriter()**
> Creates a CharArrayWriter.

public **CharArrayWriter(int initialSize)**
> Creates a CharArrayWriter whose buffer has the given initial size. The buffer will grow further if necessary to hold the output.

public void **reset()**
> Resets the stream to reuse the current buffer, discarding its contents.

public int **size()**
> Returns the number of characters generated thus far by output operations on the stream.

public char[] **toCharArray()**
> Returns a copy of the characters generated thus far by output operations on the stream.

public String **toString()**
> Returns the current contents of the buffer as a String.

public void **writeTo(Writer out)**
> Writes the current contents of the buffer to the stream out.

CharArrayWriter also has protected variables: buf, which is the buffer into which characters are being placed; and count, which is the number of used positions in the buffer array.

12.14 String Character Streams

The `StringReader` reads its characters from a `String`. It provides a single constructor that takes the string from which to read. For example, this program factors numbers read either from the command line or `System.in`:

```
class Factor {
    public static void main(String[] args) {
        if (args.length == 0) {
            factorNumbers(new InputStreamReader(System.in));
        } else {
            for (int i = 0; i < args.length; i++) {
                StringReader in = new StringReader(args[i]);
                factorNumbers(in);
            }
        }
    }
    // ...
}
```

If the command is invoked without parameters, `factorNumbers` parses numbers from the standard input stream. When the command line contains some arguments, a `StringReader` is created for each parameter, and `factorNumbers` is invoked on each one. `factorNumbers` treats its input as a stream of characters containing numbers to be parsed; it does not know whether they come from the command line or from standard input.

`StringWriter` lets you write results into a buffer that can be retrieved as a `String` or `StringBuffer` object. The following code uses a `StringWriter` to create a string that contains the output of a series of `println` calls on the contents of an array:

```
public static String arrayToStr(Object[] objs) {
    StringWriter strOut = new StringWriter();
    PrintWriter out = new PrintWriter(strOut);
    for (int i = 0; i < objs.length; i++)
        out.println(i + ": " + objs[i]);
    return out.toString();
}
```

You can create a `StringWriter` with no arguments, as shown here, or with an `int` that will be the buffer's initial size. A good size estimate can improve performance in many cases.

StringWriter stores the output it receives into a StringBuffer object. Each time output is written to the StringWriter, it is added to the buffer using append. You can obtain this StringBuffer by invoking the getBuffer method.

12.15 File Streams and FileDescriptor

The File streams allow you to treat a file as a stream of input or output. Each type is instantiated with one of three constructors:

- ◆ A constructor that takes a String that is the name of the file
- ◆ A constructor that takes a File that refers to the file (see "The Object Byte Streams" on page 259)
- ◆ A constructor that takes a FileDescriptor object

With an output stream, the first two constructor types create the file if it does not exist, or truncate it if it does exist. You can get control over truncation by using the additional output stream constructors that take two parameters: a String that is the name of the file and a boolean that, if true, causes each individual write to append to the file. If this boolean is false, the file will be truncated and new data added. If the file does not exist, the file will be created and the boolean will be ignored.

A FileDescriptor object represents a system-dependent value that describes an open file. A file descriptor object can be obtained by invoking getFD on a File stream or RandomAccessFile. FileDescriptor objects are used to create a new File or RandomAccessFile stream to the same file as another stream without needing to know the file's pathname. You must be careful to avoid unexpected interactions between two streams doing different things with the same file. You cannot predict what happens, for example, when two threads write to the same file using two different FileOutputStream objects at the same time.

The flush method of FileOutputStream and FileWriter guarantees that the buffer is flushed to the underlying file. It does not guarantee that the data is committed to disk—the underlying file system may do its own buffering. You can guarantee that the data is committed to disk by invoking the sync method on the file's FileDescriptor object, which will either force the data to disk or will throw a SyncFailedException if the underlying system cannot fulfill this contract.

The class RandomAccessFile allows you more-sophisticated manipulation of the file at the expense of not being a stream type. See "RandomAccessFile" on page 258.

12.16 Piped Streams

Piped streams are used as input/output pairs; data written on the output stream of a pair is the data read on the input. Piped streams are thread-safe; in fact, the only safe way to use Piped streams is with two threads: one for reading and one for writing. Writing on one end of the pipe blocks the thread when the pipe fills up. If the writer and reader are the same thread, that thread blocks permanently.

The following example assumes that a TextGenerator thread will write characters on any Writer.

```
class Pipe {
    public static void main(String[] args) {
        try {
            PipedWriter out = new PipedWriter();
            PipedReader in = new PipedReader(out);

            // TextGenerator will write its results on
            // the output stream we give it
            TextGenerator data = new TextGenerator(out);
            data.setPriority(Thread.MIN_PRIORITY);
            data.start();

            int ch;
            while ((ch = in.read()) != -1)
                System.out.print((char)ch);
            System.out.println();
        } catch (IOException e) {
            System.out.println("Exception: " + e);
        }
    }
}
```

We create the Piped streams, making the PipedWriter a parameter to the constructor for the PipedReader. The order is unimportant: the output pipe could be a parameter to the input pipe. What is important is that an input/output pair be attached to each other. We create the new TextGenerator object, with the PipedWriter as the output stream for the generated characters. Then we loop, reading characters from the text generator and writing them to the system output stream. At the end, we make sure that the last line of output is terminated.

12.17 `SequenceInputStream`

The `SequenceInputStream` class creates a single input stream from reading one or more byte input streams, reading the first stream until its end of input and then reading the next one, and so on through the last one. `SequenceInputStream` has two constructors: one for the common case of two input streams that are provided as the two parameters to the constructor, and the other for an arbitrary number of input streams using the `Enumeration` abstraction (described in detail in "Enumeration" on page 276). `Enumeration` is an interface that provides an ordered list of any object type. For `SequenceInputStream`, the enumeration should contain only `InputStream` objects. If it contains anything else, a `ClassCastException` is thrown when the `SequenceInputStream` tries to get that object from the list.

The following example program concatenates all its input to create a single output. This program is similar to a simple version of the UNIX utility `cat`—if no files are named, the input is simply forwarded to the output. Otherwise, it opens all the files and uses a `SequenceInputStream` to model them as a single stream. Then the program writes its input to its output:

```java
import java.io.*;
import java.util.Vector;
import java.util.Enumeration;

class Concat {
    public static void main(String[] args) {
        try {
            InputStream in; // stream to read numbers from
            if (args.length == 0) {
                in = System.in;
            } else {
                InputStream fileIn, bufIn;
                Vector inputs = new Vector(args.length);
                for (int i = 0; i < args.length; i++) {
                    fileIn = new FileInputStream(args[i]);
                    bufIn = new BufferedInputStream(fileIn);
                    inputs.addElement(bufIn);
                }
                Enumeration files = inputs.elements();
                in = new SequenceInputStream(files);
            }

            int ch;
```

```
            while ((ch = in.read()) != -1)
                System.out.write(ch);
        } catch (IOException e) {
            System.out.println(e);
            System.exit(-1);    // we failed
        }
    }
    // ...
}
```

If there are no parameters, we use System.in for input. If there are parameters, we create a Vector large enough to hold as many BufferedInputStream objects as there are command-line arguments (see "Vector" on page 278). Then we create a stream for each named file and add the stream to the inputs vector. When the loop is finished, we use the vector's elements method to get an Enumeration object for the elements of the vector. We use that Enumeration in the constructor for SequenceInputStream to create a single stream that concatenates all the streams for the files into a single InputStream object. Then a simple loop reads all the bytes from that stream and writes them on System.out.

You could instead write a new implementation of Enumeration whose nextElement method creates a StringInputStream for each argument on demand, closing the previous stream, if any. See "Enumeration" on page 276 for details on the Enumeration interface.

12.18 LineNumberReader

The LineNumberReader stream keeps track of line numbers while reading text. The getLineNumber method returns the current line number. Line numbering starts at zero. The FindChar example on page 238 uses this stream.

The current line number can be set by using setLineNumber. This technique could be useful, for example, if you have a file that contains several sections of information. You could use setLineNumber to reset the line number to 1 at the start of each section so that problems would be reported to the user based on the line numbers within the section instead of within the file.

Exercise 12.5: Write a program that reads a specified file and searches for a specified word, printing all the lines on which that word is found, preceded by the line's number.

12.19 Pushback Streams

A Pushback stream lets you push back characters when you have read too far. Pushback is typically useful for breaking input into tokens. Lexical scanners, for example, often know that a token (such as an identifier) has ended only when they have read the first character that follows it. Having seen that character, the scanner must push it back onto the input stream so it is available as the start of the next token. The following example uses PushbackInputStream to report the longest consecutive sequence of any single byte in its input:

```java
import java.io.*;

class SequenceCount {
    public static void main(String[] args) {
        try {
            PushbackInputStream
                in = new PushbackInputStream(System.in);
            int max = 0;      // longest sequence found
            int maxB = -1;    // the byte in that sequence
            int b;            // current byte in input
            do {
                int cnt;
                int b1 = in.read(); // 1st byte in sequence
                for (cnt = 1; (b = in.read()) == b1; cnt++)
                    continue;
                if (cnt > max) {
                    max = cnt; // remember length
                    maxB = b1; // remember which byte value
                }
                in.unread(b);  // pushback start of next seq
            } while (b != -1); // until we hit end of input
            System.out.println(max + " bytes of " + maxB);
        } catch (IOException e) {
            System.out.println(e);
            System.exit(1);
        }
    }
}
```

We know that we have reached the end of one sequence only when we read the first byte of the next sequence. We push this byte back using unread so that it is read again when we repeat the do loop for the next sequence.

When you create the Pushback stream you can specify the size of the push-back buffer as a constructor parameter. If you do not specify a size, the buffer will allow only one piece of data (byte or char as appropriate). Attempting to push back more than the specified amount of data will cause an IOException.

Each Pushback stream has three variants of unread: one that takes a single piece of data to push back, another that takes an array, and a third that unreads a subarray, given an array, a starting offset in that array, and a length. Each unread invocation sets the next data to be read. For example, after two consecutive unread calls on a PushbackReader with the characters '1' and '2', the next two characters read will be '2' and '1', because '2' was pushed back second. Each unread sets its own list of characters, so the code

```
pbr.unread(new char[] {'1', '2'});
pbr.unread(new char[] {'3', '4'});
for (int i = 0; i < 4; i++)
    System.out.println(i + ": " + (char)pbr.read());
```

produces the following lines of output:

```
0: 3
1: 4
2: 1
3: 2
```

Data from the last unread (the one with '3' and '4') is read back first, and within that unread the data comes from the beginning of the array through the end. When that data is exhausted, the data from the first unread is returned in the same order. The unread method copies data into the pushback buffer, so changes made to an array after it is used with unread do not affect future calls to read.

In PushbackInputStream, the pushback buffer has two protected fields: a byte[] field named buf that is the pushback buffer, and an int field pos that marks the current position in that buffer. When pos is -1, the buffer is empty. When pos is greater than -1, it moves backward toward 0 as read takes data from the buffer. A subclass could provide additional ways to modify this buffer. Push-backReader doesn't expose its internals in this way. You simply use the unread mechanism to populate the buffer.

12.20 StreamTokenizer

Tokenizing input text is a common application, and the java.io package pro-vides a StreamTokenizer class for simple tokenization problems. A stream is tokenized by creating a StreamTokenizer with a Reader object as its source and then setting parameters for the scan. A scanner loop invokes nextToken, which returns the token type of the next token in the stream. Some token types have associated values that are found in fields in the StreamTokenizer object.

This class is designed primarily to parse Java-style input; it is not a general tokenizer. However, many configuration files look similar enough to Java that they can be parsed by this tokenizer. When designing a new configuration file or other data, you can save work if you make it look enough like Java to be parsed with StreamTokenizer.

When nextToken recognizes a token, it returns the token type as its value and also sets the ttype field to the same value. There are four token types:

- ◆ TT_WORD: A word was scanned. The String field sval contains the word that was found.

- ◆ TT_NUMBER: A number was scanned. The double field nval contains the value of the number. Only decimal floating-point numbers (with or without a decimal point) are recognized. The tokenizer does not understand 3.4e79 as a floating-point number, nor 0xffff as a hexadecimal number.

- ◆ TT_EOL: An end-of-line was found.

- ◆ TT_EOF: The end-of-file was reached.

The input text is composed of *special* and *ordinary* characters. Special characters are those that the tokenizer treats specially—namely white space, characters that make up numbers, characters that make up words, and so on. Any other character is considered ordinary. When an ordinary character is the next character in the input, its token type is itself. For example, if the character '¿' is encountered in the input and is not special, the token return type (and the ttype field) is the int value of the character '¿'.

As one example, let's look at a method that sums the numeric values in a character stream it is given:

```
static double sumStream(Reader in) throws IOException {
    StreamTokenizer nums = new StreamTokenizer(in);
    double result = 0.0;
    while (nums.nextToken() != StreamTokenizer.TT_EOF) {
        if (nums.ttype == StreamTokenizer.TT_NUMBER)
            result += nums.nval;
    }
    return result;
}
```

We create a `StreamTokenizer` object from the reader and then loop, reading tokens from the stream, adding all the numbers found into the burgeoning result. When we get to the end of the input, we return the final sum.

Here is another example that reads a file, looking for attributes of the form name=value, and stores them as attributes in `AttributedImpl` objects, described in "Implementing Interfaces" on page 97:

```
public static Attributed readAttrs(String file)
    throws IOException
{
    FileReader fileIn = new FileReader(file);
    StreamTokenizer in = new StreamTokenizer(fileIn);
    AttributedImpl attrs = new AttributedImpl();
    Attr attr = null;

    in.commentChar('#');    // '#' is ignore-to-end comment
    in.ordinaryChar('/');   // was original comment char
    while (in.nextToken() != StreamTokenizer.TT_EOF) {
        if (in.ttype == StreamTokenizer.TT_WORD) {
            if (attr != null) {
                attr.setValue(in.sval);
                attr = null;          // used this one up
            } else {
                attr = new Attr(in.sval);
                attrs.add(attr);
            }
        } else if (in.ttype == '=') {
            if (attr == null)
                throw new IOException("misplaced '='");
        } else {
            if (attr == null)         // expected a word
                throw new IOException("bad Attr name");
            attr.setValue(new Double(in.nval));
            attr = null;
        }
    }
    return attrs;
}
```

The attribute file uses # to mark comments. Ignoring these comments, the stream is searched for a string token followed by an optional = followed by a word or number. Each such attribute is put into an `Attr` object, which is added to a set of attributes in an `AttributedImpl` object. When the file has been parsed, the set of attributes is returned.

Setting the comment character to # sets its character class. The tokenizer recognizes several character classes that are set by the following methods:

public void **wordChars(int low, int hi)**

Characters in this range are word characters: they can be part of a `TT_WORD` token. You can invoke this several times with different ranges. A word consists of one or more characters inside any of the legal ranges.

public void **whitespaceChars(int low, int hi)**

Characters in this range are white space. White space is ignored, except to separate tokens such as two consecutive words. As with the `wordChars` range, you can make several invocations, and the union of the invocations is the set of whitespace characters.

public void **ordinaryChar(int ch)**

The character `ch` is ordinary. An ordinary character is returned as itself, not as a token. Refer to the = in the preceding `readAttrs` example for an illustration.

public void **ordinaryChars(int low, int hi)**

Characters in this range are ordinary.

public void **commentChar(int ch)**

The character `ch` starts a single-line comment—characters after `ch` up to the next end-of-line are treated as one run of white space.

public void **quoteChar(int ch)**

Matching pairs of the character `ch` delimit `String` constants. When a `String` constant is recognized, the character `ch` is returned as the token, and the field `sval` contains the body of the string with surrounding `ch` characters removed. When reading string constants, some of the standard Java \ processing is followed (for example, you can have \t in the string). The string processing in `StreamTokenizer` is a subset of the Java strings. In particular, you cannot use \uxxxx, \', \", or (unfortunately) \Q, where Q is the quote character `ch`. You can have more than one quote character at a time on a stream, but strings must start and end with the same quote character. In other words, a string that starts with one quote character ends when the next instance of that same quote character is found; if another quote character is found in between, it is simply part of the string.

public void **parseNumbers()**

Specifies that numbers should be parsed as double-precision floating-point numbers. When a number is found, the stream returns a type of `TT_NUMBER`, leaving the value in `nval`. There is no way to turn off just this feature—to turn this off you must either invoke `ordinaryChars` for all the number-related characters (don't forget the decimal point and minus sign) or invoke `resetSyntax`.

`public void` **`resetSyntax()`**

Resets the syntax table so that all characters are ordinary. If you do this and then start reading the stream, `nextToken` always returns the next character in the stream, just as when you invoke `InputStream.read`.

There are no methods to query the character class of a given character or to add new classes of characters. Here are the default settings for a newly created `StreamTokenizer` object:

```
wordChars('a', 'z');
wordChars('A', 'Z');
wordChars(128 + 32, 255);
whitespaceChars(0, ' ');
commentChar('/');
quoteChar('"');
quoteChar('\'');
parseNumbers();
```

Other methods control the basic behavior of the tokenizer:

`public void` **`eolIsSignificant(boolean flag)`**

If `flag` is `true`, ends of lines are significant and TT_EOL may be returned by `nextToken`. If `false`, ends of lines are treated as white space and TT_EOL is never returned. The default is `false`.

`public void` **`slashStarComments(boolean flag)`**

If `flag` is `true`, the tokenizer recognizes /*...*/ comments. The default is `false`.

`public void` **`slashSlashComments(boolean flag)`**

If `flag` is `true`, the tokenizer recognizes // to end-of-line comments. The default is `false`.

`public void` **`lowerCaseMode(boolean flag)`**

If `flag` is `true`, all characters in TT_WORD tokens are converted to their lowercase equivalent if they have one (using `String.toLowerCase`). The default is `false`. Because of the case issues described in "Character" on page 297, you cannot reliably use this for Unicode string equivalence—two tokens might be equivalent but have different lowercase representations. Use the method `String.equalsIngoreCase` for reliable case-insensitive comparison.

There are three miscellaneous methods:

`public void `**`pushBack()`**

    Pushes the previously returned token back into the stream. The next invocation of `nextToken` returns the same token again instead of proceeding to the next token. There is only a one-token pushback; multiple consecutive invocations to `pushBack` are equivalent to one invocation.

`public int `**`lineno()`**

    Returns the current line number. This is usually useful for reporting errors that you detect.

`public String `**`toString()`**

    Returns a `String` representation of the last returned stream token, including its line number.

Exercise 12.6: Write a program that takes input of the form *name op value*, where *name* is one of three words of your choosing, *op* is +, -, or =, and *value* is a number. Apply each operator to the named value. When input is exhausted, print the three values. For extra credit, use the `Hashtable` class that was used for `AttributedImpl` so you can use an arbitrary number of named values.

12.21 Data Byte Streams

Reading and writing bytes is useful, but you also frequently need to transmit data of specific types across a stream. The `DataInput` and `DataOutput` interfaces define methods that transmit Java primitive types across a stream. The classes `DataInputStream` and `DataOutputStream` provide a default implementation for each interface. We cover the interfaces first, followed by their implementations.

    The interfaces for data input and output streams are almost mirror images. The parallel read and write methods for each type are:

Read	Write	Type
`readBoolean`	`writeBoolean`	`boolean`
`readChar`	`writeChar`	`char`
`readByte`	`writeByte`	`byte`
`readShort`	`writeShort`	`short`
`readInt`	`writeInt`	`int`
`readLong`	`writeLong`	`long`
`readFloat`	`writeFloat`	`float`
`readDouble`	`writeDouble`	`double`
`readUTF`	`writeUTF`	`String` (in UTF format)

UTF is Unicode Transmission Format. Unicode characters are transmitted in Unicode-1-1-UTF-8, which is a usually compact binary form designed to encode 16-bit Unicode characters in 8-bit bytes.

In addition to these paired methods, `DataInput` has several methods of its own:

`public abstract void` **`readFully(byte[] buf)`** `throws IOException`
> Reads bytes into buf, blocking until all bytes are read.

`public abstract void` **`readFully(byte[] b, int off, int len)`**
`throws IOException`
> Reads bytes into buf starting at position offset, continuing until either len bytes are read or the end of buf is reached, blocking until all bytes are read.

`public abstract int` **`skipBytes(int n)`** `throws IOException`
> Skips bytes, blocking until all n bytes are skipped.

`public abstract String` **`readLine()`** `throws IOException`
> Reads a String until bytes \n, \r, or a \r\n pair is reached. The end-of-line sequence is not included in the string. A null is returned if end-of-input is reached. The upper bits of the bytes are filled with zero to make them into characters. Better text handling for lines is available in `BufferedReader`.

`public abstract int` **`readUnsignedByte()`** `throws IOException`
> Reads an unsigned 8-bit integer and returns it as an int, filling the upper bits with zeros.

`public abstract int` **`readUnsignedShort()`** `throws IOException`
> Reads an unsigned 16-bit integer and returns it as an int, filling the upper bits with zeros.

The `DataInput` interface handles end-of-file by throwing an `EOFException` when it occurs. `EOFException` is an extended class of `IOException`.

The `DataOutput` interface supports signatures equivalent to the three forms of `write` in `OutputStream` and additionally provides the following unmirrored methods:

`public abstract void` **`writeBytes(String s)`** `throws IOException`
> Writes a String as a sequence of bytes. The upper byte in each character is lost, so unless you are willing to lose data, this method should be used only for strings that contain characters between \u0000 and \u00ff.

`public abstract void` **`writeChars(String s)`** `throws IOException`
> Writes a String as a sequence of char.

You must read strings written with these methods using a loop on `readChar`, because there is no `readBytes` or `readChars` method to read the same number of characters written using a `writeBytes` or `writeChars` invocation. You need to write the length of the string first or use an end-of-sequence character to mark its end. You can use `readFully` to read a full array of bytes if you wrote the length first, but that won't work for `writeChars` because you want `char` values, not byte values.

12.22 The Data Stream Classes

For each `Data` interface there is a corresponding `Data` stream. In addition, the `RandomAccessFile` class implements both the input and output `Data` interfaces (see "RandomAccessFile" on page 258). Each `Data` class is an extension of its `Filter` class, so `Data` streams can be used to filter other streams. Each `Data` class has constructors that take another appropriate input or output stream. For example, the filtering can be used to write data to a file by putting a `DataOutputStream` in front of a `FileOutputStream` object. The data can then be read by putting a `DataInputStream` in front of a `FileInputStream` object:

```
public static void writeData(double[] data, String file)
    throws IOException
{
    OutputStream fout = new FileOutputStream(file);
    DataOutputStream out = new DataOutputStream(fout);
    out.writeInt(data.length);
    for (int i = 0; i < data.length; i++)
        out.writeDouble(data[i]);
    out.close();
}

public static double[] readData(String file)
    throws IOException
{
    InputStream fin = new FileInputStream(file);
    DataInputStream in = new DataInputStream(fin);
    double[] data = new double[in.readInt()];
    for (int i = 0; i < data.length; i++)
        data[i] = in.readDouble();
    in.close();
    return data;
}
```

The `writeData` method first opens the file and writes the array length. It then loops, writing the contents of the array. The file can be read into an array using readData. These methods can be rewritten more simply using the Object streams you will learn about next.

Exercise 12.7: Add a method to the Body class of Chapter 2 that writes the contents of an object to a DataOutputStream and add a constructor that will read the state from a DataInputStream.

12.23 RandomAccessFile

The RandomAccessFile class provides a more sophisticated file mechanism than the File streams. RandomAccessFile is not a subclass of InputStream, OutputStream, Reader, or Writer because it can do both input and output and can work with both characters and bytes. The constructor has a parameter that declares whether the stream is for input, output, or both.

RandomAccessFile supports methods of the same names and signatures as the read and write invocations of the byte stream; for example, read returns a single byte. Although you don't have to learn a new set of method names and semantics for the same kinds of tasks you do with the other streams, you cannot use a RandomAccessFile where any of the other input or output streams are required. RandomAccessFile implements the DataInput and DataOutput interfaces and so can be used to read and write data types supported in those interfaces.

The constructors for RandomAccessFile are:

public **RandomAccessFile(String name, String mode)**
    throws IOException
        Creates a RandomAccessFile with the specified file name and mode. The mode can be either "r" or "rw" for read or read/write, respectively. Any other mode throws IOException.

public **RandomAccessFile(File file, String mode)**
    throws IOException
        Creates a RandomAccessFile with the specified File object and mode. Modes are the same as for the String-based constructor.

The "random access" referred to in the name of the class is the ability to set the read/write file pointer to any position in the file and then perform your operations. The additional methods in RandomAccessFile to support this functionality are:

public long **getFilePointer()** throws IOException
        Returns the current location of the file pointer (in bytes) from the beginning of the file.

```
public void seek(long pos) throws IOException
```
    Sets the file pointer to the specified number of bytes from the beginning of
    the file. The next byte written or read will be the pos[th] byte in the file, where
    the initial byte is the 0th.

```
public void skipBytes (int count) throws IOException
```
    Moves the current input position the specified number of bytes forward (if
    count is positive) or backward (if count is negative).

```
public long length() throws IOException
```
    Returns the file length.

Exercise 12.8: Write a program that reads a file with entries separated by lines
starting with %%, and creates a table file with the starting position of each such entry.
Then write a program that prints a random entry using that table (see the
Math.random method described in "Math" on page 332).

12.24 The Object Byte Streams

The Object streams—ObjectInputStream and ObjectOutputStream—allow
you to read and write object graphs in addition to the well-known Java types
(primitives, strings, and arrays). By "object graph" we mean that when you write
an object to an ObjectOutputStream using writeObject, bytes representing the
object—including any other objects that it references—are written to the stream.
This process of transforming an object into a stream of bytes is called *serialization*. Because the serialized form is expressed in bytes, not characters, the Object
streams have no Reader or Writer forms.

When bytes encoding a serialized graph of objects are read by the method
readObject of ObjectInputStream—that is, *deserialized*—the result is a graph
of objects equivalent to the input graph.

Suppose, for example, that you have a Hashtable object that you wish to
store into a file for future use. You could write the graph of objects that starts with
the hashtable this way:

```
FileOutputStream fileOut = new FileOutputStream("tab");
ObjectOutputStream out = new ObjectOutputStream(fileOut);
Hashtable hash = getHashtable();
out.writeObject(hash);
```

As you can see, this approach is quite straightforward. The single writeObject
on hash writes the entire contents of the hashtable, including all entries, all the
objects that the entries refer to, and so on, until the entire graph of interconnected

objects has been visited. A new copy of the hashtable could be reconstituted from the serialized bytes:

```
FileInputStream fileIn = new FileInputStream("tab");
ObjectInputStream in = new ObjectInputStream(fileIn);
Hashtable newHash = (Hashtable)in.readObject();
```

Serialization preserves the integrity of the graph itself. Suppose, for example, that in a serialized hashtable, an object was stored in the table under two different keys:

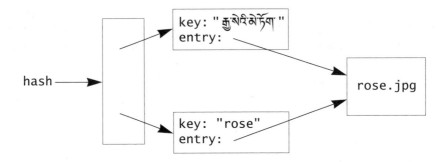

When the serialized hashtable is deserialized, the two analogous entries in the new copy of the hashtable will have references to a single copy of the rose.jpg object, not references to two separate copies of rose.jpg.[1]

12.24.1 Making Your Classes `Serializable`

When an `ObjectOutputStream` writes a serialized object, the object must implement the `Serializable` marker interface. This marker interface declares that the class is designed to have its objects serialized.

Being serializable can be quite simple. The default serialization is to serialize each field of the object that is neither `transient` nor `static`. Primitive types and strings are written in the same encoding used by `DataOutputStream`; objects are serialized by calling `writeObject`. With default serialization, all serialized fields that are object references must refer to serializable object types. Default serialization also requires either that your superclass have a no-arg constructor, or that it also be `Serializable` (in which case declaring your class to implement `Serializable` is redundant but harmless). For most classes this default serializa-

---

[1] The first key field is the word "rose" in Tibetan.

tion is sufficient, and the entire work necessary to make a class serializable is to mark it as such by declaring that it implements the `Serializable` interface:

```java
public class Name implements java.io.Serializable {
    private String name;
    private long id;
    private transient boolean hashSet = false;
    private transient int hash;

    private static long nextID = 0;

    public Name(String name) {
        this.name = name;
        synchronized (Name.class) {
            id = nextID++;
        }
    }

    public int hashCode() {
        if (!hashSet) {
            hash = name.hashCode();
            hashSet = true;
        }
        return hash;
    }

    // ... override equals, provide other useful methods
}
```

The class `Name` can be written to an `ObjectOutputStream` either directly using `writeObject`, or indirectly if it is referenced by an object written to such a stream. The `name` and `id` fields will be written to the stream; the fields `nextID`, `hashSet`, and `hash` will not be written, `nextID` because it is `static` and the others because they are `transient`. Because `hash` is a cached value that can be easily recalculated from `name`, there is no reason to consume the time and space it takes to write it to the stream.

Default deserialization reads the values written during serialization. Static fields in the class are left untouched; each transient field is set to the default value for its type. When a `Name` object is deserialized, the newly created `Name` object will have `name` and `id` set to the same values as the original object's, the static field `nextID` will remain untouched, and the transient fields `hashSet` and `hash` will have their default values (`false` and `0`). These defaults work for `Name`, because when `hashSet` is `false` the value of `hash` will be recalculated.

Occasionally you will have a class that is generally serializable but has specific instances that are not serializable. For example, a container might itself be serializable, but contain references to objects that are not serializable. Any attempt to serialize a non-serializable object will throw `NotSerializableException`.

12.24.2 Serialization and Deserialization Order

Each class is responsible for properly serializing its own state. Objects are serialized and deserialized down the type tree—from the highest-level class that is `Serializable` to the most specific class. This order is rarely important when you're serializing, but it can be important when you're deserializing. Let us consider the following type tree for a `URLInput` class:

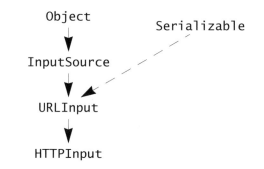

When deserializing a `URLInput` object, `ObjectInputStream` first allocates memory for the new object and then finds the first `Serializable` class in the object's type hierarchy. The stream invokes the no-arg constructor of that class's superclass (the object's last non-serializable class). In our example, the stream will allocate space for a `URLInput` object and will invoke the no-arg constructor of `InputSource`. If other state from the superclass must be preserved, `URLInput` is responsible for serializing that state and restoring it on deserialization. If your non-serializable superclass has state, you will almost certainly need to customize the first serializable class (see the next section). If the first serializable class extends `Object` (as the `Name` class does implicitly), customizing is easy because `Object` has no state to preserve or restore.

Once the first serializable class has finished with its part of its superclass's state, it will set its own state from the stream. Then `ObjectInputStream` will walk down the type tree, deserializing the state for each class. When it reaches the bottom of the type tree, the object is completely deserialized.

As the stream is deserialized, other serialized objects will be found that were referenced from the object currently being deserialized. These other objects are deserialized as they are encountered. Thus, if `URLInput` had a reference to a `Hashtable`, that hashtable and its contents would be deserialized before the `HTTPInput` part of the object was deserialized.

Before any of this can happen, the relevant classes must first be loaded. This requires finding a class of the same name as the one written and checking to see that it is the same class. We will discuss versioning issues shortly. Assuming it is the same class, the class must be loaded. If the class is not found or cannot be loaded for any reason, `readObject` will throw a `ClassNotFoundException`.

12.24.3 Customized Serialization and `Externalizable`

The default serialization methods work for many classes but not for all of them. For some classes deserialization may be improper or inefficient. The `Hashtable` class is an example of both problems. Default serialization would write all the data structures for the hashtable, including the hash codes of the entries. This serialization is both wrong and inefficient.

It is wrong because hash codes may be different for deserialized entries. This will be true, for example, of entries using the default `hashCode` implementation.

It is inefficient because a hashtable typically has a significant number of empty buckets. There is no point in wasting space on empty buckets. It would be more efficient to serialize the referenced keys and entries and rebuild a hashtable from them than to serialize the entire data structure of the hashtable.

For these reasons, `java.util.Hashtable` provides private `writeObject` and `readObject` methods. These methods are invoked by `ObjectOutputStream` and `ObjectInputStream`, respectively, when it is time to serialize or deserialize a `Hashtable` object. These methods are invoked only on classes that provide them, and the methods are responsible only for the class's own state. A class's `writeObject` and `readObject` methods, if provided, should not invoke the superclass's `readObject` or `writeObject` method. Object serialization differs in this way from `clone` and `finalize`.

Let us suppose, for example, that we wanted to improve the Name class so that it didn't have to check whether the cached hash code was valid each time. We could just set `hash` in the constructor, but then we would serialize this redundant data. We can prevent this overhead by providing Name with its own `writeObject` and `readObject` methods:

```
public class BetterName implements Serializable {
    private String name;
    private long id;
```

```
private transient int hash;

private static long nextID = 0;

public BetterName(String name) {
    this.name = name;
    synchronized (Name.class) {
        id = nextID++;
    }
    hash = name.hashCode();
}

private void writeObject(ObjectOutputStream out)
    throws IOException
{
    out.writeUTF(name);
    out.writeLong(id);
}

private void readObject(ObjectInputStream in)
    throws IOException
{
    name = in.readUTF();
    id = in.readLong();
    hash = name.hashCode();
}

public int hashCode() {
    return hash;
}

// ... override equals, provide other useful methods
}
```

Now writeObject will write only the relevant state. It declares that it can throw IOException because the write methods it invokes can do so, and, if one does throw an exception, the serialization must be halted. When readObject gets the values from the stream, it can then set hash properly. It, too, must declare that it throws IOException because the read methods it invokes can do so, and this should stop deserialization.

The `readObject` and `writeObject` methods for `BetterName` show that you can use the methods of `DataInput` and `DataOutput` to transmit arbitrary data on the stream. However, the actual implementations replicate the default serialization and then add the necessary setup for `hash`. The read and write invocations of these methods could have been replaced with a simple invocation of methods that perform default serialization and deserialization:

```
private void writeObject(ObjectOutputStream out)
    throws IOException
{
    out.defaultWriteObject();
}

private void readObject(ObjectInputStream in)
    throws IOException, ClassNotFoundException
{
    in.defaultReadObject();
    hash = name.hashCode();
}
```

A `writeObject` method can throw `NotSerializableException` if a particular object is not serializable. For example, objects of a class might be generally serializable, but a particular object might contain sensitive data. Such cases should be rare.

You will occasionally find that an object cannot be initialized properly until the graph of which it is a part has been completely deserialized. You can have the `ObjectInputStream` invoke a method of your own devising by calling the stream's `registerValidation` method with a reference to an object that implements the interface `ObjectInputValidation`. When deserialization of the top-level object at the head of the graph is complete, your object's `validateObject` method will be invoked to make any needed validation operation or check.

12.24.4 Object Versioning

Class implementations change over time. If a class's implementation changes between the time an object is serialized and the time it is deserialized, the `ObjectInputStream` can detect this change. When the object is written, the *serial version UID* (unique identifier), a 64-bit `long` value, is written with it. By default, this identifier is a secure hash of the full class name, superinterfaces, and members—the facts about the class that, if they change, signal a possible class incompatibility. Such a hash is essentially a fingerprint—it is nearly impossible for two different classes to have the same UID.

When an object is read from an `ObjectInputStream`, the serial version UID is also read. Then an attempt is made to load the class. If no class with the same name is found or if the loaded class's UID does not match the UID in the stream, `readObject` throws an exception. If the versions of all the classes in the object's type are found and all the UIDs match, the object can be deserialized.

This assumption is very conservative: any change in the class creates an incompatible version. Many class changes are less drastic than this. Adding a cache to a class can be made compatible with earlier versions of the serialized form, as can adding optional behavior or values. When you make a change to a class that can be compatible with the serialized forms of earlier versions of the class, you can explicitly declare the serial version UID for the class:

```
static final long serialVersionUID = 9199361937812857794L;
```

The value of `serialVersionUID` is provided by your development system. In many development systems, it is the output of a command called `serialver`. Other systems have different ways to provide you with this value, which is the serial version UID of the class before the first incompatible modification. (Nothing prevents you from using any number as this UID if you stamp it from the start, but it is usually a really bad idea. Your numbers will not be as carefully calculated to avoid conflict with other classes as the secure hash.)

Now when the `ObjectInputStream` finds your class and compares the UID with that of the older version in the file, the UIDs will be the same even though the implementation has changed. If you invoke `defaultReadObject`, only those fields that were present in the written version will be set. Other fields will be left in their default state. If `writeObject` in the earlier version of the class wrote values on the field without using `defaultWriteObject`, you must continue to read those values. If you try to read more values than were written, you will get an `EOFException`, which can indicate that you are deserializing an older form that wrote less information. If possible, you should design your classes to read a class version number instead of relying on an exception to signal the version of the original data.

When an object is written to an `ObjectOutputStream`, the `Class` object for that object is also written. Because `Class` objects are specific to each virtual machine, serializing the actual `Class` object would not be helpful. So `Class` objects on a stream are replaced by `ObjectStreamClass` objects that contain the information necessary to find an equivalent class when the object is deserialized. This information includes the class's full name and its serial version UID. Unless you create one yourself, you will never directly see an `ObjectStreamClass` object.

12.24.5 The `Externalizable` Interface

The `Externalizable` interface extends `Serializable`. A class that implements `Externalizable` takes complete control over its serialized state. An externalizable class assumes responsibility for all the data of its superclasses, any versioning issues, and so on. The `Externalizable` interface has two methods:

```
public interface Externalizable extends Serializable {
    void writeExternal(ObjectOutput out)
        throws IOException;
    void readExternal(ObjectInput in)
        throws IOException, ClassNotFoundException;
}
```

These methods are invoked when the object is serialized and deserialized, respectively. They are normal public methods, so the exact type of the object determines which implementation will be used. Subclasses of an externalizable class will often need to invoke their superclass's implementation before serializing or deserializing their own state.

12.25 The `File` Class

The `File` class provides several common manipulations that are useful with file names. It provides methods to separate pathnames into subcomponents and for querying the file system about the file a pathname refers to.

A `File` object actually represents a path, not necessarily an underlying file. For example, to find out whether a pathname represents an existing file, you create a `File` object with the pathname and then invoke `exists` on that object.

A path is separated into directory and file parts by a `char` stored in the static field `separatorChar` and available as a `String` in the static field `separator`. The last occurrence of this character in the path separates the pathname into directory and file components. (*Directory* is the term Java uses on all systems; some systems call such an entity a "folder" instead.)

File objects are created using one of three constructors:

public **File(String path)**

Creates a `File` object to manipulate the specified `path`. This method throws a `NullPointerException` if the `path` parameter is `null`.

public **File(String dirName, String name)**

Creates a `File` object for the file `name` in the directory named `dirName`. If `dirName` is `null`, only the `name` component is used. Otherwise, this is equivalent to using `File(dirName + File.separator + name)`.

```
public File(File fileDir, String name)
```
> Creates a File object given a directory File object fileDir and the file named name. Equivalent to using File(fileDir.getPath(), name).

Five "get" methods retrieve information about components of a File object's pathname. The following code invokes each of them:

```
File src = new File("ok", "FileMethods");
System.out.println("getName() = " + src.getName());
System.out.println("getPath() = " + src.getPath());
System.out.println("getAbsolutePath() = "
    + src.getAbsolutePath());
System.out.println("getCanonicalPath() = "
    + src.getCanonicalPath());
System.out.println("getParent() = " + src.getParent());
```

And here is the output:

```
getName() = FileMethods
getPath() = ok/FileMethods
getAbsolutePath() = /vob/java_prog/src/ok/FileMethods
getCanonicalPath() = /vob/java_prog/src/ok/FileMethods
getParent() = ok
```

The canonical path is defined by each system. Usually, it is a form of the absolute path with relative components (such as ".." to refer to the parent directory) renamed and references to the current directory removed. Unlike the other "get" methods, getCanonicalPath can throw IOException because resolving path components can require calls to the underlying file system that may fail.

Several boolean tests return information about the underlying file:

- ◆ exists returns true if the file exists in the file system.
- ◆ canRead returns true if a file exists and can be read.
- ◆ canWrite returns true if the file exists and can be written.
- ◆ isFile returns true if the file is not a directory or other special type of file.
- ◆ isDirectory returns true if the file is a directory.
- ◆ isAbsolute returns true if the path is an absolute pathname.

File objects have several other useful methods:

```
public long lastModified()
```
> Returns a "last modified" value for the file. The value is useful only when compared to other values returned by lastModified on the same or other

files. If two values returned by this method are compared, the smaller value represents the older time. The value has only this relative meaning; you cannot use it as an actual modification time of the file.

`public long length()`
Returns the file length in bytes.

`public boolean mkdir()`
Creates a directory, returning `true` on success.

`public boolean mkdirs()`
Creates all directories in this path, returning `true` if all were created. This is a way to ensure that a particular directory is created, even if it means creating other directories that don't currently exist above it in the directory hierarchy.

`public boolean renameTo(File new_name)`
Renames a file, returning `true` if the rename succeeded.

`public boolean delete()`
Deletes the file or directory named in this `File` object, returning `true` if the deletion succeeded. Directories must be empty before they are removed.

`public String[] list()`
Lists the files in this directory. If used on something that isn't a directory, it returns `null`. Otherwise, it returns an array of file names. This list includes all files in the directory except the equivalent of "`.`" and "`..`" (the current and parent directory, respectively).

`public String[] list(FilenameFilter filter)`
Uses `filter` to selectively list files in this directory (see `FilenameFilter` described next).

The overridden method `File.equals` deserves mention. Two `File` objects are considered equal if they have the same path, not if they refer to the same underlying file system object. You cannot use `File.equals` to test whether two `File` objects denote the same file.

Files are created using `FileOutputStream` objects or `RandomAccessFile` objects, not using `File` objects.

Finally, the character `File.pathSeparatorChar` and its companion string `File.pathSeparator` represent the character that separates file or directory names in a search path. For example, UNIX separates components in the program search path using a colon, as in "`.:/bin:/usr/bin`", so `pathSeparatorChar` is a colon on UNIX systems.

The path of the file is a protected `String` field named `path`. Classes extending `File` can access or modify it directly.

Exercise 12.9: Write a method that, given one or more pathnames, will print all the information available about the file it represents (if any).

12.25.1 `FilenameFilter`

The `FilenameFilter` interface provides objects that filter unwanted files from a list. It supports a single method:

boolean **accept(File dir, String name)**
> Returns `true` if the file named `name` in the directory `dir` should be part of the filtered output.

Here is an example that uses a `FilenameFilter` object to list only directories:

```
import java.io.*;

class DirFilter implements FilenameFilter {
    public boolean accept(File dir, String name) {
        return new File(dir, name).isDirectory();
    }

    public static void main(String[] args) {
        File dir = new File(args[0]);
        String[] files = dir.list(new DirFilter());
        System.out.println(files.length + " dir(s):");
        for (int i = 0; i < files.length; i++)
            System.out.println("\t" + files[i]);
    }
}
```

First we create a `File` object to represent a directory specified on the command line. Then we create a `DirFilter` object and pass it to `list`. For each name in the directory, `list` invokes the `accept` method on the filtering object and includes the name in the list if the filtering object returns `true`. For our `accept` method, `true` means that the named file is a directory.

Exercise 12.10: Using `FilenameFilter`, write a program that takes a directory and a suffix as parameters and prints all the files that have that suffix.

12.26 The **IOException** Classes

Every I/O-specific error detected by classes in `java.io` is signaled by a subclass of `IOException`. Most I/O classes are designed to be general, so most of the exceptions are not detailed specifically. For example, `InputStream` methods that throw `IOException` cannot detail which particular exceptions might be thrown, because any particular input stream class might throw a subclass of `IOException` for particular error conditions relevant to that stream. And the filter input and output streams pass through exceptions only from their downstream objects, which can also be of other stream types.

The specific subclasses of `IOException` used in the `java.io` package are:

CharConversionException extends `IOException`
> A character conversion problem occurred during one of the character stream operations that must convert local character codes to Unicode or vice versa.

EOFException extends `IOException`
> Thrown by methods in the `Data` stream interfaces when you reach the end of input, expectedly or unexpectedly.

FileNotFoundException extends `IOException`
> Thrown by the `File` streams' constructors when you provide a file name that cannot be found.

InterruptedIOException extends `IOException`
> Thrown by any stream when a thread `interrupt` occurs during an I/O operation (see "Ending Thread Execution" on page 195). In effect, each unrecoverable `InterruptedException` is turned into an `InterruptedIOException`.

InvalidClassException extends `ObjectStreamException`
> Thrown when something is wrong with the class during serialization. On serialization, the problem can be that an unserializable object was found, the class defines only one of `readObject` or `writeObject` (both or neither are the only valid choices), the class is not public, or the first non-serializable superclass does not have an accessible no-arg constructor. During deserialization these problems may occur, or a serial version UID mismatch was found.

InvalidObjectException extends `ObjectStreamException`
> Thrown by a `validateObject` method if it cannot make the object valid, thus aborting the deserialization.

NotActiveException extends `ObjectStreamException`
> Thrown if a serialization method such as `defaultReadObject` is invoked when serialization is not under way on the stream.

NotSerializableException extends ObjectStreamException
Thrown either by the runtime or explicitly by a class when a class cannot be serialized.

ObjectStreamException extends IOException
Several subclasses of this type signal serialization problems.

OptionalDataException extends ObjectStreamException
The optional data in the stream is corrupt or was not read by the reading method.

StreamCorruptedException extends ObjectStreamException
Thrown when the internal stream control information is missing or invalid.

SyncFailedException extends IOException
Thrown by FileDescriptor.sync when the data cannot be guaranteed to have been written to the underlying media.

UnsupportedEncodingException extends IOException
Thrown when an unknown character encoding is specified to a reader or writer.

UTFDataFormatException extends IOException
Thrown by DataInputStream.readUTF when the string it is reading has malformed UTF syntax.

WriteAbortedException extends ObjectStreamException
Thrown when an exception interrupts the writing of a serialization.

In addition to these specific exceptions, other exceptional conditions in java.io are signaled with an IOException containing a string that describes the specific error encountered, such as using a disconnected Pipe stream object or trying to push back more than one character onto a PushbackInputStream.

> *Nothing has really happened until it has been recorded.*
> —Virginia Woolf

CHAPTER 13

Standard Utilities

Computers are useless—they can only give you answers.
—Pablo Picasso

THE Java environment provides several standard utility interfaces and classes in the `java.util` package. We've already used a few of them in earlier chapters, such as the `Date` and `Hashtable` classes. Several other useful utilities are available as interfaces and classes.

COLLECTIONS

- `BitSet`—A dynamically sized bit vector.

- `Enumeration`—An interface that returns objects that enumerate a set of values, such as elements contained in a particular hashtable.

- `Vector`—A dynamically sized array of `Object` references.

- `Stack`—An extension of `Vector` that adds methods for a basic last-in first-out stack.

- `Dictionary`—An abstract class for algorithms that map keys to values.

- `Hashtable`—An implementation of `Dictionary` that uses hash codes to map keys to values.

- `Properties`—An extension of `Hashtable` that maps string keys to string values.

DESIGN PATTERNS

- `Observer/Observable`—This interface/class pair enables an object to be `Observable` by having one or more `Observer` objects that are notified when something interesting happens in the `Observable` object.

LOCALIZATION

- ◆ Locale—A representation of cultural nexus, used to localize behavior to expected cultural norms. Given a locale, a class can customize its behavior appropriately for the user (for example, how dates are printed).

- ◆ ResourceBundle—An abstract class that helps you look up resources based on locale. Several useful subclasses are provided.

- ◆ Calendar—An abstract class for representing system clock time as human dates in various locales.

- ◆ GregorianCalendar—A subclass of Calendar that represents dates as used in most of the world.

- ◆ TimeZone—An abstract class for representing a time zone offset.

- ◆ SimpleTimeZone—A TimeZone for use with a GregorianCalendar.

MISCELLANEOUS

- ◆ Date—A class that stores time to millisecond granularity.

- ◆ Random—A class to generate sequences of pseudorandom numbers.

- ◆ StringTokenizer—A class that splits a string into tokens based on delimiters (by default, white space).

The localization types and Date are covered in Chapter 16; all the other utility types are covered in this chapter.

13.1 BitSet

The BitSet class provides a way to create a bit vector that grows dynamically. In effect, a BitSet is a vector of $2^{32}-1$ true and false bits, all of them initially false. The storage size is large enough only to hold the highest bit index ever set to true or cleared to false—any bits beyond that are assumed to be false.

A BitSet object can be created with an initial size or by using the no-arg constructor to get the default size.

```
public void set(int bit)
```
Sets the bit at position bit to true.

```
public void clear(int bit)
```
Clears the bit at position bit to false.

```
public boolean get(int bit)
```
Returns the value of the bit at position bit.

```
public void and(BitSet other)
```
Logically ANDs this bit set with other and changes the value of this set to the result.

```
public void or(BitSet other)
```
Logically ORs this bit set with other and changes the value of this set to the result.

```
public void xor(BitSet other)
```
Logically XORs this bit set with other and changes the value of this set to the result.

```
public int size()
```
Returns the highest bit position that can be set or cleared without growing the set.

```
public int hashCode()
```
Returns a reasonable hash code for this set based on the values of its bits. Be careful not to change the values of the bits while the BitSet is in the hashtable, or the set will be lost.

```
public boolean equals(Object other)
```
Returns true if all the bits in other are the same as those in this set.

Here is a class that uses a BitSet to mark which characters occur in a string. It can be printed to show the characters that it found:

```
public class WhichChars {
    private BitSet used = new BitSet();

    public WhichChars(String str) {
        for (int i = 0; i < str.length(); i++)
            used.set(str.charAt(i));    // set bit for char
    }

    public String toString() {
        String desc = "[";
        int size = used.size();
        for (int i = 0; i < size; i++) {
            if (used.get(i))
                desc += (char)i;
        }
        return desc + "]";
    }
}
```

13.2 Enumeration

Most collection classes use the Enumeration interface as a means to iterate through the values in the collection. It is also used by other classes in the Java libraries and in user code to return an enumeration. Each such class usually creates a private enumeration class to implement the Enumeration interface and has one or more methods to return an Enumeration object. The Enumeration interface declares two methods:

boolean **hasMoreElements()**

> Returns true if the enumeration contains more elements. This method can be invoked more than once between successive calls to nextElement().

Object **nextElement()** throws NoSuchElementException

> Returns the next element of the enumeration. Invocations of this method enumerate successive elements. Throws NoSuchElementException if no more elements exist.

Here is a typical loop using Enumeration to step through the elements in a collection object, in this case with the elements of a Hashtable:

```
Enumeration e = table.elements();
while (e.hasMoreElements())
    doSomethingWith(e.nextElement());
```

The contract for Enumeration does not include a *snapshot* guarantee. In other words, if the contents of the collection are changed while the enumeration is in use, it can affect the values returned by the methods. For example, if the implementation of nextElement uses the contents of the original collection for its list, it is dangerous to remove elements from the list as you enumerate through it. A snapshot would return the elements as they were when the Enumeration object was created, immune from future changes. You can rely on having a snapshot of the contents only if the method that returns the Enumeration object explicitly makes a snapshot guarantee.

13.3 Implementing an Enumeration Interface

When you write your own collections, you may need to implement your own Enumeration interface. The WhichChars class is, in effect, a collection for the set of characters in the initial string. Here is a class that implements Enumeration to return the characters represented by the BitSet in WhichChars:

```
public class WhichChars {
    private BitSet used = new BitSet();

    private class Enum implements Enumeration {
        private int pos = 0;
        private int setSize = used.size();

        public boolean hasMoreElements() {
            while (pos < setSize && !used.get(pos))
                pos++;
            return (pos < setSize);
        }

        public Object nextElement()
            throws NoSuchElementException
        {
            if (hasMoreElements())
                return new Character((char)pos++);
            else
                throw new NoSuchElementException();
        }
    }

    public Enumeration characters() {
        return new Enum();
    }
    // ...
}
```

The inner Enum class iterates through the bits in the BitSet, returning Character objects to hold the character values represented by the set bits in the BitSet object. The hasMoreElements method advances the current position to the next element to be returned. The method is carefully written so that it can be invoked several times for each invocation of nextElement. We also add the characters method to WhichChars that returns an Enum object made with this as the implicit enclosing object. The setSize field is an optimization to all except one invocation of used.size.

Notice that characters is declared to return an Enumeration object, not an Enum object. Making Enum a private class allows us to hide the enumeration implementation. Unless you need to return an enumeration with new public functionality, you should hide the enumeration object's type so that you retain the flexibility to change its implementation. An inner class—either named as shown here or anonymous as in the `walkThrough` example on page 74—is the most common way to implement `Enumeration`, because enumeration is almost always an implementation detail.

Exercise 13.1: Rewrite the example program `Concat` on page 247 so that it uses an implementation of `Enumeration` that has only one `FileInputStream` object open at a time.

13.4 Vector

The `Vector` class provides a resizable array of `Object` references. Items can be added to the beginning, middle, or end of a vector, and any element in the vector can be accessed with an array index. Java arrays are fixed in size, so a `Vector` object is a useful replacement for an array when you do not know in advance the number of objects you will need to store or when the maximum is large and rarely reached.

There are three kinds of methods in `Vector`:

◆ Methods to modify the vector

◆ Methods to get values from the vector

◆ Methods that manage how the vector grows when it needs more capacity

The no-arg constructor creates a `Vector` object that uses default capacity management. The other constructors are covered along with the capacity management methods.

Many methods change the contents of a vector. All except `setElementAt` dynamically change the size of the vector, if needed, to accommodate the request.

`public final synchronized void` **`addElement(Object obj)`**
  Adds obj as the last element of the vector.

`public final synchronized void` **`insertElementAt(Object obj, int index)`**
  Inserts obj as an element at the position `index`. Elements in the vector from `index` on are shifted to make room.

`public final synchronized void` **`setElementAt(Object obj, int index)`**
  Sets the element at `index` to be the obj. The existing element at `index` is dropped from the vector. This throws `IndexOutOfBoundsException` if given an index larger than the current size of the vector. Use `setSize` to ensure that the index is valid before use.

`public final synchronized void` **`removeElementAt(int index)`**
> Deletes the element at `index`. Elements in the vector after `index` are moved down, and the size of the vector is reduced by one.

`public final synchronized boolean` **`removeElement(Object obj)`**
> Equivalent to using `indexOf(obj)` and, if the object is found, invoking `removeElementAt` with the index. If the object is not an element, `removeElement` returns `false` (`indexOf` is described later).

`public final synchronized void` **`removeAllElements()`**
> Removes all elements from the vector. The vector becomes empty.

Here is a `Polygon` class that stores a list of `Point` objects that are the polygon's vertices:

```
import java.util.Vector;

public class Polygon {
    private Vector vertices = new Vector();

    public void add(Point p) {
        vertices.addElement(p);
    }

    public void remove(Point p) {
        vertices.removeElement(p);
    }

    public int numVertices() {
        return vertices.size();
    }

    // ... other methods ...
}
```

There are several ways to examine the contents of a vector. These methods throw `IndexOutOfBoundsException` if given an invalid index. All methods that search the vector for an element use `Object.equals` to compare the object being searched for to the elements of the `Vector`.

`public final synchronized Object` **`elementAt(int index)`**
> Returns the element at `index`.

`public final boolean` **`contains(Object obj)`**
> Returns `true` if `obj` is in the vector.

`public final synchronized int` **`indexOf(Object obj, int index)`**
Searches for the first occurrence of `obj`, starting with the `index`th position, and returns an index to it or `-1` if it is not found.

`public final int` **`indexOf(Object obj)`**
Equivalent to `indexOf(obj, 0)`.

`public final synchronized int` **`lastIndexOf(Object obj, int index)`**
Searches backward for `obj`, starting from the `index`th position, and returns an index to it, or `-1` if it was not found.

`public final int` **`lastIndexOf(Object elem)`**
Equivalent to `lastIndexOf(obj, size() - 1)`.

`public final synchronized void` **`copyInto(Object[] anArray)`**
Copies the elements of this vector into the specified array. This method can also be used to get a snapshot of the contents of the vector.

`public final synchronized Enumeration` **`elements()`**
Returns an `Enumeration` for the current list of elements. Use the methods of `Enumeration` on the returned object to fetch elements sequentially. The enumerator is not a snapshot. Use `copyInto` if a snapshot is needed.

`public final synchronized Object` **`firstElement()`**
Returns the first element of the vector. Throws `NoSuchElementException` if the vector is empty.

`public final synchronized Object` **`lastElement()`**
Returns the last element of the vector. Throws `NoSuchElementException` if the vector is empty.

`public synchronized Object` **`clone()`**
Creates a clone of the vector. The keys and elements are not cloned.

The size of the vector is the number of elements that are used in the vector. You can change the size by adding or removing elements or by using `setSize` or `trimToSize`:

`public final int` **`size()`**
Returns the number of elements currently in the vector. Note that this is not the same as the vector's capacity.

`public final boolean` **`isEmpty()`**
Returns `true` if the vector contains no elements.

`public final synchronized void` **`trimToSize()`**
Trims the vector's capacity to the current size. Use this method to minimize the storage of a vector when its size is stable. Subsequent addition to the vector will make it grow again.

`public final synchronized void `**`setSize(int newSize)`**
> Sets the size of the vector to `newSize`. If the size shrinks, elements beyond the end are lost; if the size increases, the new elements are set to `null`.

Correctly managing the capacity of a vector affects its efficiency significantly. If the capacity increment is small and many elements are added, the vector will spend too much time repeatedly creating a larger buffer to hold new objects and copying them into the new buffer. A better way is to create the vector with a capacity at or near the usual size you will need. If you know how many values you will add at a given point, use `ensureCapacity` to grow the vector at most once. The capacity management parameters are set when the `Vector` is constructed; use any of these constructors to create a `Vector` object:

`public `**`Vector(int initialCapacity, int capacityIncrement)`**
> Constructs an empty vector with the specified initial storage capacity and capacity increment. A capacity increment of 0 means to double each time the buffer needs to grow; otherwise, `capacityIncrement` elements will be added to the buffer.

`public `**`Vector(int initialCapacity)`**
> Equivalent to `Vector(initialCapacity, 0)`.

`public `**`Vector()`**
> Constructs an empty vector with an initial capacity of ten and a capacity increment of 0.

`public final synchronized void `**`ensureCapacity(int minCapacity)`**
> Ensures that the vector has at least the specified capacity, increasing the capacity if necessary.

`public final int `**`capacity()`**
> Returns the current capacity of the vector. This is the number of elements the vector can hold without creating new storage to hold elements. You should almost never need to invoke this method.

Here is a method for `Polygon` that includes another polygon's points:

```
public void merge(Polygon other) {
    int otherSize = other.vertices.size();

    vertices.ensureCapacity(vertices.size() + otherSize);
    for (int i = 0; i < otherSize; i++)
        vertices.addElement(other.vertices.elementAt(i));
}
```

This example uses `ensureCapacity` to ensure that the vector will grow at most once instead of multiple times as new points are added.

The implementation of `Vector.toString` provides a string that fully describes the vector, including the result of invoking `toString` on each of the contained elements.

In addition to these public methods, protected fields are available to classes that subclass the `Vector` class. Be careful what you do (if anything) with these fields, because, for example, methods in `Vector` rely on `elementCount` being less than or equal to the length of the `elementData` array.

protected Object **elementData[]**
>   The buffer where elements are stored.

protected int **elementCount**
>   The number of elements currently used in the buffer.

protected int **capacityIncrement**
>   The number of elements to add to the capacity when `elementData` runs out of space. If it is 0, the size of the buffer is doubled every time it needs to grow.

Exercise 13.2: Write a program that opens a file and reads its lines one at a time, storing each line in a `Vector` object sorted using `String.compareTo`. The line-reading class you created for Exercise 12.2 should prove helpful.

13.5 Stack

The `Stack` class extends `Vector` to add methods for a simple last-in first-out stack of `Object`. Use push to push an object onto the stack and use pop to remove the top element from the stack. The `peek` method returns the top item on the stack without removing it. The `empty` method returns `true` if the stack is empty. Trying to pop or peek in an empty `Stack` object will throw `EmptyStackException`.

You can use search to find an object's distance from the top of the stack, with 1 being the top of the stack. If the object isn't found, -1 is returned. The search method uses `Object.equals` to test whether an object in the stack is the same as the one it is searching for.

The following example uses `Stack` to keep track of the person who currently has borrowed something, such as a toy. The original owner is the first entry in the stack. When someone borrows the toy, the borrower's name is pushed on the stack. If the borrower lends it to someone else, that person's name is pushed on the stack. When the toy is returned, the borrower's name is popped off the stack. The last name is never popped off the stack because that would mean losing track of who owns the toy.

```
import java.util.Stack;

public class Borrow {
    private String itemName;
    private Stack hasIt = new Stack();

    public Borrow(String name, String owner) {
        itemName = name;
        hasIt.push(owner);        // owner's name goes first
    }

    public void borrow(String borrower) {
        hasIt.push(borrower);
    }

    public String getCurrentHolder() {
        return (String)hasIt.peek();
    }

    public String returnIt() {
        String ret = (String)hasIt.pop();
        if (hasIt.empty())        // acidentally popped owner
            hasIt.push(ret);      // put it back
        return ret;
    }
}
```

Exercise 13.3: Add a method that uses search to find out how many borrowers there are for a borrowed item.

13.6 Dictionary

The Dictionary abstract class is essentially an interface.[1] It defines a set of abstract methods to store an *element* indexed by a particular *key* and retrieve the element using that key. This is the basic interface for Hashtable, but Dictionary is defined as a separate class so that other implementations can use different algorithms to map keys to elements. The Dictionary returns null to indicate events such as the inability to find a particular entry, so neither the key

---

[1] Dictionary is not an interface because it predates the addition of interfaces to Java.

nor its element can be null. If you provide a null key or element argument, you will get a NullPointerException. If you need a special marker element, you must use a value other than null.

The Dictionary methods are:

public abstract Object **put(Object key, Object element)**
Puts element into the dictionary under key. Returns the old element stored under key or null if there wasn't one.

public abstract Object **get(Object key)**
Returns the object associated with the specified key in the dictionary or null if the key is not defined in the dictionary.

public abstract Object **remove(Object key)**
Removes the element corresponding to key, returning the element stored for key or null if key was not in the dictionary.

public abstract int **size()**
Returns the number of elements defined in the dictionary.

public abstract boolean **isEmpty()**
Returns true if the dictionary contains no elements.

public abstract Enumeration **keys()**
Returns an enumeration of the keys in the dictionary.

public abstract Enumeration **elements()**
Returns an enumeration of the elements in the dictionary.

The enumerations returned by keys and elements are not guaranteed to be snapshots. If you write a class that implements Dictionary, you can choose to add a snapshot guarantee to the contract of your implementation of these methods.

13.7 Hashtable

The *hashtable* is a common mechanism for storing key/element pairs. It has the virtues of generality and simplicity, and it is very efficient, given reasonable hash code generation. The Hashtable class extends the abstract class Dictionary. It has a capacity and tools to decide when to grow the table. Growing a hashtable involves re-hashing each element in the table to its new position in the larger table, so it is important to size a hashtable only once.

The other efficiency factor of a hashtable is generation of hash codes from the keys. Hash codes for keys that are equivalent according to equals should always be the same. Hash codes for keys that are different should collide as seldom as possible. Their values should be distributed evenly over the range of possible hash codes, which for Hashtable is the full range of int. If different keys hash frequently to the same code, that part of the hashtable will become crowded and performance will suffer.

Hashtable uses the hash code returned by the hashCode method on the object used as the key. The default implementation of hashCode distributes its values as evenly as possible over all objects because no two objects are considered equivalent by default. String, BitSet, and most other objects that override equals also override hashCode. This is important, because Hashtable uses the hash code to find a set of keys that might match and then invokes equals on each object until it finds one equal to the key it is looking for. If a class's hashCode returns different values for objects that are equal, that type will behave erratically when used as Hashtable keys.

You saw an example of Hashtable in the AttributedImpl class in "Implementing Interfaces" on page 97, where a Hashtable object was used to store attributes on an object. In that example, keys were the String objects that were the attributes' names, and the Attr object itself was the attribute value.

In addition to implementing methods from Dictionary (get, put, remove, size, isEmpty, keys, and elements), Hashtable supports these methods:

public synchronized boolean **containsKey(Object key)**
>   Returns true if the hashtable contains an element under key.

public synchronized boolean **contains(Object element)**
>   Returns true if the specified element is an element of the hashtable. This operation is more expensive than the containsKey method because a hashtable is designed to be efficient at looking up keys, not elements.

public synchronized void **clear()**
>   Empties the hashtable.

public synchronized Object **clone()**
>   Creates a clone of the hashtable. The keys and elements themselves are not cloned.

A Hashtable object automatically grows when it gets too full. It is "too full" when it exceeds the table's *load factor*, which is the ratio of the number of elements in the table to the table's current capacity. When the table grows, it chooses a new capacity roughly double the current one. A capacity that is a prime number is critical to good performance, so the Hashtable object may change a specified capacity to a nearby prime number. You can set both the initial capacity and the load factor using Hashtable constructors:

public **Hashtable()**
>   Constructs a new, empty hashtable with a default initial capacity and load factor of 0.75.

public **Hashtable(int initialCapacity)**

> Constructs a new, empty hashtable with the specified initialCapacity and a default load factor of 0.75.

public **Hashtable(int initialCapacity, float loadFactor)**

> Constructs a new, empty hashtable with the specified initial capacity and load factor. The loadFactor is a number between 0.0 and 1.0 that defines the threshold for rehashing the hashtable into a bigger one. If the number of entries in the hashtable increases to more than the current capacity times the load factor, the hashtable will resize itself.

The default size is picked by the implementation to be "reasonable." After the Hashtable is constructed, there is no way to change the load factor or to set a new capacity explicitly.

When the Hashtable is resized, the work is done by the method rehash. The rehash method is protected so that extended classes can invoke it when they decide, based on their own requirements, that the time has come for the table to grow. There is no way to set the new size—it is always calculated by rehash.

The implementation of Hashtable.toString provides a string that fully describes the contents of the table, including the result of invoking toString on each of the contained keys and elements.

Exercise 13.4: The WhichChars class shown on page 275 has a problem marking characters near the top of the Unicode range because the high character values will leave many unused bits in the lower ranges. Use a Hashtable to solve this problem by storing Character objects for each character seen. Remember to write an enumerator class.

Exercise 13.5: Now use a Hashtable to store a BitSet object for each different top byte (high 8 bits) encountered in the input string, with each BitSet storing the low bytes that have been seen with the particular high byte. Remember to write an enumerator class.

Exercise 13.6: Write a program that uses a StreamTokenizer object to break an input file into words and counts the number of times each word occurs in the file, printing the result.

13.8 Properties

Another common key/element pair is a *property list,* consisting of string names and associated string elements. This kind of dictionary often has a backing set of default elements for properties not specified in the table. The `Properties` class extends `Hashtable`. Standard `Hashtable` methods are used for almost all manipulation of a property list, but to get properties, use one of the two `getProperty` methods:

`public String getProperty(String key)`
> Gets the property element for key. If the key is not found in this property list, the default list (if any) is searched. This method returns `null` if the property is not found.

`public String getProperty(String key, String defaultElement)`
> Gets the property element for key. If the key is not found in this property list, the default list (if any) is searched. If there is no element for key in either this table or its defaults, the string in `defaultElement` is returned.

The `Properties` class has two constructors: a no-arg constructor and one that takes another `Properties` object as a default property list. If a property lookup fails, the default `Properties` object is queried. The default properties object can have its *own* default property list, and so on. The chain of property lists and default lists can be arbitrarily deep.

`public Properties()`
> Creates an empty property list.

`public Properties(Properties defaults)`
> Creates an empty property list with the specified default `Properties` object for looking up properties that are not specified in this list.

If a property list contains only `String` keys and elements, you can save and restore it from files or other I/O streams using the following methods:

`private void save(OutputStream out, String header)`
> Saves the contents of the property list to an `OutputStream`. The header string is written to the output stream as a single-line comment. Do not use a multiline header string, or else the saved property list will not be loadable. Only properties in this list are saved to the file; those in the default property list are not saved.

`public synchronized void load(InputStream in) throws IOException`
> Loads a property list from an `InputStream`. The property list is presumed to have been created previously by a `save` method invocation. This method loads values only into this property list; it does not set values in the default property list.

A snapshot `Enumeration` of the keys in a property list is obtained by invoking the `propertyNames` method:

`public Enumeration propertyNames()`
> Enumerates the keys. This method provides a snapshot.

```
public void list(PrintWriter out)
```
 Lists properties on the given `PrintWriter`. Useful for debugging.

```
public void list(PrintStream out)
```
 Lists properties on the given `PrintStream`. Also useful for debugging, even though `PrintStream` is deprecated.

 The default property list cannot be changed after the object is created. To change the default list, you can subclass the `Properties` class and modify the protected field called `defaults` that contains the default properties list.

13.9 Observer/Observable

The `Observer/Observable` types provide a protocol in which an arbitrary number of `Observer` objects watch for changes and events in any number of `Observable` objects. An `Observable` object subclasses the `Observable` class, which provides methods to maintain a list of `Observer` objects that want to know about changes in the `Observable` object. All objects in the "interested" list must implement the `Observer` interface. When an `Observable` object experiences a noteworthy change or an event that `Observer` objects care about, the `Observable` object invokes its `notifyObservers` method, which invokes each `Observer` object's `update` method:

```
protected synchronized void setChanged()
```
 Marks this object as having been changed since the last time `update` was invoked.

```
public abstract void update(Observable obj, Object arg)
```
 This method is invoked when the `Observable` object `obj` has a change or an event to report. The `arg` parameter is a way to pass an arbitrary object to describe the change or event to the `Observer`.

 The `Observer/Observable` mechanism is designed to be general. Each `Observable` class is left to define the circumstances under which an `Observer` object's `update` method will be invoked.

 The `Observable` class implements methods to maintain the list of `Observer` objects, methods to maintain an "object changed" flag, and methods to invoke the `update` method on any `Observer`. The following `Observable` methods maintain the list of `Observer` objects:

```
public synchronized void addObserver(Observer o)
```
 Adds an `Observer` to the observer list.

```
public synchronized void deleteObserver(Observer o)
```
 Deletes an `Observer` from the observer list.

`public synchronized void` **`deleteObservers()`**
> Deletes all `Observer` objects from the observer list.

`public synchronized int` **`countObservers()`**
> Returns the number of observers in the observer list.

The following methods notify `Observer` objects of changes:

`public synchronized void` **`notifyObservers(Object arg)`**
> Notifies all `Observer` objects in the list that something has happened, and then clears the "object changed" flag. For each observer in the list, its `update` method is invoked with this `Observable` object as the first argument and `arg` as the second.

`public void` **`notifyObservers()`**
> Equivalent to `notifyObservers(null)`.

The following example illustrates how `Observer/Observable` might be used to monitor users of a system. First, we define a `Users` class that is an `Observable` type:

```java
import java.util.*;

public class Users extends Observable {
    private Hashtable loggedIn = new Hashtable();

    public void login(String name, String password)
        throws BadUserException
    {
        // this method throws BadUserException
        if (!passwordValid(name, password))
            throw new BadUserException(name);

        UserState state = new UserState(name);
        loggedIn.put(name, state);
        setChanged();
        notifyObservers(state);
    }

    public void logout(UserState state) {
        loggedIn.remove(state.name());
        setChanged();
        notifyObservers(state);
    }
```

```
    // ...
}
```

A Users object stores a list of users who are logged in and maintains UserState objects for each login. When someone logs in or out, all Observer objects will be passed that user's UserState object. The notifyObservers method sends messages only if the state changes, so we must also invoke setChanged on Users; otherwise notifyObservers would do nothing. In addition to setChanged, there are two other methods that operate on the "changed" flag: clearChanged marks the Observable object as unchanged, and hasChanged returns the boolean flag.

Here is how an Observer that maintains a constant display of logged-in users might implement update to watch a Users object:

```java
import java.util.*;

public class Eye implements Observer {
    Users watching;

    public Eye(Users users) {
        watching = users;
        watching.addObserver(this);
    }

    public void update(Observable users, Object whichState)
    {
        if (users != watching)
            throw new IllegalArgumentException();

        UserState state = (UserState)whichState;
        if (watching.loggedIn(state))    // user logged in
            addUser(state);              // add to my list
        else
            removeUser(state);           // remove from list
    }
}
```

Each Eye object watches a particular Users object. When a user logs in or out, Eye is notified because it invoked the Users object's addObserver method with itself as the interested object. When update is invoked, it checks the correctness of its parameters and then modifies its display depending on whether the user in question has logged in or out.

The check for what happened with the UserState object is simple here. You could avoid it by passing an object describing what happened and to whom instead of passing the UserState object itself. Such a design makes it easier to add new actions without breaking existing code.

The Observer/Observable mechanism is a looser, more flexible analog to the wait/notify mechanism for threads described in "wait, notifyAll, and notify" on page 188. The thread mechanism ensures that synchronized access protects you from undesired concurrency. The observation mechanism enables any relationship to be built between two participants, whatever the threading model. Both patterns have producers of information (Observable and the invoker of notify) and consumers of that information (Observer and the invoker of wait), but each one fills a different need. Use wait/notify when you design a thread-based mechanism, and use Observer/Observable when you need something more general.

Exercise 13.7: Provide an implementation of the Attributed interface that uses Observer/Observable to notify observers of changes.

13.10 Random

The Random class creates objects that manage independent sequences of pseudo-random numbers. If you don't care what the sequence is and want it as a sequence of double values, the method java.lang.Math.random creates a single Random object the first time it is invoked and returns pseudorandom numbers from that object. You can gain more control over the sequence (for example, the ability to set the seed) by creating a Random object and getting values from it.

public **Random()**
> Creates a new random number generator. Its seed will be initialized to a value based on the current time.

public **Random(long seed)**
> Creates a new random number generator using the specified seed. Two Random objects created with the same initial seed will return the same sequence of pseudorandom numbers.

public synchronized void **setSeed(long seed)**
> Sets the seed of the random number generator to seed. This method can be invoked at any time and resets the sequence to start from the given seed.

public int **nextInt()**
> Returns a pseudorandom uniformly distributed int value between the two values Integer.MIN_VALUE and Integer.MAX_VALUE, inclusive.

```
public long nextLong()
```
Returns a pseudorandom uniformly distributed long value between Long.MIN_VALUE and Long.MAX_VALUE, inclusive.

```
public void nextBytes(byte[] buf)
```
Fills the array buf with random bytes.

```
public float nextFloat()
```
Returns a pseudorandom uniformly distributed float value between 0.0f (inclusive) and 1.0f (exclusive).

```
public double nextDouble()
```
Returns a pseudorandom uniformly distributed double value between 0.0 (inclusive) and 1.0 (exclusive).

```
public synchronized double nextGaussian()
```
Returns a pseudorandom Gaussian-distributed double value with mean of 0.0 and standard deviation of 1.0.

All these methods are written using the protected synchronized method next, which returns an int of randomized bits. You can create your own random number generator by overriding this method to provide a different generating algorithm.

Exercise 13.8: Given a certain number of six-sided dice, you can calculate the theoretical probability of each possible total. For example, with two six-sided dice, the probability of a total of seven is one in six. Write a program that matches the theoretical distribution of sums for a particular number of six-sided dice with the actual results over a large number of "rolls" using Random to generate numbers between one and six. Does it matter which of the number-generating methods you use?

Exercise 13.9: Write a program that tests nextGaussian, displaying the results of a large number of runs as a graph (a bar chart of * characters will do).

13.11 StringTokenizer

The StringTokenizer class breaks a string into parts, using delimiters. A sequence of tokens broken out of a string is, in effect, an ordered enumeration of those tokens, so StringTokenizer implements the Enumeration interface (see page 276). You can pass StringTokenizer objects with methods to handle general enumeration or use Enumeration methods to iterate. StringTokenizer provides methods that are more specifically typed, which you can use if you know you are working on a StringTokenizer object. The StringTokenizer enumeration is effectively a snapshot because String objects are read-only. For example, the following loop breaks a string into tokens separated by spaces and commas:

```
String str = "Gone, and forgotten";
StringTokenizer tokens = new StringTokenizer(str, " ,");
while (tokens.hasMoreTokens())
    System.out.println(tokens.nextToken());
```

By including the comma in the list of separators in the StringTokenizer constructor, the tokenizer consumes commas along with spaces, leaving only the words of the string to be returned one at a time. The output of this example is

```
Gone
and
forgotten
```

The StringTokenizer class has several methods to control what is considered a word, whether it should understand numbers or strings specially, and so on:

public **StringTokenizer(String str, String delim, boolean returnTokens)**

Constructs a StringTokenizer on the string str, using the characters in delim as the delimiter set. The returnTokens boolean determines whether delimiters are returned as tokens or skipped. If they are returned as tokens, each delimiter character is returned separately.

public **StringTokenizer(String str, String delim)**

Equivalent to StringTokenizer(str, delim, false), meaning that delimiters are skipped, not returned.

public **StringTokenizer(String str)**

Equivalent to StringTokenizer(str, " \t\n\r"), meaning that delimiters are the whitespace characters.

public boolean **hasMoreTokens()**

Returns true if more tokens exist.

public String **nextToken()**

Returns the next token of the string. Throws NoSuchElementException if there are no more tokens.

public String **nextToken(String delim)**

Switches the delimiter set to the characters in delim and returns the next token. There is no way to set a new delimiter set without getting the next token.

```
public int countTokens()
```
Returns the number of tokens remaining in the string using the current delimiter set. This is the number of times `nextToken` can return before it will generate an exception. When you need the number of tokens, this method is faster than repeatedly invoking `nextToken`, because the token strings are merely counted, not constructed and returned.

The methods `StringTokenizer` inherits from the `Enumeration` interface—`hasMoreElements` and `nextElement`—are equivalent to `hasMoreTokens` and `nextToken`, respectively.

The section "StreamTokenizer" on page 250 describes a class with greater power over how input is understood. To use `StreamTokenizer` on a string, create a `StringReader` object for the string. For many cases, however, a simple `StringTokenizer` object is sufficient.

Exercise 13.10: Write a method that will take a string containing floating-point numbers, break it up using white space as the delimiter, and return the sum of the numbers.

Power is not revealed by striking hard or often, but by striking true.
—Honoré de Balzac

CHAPTER 14

Programming with Types

I'm gonna wrap myself in paper,
I'm gonna dab myself with glue—
Stick some stamps on top of my head!
I'm gonna mail myself to you.
—Woody Guthrie, *Mail Myself to You*

JAVA types are represented by classes. There are classes for all primitive types (byte, float, and so on), and a general Class class to represent types of classes and interfaces. These classes provide three advantages:

- Useful methods for a type have a logical home. For example, the methods to convert a string to a float are static methods of the Float type class.

- Descriptive methods and fields also have a logical home. MIN_VALUE and MAX_VALUE constants are available in the classes for each numeric primitive type, and a host of methods of the Class class and related objects let you examine, modify, and use objects and their types.

- For primitive types, wrapper objects can be created to hold their values. Then those objects can be used in any context where an Object reference is required. That's why classes for primitive types are called *wrapper classes*.

The type hierarchy for these classes looks like this:

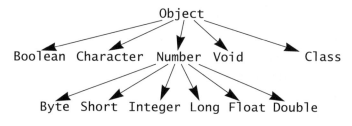

This chapter describes how to use these type-related classes. The first part of the chapter covers wrapper classes for primitive types. The rest of the chapter is devoted to programming with `Class` objects that represent particular classes and interfaces, including examining the types they represent, and using class loaders to increase your program's flexibility.

14.1 Wrapper Classes: An Overview

All primitive language types have wrapper classes to represent them. These classes have two primary functions. The first is to provide a home for methods and variables related to the type (such as string conversions and value range constants). Here, for example, is how you might check whether you could use a faster `float` calculation on a particular value or whether the value requires a larger range than a `float` provides:

```
double aval = Math.abs(value);
if (Float.MAX_VALUE >= aval && aval >= Float.MIN_VALUE)
    return fasterFloatCalc((float)value);
else
    return slowerDoubleCalc(value);
```

The second purpose of wrappers is to create objects to hold values of a particular primitive type for generically written classes that know only how to handle `Object` references. `Hashtable` objects, for example, store only `Object` references, not primitive types. To use an `int` as a key or value in a `Hashtable` object, you must create an `Integer` object to hold the value:

```
Integer keyObj = new Integer(key);
map.put(keyObj, value);
```

The following sections cover methods and constants available to each particular wrapper class, but first let's look at some things that are common to all the wrapper classes. Each wrapper class has the following constructors and methods:

- A constructor that takes the primitive type and creates an object of the type class (for example, the `Character(char)` constructor)
- A constructor that converts a single `String` parameter into the object's initial value (except `Character`, which has no such constructor)
- A `valueOf` method, which is equivalent to invoking `new` with the string-converting constructor
- A `toString` method that produces a string version of the type object's value

- ◆ A *type*Value method that produces the primitive type value, such as the methods Character.charValue and Boolean.booleanValue

- ◆ An equals method that compares objects of the same type class for equality

- ◆ A hashCode method that returns a value-based hash code for use in hashtables

All wrapper classes have these methods, so they are not listed in each class's descriptions. The system property fetch-and-decode methods described in "System Properties" on page 323 are also not discussed here.

Each wrapper class also has a static TYPE field, which is the Class object for that primitive type. These fields are equivalent to the Class objects you can obtain from .class expressions as described in "Reflection" on page 303. For example, Integer.TYPE is the same Class object you will get from the expression int.class.

The term *radix,* used in several places in the wrapper classes, is another word for numeric base. For example, decoding a long in radix 8 means the same as decoding it in base 8.

14.2 Void

The Void class is the exception to all the preceding rules because it has no values to wrap. It has only a static TYPE field and is used only for return values in reflection, something you will learn about shortly.

14.3 Boolean

The Boolean class represents the boolean type as a class. Both the constructor that decodes a string and the valueOf method understand "true", with any mixture of upper- and lowercase characters, to be true; any other string is interpreted as false.

14.4 Character

The Character class represents the char type as a class. In addition to MIN_VALUE and MAX_VALUE constants, it provides two constants MIN_RADIX and MAX_RADIX, which are the minimum and maximum radices understood by the methods (described later) that translate between a single-character digit and its integer value or vice versa. The radix must be in the range 2–36; digits for values greater than 9 are the letters A through Z or their lowercase equivalents.

```
public static int digit(char ch, int radix)
```
> Returns the numeric value of ch considered as a digit in the given radix. If the radix is not valid or if ch is not a digit in the radix, -1 is returned.

```
public static int getNumericValue(char ch)
```
> Returns the numeric value of the digit ch. These numeric values are non-negative. If ch is not a digit, -1 is returned; if it has a value that is not a non-negative integer (such as a fractional value), -2 is returned.

```
public static char forDigit(int digit, int radix)
```
> Returns the character value for the specified digit in the specified radix. If the digit is not valid in the radix, the character \u0000 is returned.

The Character class also supports methods to handle the various attributes of characters, including case. There are three cases in Unicode: upper, lower, and title. Uppercase and lowercase are familiar to most people. Titlecase is used to distinguish characters that are made up of multiple components and are written differently when used in titles, where the first letter in a word is traditionally capitalized. For example, in the string "ljepotica",[1] the first letter is the lowercase letter lj (\u01C9, a letter in the Extended Latin character set that is used in writing Croatian digraphs). If the word appeared in a book title, and you wanted the first letter of each word to be in uppercase, the correct process would be to use toTitleCase on the first letter of each word, giving you "Ljepotica" (using Lj, which is \u01C8). If you incorrectly use toUpperCase, you would get the erroneous string "LJepotica" (using LJ, which is \u01C7).

All case issues are handled as defined in Unicode. For example, in Georgian, uppercase letters are considered archaic, and translation into uppercase is usually avoided. Therefore, toUpperCase will not change lowercase Georgian letters to their uppercase equivalents, although toLowerCase will translate uppercase Georgian letters to lowercase. Because of such details, you cannot assume that all characters that are equivalent ignoring case will be the same if you invoke either toLowerCase or toUpperCase. However, the expression

```
Character.toUpperCase(Character.toLowerCase(ch));
```

leaves you with a character that you can compare with another similarly constructed character to test for equality ignoring case distinctions. If the two result-

---

[1] "Ljepotica" is a Croatian diminutive of "beauty," often used as a term of endearment and admiration.

ing characters are the same, then the original characters were the same except for possible differences in case. The case conversion methods are:

public static char **toLowerCase(char ch)**
> Returns the lowercase character equivalent of ch. If there is no lowercase equivalent, ch is returned.

public static char **toUpperCase(char ch)**
> Returns the uppercase character equivalent of ch. If there is no uppercase equivalent, ch is returned.

public static char **toTitleCase(char ch)**
> Returns the titlecase character equivalent of ch. If there is no titlecase equivalent, the result of toUpperCase(ch) is returned.

The Character class has many methods to test whether a given character is of a particular type. The methods are passed a char as a parameter and return a boolean that answers the question asked. These methods are:

Method	Is the Character...
isDefined	a defined Unicode character
isDigit	a digit in any Unicode character set
isIdentifierIgnorable	a character that can be in a Java or Unicode identifier without effect (such as a direction control directive character)
isISOControl	a Latin-1 control character
isJavaIdentifierPart	valid after the first character of a Java identifier
isJavaIdentifierStart	valid as the first character of a Java identifier
isLetter	a letter in any Unicode character set
isLetterOrDigit	a letter or digit in any Unicode character set
isLowerCase	a lowercase letter
isSpaceChar	a space in any Unicode character set
isTitleCase	a titlecase letter
isUnicodeIdentifierPart	valid after the first character of a Unicode identifier
isUnicodeIdentiferStart	valid as the first character of a Unicode identifier
isUpperCase	an uppercase letter
isWhitespace	a Java whitespace character

Unicode identifiers are defined by the Unicode standard. Unicode identifiers must start with a letter (connecting punctuation such as _ and currency symbols such as ¥ are not letters in Unicode, although they are in Java) and must contain only letters, connecting punctuation (such as _), digits, numeric letters (such as Roman numerals), combining marks, nonspacing marks, or ignorable control characters (such as text direction markers).

All these types of characters, and several others, are defined by the Unicode standard. The static method `getType` returns an `int` that defines a character's Unicode type. The return value is one of the following constants:

COMBINING_SPACING_MARK	MODIFIER_SYMBOL
CONNECTOR_PUNCTUATION	NON_SPACING_MARK
CONTROL	OTHER_LETTER
CURRENCY_SYMBOL	OTHER_NUMBER
DASH_PUNCTUATION	OTHER_PUNCTUATION
DECIMAL_DIGIT_NUMBER	OTHER_SYMBOL
ENCLOSING_MARK	PARAGRAPH_SEPARATOR
END_PUNCTUATION	PRIVATE_USE
FORMAT	SPACE_SEPARATOR
LETTER_NUMBER	START_PUNCTUATION
LINE_SEPARATOR	SURROGATE
LOWERCASE_LETTER	TITLECASE_LETTER
MATH_SYMBOL	UNASSIGNED
MODIFIER_LETTER	UPPERCASE_LETTER

14.5 Number

The `Number` class is an abstract class extended by all wrapper classes that represent numeric primitive types: `Byte`, `Short`, `Integer`, `Long`, `Float`, and `Double`. Each wrapper class has constructors that set the wrapper object's value from either a value of the relevant primitive type or a string that represents a value of that type. The string-based constructors throw `NumberFormatException` if the string cannot be decoded.

The abstract methods of `Number` return the value of the object converted to any of the other numeric types:

```
public byte byteValue()
public short shortValue()
public int intValue()
public long longValue()
public float floatValue()
public double doubleValue()
```

Each extended `Number` class overrides these methods to convert its own type to any of the others under the same rules used for an explicit cast. For example, given a `Float` object with the value `32.87`, the return value of `intValue` on the object would be 32, just as `(int)32.87` would be 32.

In addition, each numeric type class has the following methods and constants:

◆ A static `toString(type)` method that returns a `String` object when given a value of the primitive type. If the string is in an improper format for the type, the constructor throws `NumberFormatException`.

◆ A static `valueOf(String)` method that is equivalent to the `String`-based constructor for that type.

◆ Static `final` constants called `MIN_VALUE` and `MAX_VALUE` for the minimum and maximum values that variables of that type can take.

14.6   The Integer Wrapper Classes

The classes `Byte`, `Short`, `Integer`, and `Long` extend `Number` to represent the corresponding integer types as classes. In addition to the standard `Number` methods, they all support the following methods:

◆ Two static `parseType` methods that parse a `String` parameter into an integer value of the appropriate type. You can provide a `String` and an `int` radix, or just a `String`, which will be parsed with a radix of 10. For example, the `Short` class has two `parseShort` methods: one that takes both a `String` and radix, and another that takes only a `String` and is equivalent to `parseShort(string, 10)`. You will get a `NumberFormatException` if the string is not a valid number of the appropriate radix.

◆ A second overload of `valueOf` that returns a wrapper object parsed in a specified radix. For example, you could use a `String` containing a binary representation using `valueOf(string, 2)`.

◆ A static overload of `toString` that takes a primitive value that will be converted to a `String`. For example, you can get a string representation of the value of a `byte b` by invoking `toString(b)`.

In addition, the `Integer` and `Long` classes each have:

◆ Static methods `toBinaryString`, `toOctalString`, and `toHexString`, which convert an argument of the associated primitive type to a binary, octal, or hexadecimal `String`, respectively.

♦ A static `toString` method that converts an argument of the associated primitive type into a `String` in a specified radix in the range 2 through 36.

14.7   The Floating-Point Wrapper Classes

The `Float` and `Double` classes extend `Number` to represent the `float` and `double` types as classes. With only a few exceptions, the names of the methods and constants are the same for both types. In the following list, the types for the `Float` type class are shown, but `Float` and `float` can be changed to `Double` and `double`, respectively, in all of them to get equivalent fields and methods for the `Double` type class. In addition to the standard `Number` methods, `Float` and `Double` have the following constants and methods:

`public final static float POSITIVE_INFINITY`
    The value for $+\infty$.

`public final static float NEGATIVE_INFINITY`
    The value for $-\infty$.

`public final static float NaN`
    Not-a-Number. This constant provides a tool to get a NaN value, not to test one. To test whether a number is NaN, use the `isNaN` method. Don't compare it to this constant.

`public static boolean isNaN(float val)`
    Returns `true` if `val` is a Not-a-Number (NaN) value.

`public static boolean isInfinite(float val)`
    Returns `true` if `val` is either positive or negative infinity.

`public boolean isNaN()`
    Returns `true` if this object's value is a Not-a-Number (NaN) value.

`public boolean isInfinite()`
    Returns `true` if this object's value is either positive or negative infinity.

In addition to the preceding methods, `Float` has a constructor that takes a `double` argument to use as its initial value after conversion to `float`.

To manipulate the bits inside a floating-point value's representation, `Double` provides methods to get the bit pattern as a `long`, as well as a way to convert a bit pattern in a `long` into a `double` value. The `Float` class provides equivalent methods to turn a `float` value into an `int` bit pattern or vice versa:

`public static int floatToIntBits(float value)`
    Returns the bit representation of a `float` value in an `int`.

```
public static float intBitsToFloat(int bits)
```
Returns the float corresponding to a given bit representation.

```
public static long doubleToLongBits(double value)
```
Returns the bit representation of a double value as a long.

```
public static double longBitsToDouble(long bits)
```
Returns the double corresponding to a given bit representation.

Exercise 14.1: Write a program to read a file with lines of the form "*type value*", where type is one of the type class names (Boolean, Character, and so on) and value is a string that the type's constructor can decode. For each such entry, create an object of that type with that value and add it to a Vector. Display the final result when all the lines have been read.

14.8 Reflection

The package java.lang.reflect contains the Java *reflection* package, the classes you can use to examine a type in detail. You can write a complete type browser using these classes, or write an application that interprets code that a user writes, turning that code into actual uses of classes, methods, and so on. All the types mentioned in this discussion on reflection are contained in the package java.lang.reflect, except for the class Class, which is part of the package java.lang.

Reflection starts with a Class object. From the Class object you can ask for a list of all public members, or for a list of all members if the security manager allows it (see "Security" on page 331). Default security allows reflection to access only the public members of a class. (Reflection is also sometimes called *introspection*; both terms use the metaphor of asking the type to look at itself and tell you something.)

Reflection allows you to write code that performs actions you can execute directly in code if you know what you are doing. You can, for example, invoke a method using reflection, as you will soon see, but it is much harder to understand than a direct method invocation. You should use reflection only when you have exhausted all other object-oriented design mechanisms. For example, you should not use a Method object as a "method pointer," because interfaces and abstract classes are better tools. There are times when reflection is necessary—usually when you're interpreting or displaying some other code—but use more-direct means whenever possible.

14.8.1 Class

Each class and interface in the system has a `Class` object that represents it. This object can be used for basic queries about the class or interface and to create new objects of a class.

The `Class` class is the starting point for reflection. It also provides a tool to manipulate classes, primarily for creating objects of types specified in strings, and for loading classes using specialized techniques, such as across the network.

There are four ways to get a `Class` object: ask an object for its class object using its `getClass` method; use a class literal (the name of the class followed by `.class`, as in `String.class`); look it up by its fully qualified name (all packages included) using the static method `Class.forName`; or get it from one of the reflection methods that return `Class` objects for nested classes and interfaces.

The most basic `Class` methods are those that walk the type hierarchy. This class prints the type hierarchy of the type represented by a particular `Class` object:

```java
public class TypeDesc {
    public static void main(String[] args) {
        TypeDesc desc = new TypeDesc();
        for (int i = 0; i < args.length; i++) {
            try {
                Class startClass = Class.forName(args[i]);
                desc.printType(startClass, 0, basic);
            } catch (ClassNotFoundException e) {
                System.err.println(e);  // report the error
            }
        }
    }

    // by default print on standard output
    private java.io.PrintStream out = System.out;

    // used in printType() for labeling type names
    private static String[]
        basic  = { "class",   "interface"  },
        supercl = { "extends", "implements" },
        iFace  = { null,       "extends"  };

    private void printType(
        Class type, int depth, String[] labels)
    {
```

```
    if (type == null) // stop recursion -- no supertype
        return;

    // print this type
    for (int i = 0; i < depth; i++)
        out.print("  ");
    out.print(labels[type.isInterface() ? 1 : 0] + " ");
    out.println(type.getName());

    // print out all interfaces this class implements
    Class[] interfaces = type.getInterfaces();
    for (int i = 0; i < interfaces.length; i++)
        printType(interfaces[i], depth + 1,
                    type.isInterface() ? iFace : supercl);

    // recurse on the superclass
    printType(type.getSuperclass(), depth + 1, supercl);
    }
}
```

This program loops through the names provided on the command line and invokes printType on each one. It must do this inside a try block in case there is no class of the specified name. Here is its output when invoked on the utility class java.util.Hashtable (the fully qualified name is used because it is required by the forName method):

```
class java.util.Hashtable
    implements java.lang.Cloneable
    implements java.io.Serializable
    extends java.util.Dictionary
        extends java.lang.Object
```

After the main method is the declaration of the output stream to use, by default System.out. The String arrays are described shortly.

The printType method prints its own type description and then invokes itself recursively to print the description of the type's supertypes. The depth parameter keeps track of how far up the type hierarchy it has climbed, indenting each description line depending on its depth. The depth is incremented at each recursion level. The labels array specifies how to label the class—labels[0] is the label if the type is a class; labels[1] is for interfaces.

Three arrays are defined for these labels: basic is used at the top level, supercl is used for superclasses, and iFace is used for superinterfaces of interfaces, which extend, not implement, each other. After we print the right prefix, we use `getName` to print the name of the type. The `Class` class provides a `toString` method, but it already adds "class" or "interface" in front. We want to control the prefix, so we must create our own implementation.

After printing the type description, `printType` invokes itself recursively, first on all the interfaces that the original type implements and then on the superclass this type extends (if any), passing the appropriate label array to each. Eventually it reaches the `Class` object for `Object`, which implements no interfaces and whose `getSuperclass` method returns `null`, and the recursion ends.

Exercise 14.2: Modify `TypeDesc` to skip printing anything for the `Object` class. It is redundant because everything ultimately extends it. Use the reference for the `Class` object for the `Object` type.

14.8.2 Examining Classes

You can use methods of a `Class` object to fully examine the type it represents. You can make basic queries about the type by invoking `isInterface`, `isArray`, and `isPrimitive`. For nested classes, `getDeclaringClass` returns the `Class` object of the enclosing class.

If a `Class` object represents an array, `getComponentType` will return the `Class` object for the type. For example, given an array of `int`, the `getClass` method will return a `Class` object for which `isArray` returns true and whose `getComponentType` method returns `int.class`.

You can look up the members of a class using separate methods for fields, methods, constructors, and member classes and interfaces. The `getField` method looks up a `Field` object for a named public field passed as a parameter. The method `getFields` returns an array of `Field` objects, one for each public field of the class. If there are no public fields, the array has a length of zero. (This is the pattern for all reflection methods that return arrays; you get an empty array if there are no values to return.) The method `getDeclaredField` lets you look up a single `Field`, public or not, if the security manager allows it. When there is no security manager, you can access any field you like, but most security managers will not allow you to access non-public fields in order to protect the privacy of other fields—security managers do not have enough information to enforce either package or protected access. The method `getDeclaredFields` returns an array describing all declared fields, public or not, and is similarly secured.

You can look up arrays and constructors using similar methods that take overloading into account. The method `getMethod` takes the name of the method and a `Class` array to know the number and types of parameters. The method and constructor lookup methods that look up a specific name—`getDeclaredMethod`, getConstructor, and getDeclaredConstructor—take an equivalent Class array. A class array is not passed to the methods that return arrays: getMethods, getDeclaredMethods, getConstructors, and getDeclaredConstructors.

The method getClasses returns an array of Class objects that represent those classes and interfaces that are public members of the class—that is, the class's nested classes and interfaces; getDeclaredClasses returns an array of all member classes and interfaces as long as the security manager allows it.

The following program lists the public fields, methods, and constructors of a given class:

```
import java.lang.reflect.*;

public class ClassContents {
    public static void main(String[] args) {
        try {
            Class c = Class.forName(args[0]);
            System.out.println(c);
            printMembers(c.getFields());
            printMembers(c.getConstructors());
            printMembers(c.getMethods());
        } catch (ClassNotFoundException e) {
            System.out.println("unknown class: " + args[0]);
            System.exit(-1);
        }
    }

    private static void printMembers(Member[] mems) {
        for (int i = 0; i < mems.length; i++) {
            if (mems[i].getDeclaringClass() == Object.class)
                continue;
            String decl = mems[i].toString();
            System.out.print("    ");
            System.out.println(strip(decl, "java.lang."));
        }
    }
}
```

First we get the Class object for the named class. We then get the arrays of member objects that represent all of the public fields, constructors, and methods of the class and print them. The printMembers method uses the Member object's toString method to get a string that describes the member, skipping members that are inherited from Object since these are present in all classes and so not very useful to repeat each time. Here is the output when run on the `Attr` class from page 60:

```
class Attr
    public Attr(String)
    public Attr(String,Object)
    public String Attr.toString()
    public String Attr.getName()
    public Object Attr.getValue()
    public Object Attr.setValue(Object)
```

The classes `Field`, `Constructor`, and `Method` all implement the interface `Member`, which has three methods for properties all members share:

`Class getDeclaringClass()`

Returns the `Class` object for the class in which this member is declared.

`String getName()`

Returns the name of the member.

`int getModifiers()`

Returns the language modifiers for the member as a bit mask.

The values that can appear in the mask returned by `getModifiers` are defined as static fields in the `Modifier` class. For example, if a field is declared

```
public static final int OAK = 0;
```

the value returned by its `Field` object's `getModifiers` would be

```
Modifier.PUBLIC | Modifier.STATIC | Modifier.FINAL
```

You can use static methods in `Modifiers` to ask questions in a more symbolic fashion. For example, the expression

```
Modifier.isPrivate(field.getModifiers())
```

is equivalent to the expression

```
(field.getModifiers() & Modifier.PRIVATE) != 0
```

Although a class or interface can be a member of another class, for historical reasons the class `Class` does not implement `Member`, although it supports methods of the same name and contract.

The `toString` method of all `Member` classes includes all the member's modifiers, not just the simple name returned by `getName`.

Exercise 14.3: Use reflection to write a program that will print a full declaration of a named class, including everything except the import statement, comments, and code for initializers, constructors, and methods.

14.8.3 Field

The Field subclass of Member provides a getType method, which returns the Class object for the type of the field. For example, if the field were a String field, the return value would be String.class. If the field were of a primitive type, such as long, the value returned would be equivalent to the value returned for that primitive type's class, such as long.class.

You can also get and set the value of a field using the get and set methods, specifying which object to operate on. For static fields the object is ignored and can be null. The following method prints the value of a short field of an object:

```
public static void printField(Object o, String name)
    throws NoSuchFieldException, IllegalAccessException
{
    Field field = o.getClass().getField(name);
    Short value = (Short)field.get(o);
    System.out.println(value);
}
```

The return value of get is whatever object the field references or, if the field is a primitive type, a wrapper object of the appropriate type. For our short field, value is a Short object that contains the value of the field.

The set method can be used in a similar way. A method to set a short field to a provided value might look like this:

```
public static void setField(Object o, String name, short nv)
    throws NoSuchFieldException, IllegalAccessException
{
    Field field = o.getClass().getField(name);
    field.set(o, new Short(nv));
}
```

We must create a Short wrapper to hold the value of nv because get and set work only on objects. The Field class also has specific methods for getting and setting primitive types. You can invoke get*Type* and set*Type* on a Field object, where *Type* is the primitive type name (with an initial uppercase letter). The first example just shown could have used the statement

```
short value = field.getShort(o);
```

The second example could have used the simpler

```
field.setShort(o, nv);
```

You will get an IllegalAccessException if you try to use a field to which you should not have access.

With some work you can use a Field object as a way to manipulate an arbitrary value, but you should avoid this when possible. Java is designed to catch as many programming errors as possible when the program is compiled. The less you write using indirections such as the Field object, the more your errors will be prevented before they are compiled into code. Also, as you can see, it takes more reading to see what is happening in the preceding code compared with what it would take if the name of the field were simply used in the normal Java syntax.

Exercise 14.4: Create an Interpret program that creates an object of a known type and allows the user to examine and modify fields of that object.

14.8.4 Method

The Method subclass of the Member class adds methods that let you find out everything about the method itself. The getReturnType method returns a Class object for the declared return type, which can be void.class if the method is declared to be void. The method getParameterTypes returns an array of the Class objects representing each parameter type in the order declared. The method getExceptionTypes returns an array of Class objects for each exception declared in the method's throws clause. You can use a Method object to invoke the method:

public Object **invoke(Object onThis, Object[] args)**
  throws IllegalAccessException, IllegalArgumentException,
  InvocationTargetException

> Invokes the method defined by this Method object on the object onThis, setting the parameters of the method from the values in args. If the method is static, onThis is ignored and is traditionally null. The length of args must equal the number of parameters for the method, and types of parameters in args must all be assignable to those of the method. Otherwise you will get an IllegalArgumentException. If you attempt to invoke a method to which you do not have access, you will get an IllegalAccessException.

When you use invoke, primitive types are passed in the argument array inside appropriate wrapper classes. The type represented by a wrapper must be assignable to the unwrapped type. You can use a Long, Float, or Double to wrap a double argument, but you cannot use a Double to wrap a long or float argument because a double is not assignable to a long. The Object returned by invoke is handled as with Field.get, wrapping primitive types.

Simply put, you can use invoke only to invoke a method with the same types and values that would be legal in the language. The invocation

```
return str.indexOf(".", 8);
```

can be written using reflection in the following way:

```
Exception failure;
try {
    Class StrClass = str.getClass();
    Method indexM = StrClass.getMethod("indexOf",
        new Class[] { String.class, int.class }
    );
    Object result = indexM.invoke(str, new Object[] {
        ".", new Integer(8) }
    );
    return ((Integer)result).intValue();
} catch (NoSuchMethodException e) {
    failure = e;
} catch (InvocationTargetException e) {
    // rethrow any runtime exception
    if (e.getTargetException() instanceof RuntimeException)
        throw (RuntimeException)e.getTargetException();
    failure = e;
} catch (IllegalAccessException e) {
    failure = e;
}

// these failures can happen only using reflection, and
// cannot be recovered from
failure.printStackTrace(System.err);
System.exit(-1);
return 0; // not reached, but compiler can't tell
```

The reflection-based code has semantically equivalent safety checks, although the checks that are made by the compiler for direct invocation can be made only at run time when you use invoke. The access checking will be done in a somewhat different way—you might be denied access to a method in your package by the security manager, even if you could invoke that method directly.

These are good reasons to avoid using this kind of invocation when you can. It's reasonable to use invoke—or the get/set methods of Field—when you are writing a debugger or other generic applications that require interpreting user input as manipulations of Java objects. A Method object can be used somewhat like a method pointer in other languages, but there are better Java tools—notably interfaces, abstract classes, and nested classes—to address the problems typically solved by method pointers in those languages.

If the invoked method itself throws an exception, invoke throws an InvocationTargetException. This exception has a getTargetException method that will return the exception thrown by the method.

Exercise 14.5: Modify your Interpret program to invoke methods on the object. You should properly display any values returned or exceptions thrown.

14.8.5 Creating New Objects and Constructor

You can use a Class object's newInstance method to create a new instance (object) of the type it represents. This method invokes the class's no-arg constructor or throws NoSuchMethodError if the class doesn't have a no-arg constructor. If the class or the no-arg constructor is not accessible (because it isn't public or isn't in the same package), an IllegalAccessException is thrown. If the class is abstract, or an interface, or if the creation fails for some other reason, an InstantiationException is thrown. Creating a new object in this way is useful when you want to write general code and let the user specify the class. For example, you could modify the generic sorting algorithm tester from "Designing a Class to Be Extended" on page 83 so that the user could type the name of the class to be tested and use that as a parameter to the forName lookup method. Assuming that the given class name was valid, newInstance could then be invoked to create an object of that type. Here is a new main method for a generic TestSort class:

```
static double[] testData = { 0.3, 1.3e-2, 7.9, 3.17, };

public static void main(String[] args) {
    try {
        for (int arg = 0; arg < args.length; arg++) {
            String name = args[arg];
            Class classFor = Class.forName(name);
            SortDouble sorter
                = (SortDouble)classFor.newInstance();
            SortMetrics metrics
                = sorter.sort(testData);
            System.out.println(name + ": " + metrics);
            for (int i = 0; i < testData.length; i++)
```

```
                        System.out.println("\t" + testData[i]);
            }
        } catch (Exception e) {
            System.err.print(e);            // report the error
        }
    }
```

This is almost exactly like `TestSort.main` (see page 87), but we have removed all type names. This `main` method can be used to test any subclass of `SortDouble` that provides a no-arg constructor. You don't have to write a `main` for each type of sorting algorithm—this generic `main` works for them all. All you need to do is execute

```
    java TestSort TestClass ...
```

for any sorting class (such as `SimpleSortDouble`), and it will be loaded and run.

The `newInstance` method of `Class` can invoke only a no-arg constructor. You can invoke any constructor by using the `Class` object to get the `Constructor` object and invoking `newInstance` on that `Constructor`, passing any arguments using an array of `Object`, just as you would when using a `Method` object to invoke a method. `Constructor` has analogous `getParameterTypes` and `getExceptionTypes` methods to examine the constructor but needs no `getReturnType` method.

You can use reflection to create instances of inner classes only by using a `Constructor` object. In essence, every constructor for such a class has an implicit first parameter that is a reference to the enclosing object, and so in reflection there is never a no-arg constructor for an inner class. In a `newInstance` invocation for an inner class's, the enclosing object is the first parameter you will pass in the array to `newInstance`, the first declared constructor parameter becomes the second parameter in the array, the second becomes the third, and so on.

Exercise 14.6: Modify your `Interpret` program further to let users invoke constructors of an arbitrary class, display any exceptions, and, if a construction is successful, let them invoke methods on the returned object.

14.8.6 Arrays

The `Class` object returned by invoking `getClass` on an actual array returns `true` from the method `isArray`. The result of the expression

```
    String[].class.isArray()
```

is true. The Class object's field-related methods (getField, getFields, and the like) cannot be used to manipulate an array because an array has elements, not fields.

You can create and manipulate array objects reflectively by using the static methods of the Array class. You can create arrays with either of two newInstance methods. One of these methods takes a Class object for the element type—use int.class to create an int array and similarly for the other primitive types—and a single dimension. The statement

```
byte[] ba = (byte[])Array.newInstance(byte.class, 13);
```

is equivalent to

```
byte[] ba = new byte[13];
```

The second newInstance method takes an array of dimensions. The statement

```
int[] dims = { 4, 4 };
double[][] matrix =
    (double[][])Array.newInstance(double.class, dims);
```

is equivalent to

```
double[][] matrix = new double[4][4];
```

The expression xa[i] can be more laboriously and less clearly expressed as Array.get(xa, i). The return value is like that of get on a Field object, wrapping primitive values. You can set a value in a similar way: xa[i] = 42 is the same as the more awkward

```
Array.set(xa, i, new Integer(42));
```

The Array class also supports a full set of get*Type* and set*Type* methods for all the primitive types, as in:

```
Array.setInt(xa, i, 42);
```

The getLength method of Array returns the length of a given array.

Exercise 14.7: Modify Interpret further to allow users to specify a type and size of array to create, set and get the elements of that array, and specify which element of the array contains the object on which their expressions access fields and invoke methods.

14.9 Loading Classes

The Java runtime system loads classes when they are needed. Details of loading classes vary between Java implementations, but most of them use a *class path* mechanism to search for a class referenced by your code but not yet loaded into the runtime. This default mechanism works well in many cases, but much of the power of Java is the ability to load classes from places that make sense to your application. To write an application that loads classes in ways different from the default mechanism, you must provide a `ClassLoader` object that can get the bytecodes for class implementations and load them into the runtime.

For example, you might set up a game so that players could write classes to play the game using whatever strategy the player chooses. The design would look something like this:

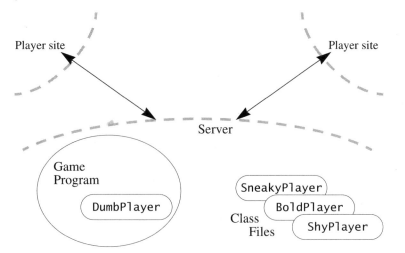

To make this work, you would provide a `Player` abstract class that players would extend to implement their strategy. When players were ready to try their strategy, they would send the compiled class's bytecodes to your system. The bytecodes would need to be loaded into the game, evaluated, and the score returned to the player.

At the server, the game program loads each waiting `Player` class, creates an object of the new type, and runs its strategy against the game algorithm. When the results are known, they are reported to the player who submitted the strategy.

The communication mechanism isn't specified here, but it could be as simple as electronic mail, with players mailing their classes and receiving the results by return mail.

The interesting part is how the game program loads the compiled class files into its runtime. This is the province of a *class loader,* which must extend the abstract ClassLoader class and implement its abstract loadClass method:

protected abstract Class **loadClass(String name, boolean resolve)**
     throws ClassNotFoundException

> Loads the class of the given name. If resolve is true, the method must invoke the resolveClass method to ensure that all classes referred to by the class are also loaded.

There is an overload of loadClass that takes only the name of the class, which is equivalent to loadClass(name, true).

In our example, we would provide a PlayerLoader class to read the byte-codes from the player classes and install each of them as a usable class. The basic loop would look like this:

```
public class Game {
    static public void main(String[] args) {
        String name;    // the class name
        while ((name = getNextPlayer()) != null) {
            try {
                PlayerLoader loader = new PlayerLoader();
                Class
                    classOf = loader.loadClass(name, true);
                Player
                    player = (Player)classOf.newInstance();
                Game game = new Game();
                player.play(game);
                game.reportScore(name);
            } catch (Exception e) {
                reportException(name, e);
            }
        }
    }
}
```

Each new game needs a new PlayerLoader object so that the new Player class will not get mixed up with loaded classes from previous runs. That new loader loads the class, returning the Class object that represents it. That Class object is used to create a new object of the Player class. Then we create a new game and play it. When the game is finished, the score is reported.

The PlayerLoader class extends ClassLoader to implement loadClass:

```
class PlayerLoader extends ClassLoader {
    public Class loadClass(String name, boolean resolve)
        throws ClassNotFoundException
    {
        try {
            Class newClass = findLoadedClass(name);
            if (newClass == null) { // not yet defined
                try {                   // check if system class
                    newClass = findSystemClass(name);
                    if (newClass != null)
                        return newClass;
                } catch (ClassNotFoundException e) {
                    ;                           // keep on looking
                }

                // class not found -- need to load it
                byte[] buf = bytesForClass(name);
                newClass =
                    defineClass(name, buf, 0, buf.length);
            }
            if (resolve)
                resolveClass(newClass);
            return newClass;
        } catch (IOException e) {
            throw new ClassNotFoundException(e.toString());
        }
    }

    // ... bytesForClass, and any other methods ...
}
```

Each ClassLoader maintains a hashtable of loaded classes to help you avoid loading a class twice. If a class has already been loaded, the findLoadedClass method returns the associated Class object from that hashtable. Otherwise, loadClass first checks whether it can find the class on the local system by invoking the ClassLoader method findSystemClass, which not only looks for system classes (those in the java packages), but also looks through the class path. If the class is found this way, the Class object for it is returned after any necessary loading is done.

If both these simple mechanisms fail, we must read the bytes for the class, and that is the purpose of bytesForClass:

```
protected byte[] bytesForClass(String name)
    throws IOException, ClassNotFoundException
{
    FileInputStream in = streamFor(name + ".class");
    int length = in.available(); // get byte count
    if (length == 0)
        throw new ClassNotFoundException(name);
    byte[] buf = new byte[length];
    in.read(buf);                    // read the bytes
    return buf;
}
```

This method uses streamFor (not shown) to get a FileInputStream to the class's bytecodes, assuming that the bytecodes are in a file named by the class name with a ".class" appended. We then create a buffer for the bytes, read them all, and return the buffer.

When loadClass gets the bytes for the class, it invokes the ClassLoader method defineClass, which takes the expected name of the class, a byte array, a start position, and a number of bytes. The bytes in that part of the array are the bytecodes for the class. In our case, we use the entire array for the class's byte-codes. The method defineClass method also adds the class to the hashtable of known classes searched by findLoadedClass.

When the class has been successfully loaded, loadClass resolves the new class if requested, and then returns the new Class object. There is no way to unload a class when it is no longer needed. You simply stop using it, allowing it to be garbage-collected.

You can obtain the class loader for a given Class object by invoking its getClassLoader method. System classes have no class loader, so the method returns null.

The class loader assists in only the first stage of making a class available. There are three steps in all:

1. Loading: Getting the bytecodes that implement the class.

2. Linking: Locating the supertypes of the class and loading them if needed.

3. Initialization: Setting the static fields of the class to their initial values and executing their initializers as well as any static blocks.

Exercise 14.8: Expand upon Game and Player to implement a simple game, such as tic-tac-toe. Score some Player implementations over several runs each.

14.9.1 Loading Related Resources

Classes are the primary resources a Java program needs, but some classes need other associated resources, such as text, images, or sounds. Class loaders have ways to find class resources, and they can use the same mechanisms to get arbitrary resources stored with the class. In our game example, a strategy might have an associated "book" that tells it how to respond to particular situations. The following code would get an InputStream for such a book:

```
String book = "BoldPlayer.book";
InputStream in;
ClassLoader loader = this.getClass().getClassLoader();
if (loader != null)
    in = loader.getResourceAsStream(book);
else
    in = ClassLoader.getSystemResourceAsStream(book);
```

System resources are associated with system classes, which are the classes that have no class loader. The static method getSystemResourceAsStream returns an InputStream for a named resource. The preceding code checks to see whether it has a class loader. If it does not, it has been loaded by the system class loader; otherwise, it uses the class loader's getResourceAsStream method to turn its resource name into a byte input stream. The resource methods return null if the resource is not found.

The Class class provides a getResourceAsStream method to simplify getting resources from a class's class loader. The preceding code could be written more simply as:

```
String book = "BoldPlayer.book";
InputStream in = BoldPlayer.class.getResourceAsStream(book);
```

Resource names must be made up of zero or more valid Java identifiers separated by / characters. This restriction helps class loaders use identical mappings for resources and class names.

The implementation of getResourceAsStream in ClassLoader just returns null. It is up to your specific class loader to override the method to use appropriate means to locate a resource. Usually this means that resources will be found in the same places and ways that classes are found. Here is an implementation of getResourceAsStream for PlayerLoader:

```
public InputStream getResourceAsStream(String name) {
    try {
        return streamFor(name);
    } catch (IOException e) {
        return null;
    }
}
```

This code uses the same streamFor method used by loadClass earlier, so the file BoldPlayer.book should live in the same place that BoldPlayer.class lives.

The two other resource methods—getResource and getSystemResource—return URL objects that name the resources. The class URL is covered briefly on page 369; it provides methods to use universal resource locators to access resources. You can invoke the getContents method on the URL objects returned by the class loader methods to get an object that represents the contents of that URL.

Exercise 14.9: Modify your results for Exercise 14.8 to allow player strategies to use attached resources.

Be and not seem.
—Ralph Waldo Emerson

CHAPTER 15

System Programming

GLENDOWER: I can call spirits from the vasty deep.
HOTSPUR: Why, so can I, or so can any man;
But will they come when you do call for them?
—William Shakespeare, *King Henry IV, Part 1*

THIS chapter describes how to access general functions of the Java runtime system and the underlying operating system. Such functions include reading properties, using mathematical functions, executing other programs, and controlling memory. Four classes in `java.lang` provide this access:

- The `Runtime` class represents the state of a Java runtime. The `Runtime` object provides access to functionality that is per-runtime, such as controlling the garbage collector and exiting the runtime.

- The `Process` class represents a running process created with an invocation of `Runtime.exec`.

- The `System` class provides static methods to represent the system. For convenience, several methods in `System` operate on the current runtime.

- The `Math` class provides static methods to compute many standard mathematical functions, such as trigonometric functions and logarithms.

15.1 Standard I/O Streams

You can use `System.in`, `System.out`, and `System.err` to do I/O in standard places. These are the three system streams available as static fields of the `System` class.

```
public static InputStream in
```
    Standard input stream for reading character data.

```
public static PrintStream out
```
    Standard output stream for printing messages.

```
public static PrintStream err
```
    Standard error stream to print error messages. The user often can redirect standard output to a file. But applications also need to print error messages that the user will see even if standard output is redirected. The `err` stream is specifically devoted to error messages that are not rerouted with the regular output. Both `out` and `err` are `PrintStream` objects, so you print errors on `err` using the same methods as for `out`.

See "Print Streams" on page 240 for a discussion about `PrintStream` and `PrinterWriter` types.

15.2 Memory Management

Although Java has no explicit way to dispose of unwanted objects, you can directly invoke the garbage collector to look for unused objects. You do this with the `Runtime` class's `gc` method. The `Runtime` class also supports a `runFinalization` method to invoke any pending finalizers. `Runtime` has two methods to report on the memory state:

```
public long freeMemory()
```
    Returns an estimate of free bytes in system memory.

```
public long totalMemory()
```
    Returns the total bytes in system memory.

The `System` class supports static `gc` and `runFinalization` methods that invoke the corresponding methods on the current runtime.

The garbage collector may not be able to free any additional memory when `Runtime.gc` is invoked. There may be no garbage to collect, and not all garbage collectors can find collectable objects on demand. However, before creating a large number of objects—especially in a time-critical application that might be affected by garbage-collection overhead—invoking `gc` may be advisable. Doing so has two benefits: you start with as much free memory as possible, and you reduce the likelihood of the garbage collector running during the task. Here is a method that aggressively frees everything it can at the moment:

```
public static void fullGC() {
    Runtime rt = Runtime.getRuntime();
    long isFree = rt.freeMemory();
    long wasFree;
```

```
        do {
            wasFree = isFree;
            rt.runFinalization();
            rt.gc();
            isFree = rt.freeMemory();
        } while (isFree > wasFree);
    }
```

This method loops while the amount of `freeMemory` is being increased by successive calls to `runFinalization` and `gc`. When the amount of free memory doesn't increase, further calls will likely do nothing.

You will not usually need to invoke `runFinalization`, because `finalize` methods are called asynchronously by the garbage collector. Under some circumstances, such as running out of a resource that a `finalize` method reclaims, it is useful to force as much finalization as possible. But remember, there is no guarantee that any object awaiting finalization is using some of that resource, so `runFinalization` may be of no help.

The `fullGC` method is too aggressive for most purposes. In the unusual circumstance that you need to force garbage collection, a single invocation of `System.gc` will gather most if not all of the available garbage. Repeated invocations are progressively less productive—on many systems they will be completely unproductive.

15.3 System Properties

Several system properties are available. They are stored by the `System` class in a `Properties` object (see "Properties" on page 286). These properties define the system environment and are used by classes that need to know their environment. For example, here is a dump of the properties on one system:

```
#System properties
#Tue Sep 30 22:23:55 EDT 1997
user.language=en
java.home=/vob/tools/java//bin/..
java.vendor.url.bug=http://java.sun.com/cgi-bin/
bugreport.cgi
file.encoding.pkg=sun.io
java.version=1.1.4
file.separator=/
line.separator=\n
file.encoding=8859_1
```

```
java.vendor=Sun Microsystems Inc.
user.timezone=EST
user.name=arnold
os.arch=sparc
os.name=Solaris
java.vendor.url=http://www.sun.com/
user.dir=/vob/java_prog/src
java.class.path=.:../classes:/vob/tools/java//bin/../
classes:/vob/tools/java//bin/../lib/classes.jar:/vob/tools/
java//bin/../lib/rt.jar:/vob/tools/java//bin/../lib/
i18n.jar:/vob/tools/java//bin/../lib/classes.zip
java.class.version=45.3
os.version=2.x
path.separator=:
user.home=/home/arnold
```

These properties are defined on all systems, although the values will certainly vary. Some of the properties are used by classes in the standard packages. The File class, for example, uses the file.separator property to build up and break down pathnames. You are also free to use properties. The following method looks for a personal configuration file in the user's home directory:

```
public static File personalConfig(String fileName) {
    String home = System.getProperty("user.home");
    if (home == null)
        return null;
    else
        return new File(home, fileName);
}
```

The methods of the System class that deal with the system properties are:

public static Properties **getProperties()**
    Gets the Properties object that defines all system properties.

public static void **setProperties(Properties props)**
    Sets the Properties object that defines all system properties to be props.

public static String **getProperty(String key)**
    Returns the value of the system property named in key.

public static String **getProperty(String key, String defaultValue)**
    Returns the value of the system property named in key. If it has no definition, it returns defaultValue.

Property values are stored as strings, but the strings can represent other types, such as integers or booleans. Methods are available to read properties and decode them into many of the primitive types. These decoding methods are static methods of the primitive type's class. Each method has a `String` parameter that names the property to retrieve. Some forms have a second parameter (shown as `def` later) that is the default value to return if no property is found with that name. Methods that lack a default value parameter return an object that contains the default value for the type. All these methods decode values in the standard Java formats for constants of the primitive type:

```
public static boolean Boolean.getBoolean(String name)
public static Integer Integer.getInteger(String name)
public static Integer
                Integer.getInteger(String name, Integer def)
public static Integer
                Integer.getInteger(String name, int def)
public static Long Long.getLong(String nm)
public static Long Long.getLong(String nm, long def)
public static Long Long.getLong(String nm, Long def)
```

The `getBoolean` method is different from the others—it returns a `boolean` value instead of an object of class `Boolean`. If the property isn't present, `getBoolean` returns `false`; the other methods return `null`.

The classes `Character`, `Byte`, `Short`, `Float`, and `Double` do not have property fetching methods. You can get the value as a string and use the mechanisms described in "String Conversions" on page 169.

15.4 Creating Processes

As we have discussed, a running Java system can have many threads of execution. Most systems that host a Java environment also have the ability to run multiple programs. Java applications can execute new programs using one of two forms of the method `Runtime.exec`. Each successful invocation of `exec` creates a new `Process` object that represents the program running in its own *process*. You can use a `Process` object to query the process's state and invoke methods to control its progress. `Process` is an abstract class whose subclasses are defined on each system to work with that system's processes. The two basic forms of `exec` are:

`public Process exec(String[] cmdarray) throws IOException`
      Runs the command in `cmdarray` on the current system. Returns a `Process` object (described later) to represent it. The string in `cmdarray[0]` is the

name of the command, and any subsequent strings in the array are passed to the command as arguments.

`public Process` **`exec(String command)`** `throws IOException`
Equivalent to the other form of `exec` with the string `command` split into an array wherever white space occurs.

The newly created process is called a *child* process. By analogy, the creating process is a *parent* process. The `exec` methods return a `Process` object for each child process created. This object represents the child process in two major ways. First, it provides methods to get input, output, and error streams for the child process:[1]

`public abstract OutputStream` **`getOutputStream()`**
Returns a buffered `OutputStream` connected to the input of the child process. Data written on this stream is read by the child process as its input.

`public abstract InputStream` **`getInputStream()`**
Returns a buffered `InputStream` connected to the output of the child process. When the child writes data on its output, it can be read from this stream.

`public abstract InputStream` **`getErrorStream()`**
Returns an unbuffered `InputStream` connected to the error output stream of the child process. When the child writes data on its error output, it can be read from this stream. The stream is unbuffered to ensure that errors are reported immediately.

Here, for example, is a program that connects the Java streams to the streams of the new process so that whatever the user types will go to the specified program and whatever the program produces will be seen by the user:

```
public static Process userProg(String cmd)
    throws IOException
{
    Process proc = Runtime.getRuntime().exec(cmd);
    plugTogether(System.in,  proc.getOutputStream());
    plugTogether(System.out, proc.getInputStream());
    plugTogether(System.err, proc.getErrorStream());
    return proc;
}
```

---

[1] For historical reasons these are byte-stream objects instead of character streams. You can use `InputStreamReader` and `OutputStreamWriter` to convert the bytes to characters using the system default translation.

This code assumes that a method `plugTogether` exists to connect two streams by reading the bytes from one stream and writing them onto the other.

The second way a `Process` object represents the child process is by providing methods to control the process and discover its termination status:

public abstract int waitFor() throws InterruptedException
> Waits indefinitely for the process to complete, returning the value it passed to either `System.exit` or its equivalent (zero means success, nonzero means failure). If the process has already completed, the value is simply returned.

public abstract int exitValue()
> Returns the exit value for the process. If the process has not completed, `exitValue` throws `IllegalStateException`.

public abstract void destroy()
> Kills the process. Does nothing if the process has already completed. If a `Process` object gets garbage-collected, this does not mean that the process is destroyed; it will merely be unavailable for manipulation.

For example, the following method returns a `String` array that contains the output of `ls` with the specified options. It throws an `LSFailedException` if the command completed unsuccessfully:

```java
// We have imported java.io.* and java.util.*
public String[] ls(String dir, String opts)
    throws LSFailedException
{
    try {
        // start up the command
        String[] cmdArray = { "/bin/ls", opts, dir };
        Process child = Runtime.getRuntime().exec(cmdArray);
        InputStream lsOut = child.getInputStream();
        InputStreamReader r = new InputStreamReader(lsOut);
        BufferedReader in = new BufferedReader(r);

        // read the command's output
        Vector lines = new Vector();
        String line;
        while ((line = in.readLine()) != null)
            lines.addElement(line);
        if (child.waitFor() != 0)   // if the ls failed
            throw new LSFailedException(child.exitValue());
        String[] retval = new String[lines.size()];
        lines.copyInto(retval);
```

```
            return retval;
        } catch (LSFailedException e) {
            throw e;
        } catch (Exception e) {
            throw new LSFailedException(e.toString());
        }
    }
}
```

In the `ls` method we want to treat the output as character data, so we wrap the input stream that lets us read the child's output via an `InputStreamReader`. If we wanted to treat the child's output as a stream of bytes, we could easily do that instead. If the example were written to use the second form of `exec`, the code would look like this:

```
String cmd = "/bin/ls " + opts + " " + dir;
Process child = Runtime.getRuntime().exec(cmd);
```

`Process` is an abstract class. Each implementation of Java may provide one or more appropriate extended classes of `Process` that can interact with processes on the underlying system. Such classes might have extended functionality that would be useful for programming on the underlying system. The local documentation should contain information about this extended functionality.

Two other forms of `exec` enable you to specify a set of *environment variables*, which are system-dependent values that can be queried as desired by the new process. Environment variables are passed to `exec` as a `String` array; each element of the array specifies the name and value of an environment variable in the form `name=value`. The name cannot contain any spaces, although the value can be any string. The environment variables are passed as the second parameter:

public Process **exec(String command, String[] env)**
    throws IOException

public Process **exec(String[] command, String[] env)**
    throws IOException

Environment variables are interpreted in a system-dependent way by the child process's program. The environment variables mechanism is supported because existing programs on many different kinds of platforms understand them. To communicate between Java programs, you should use properties, not environment variables.

You should note that any program that uses `exec` is not portable across all Java systems. Not all Java environments have processes, and those that have them can have widely varying commands and syntax for invoking them. Also, because running arbitrary commands raises serious security issues, the system may not allow all programs to use exec. Be very cautious in choosing to use exec because it has a strong negative impact on your ability to run your program everywhere.

Exercise 15.1: Write the plugTogether method. You will need threads.

Exercise 15.2: Write a program that runs exec on its command-line arguments and prints the output from the command, precededing each line of output by its line number.

Exercise 15.3: Write a program that runs exec on command-line arguments and prints the output from the command, killing the command when a particular string appears in the output.

15.5 Runtime

Objects of the Runtime class represent the state of the runtime system and operations that it can perform. You can obtain a Runtime object that represents the current runtime by invoking the static method Runtime.getRuntime.

A runtime can be shut down by invoking its exit method, passing a status code. This method kills all threads in the runtime, no matter what their state. They are not interrupted, or even stopped. They simply cease to exist as the virtual machine itself stops running—no finally clauses or finalize methods are executed. In some situations a better way to quit is to interrupt all the threads in your thread group, letting them die gracefully, before you invoke exit.

The exit status code is zero to indicate successful completion of a task and is nonzero to indicate failure. There are two ways to signal the success of an application with an exit status: immediately invoke exit and destroy the threads, or ensure that all threads are shut down cleanly before invoking exit. The following example interrupts all threads in the current group, lets them finish, and then invokes exit:

```
public static void safeExit(int status) {
    // Get the list of all threads
    Thread myThrd = Thread.currentThread();
    ThreadGroup thisGroup = myThrd.getThreadGroup();
    int count = thisGroup.activeCount();
    Thread[] thrds = new Thread[count + 20]; // +20 for slop
    thisGroup.enumerate(thrds);

    // interrupt all threads
```

```
    for (int i = 0; i < thrds.length; i++) {
        if (thrds[i] != null && thrds[i] != myThrd)
            thrds[i].interrupt();
    }

    // wait for all threads to complete
    for (int i = 0; i < thrds.length; i++) {
        if (thrds[i] != null && thrds[i] != myThrd) {
            try {
                thrds[i].join();
            } catch (InterruptedException e) {
                // just skip this thread
            }
        }
    }

    // now we can exit
    System.exit(status);
}
```

This method gets the threads from its thread groups and all its subgroups. The 20 extra slots in the array "for slop" allow extra room in case some threads are spawned after activeCount returns. It then loops, interrupting all the threads, and uses join to join each thread after it is finished. When all threads are ready, it exits with the provided status.

When you invoke exit, the virtual machine will simply stop. You can think of this as turning all objects into garbage, because they are all unreachable from running code—after all, there is no running code. However, the virtual machine will not execute the finalize methods of any objects.

You can invoke System.runFinalizersOnExit with a value of true before you exit, which will make the virtual machine attempt to run the finalize methods of all unclaimed objects when it exits. You should use this feature with great care —for example, many people have not tested their finalize methods in an environment where System.out may be finalized before their methods execute.

Exercise 15.4: Modify safeExit to handle threads that are created after the method enumerate is invoked. Also modify it to skip daemon threads, which presumably expect sudden death.

15.6 Miscellaneous

Two methods in `System` don't belong to any particular category:

`public static long currentTimeMillis()`

> Returns the current time in milliseconds GMT since the epoch (00:00:00 UTC, January 1, 1970). The time is returned in a `long`. Sophisticated applications may require more functionality: see "Time, Dates, and Calendars" on page 343.

`public static void arraycopy(Object src, int srcPos, Object dst, int dstPos, int count)`

> Copies the contents of the source array, starting at `src[srcPos]`, to the destination array, starting at `dst[dstPos]`. Exactly `count` elements will be copied. All the array references must be inside the two arrays, or else you will get an `IndexOutOfBoundsException`. The values in the source array must be compatible with the type of the destination array, or else you will get an `ArrayStoreException`. By "compatible," we mean that each object in the source array must be assignable to an entry in the destination array. For arrays of primitive types, the types must be the same, not just assignable; `arraycopy` cannot be used to copy an array of `short` to an array of `int`.
>
> The `arraycopy` method works correctly on overlapping arrays, so it can be used to copy one part of an array over another part. You can, for example, shift everything in an array one slot toward the beginning, as shown in the method `squeezeOut` on page 170.

Two tracing methods available in `Runtime` also don't fit in any other category: `traceInstructions` and `traceMethodCalls`. Each method takes a `boolean` parameter that, if `true`, turns on tracing of instructions or method calls, respectively. Tracing is turned off when the boolean is `false`. Each virtual machine is free to do what it wants with these calls, including ignoring them if the local runtime has nowhere to put the trace output, although they are likely to work in a development environment.

15.7 Security

The `System` class supports two methods for the `SecurityManager` object. The `SecurityManager` class defines methods that govern whether sockets can be opened, files accessed, threads created, and so on. For details on how all this works, see *The Java Language Specification;* a description of the details would be too arcane for this general text.

```
public static void setSecurityManager(SecurityManager s)
```
Sets the system security manager object. This value can be set only once so that whoever sets up system security can rely it not being changed.

```
public static SecurityManager getSecurityManager()
```
Gets the system security manager. If none has been set `null` is returned, and all operations are assumed to be allowed by the virtual machine, although your system's underlying security policy is still in force. For example, if there were no installed security manager, you would still not be allowed to open files that non-Java programs could not open.

15.8 Math

The `Math` class consists of static constants and methods for common mathematical manipulations. `Math.E` represents the value e (2.7182818284590452354), and `Math.PI` represents the value π (3.14159265358979323846). In the following table of `Math` methods angles are in radians, and all parameters and return values are `double`, unless stated otherwise:

Function	Value
sin(a)	sine(a)
cos(a)	cosine(a)
tan(a)	tangent(a)
asin(v)	arcsine(v), with v in the range [−1.0, 1.0]
acos(v)	arccosine(v), with v in the range [−1.0, 1.0]
atan(v)	arctangent(v), returned in the range [$-\pi/2,\pi/2$]
atan2(x,y)	arctangent(x/y), returned in the range [$-\pi,\pi$]
exp(x)	e^x
pow(y,x)	y^x
log(x)	ln x (natural log of x)
sqrt(x)	Square root of x
ceil(x)	Smallest whole number $\geq x$
floor(x)	Largest whole number $\leq x$
rint(x)	x rounded to the nearest integer; if neither integer is nearer, rounds to the even integer
round(x)	(int)floor(x + 0.5) for float x; (long)floor(x + 0.5) for double x
abs(x)	Absolute value of x for any numeric type
max(x,y)	Larger of x and y for any numeric type
min(x,y)	Smaller of x and y for any numeric type

The static method `Math.IEEEremainder` calculates remainder as defined by the IEEE-754 standard. The remainder operator %, as described in "Floating-Point Arithmetic" on page 128, obeys the rule

```
(x/y)*y + x%y == x
```

This preserves one kind of symmetry: if x%y is z, then changing the sign of either x or y will change only the sign of z, never its absolute value. For example, 7%2.5 is 2.0, and -7%2.5 is -2.0. The IEEE standard defines remainder for x and y differently, preserving symmetry of spacing along the number line—the result of `Math.IEEEremainder(-7, 2.5)` is 0.5. The remainder operator makes values symmetric around zero on the number line, whereas the IEEE remainder mechanism keeps resulting values y units apart. The method is provided because both kinds of remainder are useful.

The static method `random` generates a pseudorandom number r in the range $0.0 \leq r < 1.0$. For more control over pseudorandom numbers, see "Random" on page 291.

See "java.math—Mathematics" on page 370 for brief coverage of some other math-related classes.

Exercise 15.5: Write a calculator that has these functions as well as (at least) the basic operators +, -, *, /, and %. The simplest form is probably a reverse Polish stack calculator because operator precedence is not an issue.

Power corrupts.
Absolute power is kind of neat.
—John Lehman, U.S. Secretary of the Navy

CHAPTER 16

Internationalization and Localization

Nobody can be exactly like me.
Sometimes even I have trouble doing it.
—Tallulah Bankhead

JAVA's credo of "Write once, run anywhere" means that your code will run in many places where languages and customs than are different from yours. With a little care you can write programs that can adapt to these variations gracefully. Keeping your programs supple in this fashion is called *internationalization.* Java provides several tools for internationalizing your code. Using internationalization tools to adapt your program to a specific locale—such as by translating messages into the local language—is called *localization.*

Java provides several tools that help with internationalization and localization. The first one is inherent in the language: Java strings are in Unicode, which can express almost any written language on our planet. Someone must still translate the strings, and displaying the translated text to users requires fonts for those characters. Still, having Unicode is a big boost for localizing your code.

The nexus of internationalization and localization is the *locale,* which defines a "place." A place can be a language, culture, or country—anything with an associated set of customs that requires changes in program behavior. Each running program has a default locale that is the user's preferred place. It is up to each program to adapt to a locale's customs as best it can. Java represents the locale concept with a `Locale` class, which is part of the `java.util` package.

Given a locale, several Java tools can help your program behave in a locally comprehensible fashion. A common pattern is for an abstract class to define the methods for performing *locale-sensitive* operations. A generic "get instance" static method of this abstract class returns an object of a concrete subtype suitable for the default locale. The abstract class will also provide an overload of each "get instance" method that takes a locale argument and returns a suitable object. For example, you can get an appropriate calendar object that works with the user's preferred dates and times by invoking the `getInstance` methods of the `java.util.Calendar` class. The returned `Calendar` object will understand how to translate system time into dates using the customs of the default locale. If the user were Mexican, an object that was a subclass of `Calendar` adapted to Mexican customs could be returned. A Chinese user might get an object of a different subtype that worked under the Chinese calendar customs.

If your program displays information to the user, you will likely want to localize the output: saying "Please deflate your shoes" to someone who doesn't understand English is probably pointless, so you would like to localize the message for a native speaker of the current locale. The resource bundle mechanisms map string keys to arbitrary resources. You use the values returned by a resource bundle to make your program speak in other tongues—instead of writing the literal strings in code, look up the strings by identifier. When the program is moved to another locale, someone can translate those resource strings inside an appropriate class and your program will work for that new locale without changing a line of code.

The classes described in this chapter come almost entirely from the package `java.util`. You will see occasional brief discussion of classes in the text internationalization and localization package `java.text`, which is generally outside the purview of this book. An overview of `java.text` starts on page 354.

16.1 Locale

A `java.util.Locale` object describes a specific place—cultural, political, or geographical. Using a locale, objects can *localize* their behavior to a user's expectations. An object that does so is called *locale-sensitive*. For example, date formatting can be localized using the locale-sensitive `DateFormat` class (described later in this chapter), so the date written in Great Britain as 26/11/72 would be written 26.11.72 in Iceland, 11/26/72 in the United States, or 72.26.11 in Latvia.

A single locale represents issues of language, country, and other traditions. There can be separate locales for U.S. English, U.K. English, Pakistani English, and so forth. Although the language is arguably in common for these locales, the customs of date, currency, and numeric representation vary.

Your code will rarely get or create `Locale` objects directly but instead will use the default locale that reflects the user's preference. You typically use this locale implicitly by getting resources or resource bundles as shown with other locale-sensitive classes. For example, you get the default calendar object like this:

```
Calendar now = Calendar.getInstance();
```

The `Calendar` class's `getInstance` method looks up the default locale to figure out which type of calendar object it should return. When you write your own locale-sensitive classes, you get the default locale from the static `getDefault` method of the `Locale` class.

If you write code that lets a user configure a locale, you may need to create `Locale` objects. There are two constructors:

public **`Locale(String language, String country, String variant)`**
> Creates a `Locale` object that represents the given language and country, where `language` is the two-letter ISO 639 code for the language (such as `"et"` for Estonian) and `country` is the two-letter ISO 3166 code for the country (such as `"KY"` for Cayman Islands). "Further Reading" on page 381 lists references for these codes. The `variant` can specify anything, such as an operating system (such as `"POSIX"` or `"MAC"`) or company or era. If you specify more than one variant, separate the two with an underscore. To leave any part of the locale unspecified, use `""`, an empty string.

`Locale(String language, String country)`
> Equivalent to `Locale(language, country, "")`.

The language and country can be in any case, but they will always be translated to lowercase for the language and uppercase for the country to conform to the governing standards. The case of variants is not modified.

The `Locale` class defines `Locale` objects for several well-known locales, such as CANADA_FRENCH, and KOREA for countries, and TRADITIONAL_CHINESE and KOREAN for languages. These objects are simply conveniences and have no special privileges compared to any `Locale` object you may create.

The static method `setLocale` changes the default locale. The default locale is shared state and should always reflect the user's preference. If you have code that must operate in a different locale, you can specify that locale to locale-sensitive classes either as an argument when you get resources or on specific operations.

`Locale` provides methods for getting the parts of the locale description. The methods `getCountry`, `getLanguage`, and `getVariant` return the values defined during construction. These are terse codes that most users will not know. These methods have "display" variants—`getDisplayCountry`, `getDisplayLanguage`, and `getDisplayVariant`—that returns a human-readable version of the value. The method `getDisplayName` returns a human-readable summary of the entire locale description, and `toString` returns the terse equivalent, using underscores to separate the parts.

You can optionally provide a `Locale` argument to any of the "display" methods to get a description of the provided locale under the default locale. For example, if the locale provided was for France and the default locale was Italian, `getDisplayCountry` could return `"Italie"`, the French name for Italy.

The methods `getISO3Country` and `getISO3Language` return three-character ISO codes for the country and language of the locale, respectively.

16.2 Resource Bundles

When you internationalize code, you commonly have units of meaning—such as text or sounds—that must be translated or otherwise made appropriate for each locale. If you put English text directly into your program, localizing that code is difficult—it requires finding all the strings in your program, identifying which ones are shown to users, and translating them in the code, thereby creating a second version of your program for, say, Swahili users. When you repeat this process for a large number of locales the task becomes a nightmare.

The resource bundle classes in `java.util` help you address this problem in a cleaner and more flexible fashion. The abstract class `ResourceBundle` defines methods to look up resources in a bundle by string key and to provide a parent bundle that will be searched if a bundle doesn't have a key. This parenting allows one bundle to be just like another bundle except that a few resource values are overridden or added. For example, a U.S. English bundle might use a British English bundle for a parent, providing replacements for resources that have different spelling. `ResourceBundle` provides the following public methods:

`public final String getString(String key)`
    `throws MissingResourceException`
    Returns the string stored in the bundle under the given key.

`public final String[] getStringArray(String key)`
    `throws MissingResourceException`
    Returns the string array stored in the bundle under the given key.

`public final Object getObject(String key)`
    `throws MissingResourceException`
    Returns the object stored in the bundle under the given key.

`public abstract Enumeration getKeys()`
    Returns an `Enumeration` of the keys understood by this bundle, including all those of the parent.

Each resource bundle defines a set of string keys that map to locale-sensitive resources. These strings can be anything you like, although it is best to make them mnemonic. When you want to use the resource you look it up by name.

We will show an internationalized way to rewrite the "Hello, world" example. This internationalized example will require a program called `GlobalHello` and a resource bundle for the program's strings called GlobalRes, which will define a set of constants for the localizable strings. First, the program:

```
import java.util.*;

public class GlobalHello {
    public static void main(String[] args) {
        ResourceBundle res =
            ResourceBundle.getBundle("GlobalRes");
        String msg;
        if (args.length > 0)
            msg = res.getString(GlobalRes.GOODBYE);
        else
            msg = res.getString(GlobalRes.HELLO);
        System.out.println(msg);
    }
}
```

The program first gets its resource bundle. Then it checks whether any arguments are provided on the command line. If some are, it says good-bye; otherwise it says hello. The program logic determines which message to display, but the actual string to print is looked up by key (GlobalRes.HELLO or GlobalRes.GOODBYE).

Each resource bundle is a set of associated classes and property files. In our example, GlobalRes is the name of a class that extends ResourceBundle, implementing the methods necessary to map a message key to a localized translation of that message. You define classes for the various locales for which you want to localize the messages, naming the classes to reflect the locale. For example, the bundle class that manages GlobalRes messages for the Lingala language would be GlobalRes_ln because "ln" is the two-letter code for Lingala. French would be mapped in GlobalRes_fr, and Canadian French would be GlobalRes_fr_CA, which might have a parent bundle of GlobalRes_fr.

We have chosen to make the key strings constants in the GlobalRes class. Using constants prevents errors of misspelling. If you pass literal strings such as "hello" to getString, a misspelling will show up only when the erroneous getString is executed, and that might not happen during testing. If you use constants, a misspelling will be caught by the compiler (unless you are unlucky enough to accidentally spell the name of another constant).

You find resources by calling one of two static getBundle methods in ResourceBundle: the one we used, which searches the current locale for the best available version of the bundle you name; and the other method, which lets you specify both bundle name and desired locale. A fully qualified bundle name has the form *package.Bundle_la_CO_va*, where *package.Bundle* is the general name for the bundle class (such as `GlobalRes`), *la* is the two-letter language code (lowercase), *CO* is the two-letter country code (uppercase), and *va* is the list of variants separated by underscores. If a bundle of the fully qualified name cannot be found, the last component is dropped and the search repeated with this shorter name. This process is repeated until only the last locale modifier is left. If even this search fails and if you invoked `getBundle` with a specified locale, the search is restarted using the fully qualified name of the bundle for the default locale. If this second search ends with no bundle found or if you were searching in the default locale, `getBundle` checks using just the bundle name. If even that bundle does not exist, `getBundle` throws a `MissingBundleException`.

For example, suppose you ask for the bundle `GlobalRes`, specifying a locale for an Esperanto speaker living in Kiribati who is left-handed, and the default locale of the user is for a Nepali speaker in Bhutan who works for Acme, Inc. The longest possible search would be:

```
GlobalRes_eo_KI_left
GlobalRes_eo_KI
GlobalRes_eo
GlobalRes_ne_BT_Acme
GlobalRes_ne_BT
GlobalRes_ne
GlobalRes
```

The first resource bundle that is found ends the search, being considered the best available match. If no match is found, you will get a `MissingBundleException`.

The examples you have seen use resource bundles to fetch strings, but remember that you can use `getObject` to get any type of object. Bundles are used to store images, URLs, audio sources, graphics components, and any other kind of locale-sensitive resource that can be represented by an object.

Mapping string keys to localized resource objects is usually straightforward—simply use one of the provided subclasses of `ResourceBundle` that implement the lookup for you: `ListResourceBundle` and `PropertyResourceBundle`.

16.2.1 `ListResourceBundle`

`ListResourceBundle` maps a simple list of keys to their localized objects. It is an abstract subclass of `ResourceBundle` for which you provide a `getContents` method that returns an array of key/resource pairs as an array of arrays of `Object`. The keys must be strings, but the resources can be any kind of object. The `ListResourceBundle` takes this array and builds the maps for the various "get" methods. The following classes use `ListResourceBundle` to define a few locales for `GlobalRes`. First, the base bundle:

```
public class GlobalRes extends ListResourceBundle {
    public final static String HELLO = "hello";
    public final static String GOODBYE = "goodbye";

    public Object[][] getContents() {
        return contents;
    }

    static private final Object[][] contents = {
        { GlobalRes.HELLO,      "Ciao" },
        { GlobalRes.GOODBYE,    "Ciao" },
    };
}
```

This is the top-level bundle—when no other bundle is found, this will be used. We have chosen Italian for the default. The values in the `contents` array will be used to seed the data structures used by the "get" methods of `ListResourceBundle`. Before any "get" method is executed, `GlobalRes.getContents` will be invoked and the resulting array's contents will seed the data structures used by the "get" methods. `ListResourceBundle` uses an internal lookup table for efficient access; it does not search through your array of keys. The `GlobalRes` class also defines the constants that name known resources in the bundle. Here is another bundle for a more specific locale:

```
public class GlobalRes_en extends ListResourceBundle {
    public Object[][] getContents() {
        return contents;
    }
    static private final Object[][] contents = {
        { GlobalRes.HELLO,      "Hello" },
        { GlobalRes.GOODBYE,    "Goodbye" },
    };
}
```

This bundle covers the English language locale `en`. It provides specific values for each localizable string. The next bundle uses the parenting feature:

```
public class GlobalRes_en_AU extends ListResourceBundle {
    // mostly like the basic English locale
    { parent = new GlobalRes_en(); }
```

```
    public Object[][] getContents() { return contents; }

    static private final Object[][] contents = {
        { GlobalRes.HELLO,      "G'day" },
    };
}
```

This bundle is for English speakers from Australia (AU). It provides a more collo-
quial version of the HELLO string and inherits all other strings from the general
English locale GlobalRes_en by setting its parent field to be a bundle for
English in an initializer block.

　　Given these classes, someone with an English (en) language locale would get
the values returned by GlobalRes_en unless the locale also specified the country
Australia (AU), in which case values from GlobalRes_en_AU would be used.
Everyone else would see those in GlobalRes.

16.2.2 PropertyResourceBundle

PropertyResourceBundle is a subclass of ResourceBundle that reads its list of
resources from a text property description. The text contains key/value pairs with
lines of the form

　　　key=value

Both keys and values must be strings. Each PropertyResourceBundle object
reads an InputStream that contains the description and builds a lookup table for
efficient access. A possible PropertyResourceBundle for GlobalRes might be:

```
import java.util.*;
import java.io.*;

public class GlobalRes_tl extends PropertyResourceBundle {
    public GlobalRes_tl() throws IOException {
        super(propStream());
    }

    private static InputStream propStream() {
        Class cl = GlobalRes_tl.class;
        return cl.getResourceAsStream("GlobalRes_tl.pr");
    }
}
```

The bundle search looks for classes or for property files named like the class with `.properties` at the end. If one is found, `ResourceBundle.getBundle` creates a `PropertyResourceBundle` that uses that file as input. The effect will be the same as that of the preceding class, so we could avoid writing any class if we simply rename the file `GlobalRes_tl.pr` to `GlobalRes_tl.properties`.

16.2.3   Subclassing `ResourceBundle`

`ListResourceBundle`, `PropertyResourceBundle`, and `.properties` files will be sufficient for most of your bundles, or you can create your own subclass of `ResourceBundle`. You must implement two methods:

protected abstract Object **handleGetObject(String key)**
   throws MissingResourceException
>   Returns the object associated with the given key. If the key is not defined in this bundle, it returns `null`, and that causes the `ResourceBundle` to check in the parent (if any). Do not throw `MissingResourceException` unless you check out the parent instead of letting the bundle do it. All the "get" methods are written in terms of this one method.

public abstract Enumeration **getKeys()**
>   Returns an `Enumeration` that iterates over the keys in this bundle.

Exercise 16.1: Get `GlobalHello` to work with the example locales. Add some more locales, using `ListResourceBundle`, `.properties` files, and your own specific subclass of `ResourceBundle`.

16.3   Time, Dates, and Calendars

Java time is a `long` integer measured in milliseconds since midnight Greenwich Mean Time (GMT) January 1, 1970. This value is signed, so negative values signify time before the beginning of the *epoch*, the starting point for time measurement. The method `System.currentTimeMillis` returns the current time. This value will express dates into the year A.D. 292,280,995, which should suffice for most purposes.

You can use `java.util.Date` to hold a time and perform some simple time-related operations. When a new `Date` object is created, you can specify a `long` value for its time. If you use the no-arg constructor, the `Date` object will mark the time of its creation. A `Date` object can be used for simple operations. For example, the simplest program to print the current time (repeated from page 25) is

```
import java.util.Date;

class Date2 {
    public static void main(String[] args) {
        Date now = new Date();
        System.out.println(now);
    }
}
```

This program will produce output such as the following:

```
Tue Sep 30 22:20:28 EDT 1997
```

Note that this is not localized output. No matter what the default locale, the date will be in this format, adjusted for the default time zone.

You can compare two dates using `before` and `after` methods, which return `true` if the object on which they are invoked is before or after the other date. Or you can compare the `long` values you get from invoking `getTime` on the two objects. The method `setTime` lets you change the time to a different `long`.

16.3.1 Calendars

Calendars express dates in forms that people can understand. Most of the world uses the same calendar, commonly called the Gregorian calendar after Pope Gregory XIII, under whose auspices it was first instituted. Many other calendars exist in the world, and Java's calendar abstractions are designed to express such variations. A given moment in time is expressed as a date according to a particular calendar, and the same moment can be expressed as different dates by different calendars. The calendar abstraction is couched in the following form:

- An abstract `Calendar` class that represents various ways of marking time
- An abstract `TimeZone` class that represents time zone offsets and other adjustments, such as daylight saving time
- An abstract `java.text.DateFormat` class that defines how one can format and parse date and time strings

Because the Gregorian calendar is commonly used, Java also provides the following concrete implementations of the abstractions:

- A `GregorianCalendar` class
- A `SimpleTimeZone` class for use with `GregorianCalendar`

- ◆ A `java.text.SimpleDateFormat` class that formats and parses Gregorian dates and times

For example, the following program uses a `GregorianCalendar` to show the full date for midnight, October 26, 1972 GMT, in the local time zone:

```
Calendar cal =
    new GregorianCalendar(1972, Calendar.OCTOBER, 26);
System.out.println(cal.getTime());
```

The method `getTime` returns a `Date` object for the calendar object's time, which was set by converting a year, month, and date into a millisecond-measured `long`.

The `Calendar` class provides an abstract class that can be extended to provide concrete examples of particular calendars. It provides a large set of constants that are useful in many calendars, such as `Calendar.AM` and `Calendar.PM` for calendars that use 12-hour clocks. Some constants are useful only for certain calendars, but no calendar class is required to use such constants. In particular, the month names in `Calendar` (such as `Calendar.JUNE`) are names for the various month numbers (such as 6), with a special month UNDECIMBER for the thirteenth month that many calendars have. But no calendar is required to use these constants.

Each `Calendar` object represents a particular moment in time on that calendar. The `Calendar` class provides only constructors that create an object for the current time, either in the default locale and time zone or in specified ones.

Calendar objects represent a moment in time, but they are not responsible for displaying the date. That locale-sensitive procedure is the job of the `DateFormat` class, which will be described soon.

You can obtain a calendar object for a locale by invoking one of the static `Calendar.getInstance` methods. With no arguments, `getInstance` returns an object of the best available calendar type for the default locale and time zone. The other overloads allow you to specify the locale, the time zone, or both. The static `getAvailableLocales` method returns an array of `Locale` objects for which calendars are installed on the system.

With a calendar object in hand, you can manipulate the date. The following example prints the next week of days for a given calendar object:

```
public static void oneWeek(PrintStream out, Calendar cal) {
    Calendar cur = (Calendar)cal.clone(); // modifiable copy
    int dow = cal.get(Calendar.DAY_OF_WEEK);
    do {
        out.println(cur.getTime());
        cur.add(Calendar.HOUR, 24);
    } while (cur.get(Calendar.DAY_OF_WEEK) != dow);
}
```

First, we make a copy of the calendar argument so that we can make changes without affecting the calendar we were passed. Instead of assuming that there are seven days in a week (who knows what kind of calendar we were given?), we loop, printing the time and adding one day to that time, until we have printed a week's worth of days. We detect that a week has passed by looking for the next day whose "day of the week" is the same as that of the original.

The `Calendar` class defines many kinds of *calendar fields* for calendar objects, such as YEAR in the preceding code. These calendar fields are constants used in the methods that manipulate parts of the time:

MILLISECOND	DAY_OF_WEEK_IN_MONTH	MONTH_OF_YEAR
SECOND	DAY_OF_MONTH	YEAR
MINUTE	DATE	ERA
HOUR	DAY_OF_YEAR	ZONE_OFFSET
HOUR_OF_DAY	WEEK_OF_MONTH	DST_OFFSET
AM_PM	WEEK_OF_YEAR	FIELD_COUNT
DAY_OF_WEEK	MONTH	

An `int` is used to store values for all these calendar field types. You use these constants—or any others defined by a particular calendar class—to specify a calendar field to the following methods (always as the first argument):

get	Returns the value of the field
set	Sets the value of the field to the provided `int`
clear	Clears the value of the field to "unspecified"
isSet	Returns a `boolean` that is `true` if the field has been set
add	Adds an `int` amount to the specified field
roll	Rolls the field up to the next value if the second `boolean` argument is `true`, or down if it is `false`
getMinimum	Gets the minimum valid value for the field
getMaximum	Gets the maximum valid value for the field
getGreatestMinimum	Gets the highest minimum value for the field; if the minimum varies this can be different from `getMinimum`
getLeastMaximum	Gets the smallest maximum value for the field; if the maximum varies this can be different from `getMaximum`

The greatest minimum and least maximum describe cases in which a value can vary within the overall boundaries. For example, the least maximum value for DAY_OF_MONTH on the Gregorian calendar is 28 because February, the shortest month, can have as few as 28 days. The maximum value is 31 because no month has more than 31 days.

The set, clear, and isSet methods allow you to specify a date by certain calendar fields and then calculate the time associated with that date. For example, you can calculate on which day of the week a particular date falls:

```
public static int dotw(int year, int month, int date) {
    Calendar cal = new GregorianCalendar();
    cal.set(Calendar.YEAR, year);
    cal.set(Calendar.MONTH, month);
    cal.set(Calendar.DATE, date);
    return cal.get(Calendar.DAY_OF_WEEK);
}
```

The method dotw calculates the day of the week on the Gregorian calendar for the given date. It creates a Gregorian calendar object, sets the date fields for year, month, and day, and the returns the resulting day of the week. You can use clear with no parameters to clear all calendar fields.

Three variants of set change particular fields you commonly need to manipulate, leaving unspecified fields alone:

public void **set(int year, int month, int date)**

public void **set(int year, int month, int date, int hrs, int min)**

public void **set(int year, int month, int date, int hrs, int min, int sec)**

You can also use setTime to set the calendar's time from a Date object.

A calendar field that is out of range can be interpreted correctly. For example, January 32 can be equivalent to February 1. Whether it is treated as such or as an error depends on whether the calendar is considered to be *lenient*. A lenient calendar will do its best to interpret values as valid. A strict (nonlenient) calendar will not accept any values out of range, throwing IllegalArgumentException. The setLenient method takes a boolean that specifies whether parsing should be lenient; isLenient returns the current setting.

A week can start on any day, depending on the calendar. You can discover the first day of the week using the method getFirstDayOfWeek. In a Gregorian calendar for the United States this method would return SUNDAY, whereas Ireland uses MONDAY. You can change this by invoking setFirstDayOfWeek with a valid weekday index.

Some calendars require a minimum number of days in the first week of the year. The method getMinimalDaysInFirstWeek returns that number; the method setMinimalDaysInFirstWeek lets you change it.

You can compare two Calendar objects by comparing the Date objects returned by their respective getTime methods. If you prefer, you can use the before and after methods to compare the objects.

16.3.2 Time Zones

TimeZone is an abstract class that encapsulates not only offset from GMT but also other offset issues, such as daylight saving time. As with other locale-sensitive classes, you can get the default one by invoking the static method getDefault. You can change the default time zone by passing setDefault a new TimeZone object to use. Time zones are understood by particular calendar types, so you should ensure that the default calendar and time zone are compatible.

Each time zone has a string identifier that is interpreted by the time zone object and can be displayed to the user. An array of string identifiers available can be obtained by invoking the static method getAvailableIDs. If you want only those for a given offset from GMT, you can invoke getAvailableIDs with that offset. An offset might, for example, have identifiers for both daylight saving and standard time zones.

The identifier of a given TimeZone object can be found by invoking getID and can be set by using setID. Setting the identifier changes only the identifier on the time zone—it does not change the offset or other values. You can get the time zone for a given identifier by passing it to the static method getTimeZone.

Each time zone has a *raw offset* from GMT. It can be either positive or negative, but is always in the range –24 through 24. You can get or set the raw offset using getRawOffset or setRawOffset.

Daylight saving time supplements the raw offset with a seasonal time shift. You can ask whether a time zone ever uses daylight saving time by invoking use-DaylightTime, which returns a boolean. The method inDaylightTime returns true if the Date argument you pass would fall inside daylight saving time in the zone. Or you can specify a date using values for calendar fields to ask the same question:

```
public int getOffset(int era, int year, int month, int day,
   int dayOfWeek, int milliseconds)
```
   Returns the offset from GMT for the given time in this time zone, taking any daylight saving time offset into account. All parameters are interpreted relative to the calendar for which the particular time zone implementation is designed. The era parameter represents calendar-specific eras, such as B.C. and A.D. in the Gregorian calendar.

16.3.3 GregorianCalendar and SimpleTimeZone

The GregorianCalendar class is a concrete subclass of Calendar that reflects UTC (Coordinated Universal Time), although it cannot always do so exactly. Imprecise behavior is inherited from the time mechanisms of the underlying system.[1] Parts of a date are specified in UTC standard units and ranges. Here are the ranges for GregorianCalendar:

YEAR   A year after 1900, always specified as (year – 1900) with all digits (for example, 2003 is year 103)

MONTH   0–11

DATE   Day of the month, 1–31

HOUR   0–23

MINUTE   0–59

SECOND   0–61 (provides for leap seconds)

MILLISECOND 0-999

The GregorianCalendar class supports several constructors:

public **GregorianCalendar()**

> Creates a GregorianCalendar object that represents the current time in the default time zone with the default locale.

public **GregorianCalendar(int year, int month, int date, int hrs, int min, int sec)**

> Creates a GregorianCalendar object that represents the given date in the default time zone with the default locale.

public **GregorianCalendar(int year, int month, int date, int hrs, int min)**

> Equivalent to GregorianCalendar(year, month, date, hrs, min, 0)— that is, the beginning of the specified minute.

public **GregorianCalendar(int year, int month, int date)**

> Equivalent to GregorianCalendar(year, month, date, 0, 0, 0)—that is, midnight on the given date.

public **GregorianCalendar(Locale locale)**

> Creates a GregorianCalendar object that represents the current time in the default time zone with the given locale.

---

[1]   Almost all modern systems assume that one day is 24*60*60 seconds. In UTC, about once a year an extra second, called a *leap second,* is added to a day to account for the wobble of the Earth. Most computer clocks are not accurate enough to reflect this distinction, so neither is the Date class. Some computer standards are defined in GMT, which is the "civil" name for the standard; UT is the scientific name for the same standard. The distinction between UTC and UT is that UT is based on an atomic clock and UTC is based on astronomical observations. For almost all practical purposes, this is an invisibly fine hair to split. See "Further Reading" on page 381 for references.

public **GregorianCalendar(TimeZone timeZone)**

> Creates a GregorianCalendar object that represents the current time in the given timeZone with the default locale.

public **GregorianCalendar(TimeZone zone, Locale locale)**

> Creates a GregorianCalendar object that represents the current time in the given timeZone with the given locale.

In addition to the methods it inherits from Calendar, GregorianCalendar provides an isLeapYear method that returns true if the calendar object represents a date that happens in a leap year.

The Gregorian calendar was preceded by the Julian calendar in many places. In a GregorianCalendar object, the default date at which this change happened is midnight local time on October 15, 1582. This is when the first countries switched, but others changed later. The getGregorianChange method returns the time the calendar is currently using for the change as a Date. You can set a calendar's change-over time by using setGregorianChange with a Date object.

The SimpleTimeZone class is a concrete subclass of TimeZone that is used to express values for Gregorian calendars. It does not handle historical complexities, but instead projects current practices onto all times. For historical dates that precede the use of daylight saving time, for example, you will want to use a calendar with a time zone you have selected that ignores daylight saving time. For future dates, SimpleTimeZone is probably as good a guess as any.

16.4 Formatting and Parsing Dates and Times

Date and time formatting is a separate issue from calendars, although they are closely related. Formatting is localized in a different way. Not only are the names of days and months different in different locales that share the same calendar, but also the order in which things are expressed changes. In the United States it is customary in short dates to put the month before the date: July 5 becomes 7/5. In many European countries the date comes first, so 5 July becomes 5/7 or 5.7 or...

Date and time formatting issues are text issues, so the classes for formatting are in java.text. The Date2 program on page 344 is simple because it does not localize its output. If you want localization, you need a DateFormat object.

DateFormat provides several ways to format and parse dates and times. It is a subclass of the general Format class, discussed in "Formatting and Parsing" on page 355. There are three kinds of date formatters, each returned by different static methods: date formatters from getDateInstance, time formatters from getTimeInstance, and date/time formatters from getDateTimeInstance. Each of these formatters understands four formatting styles: SHORT, MEDIUM, LONG, and

FULL. And for each of them you can either use the default locale or specify one. For example, to get a medium date formatter in the default locale, you would use

```
Format fmt = DateFormat.getDateInstance(DateFormat.MEDIUM);
```

To get a date and time, with dates in short form and times in full form in a Japanese locale, you would use

```
Locale japan = new Locale("JP", "jp");
Format fmt = DateFormat.getDateTimeInstance(
            DateFormat.SHORT, DateFormat.FULL, japan
        );
```

For all the various "get instance" methods, if both format and locale are specified the locale is the last parameter. The date/time methods require two format styles: the first for the date part and the second for the time. The simplest `getInstance` method takes no arguments and returns a date/time formatter for short formats in the default locale. The `getAvailableLocales` method returns an array of all `Locale` objects for which date and time formatting is configured.

The following list shows how each formatting style is expressed for the same date. The output is from a date/time formatter for U.S. locales using the same formatting mode for both dates and times:

```
FULL:    Friday, August 29, 1986 2:00:00 o'clock PM PDT
LONG:    August 29, 1986 2:00:00 PM PDT
MEDIUM:  29-Aug-86 2:00:00 PM
SHORT:   8/29/86 2:00 PM
```

Each `DateFormat` object has an associated calendar and time zone set by the "get" method. They are returned by `getCalendar` and `getTimeZone`, respectively. You can set these values using `setCalendar` and `setTimeZone`. Each `DateFormat` object has a reference to a `NumberFormat` object for formatting numbers. You can use `getNumberFormat` and `setNumberFormat`. (Number formatting is covered briefly in "`java.text`—Internationalization and Localization for Text" on page 354.)

You format dates using one of several format methods based on the formatting parameters described earlier:

`public final String `**`format(Date date)`**
Returns a formatted string for date.

`public abstract StringBuffer `
`format(Date date, StringBuffer appendTo, FieldPosition pos)`
Adds the formatted string for date to the end of appendTo.

```
public abstract StringBuffer
```
format(Object obj, StringBuffer appendTo, FieldPosition pos)
Adds the formatted string for obj to the end of appendTo. The object can be either a Date or a Number whose longValue will be treated as a time.

A DateFormat object can also be used to parse dates. Date parsing can be lenient or not, depending on your preference. Lenient date parsing is as forgiving as it can be, whereas strict parsing requires the format and information to be proper and complete. The default is to be lenient. You can use setLenient to set leniency to be true or false. You can test leniency using isLenient.

The parsing methods are:

```
public Date parse(String text) throws ParseException
```
Tries to parse text into a date and/or time. If successful, a Date object is returned; otherwise, a ParseException is thrown.

```
public abstract Date parse(String text, ParsePosition pos)
```
Tries to parse text into a date and/or time. If successful, a Date object is returned; otherwise, returns a null reference. When the method is called, pos is the position at which to start parsing; at the end it will either be positioned after the parsed text or will remain unchanged if an error occurred.

```
public Object parseObject(String text, ParsePosition pos)
```
Returns the result of parse(text, pos). This method is provided to fulfill the generic contract of Format.

The class java.text.SimpleDateFormat is a concrete implementation of DateFormat that is used in many locales. If you are writing a DateFormat class, it may be useful to extend SimpleDateFormat. SimpleDateFormat uses methods in the DateFormatSymbols class to get localized strings and symbols for date representation. When formatting or parsing dates, you should usually not create SimpleDateFormat objects; you should use one of the "get instance" methods to return an appropriate formatter.

DateFormat has protected fields calendar and numberFormat that give direct access to the values publicly manipulated via the set and get methods.

Exercise 16.2: Write a program that takes a string argument that is parsed into the date to print, and print that date in all possible styles. How lenient will the date parsing be?

> *Love thy neighbor as yourself, but choose your neighborhood.*
> —Louise Beal

CHAPTER **17**

Standard Packages

No unmet needs exist,
and current unmet needs that are being met will continue to be met.
—Transportation Commission on Unmet Needs, California

THE Java platform comes with several standard packages. These define the Java core classes:

- `java.lang` — The core language classes, such as `String`, `Thread`, `Class`, and so on. The subpackage `java.lang.reflect` provides a way to examine types in detail, and is covered in "Reflection" on page 303.

- `java.io` — Input and output and some file system manipulation. This package is covered primarily in Chapter 12.

- `java.util` — Classes of general utility. They are covered primarily in Chapter 13, with localization classes covered in Chapter 16.

- `java.text` — Internationalization and localization for formatting and parsing numbers and dates, sorting strings, and message lookup by key. They are touched on briefly in Chapter 16.

- `java.awt` — The Abstract Window Toolkit abstraction layer for writing platform-independent graphical user interfaces.

- `java.applet` — The `Applet` class and related types for writing applets that can be run in HTML browsers.

- `java.beans` — The JavaBeans components in Java for user-composable code.

- `java.rmi` — Remote Method Invocation, which lets you invoke methods on objects running in different virtual machines, usually on different host computers.

- `java.net` — Networking classes for sockets, URLs, and so on.

- ◆ `java.math` — Mathematical manipulations. Currently this package has only two classes, which handle some kinds of arbitrary-precision arithmetic.

- ◆ `java.sql` — The JDBC package for using relational databases from Java.

- ◆ `java.security` — Encryption, authentication, digital signatures, and other useful security-related code.

This book cannot be large enough to contain full coverage of every one of these packages—some of them require complete books of their own. This chapter will discuss each package not otherwise covered in this book, giving an overview of the purpose and contents. All these packages are covered in detail in your local Java documentation and *The Java Class Libraries*. Most of the packages, including the AWT and applet packages, are taught in *The Java Tutorial*. These books and all others cited in this chapter are part of this official JavaSoft book series of documentation from the source—the people who invented Java and its packages.

17.1 `java.text`—Internationalization and Localization for Text

The package `java.text` provides several types for localizing text behavior, such as collation (comparing strings), and formatting and parsing numbers and dates. The topics not covered in Chapter 16 are covered briefly here.

17.1.1 Collation

Comparing strings in a locale-sensitive fashion is called *collation*. The central class for collation is `Collator`, which provides a `compare` method that takes two strings and returns an `int` less than, equal to, or greater than zero as the first string is less than, equal to, or greater than the second. Only the sign of the number matters—the value itself is meaningless—so you should compare the return value only against zero.

As with most locale-sensitive classes, you get the best available `Collator` object for a locale using a `getInstance` method, either passing a specific `Locale` object, or specifying no locale and so using the default locale. For example, you get the best available collator to sort a set of Russian-language strings like this:

```
Locale russian = new Locale("ru", "");
Collator coll = Collator.getInstance(russian);
```

Then you would use `coll.compare` to determine the order of strings. A `Collator` object takes locality—not Unicode equivalence—into account when comparing. For example, in a French-speaking locale, the characters ç and c are considered equivalent for sorting purposes. A naïve sort that used `String.com-pare` would put all strings starting with ç after all those starting with c (indeed, it would put them after z), but in a French locale this would be wrong. They should be sorted based on the characters that follow the initial c or ç characters in the strings.

Determining collation factors for a string can be expensive. A `CollationKey` object examines a string once, so you can compare pre-computed keys instead of comparing strings using a `Collator`. The method `Collator.getCollationKey` returns a key for a string. For example, if you want to maintain a sorted list of strings in a `Vector`, you could have a parallel `Vector` that stored each string's key. Insertion might then look like this:[1]

```
private Collator collator;   // collator to use
private Vector strings;      // the strings
private Vector keys;         // keys for each string

public void add(String newStr) {
    CollationKey newKey = collator.getCollationKey(newStr);
    for (int i = 0; i < strings.size(); i++) {
        CollationKey key = (CollationKey)keys.elementAt(i);
        int diff = newKey.compareTo(key);
        if (diff == 0)          // already in the list
            return;
        else if (diff < 0) {  // belongs before this one
            strings.insertElementAt(newStr, i);
            keys.insertElementAt(newKey, i);
            return;
        }
    }
    // must belong at the end
    strings.addElement(newStr);
    keys.addElement(newKey);
}
```

17.1.2 Formatting and Parsing

The abstract `Format` class provides methods to format and parse objects according to a locale. `Format` declares an abstract `format` method that takes an object

---

[1] We use a naïve insertion sort algorithm to keep the code simple; a binary insertion sort would have been more efficient.

and returns a formatted `String`, throwing `IllegalArgumentException` if the object is not of a type known to the formatting object. `Format` also declares an abstract `parse` method that takes a `String` and returns an object initialized from the parsed data, throwing `ParseFormatException` if the string is not understood. Each of these methods is implemented as appropriate for the particular kind of formatting. The package `java.text` provides three `Format` subclasses:

- `DateFormat` was discussed in "Formatting and Parsing Dates and Times" on page 350.

- `MessageFormat` helps you localize output when printing messages that contain values from your program. Because word order varies among languages, you cannot simply use a localized string concatenated with your program's values. For example, the English phrase "a fantastic menu" would in French have the word order "un menu fantastique." A message that took adjectives and nouns from lists and displayed them in such a phrase could use a `MessageFormat` object to localize the order.

- `NumberFormat` is an abstract class that defines a general way to format and parse various kinds of numbers for different locales. It has two subclasses. `ChoiceFormat` is used to choose among alternatives based on number (such as picking between a singular or plural variant of a word). `DecimalFormat` is used to format and parse decimal numbers.

`NumberFormat` in turn has three different kinds of "get instance" methods. Each method uses either a provided `Locale` object or the default locale.

- `getNumberInstance` returns a general number formatter/parser. This is the kind of object returned by the generic `getInstance` method.

- `getCurrencyInstance` returns a formatter/parser for currency values.

- `getPercentInstance` returns a formatter/parser for percentages.

Here is a program that prints a number in a list of locales:

```
import java.text.*;
import java.util.Locale;
import java.util.StringTokenizer;

class LocalNumber {
    public static void main(String[] args) {
        double num = new Double(args[0]).doubleValue();
        for (int i = 1; i < args.length; i++) {
```

```
            Locale pl = parseLocale(args[i]);
            NumberFormat fmt = NumberFormat.getInstance(pl);
            System.out.print(fmt.format(num));
            System.out.println("\t" + pl.getDisplayName());
        }
    }

    public static Locale parseLocale(String desc) {
        StringTokenizer st = new StringTokenizer(desc, "_");
        String lang = "", ctry = "", var = "";
        try {
            lang = st.nextToken();
            ctry = st.nextToken();
            var = st.nextToken();
        } catch (java.util.NoSuchElementException e) {
            ; // fine, let the others default
        }
        return new Locale(lang, ctry, var);
    }
}
```

The first argument to format is the number to format; optional following arguments specify locales. We use a StringTokenizer to break locale argument strings into constituent components. For example, cy_GB will be broken into the language cy (Welsh), the country GB (United Kingdom), and the empty variant "". We create a Locale object from each result, get a number formatter for that locale, and then print the formatted number and the locale. When run with the number 5372.97 and the locale arguments en_US, lv, it_CH, and lt, the program's output is

```
5,372.97        English (United States)
5 372,97        Latvian (Latvia)
5'372.97        Italian (Switzerland)
5.372,97        Lithuanian (Lithuania)
```

A similar program can be written that takes a locale and a number formatted in that locale, uses the parse method to get a Number object, and prints the resulting value formatted according to a list of other locales:

```
import java.text.*;
import java.util.Locale;
import java.util.StringTokenizer;
```

```
class ReformatNumber {
    public static void main(String[] args) {
        Locale loc = LocalNumber.parseLocale(args[0]);
        NumberFormat parser = NumberFormat.getInstance(loc);
        Number num = null;
        try {
            num = parser.parse(args[1]);
        } catch (ParseException e) {
            e.printStackTrace(System.err);
            System.exit(-1);
        }

        for (int i = 2; i < args.length; i++) {
            Locale pl = LocalNumber.parseLocale(args[i]);
            NumberFormat fmt = NumberFormat.getInstance(pl);
            System.out.println(fmt.format(num));
        }
    }
}
```

17.1.3 Text Boundaries

Parsing requires finding boundaries in text. The class `BreakIterator` provides a locale-sensitive tool for locating such break points. It has four kinds of "get instance" methods that return specific types of `BreakIterator` objects:

- `getCharacterInstance` returns an iterator that shows valid breaks in a string for individual characters (not necessarily a Java `char`).
- `getWordInstance` returns an iterator that shows word breaks in a string.
- `getLineInstance` returns an iterator that shows where it is proper to break a line in a string, for purposes such as wrapping text.
- `getSentenceInstance` returns an iterator that shows where sentence breaks occur in a string.

The following code prints each break shown by a given `BreakIterator`:

```
static void showBreaks(BreakIterator breaks, String str) {
    breaks.setText(str);
    int start = breaks.first();
    int end = breaks.next();
```

```
    while (end != BreakIterator.DONE) {
        System.out.println(str.substring(start, end));
        start = end;
        end = breaks.next();
    }
    System.out.println(str.substring(start)); // the last
}
```

You should always use these boundary classes when breaking up text because the issues involved are subtle and widely varying. For example, the logical characters used in these classes are not necessarily equivalent to a single Java char— Unicode characters can be combined, so that more than one 16-bit Unicode value can together constitute a logical character. And word breaks are not necessarily spaces—some languages, such as Chinese, do not even use spaces.

17.2 `java.awt`—The Abstract Window Toolkit

The Abstract Window Toolkit allows you to write graphical user interfaces (GUIs) that will run on every Java system in a reasonable way. The AWT displays GUI components (such as buttons, labels, and text fields) using (by default) the local platform's look and feel, showing Macintosh buttons on a Mac, Motif buttons on X platforms, Windows buttons on Windows systems, and so on.

For this to work, you may need to change how you think about laying out your GUI. You may be used to interactive tools that let you place the various GUI components on the screen exactly where you want them to be. Such *absolute placement* will not work for a portable interface because, for example, the size of a button is different on different systems. When your interface is used on a different system than the one on which you designed it, some buttons will overlap and others will have ugly gaps between them.

Although you can use absolute placement in AWT, it is not recommended. When you place a component into an AWT display frame, the frame's *layout manager* decides where to put it. Almost all the layout managers provided with the AWT use *relative placement:* components are placed and sized relative to other components. All the provided layout managers implement either the interface `LayoutManager` or its subinterface `LayoutManager2`. Layout managers range from the simple (`FlowLayoutManager` adds components to a line until they don't fit and then starts a new line) to the sophisticated (`GridBagLayoutManager` has a great deal of flexibility). You can also write your own layout manager.

Instead of thinking about where a check box should go on the screen, you should think about how it should be placed relative to other components. Then choose a layout manager for the frame in which the check box will be placed and add the components so that they have the expected relationships. If you do this right, your interface will look clean on all Java platforms.

AWT has a set of standard GUI components: labels, buttons, check boxes, choice lists, scroll bars, text fields, text regions, and so on. Several top-level containers, such as dialog boxes and windows, let you place other components inside them (preferably using a relative-placement layout manager).

The Canvas is one of the most important components. It provides a general-purpose drawing area on which you can draw such things as lines, ovals, and text. Canvas is the basis for many customized user-interface components when no standard component does what you need.

Components are notified of events (mouse up, mouse down, mouse drag, keyboard events, and the like) by having methods invoked on them. You can also register *listener* objects that are notified when an event occurs within a component. For example, a button that lets the user exit the program might be set up like this:

```
Button b = new Button("Exit");
b.addActionListener(
    new ActionListener() {
        public void actionPerformed(ActionEvent e) {
            System.exit(0);
        }
    }
);
gui.add(b);
```

Action events come from the basic action on the component, such as pressing a button or selecting a check box. The ActionEvent class has details of an action event, such as the keyboard modifiers (such as the Alt or Control key) that were being pressed when the action occurred. To receive this event you must register interest in action events, either by adding an ActionListener to the component as shown here or by invoking enableEvents with an appropriate mask.

The ActionListener interface in the previous example is a *listener interface*. Listener interfaces exist for many kinds of events: mouse, keyboard, window, item, text, container, and general component events. You use objects that implement listener interfaces to trigger method execution when events occur.

Other classes in java.awt allow you to set colors, fonts, and so on. All these properties are inherited by default from outer components—the default colors of a button are those of the frame in which it has been placed. You can override this setting at any level by explicitly specifying a color for a component. That component and all its contained components will turn the specified color unless a subcomponent has its color specified.

Various subpackages of `java.awt` allow you to manipulate images, sounds, and other media. The package `java.awt.event` contains the various event listener and adapter classes for connecting events to your code. The package `java.awt.images` has `ImageConsumer`, `ImageObserver`, and `ImageProducer` interfaces and several classes for reading and manipulating images. The package `java.awt.datatransfer` enables moving data between applications—for example, using cut, copy, and paste.

17.3 `java.applet`—Applets

Applets are a way to run Java code inside a Web browser. Applets are the first exposure many people have to Java and its uses. An applet is defined primarily by the protocol that governs its lifetime and the methods by which it can query and manipulate its runtime environment. The types in `java.applet`—primarily the `Applet` superclass itself—define this environment.

When an APPLET tag is found in a Web page's HTML, the browser downloads the code for the named class from a URL, creates an object of that class, creates a region on the Web page for that object to control, and then invokes the object's `init` method. As the applet runs, it can download other classes from the server as needed. Applets are run in a tightly secured "sandbox" in which potentially dangerous operations (such as file access, network access, and running local programs) are restricted by a browser-defined security manager.

The method `init` is one of four lifecycle methods defined for the applet in the `Applet` class. The next two methods—`start` and `stop`—are invoked when users visit the page and when they leave. These methods can be invoked multiple times as the user presses the "Back" and "Forward" buttons (or their equivalents) to visit and leave the page. Finally, when the page is no longer reachable, the applet's `destroy` method is invoked to free up any resources.

These methods are typically overridden by applet classes. For example, if an applet uses a thread to do its work, `init` would typically create the thread; `start` would invoke the thread's `start` method the first time and ask it to continue execution on subsequent invocations; `stop` could ask the thread to pause to prevent it from consuming resources while the page is not visible; and `destroy` could interrupt the thread because the thread would no longer be needed.

An applet can get parameters from the APPLET tag to customize its behavior. It might get colors, fonts, or the URL of an image to display.

Applets usually run in a highly constrained security environment to protect your computer and network from unwelcome inspection or invasion by a hostile applet. This means that certain conveniences, such as a local scratch disk, may not be available. As security models in Java become more sophisticated, applet security is developing finer-grained notions of trust. Each browser will define what applets can and cannot do in the browser's environment.

The applet model is a good example of how the Java platform provides power. The fact that the same code runs on all systems in the same way allows a single piece of code (an applet) to run in a variety of browsers on a variety of windowing systems running on a larger variety of operating systems. The portability of Java bytecodes allows you to execute part of your application on the server and another part on the client system via downloaded code, whichever is appropriate. It is the same platform on both sides: the Java Virtual Machine. The ability to move code from one place to another and execute it in a secure environment enables new ways of thinking about where to execute what part of your design.

17.4 `java.rmi`—Remote Method Invocation

When you can download and run code on other systems, the face of distributed computing changes. Java's remote method invocation (RMI) gives you a way to create objects whose methods can be invoked from other virtual machines, including those running on completely different hosts. Because RMI is designed for communicating between Java systems, it can take advantage of Java's features and can operate in a natural fashion natural for Java programmers. RMI is contained in the package `java.rmi` and its subpackages, most notably the package `java.rmi.server` for RMI server implementations.

To use RMI you must first design one or more *remote interfaces*—interfaces whose methods can be invoked remotely. A remote interface extends the `Remote` interface, and its methods throw `RemoteException` in addition to any other exceptions. Here, for example, is a simple definition of a compute server interface that will accept `Task` objects for execution, returning the resulting `Object`:

```
import java.rmi.*;

public interface ComputeServer extends Remote {
    Object compute(Task task) throws RemoteException;
}
```

The `Task` interface is generic, allowing a `ComputeServer` to do any computation requested of it:

```
public interface Task {
    Object run();
}
```

Task itself is not a remote interface. Each ComputeServer object will run on a host and will be asked to execute tasks locally on its own host and return any results. (Traditionally, the application invoking a remote method is called the *client* of the invocation, and the application executing the method is called the *server,* although a client of one invocation may be the server of another.)

Each method of a remote interface is required to throw RemoteException because any invocation of a remote method can have failures that must be signaled. Recovery from these failures is unlike recovery in local computation, where methods always arrive at their intended objects, and either results are always returned or you clearly know that they were not returned.

When you invoke a remote method, network failures create new uncertainties—if the network fails after the request is transmitted from the client, the client doesn't know whether the request was received. The failure may have happened before the invocation reached the server, or it may have happened after it reached the server but before results could be returned. There is no way for the client to know which of these two cases actually happened. If the request is to withdraw money from your bank account, you would not want to simply retransmit the request—it might get there twice. Remote interfaces must be designed to allow clients to recover from such *partial failures*. Methods may be *idempotent*—meaning the method can safely be reinvoked—or some other recovery method may be provided for the interface, such as transactions that can be aborted when non-idempotent methods fail. The users of a remote object must recover from such failures, and the declared RemoteException helps them do so.

Here is a simple implementation of the ComputeServer interface:

```java
import java.rmi.*;
import java.rmi.server.*;

public class ComputeServerImpl
    extends UnicastRemoteObject
    implements ComputeServer
{
    public ComputeServerImpl() throws RemoteException { }

    public Object compute(Task task) {
        return task.run();
    }

    public static void main(String[] args) {
        // use the default, restrictive security manager
        System.setSecurityManager(new RMISecurityManager());
```

```
        try {
            ComputeServer server = new ComputeServerImpl();
            Naming.rebind("ComputeServer", server);
        } catch (Exception e) {
            e.printStackTrace(System.err);
            System.exit(-1);
        }
        System.out.println("Ready to receive tasks");
        return;
    }
}
```

This code is also straightforward. When an `execute` invocation arrives from a client, `ComputeServerImpl` implements the `ComputeServer` interface by taking the `Task` object it is given and invoking its `run` method, returning the resulting `Object`. Each incoming request typically gets its own thread, so this compute server implementation could have many concurrently executing tasks for different clients. `ComputeServerImpl` extends `UnicastRemoteObject`, which provides references for single-server remote method invocation. `UnicastRemoteObject`, like all types needed only by servers, is defined in `java.rmi.server`. The `ComputeServerImpl` constructor declares that it throws `RemoteException` because it can be thrown by the (implicitly invoked) `UnicastRemoteObject` constructor when registering the object with the RMI system.

Now comes the fun part. Clients can ask the server to perform any computation at all. Suppose, for example, that you want to compute π to some number of decimal places. You can have the compute server do this for you:

```
import java.math.BigDecimal;

public class Pi implements Task {
    private int decimals;

    /** Calculate Pi to a given number of decimal places */
    public Pi(int decimals) {
        this.decimals = decimals;
    }

    public Object run() {
        BigDecimal res = computePi();
        return res;
    }
```

```
    BigDecimal computePi() {
        // ...
    }
}
```

The `Pi` class implements the `Task` interface with a `run` method that returns a `java.math.BigDecimal` object containing the computed result (you will learn more about `BigDecimal` soon). You then put the compiled `Pi` class someplace where it can be downloaded from a URL, just as an applet class would be. The URL from which to download the code will be set as a property for your client.

When you invoke the compute server's `execute` request, passing a `Pi` object, the server will need the `Pi` class. It will look at the URL that has been implicitly passed with the request, download the class, and run it in a secure sandbox. It will then invoke the `Pi` object's `run` method and return the result.

This `ComputeServer` example leverages Java's homogeneous computing model, in which all code means the same thing on all platforms, and its security model, in which downloaded code can be run in a secure manner.

Many environments can use the basic infrastructure just described. A compute farm that uses a large number of computers to render animation can use such a system to feed those computers images to be rendered, sound computations, and other tasks. This simple example needs some hardening to be used in other situations, especially when `Task` objects could not be trusted to be friendly. All you need is Java at both ends of the network.

Because of the dangers inherent in running downloaded code, RMI requires that a security manager be installed. The `RMISecurityManager` class is a very conservative security manager that you can install to prevent any sensitive access to your system, or you can provide your own security manager.

Your server class may not be able to extend an RMI server class because your class must extend a different class. For example, an applet class must extend `Applet` and so cannot extend `UnicastRemoteObject`. You can create servers that do not extend `UnicastRemoteObject` by having your class's constructor invoke a static method:

```
public class SnazzyApplet extends Applet
    implements SnazzyRemote
{
    public SnazzyApplet() throws RemoteException {
        UnicastRemoteObject.exportObject(this);
    }
    // ... implement SnazzyRemote and Applet methods ...
}
```

Classes are downloaded from client to server (or server to client) only if they are needed. Classes will often be known on both sides. For example, `BigDecimal` is part of the Java core, so both the client and the server already know about it and it will not be downloaded. User-defined classes are treated in the same way—if both the client and server have a class installed, it will not be downloaded across the network.

Arguments and return values of remote methods are handled somewhat differently from those of local methods. RMI passes arguments and return values using object serialization (see "The `Object` Byte Streams" on page 259). When a remote reference is passed as an argument or return value, the receiver will get a reference to the same remote object that was passed. This is how local references act in local methods—an object reference refers to the same object in both the invoking code and the invoked method. Primitive types, too, are passed in the same way locally and remotely; the receiver gets a copy of the value.

References to local objects must be passed differently. Local objects are not designed to deal with partial failures, so it is not possible to pass across the network a remote reference to a local object. Local objects are instead passed by a deep copy made using serialization. Any remote references contained within the object or in any part of the graph of objects it denotes will be passed as described earlier. All other parts of the graph will be serialized on the sender's system and deserialized on the receiver's. Changes made on one side will not be visible to the other side, because each side has its own local copy of the object.

The RMI registry provides a simple naming system to store remote references for bootstrapping your clients. This is not a full naming system, but it will let you store objects that can be used to register or find top-level services. The registry is accessed via the `Naming` class.

Server objects are governed by a "best effort" distributed garbage collector. When no outstanding references to a remote object exist, that object can be collected. This is similar in principle to Java's garbage collection for local objects, but the failures of distributed computing make surety impossible. If a client hasn't been in contact for a long time, it is presumed to have gone away without notifying the server (possibly the system crashed). If a long-lived network failure is actually at fault, the client may find that the server has been garbage-collected when the network reconnects. Every reasonable effort is made to preclude this possibility. A server can ensure that it will never be garbage-collected by simply holding on to a remote reference to itself, thus ensuring that at least one remote reference will keep it alive. This reference can be dropped when the server decides that it no longer must be forced to be alive.

RMI is explicitly designed to take advantage of having both client and server in Java. This gives it a form that is simple and direct for people who know Java. You can, of course, implement any server methods you like as `native` methods.

Native methods can help you use RMI as a bridge between Java code and existing non-Java code, such as in two- and three-tier systems.

17.5 `java.beans`—Java Components

JavaBeans is a component architecture that helps independent vendors write classes that can be treated as components of larger systems assembled by users. The `java.beans` package provides necessary and useful classes for writing such *beans.* A bean exports properties, generates events, and implements methods. By following certain design patterns or by implementing methods that provide a description of these facets of behavior, you can compose beans using interactive tools to build a system the user needs.

Much of a bean's behavior is simplified if you follow expected design patterns. For example, if your bean class is called `Ernest` and you provide a class named `ErnestBeanInfo` that implements the `BeanInfo` interface, the JavaBeans tools will use it as a source of information about the behavior of the bean: the events it supports, the icons it uses, and so on.

Providing a `BeanInfo` object is itself optional—the JavaBeans system will use reflection to infer events and properties. For example, if a class `Ernest` has methods named `getImportance` and `setImportance`, the JavaBeans system will assume that you have an `importance` property that can be set, either directly or via another bean. Builder tools are expected to present the properties and events to users, who can use them to connect beans as components to build custom applications.

AWT components are beans, and the event model described earlier for AWT components is also the JavaBeans event model.

JavaBeans is designed to interoperate with existing component architectures, extending the Java "Write once, run anywhere" capability to create a homogenous component platform.

17.6 `java.net`—The Network

The `java.net` package provides classes for working with network infrastructure, such as sockets, network addresses, and URLs.

The `java.net` package is centered around the `Socket` class, which represents a connection to another socket—possibly on another machine—across which bytes can flow. You typically create a socket with a host name or `InetAddress` and a port number. You can also specify a local `InetAddress` and port to which the socket will be bound. A `ServerSocket` class lets you listen on a port for incoming connection requests, creating a socket for each request. For example, the following program accepts input on a socket:

```java
import java.net.*;
import java.io.*;

public class acceptInput {
    public static final int PORT = 0xCAFE;

    public static void main(String[] args) {
        ServerSocket server = null;
        try {
            server = new ServerSocket(PORT);
        } catch (IOException e) {
            e.printStackTrace();
            System.exit(-1);
        }

        byte[] bytes = new byte[1024];
        for (;;) {
            try {
                System.out.println("--------------------");
                Socket sock = server.accept();
                InputStream in = sock.getInputStream();
                int len;
                while ((len = in.read(bytes)) > 0)
                    System.out.write(bytes, 0, len);
                in.close();
            } catch (IOException e) {
                e.printStackTrace(System.out);
            }
        }
    }
}
```

This program creates a ServerSocket and repeatedly accepts connections to it, printing whatever bytes it receives. A client that shipped its standard input to the server might look like this:

```java
import java.net.*;
import java.io.*;
```

```
public class writeOutput {
    public static void main(String[] args) {
        try {
            String host = args[0];
            Socket sck = new Socket(host, acceptInput.PORT);
            OutputStream out = sck.getOutputStream();
            int ch;
            while ((ch = System.in.read()) != -1)
                out.write(ch);
            out.close();
        } catch (IOException e) {
            e.printStackTrace();
            System.exit(-1);
        }
    }
}
```

A URL object stores a URL, providing methods to examine and set its various parts (protocol, host, port number, and file). A URL object simply names a resource—you invoke openConnection to connect to the named resource. The openConnection method returns a URLConnection object that lets you get the header fields and content of the resource as input and output streams. The following program reads the contents of a URL:

```
import java.net.*;
import java.io.*;

public class readURL {
    public static void main(String[] args) {
        for (int i = 0; i < args.length; i++) {
            try {
                readURL(args[i]);
            } catch (Exception e) {
                System.err.println(args[i] + ":");
                e.printStackTrace(System.err);
            }
        }
    }

    private static void readURL(String name)
        throws MalformedURLException, IOException
    {
```

```
URL url = new URL(name);
URLConnection connect = url.openConnection();
InputStream in = connect.getInputStream();
byte[] bytes = new byte[1024];

int len;          // number of bytes actually read
while ((len = in.read(bytes)) >= 0)
    System.out.write(bytes, 0, len);
    }
}
```

The URLEncoder class lets you turn an ISO Latin-1 string (such as a user-typed query) into a form that can be included as part of a URL. ASCII letters and digits remain unchanged, the space character is converted to a +, and all other characters are represented by their lower eight bits in hex preceded by a %.

You can create DatagramSocket objects for sockets that send and receive DatagramPacket objects, which contain an array of bytes. Datagrams are a connectionless packet delivery service, in which each packet is individually addressed and routed and the receiver can get packets in any order. The MulticastSocket subclass of DatagramSocket lets you set up a socket that can send and receive packets to and from multiple addresses.

17.7 java.math—Mathematics

The package java.math is destined for classes that help with mathematical calculations. Currently it has two classes: BigInteger and BigDecimal. The class BigInteger provides arbitrary-precision integer arithmetic, providing analogous operations for all Java integer operations except >>>, which is equivalent to >> because there is no sign bit to copy in an arbitrary-precision integer. Neither will the provided single-bit operations (clearBit and setBit) change the sign of the number on which they operate. Binary bitwise operations start by extending the sign of the smaller number and then executing the operation. BigInteger objects are immutable, so all operations on them produce new BigInteger objects. The following simple method enumerates the prime factors of a number:

```
final static BigInteger ONE = BigInteger.valueOf(1);
final static BigInteger TWO = BigInteger.valueOf(2);
final static BigInteger THREE = BigInteger.valueOf(3);

public static Enumeration factors(BigInteger num) {
    Vector factors = new Vector();
```

```
        if (num.compareTo(ONE) <= 0) {  // <=1 means skip it
            factors.addElement(num);
            return factors.elements();
        }

        BigInteger div = TWO;                    // divisor
        BigInteger divsq = BigInteger.valueOf(4); // div squared

        while (num.compareTo(divsq) >= 0) {
            BigInteger[] res = num.divideAndRemainder(div);
            if (res[1].signum() == 0) { // if remainder is zero
                factors.addElement(div);
                num = res[0];
            } else {                      // try next divisor
                div = (div == TWO ? THREE : div = div.add(TWO));
                divsq = div.multiply(div);
            }
        }
        if (!num.equals(ONE))   // leftover must be a factor
            factors.addElement(num);
        return factors.elements();
    }
```

The constants ONE, TWO, and THREE are used often, so we create objects for them once. If the number we are factoring is less than or equal to one, we treat it as its own factor (compareTo returns –1, 0, or 1 as the integer is less than, equal to, or greater than the integer it is passed). After this validity test we perform the real work of the method: testing potential divisors. If a divisor divides into the number evenly, it is a prime factor, and we proceed with the result of the division to find more factors. We first try two, and then all odd numbers, until we reach a divisor whose square is larger than the current number. You could optimize this method in any number of ways, but it shows how to use some BigInteger functionality.

BigDecimal provides an arbitrary-precision signed decimal number consisting of an arbitrary-precision integer and an int scale that says how many decimal places are to the right of the decimal point.

Decimal division and changing a number's scale require rounding, which you specify on each operation. You can require that rounding be up, down, toward or away from zero, or toward the nearest value, with 0.5 treated as up, down, or toward the even number. You can also assert that no rounding will be necessary, in which case ArithmeticException will be thrown if you are found to be wrong.

17.8   `java.sql` — Relational Database Access

The package `java.sql` provides the JDBC package for using relational databases. These classes and methods can be implemented directly by your database vendor or via the industry-standard ODBC interface. JDBC is, in effect, a mapping of ODBC into Java. The JDBC package and other issues about Java and relational databases are covered in *JDBC Database Access with Java*.

17.9   `java.security` — Security Tools

The package `java.security` contains several useful tools for security-related functions. The package currently has tools for digital signatures, message digests, key management, and access control lists.

Because there are many ways to approach cryptography and there will be many more in the future, the security package is designed to provide abstractions of security interactions. Implementations of the abstractions are supplied by *providers*. Each Java platform has one or more providers. You can invoke methods to find out which providers are available. Providers can interoperate through the provided abstractions.

> *Programming today is a race between software engineers*
> *striving to build bigger and better idiot-proof programs,*
> *and the universe trying to produce bigger and better idiots.*
> *So far the universe is winning.*
> —Rich Cook

Runtime Exceptions

The computer can't tell you the emotional story.
It can give you the exact mathematical design, but what's missing is the eyebrows.
—Frank Zappa

THE Java runtime throws two primary kinds of exceptions: runtime exceptions, which are extensions of the RuntimeException class, and errors, which are extensions of the Error class. Both are unchecked exceptions, as defined in "The throws Clause" on page 153. Here is the top of the exception type hierarchy:

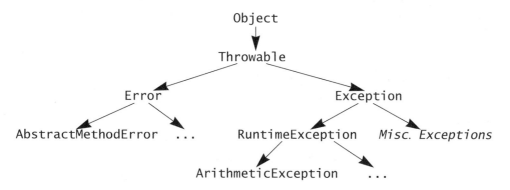

The Error exceptions indicate very serious problems that are usually unrecoverable and should never (well, hardly ever) be caught. Error exception classes are not extensions of RuntimeException, so people who write catch-all catch clauses for Exception or RuntimeException (often not a good idea anyway) won't catch Error exceptions. Of course, the finally clauses of try statements will always be executed as any exception—including Error exceptions—percolates up the call stack, so you can always clean up after any exception.

You can extend the RuntimeException and Error classes yourself to create your own unchecked exceptions—that is, exceptions that you can throw without declaring them in throws clauses. The only reason you should know this is so that you can be warned against doing it. The throws clause is there to make all the possible behaviors of a method clear to those who invoke it. By making exceptions extensions of RuntimeException or Error, you lie about the exception (that it is thrown by the runtime). You also invalidate the assumptions of programmers using your method that they can understand the method's behavior by reading its throws clause.

Even if you are writing code only for yourself, you should not create unchecked exceptions, because programmers with only a partial understanding of your code would miss an important clue about how it works. And, after all, a few months after you write the code, *you* are one of the people who must maintain it with only a partial understanding. One way to keep your code clear is to pretend that the RuntimeException and Error classes can't be extended.

All RuntimeException and Error classes support at least two constructors: a no-arg constructor and a constructor that accepts a descriptive String object.

CloneNotSupportedException extends Exception directly, because code invoking a clone method that throws it should be prepared to handle objects that are not clonable. This exception is described in "Cloning Objects" on page 77.

This appendix is in two parts—the RuntimeException classes and the Error classes. Each exception is named along with a description of when it is thrown, what it means, and any additional constructors it provides. If an exception is not part of java.lang, the package name follows the description in parentheses. Only exceptions in packages covered in this book are listed.

A.1   RuntimeException Classes

ArithmeticException extends RuntimeException
> An exceptional arithmetic condition arose, such as integer division by zero.

ArrayStoreException extends RuntimeException
> An attempt was made to store the wrong type of object in an array.

ClassCastException extends RuntimeException
> An invalid cast was attempted.

EmptyStackException extends RuntimeException
> A pop was attempted on an empty stack (java.util).

IllegalArgumentException extends RuntimeException
> An invalid argument was passed to a method, such as an invocation of String.equals with an Object that was not a String object.

IllegalMonitorStateException extends RuntimeException
> The wait/notify mechanism was used outside synchronized code.

IllegalStateException extends RuntimeException
> An object was not in the proper state for the requested operation.

IllegalThreadStateException extends IllegalArgumentException
> A thread was not in the proper state for the requested operation.

IndexOutOfBoundsException extends RuntimeException
> An array index or an index into a String object was out of bounds.

MissingResourceException extends RuntimeException
> No matching resource bundle or resource was found (java.util).

NegativeArraySizeException extends RuntimeException
> Someone tried to create an array with a negative size.

NoSuchElementException extends RuntimeException
> An element lookup failed in one of the container class objects (java.util).

NullPointerException extends RuntimeException
> A null reference was used to access a field or method. This exception also signals that a method received a null parameter when null was invalid for that method. In this usage it is like IllegalArgumentException.

NumberFormatException extends IllegalArgumentException
> A string that was supposed to describe a number did not do so. This is thrown by such methods as Integer.parseInt.

SecurityException extends RuntimeException
> An attempt to do something was vetoed by the security system, usually the SecurityManager object for this runtime.

A.2   Error Classes

AbstractMethodError extends IncompatibleClassChangeError
> An actual abstract method—one with no implementation—was invoked.

ClassFormatError extends LinkageError
> A class or interface that was being loaded was defined in an invalid format.

ExceptionInInitializerError extends LinkageError
> An uncaught exception was thrown in an initializer.

IllegalAccessError extends IncompatibleClassChangeError
> An invalid access exception occurred.

IncompatibleClassChangeError extends LinkageError
> When loading a class or interface, a change was detected that was incompatible with previous information about that class or interface. For example, a

nonprivate method was deleted from a class between the time you compiled your code and the time your code was run and tried to use that class.

InstantiationError extends `IncompatibleClassChangeError`
Something tried to instantiate an abstract class or an interface.

InternalError extends `VirtualMachineError`
An internal runtime error occurred. This should "never happen."

LinkageError extends `Error`
`LinkageError` and its subclasses indicate that a class had some dependency on another class that could not then be satisfied.

NoClassDefFoundError extends `LinkageError`
A class could not be found when it was needed.

NoSuchFieldError extends `IncompatibleClassChangeError`
A particular field could not be found in a class or interface.

NoSuchMethodError extends `IncompatibleClassChangeError`
A particular method could not be found in a class or interface.

OutOfMemoryError extends `VirtualMachineError`
You ran out of memory.

StackOverflowError extends `VirtualMachineError`
An invocation stack overflow occurred. This may indicate infinite recursion.

ThreadDeath extends `Error`
A `ThreadDeath` object was thrown in the victim thread when `thread.stop` was called. If `ThreadDeath` is caught, it should be rethrown so that the thread will die. An uncaught `ThreadDeath` is usually not reported.

UnknownError extends `VirtualMachineError`
An unknown but serious error occurred.

UnsatisfiedLinkError extends `LinkageError`
An unsatisfied linkage for a native method was encountered. This usually means that the library that implemented a native method had undefined symbols that were not satisfied by any other library.

VerifyError extends `LinkageError`
When a class was being loaded it did not pass a verification test. Such tests are designed to ensure that loaded code does not violate Java safety features.

VirtualMachineError extends `Error`
The virtual machine is broken or ran out of resources.

On the outskirts of every agony sits some observant fellow who points.
—Virginia Woolf

Useful Tables

All my life, as down an abyss without a bottom,
I have been pouring van-loads of information
into the vacancy of oblivion I call my mind.
—Logan Pearsall Smith

TABLE 1: **Keywords**

abstract	double	int	static
boolean	else	interface	super
break	extends	long	switch
byte	final	native	synchronized
case	finally	new	this
catch	float	null	throw
char	for	package	throws
class	goto[†]	private	transient
const[†]	if	protected	try
continue	implements	public	void
default	import	return	volatile
do	instanceof	short	while

NOTE: Keywords marked with [†] are unused

TABLE 2: **Operator Precedence**

Operator Type	Operator
Postfix operators	`[] . (params) expr++ expr--`
Unary operators	`++expr --expr +expr -expr ~ !`
Creation or cast	`new (type)expr`
Multiplicative	`* / %`
Additive	`+ -`
Shift	`<< >> >>>`
Relational	`< > >= <= instanceof`
Equality	`== !=`
Bitwise AND	`&`
Bitwise exclusive OR	`^`
Bitwise inclusive OR	`|`
Logical AND	`&&`
Logical OR	`||`
Conditional	`?:`
Assignment	`= += -= *= /= %= >>= <<= >>>= &= ^= |=`

TABLE 3: **Unicode Digits**

Unicode	Description
`\u0030-\u0039`	ISO Latin-1 (and ASCII) digits
`\u0660-\u0669`	Arabic–Indic digits
`\u06f0-\u06f9`	Extended Arabic–Indic digits
`\u0966-\u096f`	Devanagari digits
`\u09e6-\u09ef`	Bengali digits
`\u0a66-\u0a6f`	Gurmukhi digits
`\u0ae6-\u0aef`	Gujarati digits
`\u0b66-\u0b6f`	Oriya digits
`\u0be7-\u0bef`	Tamil digits (only nine—no zero digit)
`\u0c66-\u0c6f`	Telugu digits
`\u0ce6-\u0cef`	Kannada digits
`\u0d66-\u0d6f`	Malayalam digits
`\u0e50-\u0e59`	Thai digits
`\u0ed0-\u0ed9`	Lao digits
`\u0420-\u0f29`	Tibetan digits
`\uff10-\uff19`	Fullwidth digits

TABLE 4: **Unicode Letters and Digits**

Unicode	Description
\u0041–\u005A	ISO Latin-1 (and ASCII) uppercase Latin letters ('A'–'Z')
\u0061–\u007A	ISO Latin-1 (and ASCII) lowercase Latin letters ('a'–'z')
\u00C0–\u00D6	ISO Latin-1 supplementary letters
\u00D8–\u00F6	ISO Latin-1 supplementary letters
\u00F8–\u00FF	ISO Latin-1 supplementary letters
\u0100–\u1FFF	Latin extended-A, Latin extended-B, IPA extensions, spacing modifier letters, combining diacritical marks, basic Greek, Greek symbols and Coptic, Cyrillic, Armenian, Hebrew extended-A, Basic Hebrew, Hebrew extended-B, Basic Arabic, Arabic extended, Devanagari, Bengali, Gurmukhi, Gujarati, Oriya, Tamil, Telugu, Kannada, Malayalam, Thai, Lao, Tibetan, Basic Georgian, Georgian extended, Hangul Jamo, Latin extended additional, Greek extended
\u3040–\u9FFF	Hiragana, Katakana, Bopomofo, Hangul compatibility Jamo, CJK miscellaneous, enclosed CJK characters and months, CJK compatibility, Hangul, Hangul supplementary-A, Hangul supplementary-B, CJK unified ideographs
\uF900–\uFDFF	CJK compatibility ideographs, alphabetic presentation forms, Arabic presentation forms-A
\uFE70–\uFEFE	Arabic presentation forms-B
\uFF10–\uFF19	Fullwidth digits
\uFF21–\uFF3A	Fullwidth Latin uppercase
\uFF41–\uFF5A	Fullwidth Latin lowercase
\uFF66–\uFFDC	Halfwidth Katakana and Hangul

NOTES: A Unicode character is a letter or digit if it is in one of the above ranges and is also a defined Unicode character.

A character is a letter if it is in Table 4, "Unicode Letters and Digits," and not in Table 3, "Unicode Digits."

TABLE 5: **Special Characters Using **

Sequence	Meaning
\n	Newline (\u000A)
\t	Tab (\u0009)
\b	Backspace (\u0008)
\r	Return (\u000D)
\f	Form feed (\u000C)
\\	Backslash itself (\u005C)
\'	Single quote (\u0027)
\"	Double quote (\u0022)
ddd	An octal char, with each *d* being an octal digit (0–7)
\u*dddd*	A Unicode char, with each *d* being a hex digit (0–9, a–f, A–F)

TABLE 6: **Documentation Comment Tags**

Tag	Description
@see	Cross reference to another doc comment or URL
@param *p*	Description of the single parameter *p*
@return	Description of the return value of a method
@exception *E*	Description of the exception *E* that the method may throw
@deprecated	Marks a deprecated entity, with text directing user to a replacement, if any; the compiler will generate warning if a deprecated entity is used
@author	An author of the code
@version	A human-interpretable version of the entity
@since	A human-interpretable version of the system in which the entity first appeared

Comparing information and knowledge
is like asking whether the fatness of a pig
is more or less green than the designated hitter rule.
—David Guaspari

Further Reading

The best book on programming for the layman is Alice in Wonderland,
but that's because it's the best book on anything for the layman.
—Alan J. Perlis

WE offer this list of works for further reading on related topics. The list is necessarily duosyncratic—other excellent works exist on many of these topics. Of course, all the books in this series are recommended for their respective topics.

JAVA TOPICS

- `http://java.sun.com/`, Sun Microsystems, Inc. (JavaSoft)
  Current information on Java and related topics, including Java releases, security issues, and online documentation.

- `http://java.sun.com/Series/`, Sun Microsystems, Inc. (JavaSoft)
  Current information about books in this series, including errata and updates. Of special interest will be those errata and updates for this book.

- *The Unicode Standard: Second Edition*, Version 2.0, Addison-Wesley, 1996, ISBN 0-201-48345-9.
  More data on Unicode 2.0 is available at `http://www.unicode.org`.

- *IEEE/ANSI Standard for Binary Floating-Point Arithmetic*. Institute of Electrical and Electronics Engineers, 1985, IEEE Std 754-1985.

- `http://tycho.usno.navy.mil`
  U.S. Naval Observatory data on time paradigms used in the `Date` class.
  See `http://tycho.usno.navy.mil/systime.html`

- `http://www.unicode.org/unicode/Languages.html`
  One site where you can find two-letter ISO 639 codes for languages.

- `http://www.unicode.org/unicode/Countries.html`
  One site where you can find two-letter ISO 3166 codes for countries.

- `http://www.w3.org/`
  Main site for the World Wide Web Consortium, where you can find documentation for HTML tags, which are usable in doc comments.

OBJECT-ORIENTED DESIGN

- *An Introduction to Object-Oriented Programming*, by Timothy Budd. Addison-Wesley, 1991, ISBN 0-201-54709-0
  An introduction to object-oriented programming as well as a comparison of C++, Objective C, Smalltalk, and Object Pascal.

- *Pitfalls of Object-Oriented Development*, by Bruce F. Webster. M&T Books, 1995, ISBN 1-55851-397-3.
  A collection of traps to avoid in object technology. Alerts you to problems you're likely to encounter and presents some solutions for them.

- *Design Patterns,* by Erich Gamma, Richard Helm, Ralph Johnson, and John Vlissides. Addison-Wesley, 1995, ISBN 0-201-63361-2.

- *Object-Oriented Analysis and Design with Applications, Second Edition*, by Grady Booch. Benjamin/Cummings, 1994, ISBN 0-8053-5340-2.

- *Structured Programming*, by Ole-Johan Dahl, Edsger Wybe Dijkstra, and C. A. R. Hoare. Academic Press, 1972, ISBN 0-12-200550-3.

- *Object-Oriented Programming: An Evolutionary Approach, Second Edition*, by Brad J. Cox and Andrew Novobilski. Addison-Wesley, 1991, ISBN 0-201-54834-8.

MULTITHREADED PROGRAMMING

- *Programming with Threads*, by Steve Kleiman, Devang Shah, and Bart Smaalders. Prentice Hall, 1996, ISBN 0-13-172389-8.

- *The Architecture of Concurrent Programs,* by Per Brinch Hansen. Prentice Hall, 1977, ISBN 0-13-044628-9.

- "Monitors: An Operating System Structuring Concept," by C. A. R. Hoare. *Communications of the ACM,* Volume 17, number 10, 1974, pp. 549–557.
  The seminal paper on using monitors to synchronize concurrent tasks.

RELATED LANGUAGES

- *The C Programming Language, Second Edition*, by Brian W. Kernighan and Dennis M. Ritchie. Prentice Hall, 1988, ISBN 0-13-110362-8 and ISBN 0-13-110370-9 (hardcover).

- *The C++ Programming Language, Third Edition,* by Bjarne Stroustrup. Addison-Wesley, 1997, ISBN 0-201-88954-4.

- *The Evolution of C++*, edited by Jim Waldo. A USENIX Association book from MIT Press, ISBN 0-262-73107-X.
  A history of C++ as told by many of the people who contributed.

- *Eiffel: The Language*, by Bertrand Meyer. Prentice Hall, 1992, ISBN 0-13-247925-7.

- "A Structural View of the Cedar Programming Environment," by Daniel Swinehart, Polle Zellweger, Richard Beach, and Robert Hagmann. *ACM Transactions on Programming Languages and Systems,* Volume 8, no. 4, Oct. 1986.

- *Mesa Language Manual,* version 5.0, by James G. Mitchell, William Maybury, and Richard Sweet. Xerox Palo Alto Research Center Report CSL-79-3, April 1979.

- *Systems Programming with Modula-3*, edited by Greg Nelson. Prentice Hall, 1991, ISBN-0-13-590464-1.
  Introduces Modula-3. Chapter 4 is an excellent discussion of thread programming. Chapter 8 is a fascinating case history of language design.

- *Programming in Oberon—Steps Beyond Pascal and Modula*, by Martin Reiser and Niklaus Wirth. Addison-Wesley, 1992, ISBN 0-201-56543-9.

- *Objective C: Object-Oriented Programming Techniques,* by Lewis J. Pinson and Richard S. Wiener. Addison-Wesley, 1991, ISBN 0-201-50828-1.

- "Self: The Power of Simplicity," by David Ungar and Randall B. Smith. Sun Microsystems Laboratories Technical Report SMLI-TR-94-30, 1994.

- *Data Processing—Programming Languages—SIMULA*. Swedish standard SS 636114, SIS, 1987, ISBN 91-7162-234-9.

- *Smalltalk-80: The Language,* by Adele Goldberg and Dave Robson. Addison-Wesley, 1989, ISBN 0-201-13688-0.

SOFTWARE ENGINEERING

- *The Decline and Fall of the American Programmer*, by Ed Yourdon. Yourdon Press, 1993, ISBN 0-13-203670-3.
  Analysis of the revolution taking place in programming. Several chapters discuss object-oriented design. Two chapters of particular interest are "The Lure of the Silver Bullet" and "Programming Methodologies."

- *The Mythical Man-Month, Anniversary Edition*, by Frederick P. Brooks, Jr. Addison-Wesley, 1995, ISBN 0-201-83595-9.

  Essays describing how software projects are really managed and how they should be managed. Especially read Chapter 16, "No Silver Bullet: Essence and Accidents of Software Engineering." You cannot design good classes without understanding how they will be used and changed over time.

- *Peopleware*, by Tom DeMarco and Timothy Lister. Dorset House, 1987, ISBN 0-932633-05-6.

VISUAL DESIGN & GUI DESIGN

- *Designing Visual Interfaces,* by Kevin Mullet and Darrel Sano. Prentice Hall, 1995, ISBN 0-13-303389-9.

  This book describes fundamental techniques that can be used to enhance the visual quality of graphical user interfaces.

- *About Face,* by Allen Cooper. Prentice Hall, 1995, ISBN 0-13-303389-9.

  Basics of good GUI design in a straightforward presentation.

- *Usability Engineering*, by Jakob Nielsen. Academic Press, 1993, ISBN 0-12-518405-0.

  A direct how-to guide on testing your interfaces to make sure they are usable by actual human beings.

- *The Visual Display of Quantitative Information,* by Edward R. Tufte. Graphics Press, 1983.

  You shouldn't communicate using graphical media without reading this.

- *The Non-Designer's Design Book,* by Robin Williams. Peachpit Press, 1994, ISBN 1-56609-159-4.

  How to use type, space, alignment, and other basic techniques to make your designs visually appealing and user-friendly. Applicable to paper documents, HTML documents, displaying data, and user interfaces.

- *The Design of Everyday Things,* by Donald A. Norman. Doubleday/Currency, 1988, ISBN 0-385-26774-6.

  Discusses usability design for everyday items (doors, typewriters, and so on) with lessons applicable to any design that humans are meant to use.

The cure for boredom is curiosity.
There is no cure for curiosity.
—Dorothy Parker

Index

It's a d–mn poor mind that can only think of one way to spell a word!
—Andrew Jackson

A

aborting
  runtime; 328
abs method (Math class); 333
  See also numbers and logical operations
absolute placement
  term definition; 359
abstract
  See also classes (concepts and use);
    interfaces (concepts and use)
  abstract keyword, as reserved word; 106
  AbstractMethodError class; 375
  calendar abstraction components; 344
  classes; **75**
    extensible class design using; 84
    I/O; 225
    interfaces compared with; 76
    interfaces vs; **101**
  methods, implicit in interfaces; 92
  types, interface declaration of; 91
accept method (FilenameFIlter interface);
    270
  See also I/O
access
  See also encapsulation; object-oriented
    concepts and components
  accessor methods
    blank finals as alternative to; 112
    term definition; 41
    this use with; 43
  arrays; 15
  checking, in reflection-based code; 311
  control
    accessor method use for; **41**
    constructor declaration; 35
    extensible classes, implementation
      summary; 88
    in extensible class design; 86
    modifiers that manage; **31**
    of sockets; 331
    packages use for; 209
  IllegalAccessError class; 375
  Java runtime system *(chapter)*; **321**
  members; **125**
    static; 45

modifiers, ordering in class member
    declarations; 111
  of operating system facilities *(chapter)*; **321**
  package; **211**
  random file; **258**
  resolution
    primitive types; 127
    reference types; 126
  sharing among threads; 180
  specifiers, subclass handling; 68
Account example; 37
  multithreading environment; 184
acos method (Math class); 332
  See also numbers and logical operations
action events
  ActionEvent class, term definition; 360
  ActionListener interface, term definition;
    360
  term definition; 360
active
  See also threads
  activeCount method
    Thread class; 206
    ThreadGroup class; 206
  activeGroupCount method, ThreadGroup
    class; 206
adding
  add (Calendar class); 346
  add example; 355
  addDate example, inserting into strings with;
    174
  addElement (Vector class); 278
  addObserver (Observable class); 288
  Observer objects; 288
addition
  See also arithmetic
  additive operators, precedence of; 119
  plus (+) arithmetic operator; 128
algorithms
  See also design patterns; programming
  character streams vs. byte streams; 231
  mapping
    Dictionary class; 273
    Hashtable class; 273
    Properties class; 273
  next use for pseudo-random number
    generation; 292

algorithms *(continued)*
   overloaded method access resolution; 126
   sorting
      comparing, class design for; 84
      user class specification; 312
Alice in Wonderland
   quotation; **139**
allocation of memory
   See also creating; memory
   for new objects; 9
   runtime system handling of; 32
ambiguity; *See* conflicts
and
   See also numbers and logical operations
   AND (&&) conditional operator; 133
   and method (BitSet class); 274
angles
   See also numbers and logical operations
   Math class representation; 332
API (Application Program Interface)
   JNI (Java Native Interface), as C language native
      method API; 57
appending
   See also array(s); programming, techniques;
      strings
   append (StringBuffer class); 174
   to strings; 173, 174
   vector elements; 279
applets
   See also processes; programs; threads
   Applet class; **361**
   java.applet package; 353, **361**
   native methods not permitted in; 56
   term definition; *xv*
applications; *See* processes; programs; threads
Arabic characters
   converting; 238
arguments
   See also parameters
   program, term definition; 56
   RMI handling; 366
arithmetic
   See also Math; numbers and logical operations
   ArithmeticException class; 121, 128, 154, 374
      evaluation order impact on; 120
   character; 128
   decimal, BigDecimal class; 370
   exceptions, IEEE not supported; 130
   extended formats, not supported; 130
   floating-point; 129
   integer; 128
      BigInteger class; 370
   java.math package; 354
   modular, integer arithmetic as; 128
   operations
      Fibonacci example; 3
      operators; **128**
array(s)
   See also data, structures

accessing
   conditional operator use for; 133
   elements of; 125
Array class; 314
arraycopy (System class); 331
ArrayStoreException class; 374
bounds, term definition; 15
byte
   converting strings to and from; **171**
   streams; **242**
character
   copying; 171
   creating from a StringBuffer object; 175
   streams; **242**
cloning issues; 79
copying; 331
   vectors into; 280
dimension specification; 116
examining the type of; 306
hierarchy, relationship to class hierarchy *(figure)*;
   114
index; 114
IndexOutOfBoundsException; 375
initialization of; **117**
introduction; **14**
length; 114
multi-dimensional, as arrays of arrays; **116**
multiple return value use; 37
NegativeArraySizeException; 375
nested; 116
object vs reference, implications of the difference;
   114
one-dimensional, declaration of; 114
reading; 228
reflection handling; **313**
resizable, creating with Vector class; 278
restrictions on extension of; 115
size, applicable to object not reference; 114
sorting; 84
term definition; 114
two-dimensional, declaration of; 116
variables; **114**
writing; 230
ASCII character set
   See also characters; Unicode character set
   Unicode
      digits; 378
      relationship to; 6, 103
asin method (Math class); 332
   See also numbers and logical operations
assignment
   See also encapsulation; initialization; object-
      oriented concepts and components
   object values; 10
   operators
      =; 4
      ++; 8
      --; 8
      +=; 8, **136**

precedence of; 120
+=, string concatenation use; 16
string, new `String` objects created by; 17
associativity
See also arithmetic
of operators; **118**
asterisk (*)
doc comments use; 215
atan method (`Math` class); 332
See also numbers and logical operations
atomic
term definition; 188
attributes
See also design; mapping; properties; variables
`Attr` example; 252
attribute name/value pair storage; 60
doc commented version; 219
output from reflection method use; 308
`AttributedBody` example, interface inheritance;
92, 99
`AttributedImpl` example; 252
hashtable use in; 285
interface implementation; 98
multiple inheritance of; 97
package declaration for; 209
scanning for; 252
storing name value pairs of; 60
audio sources
resource bundle handling; 340
Australia; 342
authentication
`java.security` package; 354
@author tag; **218**
See also comments; documentation
auto reference; *See* `this` reference
`available` (`InputStream` class); 228
See also I/O
situations where inappropriate; 229
avoiding deadlock; 194
See also locks; threads
AWT (Abstract Window Toolkit)
components are beans; 367
event model; 360
`java.awt` package; **359**

B

Babble example
`yield` use; 192
Bach, Johann Sebastian
quotation; **103**
backslash (\\) character
See also character(s); special character(s); string(s)
backslash (\\\\) escape sequence, Unicode value;
109
character(s)
special characters using *(table);* 380
backspace (\\b) escape sequence
Unicode value; 109

BadCatch example
See also events
catch clause design; 157
BadDataSetException example
exception handling; 23
Balzac, Honoré de
quotation; **294**
BankAccount example; 51
Bankhead, Tallulah
quotation; **335**
beans
See also distributed computing; networks
`BeanInfo`; 367
`java.beans` package; **367**
behavior
See also methods
extending
by subclassing; 18
by subclassing *(chapter);* **59**
benchmarks
`Benchmark` example, abstract classes; 76
harness, abstract class use for; 76
BetterName example; 264
Bhutan; 340
bibliography; 381
BigDecimal example; 364
binary
conversion of integer values to, static methods for;
302
operators
assignment use with; 8
creating assignment operators using =; 136
precedence of; 119
searching, ordering issues and algorithm; 163
bit operations
See also numbers and logical operations; types
`BitSet` class; 273, **274**, 275
`hashCode` overriding; 285
manipulating inside a floating-point
representation; 302
operators
AND (&); 134
exclusive or (XOR) (^); 134
inclusive OR (|); 134
precedence; 119
precedence, precautions about; 119
types that may be used with; 134
testing; **134**
blank finals
term definition and use; 111
blocking
See also I/O
blocked, term definition; 191
reading without; 229
blocks
See also control, flow
braces use as delimiters for; 140
exiting, `break` use for; 147
as flow of control statement; 7

blocks *(continued)*
    identifier name search order; 113
    initialization; **46**
    statements and; **139**
    `synchronized`; 185
Body example
    method overloading in; 44
    overloading; 43
    `private` field use; 41
    simple class; 30
Bombeck, Erma
    quotation; **89**
boolean
    See also type(s)
    `Boolean` class; 106, **297**, 325
    `boolean` keyword
        as primitive data type, value of; 106
        as reserved word; 106
    `boolean` type
        converting to and from strings; 169
        expressions, `while` statement use of; 4
        field, default value; 117
        operators, precedence of; 119
        reading and writing; 255
        values, bitwise operator use with; 134
        values, operator restrictions; 133
    literals, characteristics; **108**
Borrow example; 283
boundaries, text; 358
bounds
    See also array(s)
    array, term definition; 15
braces ({})
    See also special characters; syntax
    blocks delimited by; 140
    class member identification by, in Java program; 2
    flow of control blocks delimited by; 7
    methods delimited by; 12
brackets ([])
    See also special characters; syntax
    arrays delimited by; 15
break(ing)
    See also debugging; events
    break; **147**
        as reserved word; 106
        `finally` clause use to clean up for; 158
        goto statement replacement; 149
        `switch` statement, case use; 143
        `switch` statement, termination use; 144
    `BreakIterator` class; 358
buffers
    See also data, structures; I/O
    buf field
        `CharArrayReader` class; 243
        `CharArrayWriter` class; 243
    `Buffered` class; 225, 236, **240**, 241
    `BufferedInputStream` class; 225, 241
        in type tree for byte streams *(figure)*; 227
    `BufferedOutputStream` class; 225, 241

        in type tree for byte streams *(figure)*; 227
    `BufferedReader` class; 225
        in type tree for character streams *(figure)*; 232
    `BufferedStream` class; 240
    `BufferedWriter` class; 225
        in type tree for character streams *(figure)*; 232
    data from a `StringBuffer`; **175**
    I/O; 236
    modifying, of `StringBuffer` object; **173**
    pushback; 237
        single-character; 249
    reading; 255
    streams; 241
    string
        `StringBuffer` class; **172**, **176**, 245
        `StringBufferInputStream` class; 237
bundles; *See* resource(s), bundles
buttons
    as AWT component; 360
byte(s)
    See also types
    byte
        arrays, converting strings to and from; **171**
        as primitive data type, value of; 106
        as reserved word; 106
        field, default value; 117
        reading and writing; **255**
    `Byte` class; 301
    `ByteArray` class; 236, **242**
    `ByteArrayInputStream` class; 242
        in type tree for byte streams *(figure)*; 227
    `ByteArrayOutputStream` class; 242
        in type tree for byte streams *(figure)*; 227
    `bytesForClass` example; 318
    `byteValues` (`Number` class); 300
    in a file, counting *(example)*; 228
    reading; 256
        `InputStream`; 227
    skipping; 256
        `skipBytes` method (`RandomAccessFile`
        class); 259
    streams; **226**
        conversion between Unicode streams and; **237**
        Data; **255**
        Object; **259**
        term definition; 225
        type tree *(figure)*; 227
    writing; 256
        `OutputStream`; 229
bytecodes
    See also runtime; virtual machine
    term definition; 2, 26

C

C++ language
    Java differences; *xvi*
C language
    Java differences; *xvi*

JNI (Java Native Interface); 57
CalcThread example; 197
calendars
    See also dates; internationalization; localization;
        time
    Calendar class; 274, 336, 344
        default locale use; 337
    fields
        methods that access; 346
        term definition; 346
    GregorianCalendar class; 274, **348**
    Julian, determining when Gregorian change
        happened; 350
    lenient; 347
    locale-sensitive; 336
        retrieving; 345
    operations related to; **343**, **344**
calling paradigms
    See also language concepts
    "pass-by-value," method parameters use of; 38
Calvin and Hobbes
    quotation; **27**
can
    See also I/O
    canRead method (File class); 268
    canWrite method (File class); 268
Canvas class
    as AWT component; 360
capacity
    See also vectors
    capacity (Vector class); 281
    capacityIncrement field (Vector class); 282
    StringBuffer objects, managing; **176**
    vectors, managing; 281
Carroll, Lewis
    quotation; **139**
case (character)
    See also character(s); conversion; lowercase;
        string(s); titlecase; uppercase
    conversion, methods; 299
    converting, between upper and lower; 168
    insensitive string region matching; 164
    testing characters for; 299
    Unicode
        Character class handling; 298
        issues; 163
case keyword
    See also control, flow
    case clause (switch statement); 142
        label requirements; 144
    as reserved word; 106
casting
    See also expressions; language concepts; type(s)
    arrays; 115
    down, term definition; 124
    explicit, as explicit type conversions; **122**
    as method of using protected member; 63
    object cloning use; 81
    operator precedence; 119

    references; 124
        conditional; 125
    as run time type conversions; 121
    safe, term definition; 124
    unsafe, term definition; 124
    up, term definition; 124
catching exceptions
    See also exceptions (concepts and uses)
    catch block; 155
    catch keyword, as reserved word; 106
    term definition; 22, 151
ceil method (Math class); 332
    See also numbers and logical operations
chaining streams; 237
    See also I/O
    Filter class; **238**
Changeable example; 93
character(s)
    See also case (character); data, structures; type(s);
        Unicode character set
    accessing, successive Unicode; 132
    arithmetic; 128
    arrays
        copying; 171
        creating from a StringBuffer object; 175
    case conversion methods; 299
    char type
        arrays, appending into strings; 174
        arrays, building strings in; **170**
        arrays, inserting into strings; 174
        as primitive data type, value of; 106
        casting to integer types; 123
        Character class representation of; 297
        field, default value; 117
        keyword, as reserved word; 106
        reading and writing; 255
        values, conversion of compared with short
            conversion; 121
    Character class; 106, 234, **297**, 298, 299
    CharArray class; 236, **242**
    CharArrayReader class; 243
        in type tree for character streams *(figure)*; 232
    CharArrayWriter class; 243
        in type tree for character streams *(figure)*; 232
    CharCast example, casting characters; 123
    classes, tokenizer methods that set; 253
    extracting from strings, with charAt; 161
    in a file, locating; 237
    literals; **109**
    marking; 276
    occurrences in a string, methods for obtaining; 162
    ordinary, ordinaryChars (StreamTokenizer
        class); 253
    printing; 240
    pushback; 249
    reading
        from standard in; 321
        Reader class; **233**

character(s) *(continued)*
  streams; **231**
    standard stream relationship; **231**
    String character streams; **244**
    term definition; 225
    type tree *(figure)*; 232
  translating; 298
  type testing methods; 299
  Unicode, converting to bytes; 238
  whitespace
    components and handling; 105
    counting; 234
    isWhitespace (Character class); 234
    specifying for tokenizing; 253
    StreamTokenizer class handling; 251
    testing characters for; 299
    whitespaceChars (StreamTokenizer class);
      253
  writing; 256, 322
    Writer class; **235**
check boxes
  as AWT component; 360
checkAccess method (ThreadGroup class); 204,
    205
  See also access
checked exceptions
  See also exceptions (concepts and uses)
  handling; 153
  term definition; 22, 152
Chesterton, G.K.
  quotation; **160**
child process
  See also process(es)
  term definition; 325
  termination status determination; 326
Chinese
  calendar conventions; 336
choice lists
  as AWT component; 360
classes (concepts and use)
  See also fields (concepts and use); interfaces
    (concepts and use); methods (concepts and
    use); object-oriented concepts and
    components
  abstract; **75**
    extensible class design using; **83**
    I/O; 225
    interfaces compared with; 76
    interfaces vs; **101**
    stream; 225
  (chapter); **29**
  class
    loader; 316
    methods, *See* static
    path mechanism; 315
    variables, characteristics and use; 44
  constructors; 33
  debugging, multiple main advantages for; 56
  declaration, type names created by; 30

defining, NoClassDefFoundError class; 376
  enclosing, term definition; 50
  examining; **306**
  examples; 1
    Container; 147
  extending
    (chapter); **59**
    design issues; **83**
    how and when to do so; **82**
    introduction; **18**
  fields, *See* class(es), variables
  hierarchy; 62
    relationship to array hierarchy *(figure)*; 114
  identifier name search order; 113
  inner
    creating instances of; 313
    local; **53**
    term definition; 52
  interfaces compared with; 91
  introduction; **9**
  literals; **110**
  loading; **315**
  members
    modifier order; 111
    type of, as determinant during access; 125
  methods; 45
    introduction; **14**
    overriding not permitted with; 68
    protected, characteristics and use; 63
    synchronizing; 185
    Thread; 207
    Thread class; 192
  of named constants, as way of grouping named
    constants; 5
  nesting; **50**, **67**
    hiding in subclasses; 70
    interface declarations; 93
    top-level nested classes term definition
      (footnote); 52
  ObjectOutputStream; 260
  runtime representation; 73
  scope of; 113
  serialization requirements; **260**
  term definition; 1
  unit-testing, multiple main advantages for; 56
  variables, *See* fields (concepts and use), static
  wrappers; 60
    floating point; **302**
    integer; **301**
    overview; **296**
classes (Java and user-defined)
  AbstractMethodError; 375
  Account example; 37, 184
  ActionEvent class; 360
  Applet class; **361**
  ArithmeticException; 121, 128, 154, 374
  ArrayStoreException; 374
  Attr example; 60, 219, 252, 285, 308
  AttributedBody example; 92, 99

AttributedImpl example; 98, 252, 285
Babble example; 192
BadCatch example; 157
BadDataSetException example; 23
BankAccount example; 51
Benchmark example; 76
BetterName example; 264
BigDecimal example; 364, 370, 371
BigInteger class; 370
BitSet; 273, **274**, 274
Body example; 30, 41, 43, 44
Boolean; 106, **297**, 325
Borrow example; 283
BreakIterator; 358
Buffered; 225, 236, **240**
BufferedInputStream; 225, 227, 241
BufferedOutputStream; 225, 227, 241
BufferedReader; 225, 232, 237, 241
BufferedStream; 240
BufferedWriter; 225, 232
Byte; 301
ByteArray; 236, 242
ByteArrayInputStream; 227, 242
ByteArrayOutputStream; 227, 242
CalcThread example; 197
Calendar; 274, 336, 337, 344
Canvas; 360
Character; 107, 234, 298, 299
CharArray; 236, 243
CharArrayReader; 232, 243
CharArrayWriter; 232, 243
CharCast example; 123
CharConversionException; 271
Class; 73, **110**, 264, 303, **304**, 308
class keyword; 30, 107
ClassCastException; 124, 154, 247, 374
ClassContents example; 307
ClassFormatError; 375
ClassLoader; 315, 316, 318
ClassNotFoundException; 263
CloneNotSupportedException; 73, 78, 82, 374
CollationKey; 355
Collator; **354**
ColorAttr example; 61, 62
ComputeServer example; 362
ComputeServerImpl example; 363, 364
Concat example; 247
Constructor; **312**, 313
Container example; 147
CountBytes example; 228
CountSpace example; 234
Data; 236
DatagramSocket; 367
DataInputStream; 227, 236, 255, 257
DataOutputStream; 227, 236, 255, 257
Date; 274, 343
Date1 example; 25
Date2 example; 344
DateFormat; 344, 350

Deck example; 15
Dictionary; 273, **283**, 285
DirFilter example; 270
Double; 107, 302, 303
EmptyStackException; 282
Enum; 54
Enumeration; 98
EOFException; 256, 271
Error; 24, 152, 373
Exception; 23, 152
ExceptionInInitializerError; 375
ExtendShow example; 68
Eye example; 290
Factor example; 244
Fibonacci example; 3
File; 227, 232, 236, 237, 241, 267, 268, 269, 324
FileDescriptor; 227, 232, **245**
FileInputStream; 227, 229, 245, 257, 318
FileNotFoundException; 271
FileOutputStream; 227, 241, 245, 257
FileReader; 232, 238
FileWriter; 232, 238
Filter; 236, **238**, 240, 241
FilterInputStream; 227, 257
FilterOutputStream; 227, 257
FilterReader; 232, 236, 238
FilterWriter; 232, 238
final; **71**
FindChar example; 238, 248
Float; 106, 107, 303
FlowLayoutManager; 359
Format; 350, **355**
Game example; 316
getBuffered; 241
GlobalHello example; 339
GlobalRes example; 339, 341
GlobalRes_tl example; 342
GregorianCalendar; 274, 344, 350
GridBagLayoutManager; 359
Hashtable; 263, 273, **284**, 285, 296
HelloWorld example; 1
IllegalAccessError; 375
IllegalAccessException; 310, 312
IllegalArgumentException; 310, 347, 356, 374
IllegalMonitorStateException; 191, 374
IllegalStateException; 375
IllegalThreadStateException; 375
ImprovedFibonacci example; 7, 8
IncompatibleClassChangeError class; 375
IncOrder example; 131
IndexOutOfBoundsException; 114, 125, 162,
    230, 233, 235, 279, 375
InetAddress; 367
InputSource; 262
InputStream; **227**, 227, 229, 231, 237, 238, 247,
    258, 326
InputStreamReader; 232, 236, **237**
InputStreamWriter; 238
InstantiationError; 376

classes (Java and user-defined) *(continued)*
    InstantiationException; 312
    Integer; 106, 301, 325
    IntegerStack example; 79
    InternalError; 376
    InterruptedException; 182, 196
    InterruptedIOException; 271
    InvalidClassException; 271
    InvalidObjectException; 271
    InvocationTargetException; 310, 312
    IOException; 226, 227, 230, 233, 235, 256, 258,
        264, 268, **271**
    java.lang; 321
    LayoutManager; 359
    LayoutManager2; 359
    LineNumberReader; 232, 237, 248
    LinkageError; 376
    ListResourceBundle; **340**
    Locale; 168, 274, 335, 338
    LocalNumber example; 356
    Long; 106, 301, 325
    LSFailedException; 327
    Math; 13, 14, 291, 321, 332, 333
    MethodBenchmark example; 76
    MissingBundleException; 340
    MissingResourceException; 375
    Moose example; 43
    More example; 70
    MyClass example; 79
    Name example; 43, 261
    Naming class; 366
    NegativeArraySizeException; 375
    NoClassDefFoundError; 376
    NoSuchAttributeException example; 152
    NoSuchElementException; 276, 293, 375
    NoSuchFieldError; 376
    NoSuchMethodError; 376
    NotActiveException; 271
    NotSerializableException; 262, 264, 271
    NullPointerException; 125, 375
    Number; 300, 301, 302
    NumberFormatException;, 300, 301, 302, 375
    Object; 59, 73, 96, 114, 188, 190, 227, 232, 236,
        296, 304
        introduction; **20**
    ObjectInputStream; 227, **259**, 262, 263, 265
    ObjectOutputStream; 227, **259**, 263, 264, 266
    ObjectStreamClass; 227, 264, 266
    ObjectStreamException; 271
    Observable; 273, 288, 289
    OptionalDataException; 271
    Outer example; 186
    OutOfMemoryError; 32, 376
    OutputStream; 227, 229, 231, 237, 238, 240, 258,
        326
    OutputStreamReader; 232
    OutputStreamWriter; 232, 236, **237**, 238
    ParseFormatException; 356
    PassByValue example; 38

    PassRef example; 39
    Permissions example; 37
    PingPong example; 181
    Pipe example; 246
    Piped; 236, 246
    PipedInputStream; 227, 236
    PipedOutputStream; 227, 236
    PipedReader; 232, 246
    PipedWriter; 232, 246
    Pixel example; 18
    Player example; 315
    PlayerLoader example; 317
    Point example; 9, 279
    Polygon example; 279
    Primes example; 46
    Print; **240**
    PrintStream; 9, 227, 232, 237, 240, 322
    PrintWriter; 232, 237, 240
    Process; 321, 325, 326
    ProcessFile example; 49
    Properties; 273, **286**, 323
    PropertyResourceBundle; **342**
    Pushback; 237, 249, 250
    PushbackInputStream; 227, 249, 250
    PushbackReader; 232, 250
    Queue example; 189
    Random; 274, 291
    RandomAccessFile; 227, 237, 245, **258**, 258, 259
    Reader; 232, **233**, 237, 238, 250, 258
    RegionMatch example; 164
    RemoteException; 362, 363
    replaceValue example; 153
    ResourceBundle; 274, 338, 339
    Runnable; 181
    RunPingPong example; 201
    Runtime; 321, 322, **329**, 331
    RuntimeException; 24, 152, 373, 374
    ScaleVector example; 115
    SecurityException; 204, 205, 375
    SecurityManager; 331
    SequenceCount example; 249
    SequenceInputStream; 227, 237, **247**
    ServerSocket; 367
    Shimmer example; 95
    Short; 301
    SimpleClass example; 36
    SimpleDateFormat; 345, 352
    SimpleSortDouble example; 87
    SimpleTimeZone; 274, 344, 350
    Socket; 367
    SortDouble example; 84
    SortMetrics example; 86
    Stack; 273, **282**
    StackOverflowError; 376
    StreamCorruptedException; 271
    StreamTokenizer; 232, 237, **250**, 251, 253, 254,
        255, 293
    String; **56**, 110
    String; 161

String; 163, 164, 165, 167, 168, 170, 171, 236, 244, 245, 269
StringBuffer; 17, **172**, 173, 174, 175, 176, 245
StringBufferInputStream; 242
StringReader; 232, 244
StringsDemo example; 16
StringTokenizer; 274, 292
StringWriter; 232, 244
SubException example; 157
SuperException example; 157
SuperShow example; 68
SyncFailedException; 245, 271
System; 321, 322, 324, 331, 343
System.err; 237
System.out; 237
Task example; 362
tenPower example; 146
TestSort example; 87, 312
TextGenerator; 246
That example; 70
Thread; 181, 182, 188, 190, 191, 192, 201, 202, 204, 207
ThreadDeath; 329, 376
ThreadGroup; 201, **203**, 204, 205, 206, 207, 329
Throwable; 23, 73, 152
TimeZone; 274, 344, 350
TranslateByte example; 230
TypeDesc example; 304
UnicastRemoteObject; 364
UnknownError; 376
UnsatisfiedLinkError; 376
UnsupportedEncodingException; 271
URL; 367
URLConnection; 367
URLEncoder; 367
URLInput; 262
Users example; 289
UTFDataFormatException; 272
Value example; 45
Vector; 273, 278, 280, 281, 282
VerifyError; 376
VirtualMachineError; 376
Void; **297**
WhichChars example; 275, 276, 277
WriteAbortedException; 271
Writer; 232, 238, 240, 258
cleanup
See also exceptions (concepts and uses); try-catch-finally sequence
finally clause; 157
clearing
clear; 12
BitSet class; 274
Calendar class; 346
example, this reference use; 13
Hashtable class; 285
Pixel class; 18
client
term definition; 363

clocks
See also calendars; time
UTC compared with UT *(footnote)*; 349
cloning; **77**
See also objects, object-oriented concepts, components
cautions; 79
clone
Object class; 73, 77
Vector class; 180
Cloneable interface
as marker interface; 100
required for object cloning; 78
CloneNotSupportedException class; 73, 78, 82, 374
hashtables; 285
as resurrection strategy; 50
clone use; 73
preventing, in subclasses; 79
closing
See also I/O
close
finalizes use with; 48
OutputStream class; 230
Reader class; 233
Writer class; 235
streams; 228, 230
code
alternatives to commenting out; 104
methods as; 30
coding technique; *See* programming style
coercion
type, during expression evaluation; 121
collation
CollationKey class; 355
Collator class; **354**
getCollationKey (Collator class); 355
collection(s)
See also data, structures
of data; 247
iteration through the values in; 276
list of classes that are; 273
ColorAttr example
extending attribute classes; 61
COMBINING_SPACING_MARK constant (Character class)
as getType return value; 300
comments
See also documentation; programming, issues
comment skew
preventing; 223
term definition; 223
commentChar method (StreamTokenizer class); 253
documentation
(chapter); **215**
tags *(table)*; 380
usage recommendations; **223**
introduction; **5**

comments *(continued)*
    nesting not permitted, alternative for; 104
    term definition; 5
    types and characteristics; 104
communication
    See also beans; RMI; threads; URL
    inter-thread; 188
comparison
    See also control, flow; operators; testing
    in array sorting *(example)*; 85
    `Calendar` objects; 347
    `compareTo` (`String` class); 163
    dates; 344
    hashtable keys; 285
    objects
        `==` operator and `!=` operator use; 73
        values, `equals` use; 73
    references, with `==` operator; 165
    strings; **163**
        `equals`; 17
        locale-sensitive; 354
        regions of; 164
compiler
    @deprecated tag impact on; 218
component architecture
    `java.beans` package; 353, **367**
composition
    creating composite streams; 237
    inheritance compared with; 91
computing
    `ComputeServer` example; 362
    `ComputeServerImpl` example; 363, 364
    distributed
        applets; **361**
        garbage collection issues; 366
        Java Beans; **367**
        RMI; **362**
concatenation
    `+` operator use in `println` invocation; 8
    `Concat` example; 247
    `concat` (`String` class); 168
    streams; 236
    string; **130**
        `+` operator use; 16
concurrency; *See* locks; threads
condition handlers; *See* events, handling
conditional
    See also control, flow; testing
    cloning; 78
    control flow, `if`; 140
    operators
        (`?:`); **135**, 136
        AND (`&&`); 133
        OR (`||`); 133
        precedence of; 119
    reference casting; 125
configuration
    file, system property access in; 324
    of locales; 337

of threads; 181
of weeks; 347, 348
conflicts
    See also conventions; packages
    name
        handling for duplicate package names; 25
        handling in multiple interface inheritance; **96**
        hierarchical packages as means of preventing;
          25
        packages as mechanism for avoiding; 210
CONNECTOR_PUNCTUATION constant (Character
      class)
    as getType return value; 300
constants (concepts and use)
    See also data, structures; literals; numbers and
        logical operations; variables
    advantages of in resource bundles; 339
    infinity, `Float` and `Double` class support of; 107
    interface
        fields as; 92
        multiple inheritance of; 97
    named, introduction; **5**
    term definition; 5
    unnamed, *See* literals
constants (Java and user-defined)
    AM_PM (`Calendar` class); 346
    COMBINING_SPACING_MARK, Character class;
       300
    CONNECTOR_PUNCTUATION, Character class; 300
    const keyword, as reserved word; 106
    CONTROL, Character class; 300
    CURRENCY_SYMBOL, Character class; 300
    DASH_PUNCTUATION, Character class; 300
    DAY_OF_WEEK (`Calendar` class); 346
    DECIMAL_DIGIT_NUMBER, Character class; 300
    ENCLOSING_MARK, Character class; 300
    END_PUNCTUATION, Character class; 300
    FORMAT, Character class; 300
    HOUR (`Calendar` class); 346
    HOUR_OF_DAY (`Calendar` class); 346
    LETTER_NUMBER, Character class; 300
    LINE_SEPARATOR, Character class; 300
    LOWERCASE_LETTER, Character class; 300
    MATH_SYMBOL, Character class; 300
    MAX_VALUE, Number class; 301
    MILLISECOND (`Calendar` class); 346
    MIN_VALUE, Number class; 301
    MINUTE (`Calendar` class); 346
    MODIFIER_LETTER, Character class; 300
    MODIFIER_SYMBOL, Character class; 300
    NaN
        Double class; 302
        Float and Double class support of; 107
        Float class; 302
    NEGATIVE_INFINITY
        Double class; 302
        Float and Double class support of; 107
        Float class; 302
    NON_SPACING_MARK, Character class; 300

NORM_PRIORITY, Thread class); 191
OTHER_LETTER, Character class; 300
OTHER_NUMBER, Character class; 300
OTHER_PUNCTUATION, Character class; 300
OTHER_SYMBOL, Character class; 300
PARAGRAPH_SEPARATOR, Character class; 300
POSITIVE_INFINITY
   Double class; 30 2
   Float class; 302
POSTIVE_INFINITY, Float and Double class
    support of; 107
PRIVATE_USE, Character class; 300
SECOND (Calendar class); 346
SPACE_SEPARATOR, Character class; 300
START_PUNCTUATION, Character class; 300
SURROGATE, Character class; 300
TITLECASE_LETTER, Character class; 300
TT_EOF, StreamTokenizer class; 251
TT_EOL, StreamTokenizer class; 251
TT_NUMBER, StreamTokenizer class; 251
TT_WORD, StreamTokenizer class; 251
UNASSIGNED, Character class; 300
UPPERCASE_LETTER, Character class; 300
constructors (concepts and use)
   See also object-oriented concepts and components
   in common among, wrapper classes; 296
   creating, reflection methods for; **312**
   explicit, invocation, this reference use; 34
   in extended classes; **64**
   identifier name search order; 113
   instance variable assignment within, advantages
    of; 117
   invocation order dependencies; **65**
   multiple, ColorAttr example; 62
   no-arg, term definition; 25
   specialized, reasons for providing; 35
   term definition; **33**
   terminating, return use for; 149
   this use with; 43
constructors (Java and user-defined)
   ByteArrayInputStream; 242
   ByteArrayOutputStream; 242
   CharArrayReader class; 243
   CharArrayWriter class; 243
   Constructor class; 313
   File; 267
   FileDescriptor; 245
   FileInputStream; 245
   FileOutputStream; 245
   Float; 303
   GregorianCalendar; 349
   Hashtable; 285
   InputStream; 227
   Locale; 337
   output, OutputStream; 229
   Print; 240
   Properties; 287
   Random; 291
   RandomAccessFile; 258

Reader; 233
SequenceInputStream; 247
String
   byte arrays; 171
   characters array manipulation with; 171
   creating strings with; 161
StringBuffer; 176
StringTokenizer; 293
Thread; 202
ThreadGroup; 205
Vector; 278
Writer; 235
containing
   Container example; 147
   contains (Vector class); 279
   containsKey (Hashtable class); 285
   containsObject (Hashtable class); 285
   EventListener interface; 360
contents
   hashtable, accessing; 286
contexts
   See also encapsulation; packages; scope
   naming, term definition; 24
   separation, packages use for; 209
continue
   See also control, flow; debugging
   keyword, as reserved word; 106
   statement; **148**
    finally clause use to clean up for; 158
    for loop use; 146
    goto statement replacement; 149
contract
   See also signature
   design, access control issues; 86
   marker interfaces as degenerate case of; 100
   marker interfaces as degenerate form of; 101
   public vs protected; 84
   term definition; 29, 59
control
   See also expressions; language concepts; object-
    oriented concepts and components;
    programming, issues; programming,
    techniques; security; threads
   access
    constructor declaration; 35
    extensible classes, implementation summary;
     88
    in extensible class design; 86
    method use for; **41**
    modifiers that manage; **31**
    packages use for; 209
   of autoflushing; 240
   CONTROL constant (Character class), as getType
    return value; 300
   flow
    (chapter); **139**
    do-while; 144
    if; 140
    introduction; **7**

control *(continued)*
   flow *(continued)*
     labeled break contrasted with goto; 148
     switch; 142
     term definition; 139
     threads; 181
     while; 144
   of processes; 325
   socket access; 331
   variables, declaring in a for statement; 15
conventions
   naming, packages; 210
conversions
   case, methods for; 299
   characters *(example)*; 230
   floating point values; 303
   implicit; **121**
   integer values, static methods for; 302
   methods, *See* to*Xxx* methods
   reference; 122
   strings
     String; **125**, 174
     to other types; **169**
     toString; 56
     upper and lower case; 168
     valueOf use for; 169
   type; 121
     characteristics; 123
     during expression evaluation; 121
   between Unicode and byte streams; **237**
Cook, Rich
   quotation; **372**
copying
   See also cloning
   arrays; 331
     byte; 171
     character; 171
   copyInto (Vector class); 280
   copyValueOf (String class); 171
   input to output; 230
   java.awt.datatransfer package; 361
   objects, *See* cloning
   strings; 161
   vectors; 280
cos method (Math class); 332
   See also numbers and logical operations
counting
   See also enumeration; programming, techniques
   bytes in a file *(example)*; 228
   count field, CharArrayWriter class; 243
   count field (CharArrayReader class); 243
   countBetween example; 162
   CountBytes example; 228
   countObservers (Observable class); 289
   CountSpace example; 234
   countStackFrames (Thread class); 207
   countTokens (StringTokenizer class); 294
   Enumeration interface; 273
   Observer objects; 289

   thread groups; 206, 207
   threads in a thread group; 206, 207
   tokens remaining in a string; 293
   whitespace characters; 234
country
   differences, managing with Locale class; 336
   ISO codes, retrieving; 338
creating
   See also debugging; extending; object-oriented
     concepts and components; programming,
     techniques
   arrays, dimension specification; 117
   buffered output streams; 241
   character arrays from a StringBuffer object; 175
   class loaders; 316
   creation operators precedence; 119
   directories; 268
   files; 269
   filters; 236
   lists, ordered; 247
   objects
     introduction; **10**
     new operator use for; **32**
     reflection use for; **312**
   pipes; 236, 246
   processes; **325**
   streams, composite; 237
   String objects; 16
   strings; 161
   threads; **181**
crisis
   millennium, solution for; 331, 343
Croatian
   character case issues; 298
cryptography
   java.security package; 372
CURRENCY_SYMBOL constant (Character class)
   as getType return value; 300
currentTimeMillis method (System class); 331,
   343
cutting
   java.awt.datatransfer package; 361
cycles
   in static initializers; 46

D

D/d suffix
   as double-precision floating-point constant
     indicator; 109
daemon
   See also runtime; system
   thread groups; 204
     methods for handling; 205
   threads, term definition; 200
dangling references
   See also memory
   garbage collection prevention of; 47

DASH_PUNCTUATION constant (Character class)
as getType return value; 300
data
See also buffers; I/O; language concepts; object-
oriented concepts and components; properties;
streams; type(s)
breaking into tokens; 250
buffered, writing to a file; 241
collecting; 247
containers, simple objects use as; 12
controlling access to, accessor method use for; 41
Data class; 236
relationships with other classes; 256
DataInput interface; 236, 255, 256, 257
implementation by RandomAccessFile; 258
in type tree for byte streams *(figure)*; 227
RandomAccessFile class implementation of;
237
DataInputStream class; 236, 255, 257
in type tree for byte streams *(figure)*; 227
DataOutput interface; 236, 255, 256, 257
implementation by RandomAccessFile; 258
in type tree for byte streams *(figure)*; 227
RandomAccessFile class implementation of;
237
DataOutputStream, serialization use; 260
DataOutputStream class; 236, 257
in type tree for byte streams *(figure)*; 227
DataOutputStream interface; 255
dataSet example, exception handling; 23
extending, by subclassing; 18
extracting from a StringBuffer; **175**
fields as; 30
java.awt.datatransfer package; 361
parsing; 250
printing; 237, 240
reading; 228
scanning; 250
streams
classes; **257**
reading and writing; **255**
structures, *See*
arrays
collections
hashtables
objects
queues
stacks
type(s)
vectors
structures, See, sequences
types
primitive (list); 4
vs object types; 4
writeObject, serialization use; 260
writing; 229
databases
java.sql package; 354, **372**

datagrams
DatagramSocket class; 367
term definition; 367
date(s)
See also internationalization; localization; time
calendar fields representing; 346
comparing; 344
Date class; 274
time related functions; 343
Date1 example; 25
Date2 example; 344
DateFormat class; 344, 350, 356
displaying, as locale-sensitive operation; 345
formatting; **350**, 351
getDateInstance (DateFormat class); 351
getDateTimeInstance (DateFormat class); 351
handling historical issues; 350
inserting into a buffer; 174
modification, obtaining; 268
operations related to; **343**
parsing; **350**, 352
Davis, Miles
quotation; **208**
daylight saving time
inDaylightTime (TimeZone class); 348
useDaylightTime (TimeZone class); 348
deadlock
See also programming, issues; threads
term definition; **194**
deadly embrace
See also programming, issues; threads
term definition; 194
deallocation (memory); *See* garbage collection
debugging
See also documentation; errors (concepts and use);
exceptions (concepts and use); programming,
issues; programming, techniques; runtime
Class advantages for; 304
classes, multiple main advantages for; 56
debugger creation, invoke use in; 312
error prevention, guarded class hierarchy design as
tool for; 86
list (Properties class) use for; 288
multithreaded applications; **207**
network failure handling; 363
property lists, list use for; 288
Runtime tracing methods; 331
subtle errors, preventing in the design of extensible
classes; 89
writing debuggers and inspectors, *See* reflection
decimal
BigDecimal class; 370, 371
DECIMAL_DIGIT_NUMBER constant (Character
class), as getType return value; 300
Deck example
array use; 15
declaration
See also instantiation; object-oriented concepts and
components

declaration *(continued)*
    class, type names created by; 30
    of exceptions, with `throws` clause; 153
    of methods, vs implementation; 20
    of packages; 26, 209
    statements; 140
        term definition; 139
    term definition; 110
    of variables; **110**
        control; 15
        Fibonacci example; 3
decoding
    efficient handling of; 61
decrement (--) operator; 131
    See also numbers and logical operations;
        operator(s)
    char variable use; 132
    comparison with self assignment +1; 131
defaults
    access; 211
    constructor handling of; 64
    `default` keyword, as reserved word; 106
    values
        fields *(table)*; 117
        local variables, not assigned; 117
defineClass method (ClassLoader class); 318
    See also classes (concepts and use)
deleting
    See also termination
    characters from a string; 170
    `deleteObserver` (Observable class); 288
    `deleteObservers` (Observable class); 289
    elements from a queue; 189
    files; 269
    `Observer` objects; 289
    vector elements; 279
delimiters
    See also string(s)
    string parsing use; 293
dependencies
    See also hierarchies; order(ing); subclassing
    constructor invocation order; **65**
deprecated
    @deprecated tag; **217**
    style, object resurrection; 50
descriptors
    See also files; I/O
    file; **245**
deserialization
    See also objects; serialization
    class loading requirements; 263
    object; **259**, 261
    order considerations; **262**
    term definition; 259
design patterns
    See also algorithms; debugging; object-oriented
        concepts and components; programming,
        techniques
    Observable class; 273, **288**

Observer interface; 273, **288**
`wait`/`notify` threads mechanism compared with
    Observer/Observable mechanism; 291
designing
    extensible classes; **83**
destination
    term definition; 225
destroy method
    See also processes; threads
    `Process` class; 327
    `ThreadGroup` class; 205
dialog boxes
    as AWT component; 360
diamond inheritance
    See also object-oriented concepts and components
    interface use; 95
    term definition; 94
dictionaries
    See also data, structures; hashtables
    `Dictionary` class; 273, **283**, 284, 285
        extended by `Hashtable`; 284
    property lists; 287
digital signatures
    `java.security` package; 354, 372
digits
    See also Unicode character set
    `digit` (Character class); 298
    testing characters for; 299
dimensions
    See also array(s)
    array; 114
directories
    See also file(s); I/O
    accessing; 267
    creating; 268
    `DirFilter` example; 270
    listing files in; 269
    testing; 268
disambiguating
    parameters and fields, `this` use for; 43
displaying
    dates, as locale-sensitive operation; 345
    Locale components; 337
distance example; 13
distributed computing
    See also beans; RMI; threads
    applets; **361**
    garbage collection issues; 366
    Java Beans; **367**
    `java.beans` package; 353
    RMI; **362**
division
    See also arithmetic; numbers and logical
        operations
    in floating-point arithmetic, results *(table)*; 129
    in integer arithmetic; 128
    operators, precedence of; 119
    slash (/) arithmetic operator; 128

do
 do-while statement; **144**
  as flow of control statement; 7
  while compared with; 144
 keyword, as Java reserved word; 106
documentation
 See also debugging; programming, techniques
 Class advantages for; 304
 comments
  (chapter); **215**
  example; **219**
  tags *(table)*; 380
  term definition; 5
  usage recommendations; **223**
 importance in class contracts; 29
 javadoc, linking to; **216**
dot (.) operator
 See also methods (concepts and use); operators
 accessing members with; 125
 method invocation; 2, 12, 36
 package vs field and method access use; 26
dotw example; 347
double
 Double class; 106, 302
  doubleToLongBits; 303
  longBitsTo Double; 303
  NaN constant; 107, 302
  NEGATIVE_INFINITY constant; 302
  POSITIVE_INFINITY constant; 302
 as double keyword
  primitive data type, value of; 107
  reserved word; 106
 double type
  converting to and from strings; 169
  Number class as wrapper for; 300
  reading and writing; 255
 double-quote (\")
  creating strings with; 161
  Unicode value; 109
 doubleToLongBits (Double class); 303
 doubleValue (Number class); 300
Dr. Who
 quotations; **29**, **161**
drawing
 Canvas class; 360
dumpStack method (Thread class); 207
dwim method; 105

E

E constant (Math class); 332
Edison, Thomas
 quotation; *xvii*
efficiency
 See also performance; programming, issues
 constructor avoidance of overhead; 64
 of finals; 86
Einstein, Albert
 quotation; **57**

elements
 See also data, structures
 elementAt (Vector class); 279
 elementCount field (Vector class); 282
 elementData field (Vector class); 282
 elements (Dictionary class); 284
 elements (Vector class); 280
 NoSuchElementException; 375
else keyword
 See also control, flow
 else clause (if statement); 140
 as reserved word; 106
Emerson, Ralph Waldo
 quotation; **320**
EmptyStackException class; 282
 See also debugging; stacks
 Stack class; 282
encapsulation
 See also object-oriented concepts and components
 packages use for; 209
 term definition; 12
 of threads, into thread groups; 203
enclosing
 class, term definition; 50
 ENCLOSING_MARK constant (Character class), as
  getType return value; 300
 type, term definition; 50
encryption
 java.security package; 354
end
 end of file (EOF)
  EOFException; 271
  scanning for; 251
 END_PUNCTUATION constant (Character class), as
  getType return value; 300
 endsWith method (String class); 165
English language; 342
ensureCapacity method (Vector class); 281
enumeration
 See also counting; programming, techniques
 enumerate, ThreadGroup class; 206
 Enumeration interface; 98, 273, **276**, 276, 293
  implementation by ResourceBundle; 338
  implementing; **276**
  local inner class use; 54
  SequenceInputStream class use; 247
  StringTokenizer class implementation of;
   293
 hasMoreElements example; 54
 of property list keys; 288
 WhichChars example; 277
environment
 See also runtime; system
 system, accessing information about; 323
 variables, term definition; 328
EOF (end-of-file)
 See also file(s); I/O
 EOFException class; 256

EOL (end-of-line)
See also I/O
eolIsSignificant method (StreamTokenizer
class); 254
scanning for; 251
epoch
term definition; 343
equality
See also arithmetic; control, flow; numbers and
logical operations; testing
equal (=) operator; **132**
initialization expression use; 4
equals
BitSet class; 275
File class; 269
Object class; 73
regionMatches; 163
String class; 17, 163
wrapper classes use of; 297
equals (=) operator, creating assignment operators
with; 136
equals-equals (==) operator
comparing objects; 73
compared to string content comparison; 165
equalsIgnoreCase (String class); 163
files, meaning of; 269
not equal (!=) operator
comparing objects; 73
relational operator; 132
object, hash code values and; 73
operators, precedence of; 120
testing
bit vectors; 275
NaN anomalies; 133
references; 133
references, intern; 166
String; 133
errors (concepts and use)
See also debugging; exceptions (concepts and use)
duplicate assignment, avoiding through
constructor use; 34
handling through exception mechanism *(chapter)*;
151
memory management, garbage collection
prevention of; 48
messages, standard err; 322
system, than can prevent invocation of finalizes;
50
errors (Java and user-defined)
AbstractMethodError class; 375
classes; **375**
ClassFormatError class; 375
err field (System class); 322
Error class; 24, 152, 373
as unchecked exceptions, reasons for; 154
ExceptionInInitializerError class; 375
IllegalAccessError class; 375
IncompatibleClassChangeError class; 375
InstantiationError class; 376

InternalError class; 376
LinkageError class; 376
NoClassDefFoundError class; 376
NoSuchFieldError class; 376
NoSuchMethodError class; 376
OutOfMemoryError class; 32, 376
StackOverflowError class; 376
System.err class, character stream relationship;
231
ThreadDeath class; 376
UnknownError class; 376
UnsatisfiedLinkError class; 376
VerifyError class; 376
VirtualMachineError class; 376
escape sequences; 104, 105, 109, 241
See also Unicode character set
newline (\n); 241
special character representation *(table)*; 109
Unicode encoding with; 103
Esperanto language; 340
Estes, James
quotation; **213**
Euclidian distance
computation example; 13
evaluation order
See also expressions; serialization
conditional operators; 133
operands; **120**
operators; 119
events
See also control, flow; debugging; language
concepts; threads
action
ActionEvent class; 360
ActionListener interface; 360
term definition; 360
EventListener interface; 360
model
AWT; 360
Java Beans same as AWT; 367
monitoring; 288
notifying, Observer objects; 289
waiting; 188
examining
classes; **306**
exceptions (concepts and use)
See also debugging; errors (concepts and use)
(chapter); **151**
checked
restrictions on field initializers; 117
term definition; 22, 152
declaring; **153**
documenting; **217**
@exception tag; **217**
finalize handling; 50
handling
as differentiator of Java from C and C++; *xvi*
error condition handling advantages of; *xvi*
hierarchy *(figure)*; 373

as unusable in method overloading; 127
introduction; **22**
runtime *(chapter)*; **373**
in static initializers; 46
term definition; 22, 151
types, creating; **152**
unchecked
    (chapter); **373**
    precautions against creating; 374
    term definition; 24, 152
when to use; **159**
exceptions (Java and user-defined)
ArithmeticException; 121, 128, 154, 374
ArrayStoreException; 374
BadDataSetException example; 23
CharConversionException; 271
ClassCastException; 124, 154, 247, 374
ClassNotFoundException; 263
CloneNotSupportedException; 73, 78, 82, 374
EmptyStackException; 282
EOFException; 256, 271
Error *(chapter)*; **373**
Exception; 22, 23, 152
    (chapter); **373**
FileNotFoundException; 271
IllegalAccessException; 310, 312
IllegalArgumentException; 310, 347, 356, 374
IllegalMonitorStateException; 191, 374
IllegalStateException class; 375
IllegalThreadStateException; 201
IllegalThreadStateException; 375
IndexOutOfBoundsException; 15, 114, 125,
    162, 230, 233, 235, 279, 375
InstantiationException; 312
InterruptedException; 182, 196
InterruptedIOException; 271
InvalidClassException; 271
InvalidObjectException; 271
InvocationTargetException; 310, 312
IOException; 226, 230, 233, 235, 256, 258, 264,
    268, **271**
InputStream class; 228
LSFailedException; 327
MissingBundleException; 340
MissingResourceException; 375
NegativeArraySizeException; 375
NoSuchAttributeException; 152
NoSuchAttributeException example; 152
NoSuchElementException; 276, 293, 375
NotActiveException; 271
NotSerializableException; 262, 264, 271
NullPointerException; 125, 375
NumberFormatException;, 300, 301, 302, 375
ObjectStreamException; 271
OptionalDataException; 271
OutOfMemoryError; 32
ParseFormatException; 356
RemoteException; 362, 363
RuntimeException; 24, 152, **374**

(chapter); **373**
SecurityException; 204, 205, 375
StreamCorruptedException; 271
SubException; 157
SuperException; 157
SyncFailedException; 245, 271
ThreadDeath; 329
uncaughtException; 207
UnsupportedEncodingException; 271
UTFDataFormatException; 272
WriteAbortedException; 272
execution
See also runtime
exec
    Process class; 328
    System class; 325
order, static field initialization; 45
thread
    ending; **199**
    yielding; 192
exists method (File class); 268
exiting
See also termination
blocks, break use for; 147
exit (Runtime class); 329
exitValue (Process class); 327
exp method (Math class); 332
See also numbers and logical operations
expressions
See also arithmetic; casting; evaluation order;
    language concepts; numbers and logical
    operations; parsing; syntax; type(s)
(chapter); **103**
creating statements from; 139
initialization, = operator use in; 4
statements, term definition; 139
types, determination of; **121**
extensibility
See also object-oriented concepts and components
as advantage of declaring fields private; 42
classes
    (chapter); **59**
    how and when to do so; **82**
    introduction; **18**
designing classes for; **83**
extends keyword
    as reserved word; 106
    class extension with; 59
    interface extension with; 22, 95
ExtendShow example, method overriding vs field
    hiding; 68
interfaces; 22, **95**
preserving while using final; 72
strings; 174
superclass methods; 19
term definition; 59
Externalizable interface; **267**
See also serialization
in type tree for byte streams *(figure)*; 227

extracting
 See also string(s)
 data from a `StringBuffer`; **175**
 strings from a `StringBuffer`; 175
 substrings; 167
Eye example; 290

F

F/f suffix
 as single-precision floating-point constant
  indicator; 109
factoring
 See also arithmetic; expressions; numbers and
  logical operations
 Factor example; 244
 factors example; 370
failure
 partial, term definition; 363
fall-through handling
 See also control, flow
 in `switch` statements; 143
false literal
 as boolean literal; 108
 keyword restrictions apply to; 107
Fibonacci example; 3
 See also numbers and logical operations
Fibonacci numbers; 1, 2, 3, 5, 8, 13, 21, 34, 55, 89,
  144, 233, 377
fields (concepts and use); **30**
 See also classes (concepts and use); data,
  structures; object-oriented concepts and
  components
 accessing, object types compared with method
  invocation; 68
 calendar, methods that access; 346
 class, *See* fields (concepts and use), static
 errors, `NoSuchFieldError` class; 376
 examining the values of; **309**
 Field class; 308, **309**
 `final`; **111**
  initialization requirement; 110
 hiding; 68
  reasons for; 70
  with `private`; 41
 initializers, checked exceptions not permitted; 117
 interface, `static` and `final` implicit in; 92
 multiple return value use; 37
 non-static, class methods restricted from
  accessing; 110
 numeric, default value; 11
 object
  initialization of; 117
  See instance variables
 overriding
  not permitted with; 68
  `super` reference use to access; 43
 parameters and, `this` reference as access
  differentiator; 43

protected, characteristics and use; 63
 shared, `volatile` marking of; 203
 static; **44**
  declaring; 31
  initialization of; 117
  introduction; **11**
  protected, characteristics and use; 63
  restrictions on; 45
 term definition; 1, 9
fields (Java and user-defined)
 See also constants (Java and user-defined)
 `calendar` (`DateFormat` class); 352
 `lock`, character stream synchronization use; 231
 `numberFormat` (`DateFormat` class); 352
 `serialVersionUID`; 265
file(s)
 See also data, structures; I/O; object(s); streams
 `close`, `finalizes` use with; 48
 creating; 269
 deleting; 269
 descriptors; 245
 exceptions; 271
 `File` class; 236, 237, **245**, **267**, 268, 269, 324
  in type tree for byte streams *(figure)*; 227
  in type tree for character streams *(figure)*; 232
 `File` stream classes, getFD; 245
 `FileDescriptor` class; **245**
  in type tree for byte streams *(figure)*; 227
  in type tree for character streams *(figure)*; 232
 `FileInputStream`; 229
 `FileInputStream` class; 234, 245, 318
  in type tree for byte streams *(figure)*; 227
 `FilenameFIlter` interface; 270
 `FileNotFoundException` class; 271
 `FileOutputStream` class; 245
  in type tree for byte streams *(figure)*; 227
 `FileReader` class; 238
  in type tree for character streams *(figure)*; 232
 `FileWriter` class; 238
  in type tree for character streams *(figure)*; 232
 I/O; 245
 length, obtaining; 259, 269
 listing; 269
 not found exception; 271
 pathname, retrieving; 268
 pathnames, `File` class abstraction of; 237
 pointer
  accessing; 258
  setting; 259
 property, for resource bundles; 343
 random access, `RandomAccessFile`; 245
 random access of; **258**
 `RandomAccessFile`, implementation of
  `DataOutput` and `DataInput`; 257
 `RandomAccessFile` class; 237
 readable, testing if possible; 268
 renaming; 269
 saving property lists in; 287
 writable, testing if possible; 268

writing buffered data to; 241
filenames
See also I/O; path
`FilenameFIlter` interface, accept; **270**
`FilenameFilter` interface
in type tree for byte streams *(figure)*; 227
in type tree for character streams *(figure)*; 232
filtering; 270
manipulating; 267
filters
See also I/O; streams
`DirFilter` example; 270
filename; 270
`FilenameFIlter` interface; **270**
`Filter` class; 236, **238**
`FilterInputStream`, extended by
`DataInputStream`; 256, 257
`FilterInputStream` class, in type tree for byte
streams *(figure)*; 227
`FilterOutputStream`, extended by
`DataOutputStream`; 256, 257
`FilterOutputStream` class, in type tree for byte
streams *(figure)*; 227
`FilterReader` class; 236, 238
in type tree for character streams *(figure)*; 232
`FilterWriter` class; 238
in type tree for character streams *(figure)*; 232
final
`final` keyword
as reserved word; 106
class and method use; **71**
fields, implicit in interfaces; 93
fields, initialization requirement; 110
fields, trade-offs; 42
in variable declarations; 110
in variable declarations, named constants
creation using; 5
method parameters declaration, trade-offs; 40
methods, access control use of; 86
parameters, modification of by subclasses; 67
recommended order in class member
declarations; 111
variable use; **111**
`finalize` methods; 48, 49
invoking; 322
invoking, reasons for; 323
`Object` class; 73
resurrecting objects during; **50**
`finally` keyword
as reserved word; 106
block; 155
`finally` clause (`throw` statement); **157**
`goto` statement replacement; 150, 158
find
See also access; searching
`FindChar` example; 238
`LineNumberReader` use; 248
finite arithmetic
See also numbers and logical operations

floating-point; 129
Firesign Theater
quotation; **179**
`firstElement` method (`Vector` class); 280
fishing
as coding alternative; 91
floating-point
See also arithmetic; numbers and logical
operations; type(s)
arithmetic; **128**
`doubleValue` (`Number` class); 300
`Float` class; 106, 302
`floatToIntBits`; 303
`intBitsToFloat`; 303
`NaN` constant; 107, 302
`NEGATIVE_INFINITY` constant; 302
`POSITIVE_INFINITY` constant; 302
`float` keyword, as primitive data type, value of;
107
`float` type
converting to and from strings; 169
default value; 117
`Number` class as wrapper for; 300
reading and writing; 255
`floatToIntBits` (`Float` class); 302
`floatValue` (`Number` class); 300
`intBitsToFloat` (`Float` class); 303
Java and IEEE 754 standard differences; **130**
literals, characteristics; **108**
types, casting to integer types; 123
values
bit manipulation; 303
bit manipulation not possible with; 134
ordering of; 133
wrapper classes; **302**
`floor` method (`Math` class); 332
See also numbers and logical operations
flow of control; *See* control, flow
`FlowLayoutManager` class; 359
See also AWT (Abstract Window Toolkit)
flushing
See also I/O
auto, controlling; 240
`FileOutputStream` class; 245
`FileWriter` class; 245
`flush` method (`OutputStream`); 230
`flush` (`Writer` class); 235
streams; 230
for
See also control, flow
`for` keyword, as reserved word; 106
`for` statement; 145
control variable declaration in; 15
flow of control statement; 7
in Fibonacci example; 7
`forDigit` (`Character` class); 298
`forName` (`Class` class); 304
loop, identifier name search order; 113

form feed (\f) escape sequence
See also escape sequences; special characters
Unicode value; 109
as white space; 105
formatting
See also syntax
DateFormat class; 356
dates; 351, 352
extended arithmetic, not supported; 130
Format class; **355**
FORMAT constant (Character class), as getType return value; 300
locale-sensitive; **355**
MessageFormat class; 356
NumberFormat class; 356
forwarding
See also object-oriented concepts and components
advantages; 99
disadvantages of; **101**
methods, as interface implementation technique; 99
term definition; 99
frames
positioning components in; 359
freeMemory method (Runtime class); 322
See also memory; runtime
fullGC example
See also garbage collection; memory
fullGC example; 322

G

games
Game example; 316
strategies for writing; 315
garbage collection; 47
See also debugging; memory; runtime
arrays; 115
class unloading automatically handled through; 318
as differentiator of Java from C and C++; *xvi*
fullGC example; 322
gc
    Runtime class; 322
    System class; 322
invoking; **322**
RMI; 366
as robust code facilitator; *xvi*
term definition, introduction; **11**
Gaussian-distributed value
See also numbers and logical operations; values
as seed for random number generation use; 292
Georgian
character case issues; 298
getting
See also access; setting
get
    BitSet class; 274
    Dictionary class; 284

Field class; 309
get (Calendar class); 346
getType methods (Array class); 314
getAbsolutePath (File class); 268
getAvailableIDs (TimeZone class); 348
getAvailableLocales (DateFormat class); 351
getBoolean (Boolean class); 325
getBuffered; 241
getBundle (ResourceBundle class); 339
getBytes (String class); 171
getCalendar (DateFormat class); 351
getCanonicalPath (File class); 268
getChars
    String class; 171
    StringBuffer class; 175
getClass
    Class class; 306, 314
    Object class; 73, 304
getClasses (Class class); 307
getClassLoader (ClassLoader class); 318
getCollationKey (Collator class); 355
getComponentType (Class class); 306
getConstructor method (Class class); 307
getContents method (Class class); 320
getCountry (Locale class); 337
getCurrentThread (Thread class); 207
getDaemon (Thread class); 200
getDateInstance (DateFormat class); 351
getDateTimeInstance (DateFormat class); 351
getDeclaredClasses method (Class class); 307
getDeclaredConstructor method (Class class); 307
getDeclaredConstructors method (Class class); 307
getDeclaredField method (Class class); 306
getDeclaredFields method (Class class); 306
getDeclaredMethod method (Class class); 306
getDeclaredMethods method (Class class); 307
getDeclaringClass (Member interface); 308
getDeclaringClass method (Class class); 306
getDefault (TimeZone class); 348
getDisplayCountry (Locale class); 337
getDisplayLanguage (Locale class); 337
getDisplayVariant (Locale class); 337
getErrorStream (Process class); 326
getExceptionTypes method (Method class); 310
getFD (File stream classes); 245
getField method (Class class); 306
getFields method (Class class); 306
getFilePointer (RandomAccessFile class); 258
getFirstDayOfWeek (Calendar class); 347
getGreatestMinimum (Calendar class); 346
getGregorianChange (GregorianCalendar class); 350
getID (TimeZone class); 348
getInputStream (Process class); 326
getInstance, Calendar class; 337
getInstance (Collator class); 354

getInteger (Integer class); 325
getISO3Country (Locale class); 338
getISO3Language (Locale class); 338
getLanguage (Locale class); 337
getLeastMaximum (Calendar class); 346
getLineInstance (BreakIterator class); 358
getLineNumber (LineNumberReader class); 248
getLong (Long class); 325
getMaxPriority (ThreadGroup class); 205
getMethod method (Class class); 306
getMethods method (Class class); 307
getMinimalDaysInFirstWeek (Calendar class); 347
getMinimum (Calendar class); 346
getModifiers (Member interface); 308
getName
    File class; 268
    Member interface; 308
    Thread class; 182
    ThreadGroup class; 205
getNumberFormat (DateFormat class); 351
getNumberInstance (NumberFormat class); 356
getNumericValue (Character class); 298
getOffset (TimeZone class); 348
getOutputStream (Process class); 326
getParameterTypes method (Method class); 310
getParent
    File class; 268
    ThreadGroup class; 205
getPath (File class); 268
getPercentInstance (NumberFormat class); 356
getPriority (Thread class); 192
getProperty
    Properties class; 287
    System class; 324
getRawOffset (TimeZone class); 348
getResource method (Class class); 320
getReturnType method (Method class); 310
getRuntime (Runtime class); 329
getSecurityManager (System class); 332
getSentenceInstance (BreakIterator class); 358
getSystemResourceAsStream method (Class class); 319, 320
getTargetException method (InvocationTargetException class0; 312
getThreadGroup (ThreadGroup class); 207
getTime (Date class); 344, 347
getTimeInstance (DateFormat class); 351
getTimeZone (DateFormat class); 351
getType
    Character class; 300
    Field class; 309
getVarient (Locale class); 337
getWordInstance (BreakIterator class); 358
Gilbert and Sullivan
    quotation; **59**
GlobalHello example; 339

GlobalRes example; 339, 341
GlobalRes_tl example; 342
GMT (Greenwich Mean Time)
    Java time relative to; 343
    offsets from; 348
Goethe, Johann Wolfgang von
    quotation; **177**
goto
    See also control, flow
    keyword, as reserved word; 106
    statement
        finally clause replacement of; 158
        labeled break contrasted with; 148
        replacements for; 149
graphics
    resource bundle handling; 340
graphs
    object, term definition; 259
greater than
    See also numbers and logical operations; operators
    greater than or equal (>=) operator; 132
    greater than (>) operator; 132
GregorianCalendar class; 274, 344, **348**
    See also calendars; internationalization; localization
GridBagLayoutManager class; 359
Guaspari, David
    quotation; **380**
GUI (graphical user interface)
    AWT components; 360
    java.awt package; 353, **359**
    threads advantages for; *xvi*
guillemet characters
    See also Unicode character set
    substituting in quotes; 131
Guthrie, Woody
    quotation; **295**

H

handleObject (ResourceBundle class); 343
has
    hasMoreElements method (Enumeration interface); 276, 293
    hasMoreTokens method (StringTokenizer class); 293
HasA relationships
    IsA relationships contrasted with; 82
hashtables
    See also data, structures; programming, techniques; serialization
    attribute set implementation using; 98
    AttributedImpl use of; 285
    class loader use; 317
    cloning; 285
    hash codes
        access, with hashCode; 73, 166
        mapping, Properties class; 273

hashtables *(continued)*
  hashCode; 166
    BitSet class; 275
    Object class; 73
    wrapper classes use of; 297
  Hashtable class; 273, **284**, 285, 297
    serialization, customized; 263
  resizing; 286
  serialization; 259
    customized; 263
  term definition; 284
heap
  See also garbage collection; memory
  term definition; 10
HelloWorld class example; 1
hexadecimal
  See also numbers and logical operations
  conversion of integer values to, static methods for;
    302
  literals, representation and range; 109
hiding
  See also encapsulation; object-oriented concepts
    and components
  fields; 68
    reasons for; 70
    with private; 41
  local variable restrictions, in nested constructs; 113
  method identifiers, implications of; 113
  of parameter values, in pass-by-value; 38
  term definition; 14
hierarchy
  See also classes (concepts and use); object-
    oriented concepts and components
  array, relationship to class hierarchy *(figure)*; 114
  class; 62
    relationship to array hierarchy *(figure)*; 114
  package name, advantages of; 25
  type
    for byte streams *(figure)*; 227
    for character streams *(figure)*; 232
    for primitive type wrapper classes; 295
    walking; 304
Hoare, C.A.R.
  quotation; **102**
HTML (Hypertext Markup Language)
  See also RMI; URL
  APPLET tag; 361
  doc comment
    generation; 215
    text as input to; 216
  javadoc generation of; 5

I

I/O
  See also buffers; data; file(s); reading; streams;
    threads; writing
  (chapter); **225**
  classes that handle, summary; **236**

  exceptions, IOException class; 271
  file; 245
  IOException; 230, 256
  IOException class; 233, 235, **271**
    I/O use; 226
    InputStream class use; 228
  java.io package; 353
  standard; **321**
  streams
    buffered; 241
    print; 240
idempotent
  term definition; 363
identifiers
  See also object-oriented concepts and components;
    variables
  declaration of; 110
  duplicate, regulations; 113
  scope; 110, 113
  term definition; 106
  Unicode, requirements for; 299
IEEE 754 standard
  IEEERemainder method (Math class); 333
  Java
    key differences from; **130**
    use of; 128
  remainder operator; 333
if keyword
  See also control, flow
  if statement; **140**
    conditional operator compared with; 135
  if-else statement
    as flow of control statement; 7
    in ImprovedFibonacci example; 7
  as reserved word; 106
illegal operations
  See also errors (Java and user-defined); exceptions
    (Java and user-defined)
  IllegalAccessError class; 375
  IllegalAccessException class; 310, 312
  IllegalArgumentException class; 310, 374
  IllegalMonitorStateException class; 191,
    374
  IllegalStateException class; 375
  IllegalThreadStateException class; 201, 375
images
  ImageConsumer interface; 361
  ImageObserver interface; 361
  ImageProducer interface; 361
  loading; 319
  resource bundle handling; 340
immutable
  See also constants (Java and user-defined); literals;
    string(s)
  term definition; 17
implementation
  See also runtime
  implements keyword, as reserved word; 106
  interfaces; **97**

of methods, vs declaration; 20
multiple inheritance of, interface inheritance
   contrasted with; 94
partial, abstract classes use for; 76
implicit conversion
   term definition; **121**
importing
   See also object-oriented concepts and components;
      packages; runtime
   import keyword, as reserved word; 106
   import statement; 210
      package access with; 25
   packages; 210
   types, identifier name search order; 113
ImprovedFibonacci example; 7
in field (System class); 321
incompatibility
   IncompatibleClassChangeError class; 375
increment (++) operator; **131**
   See also numbers and logical operations; operator
   char variable use; 132
   comparison with self assignment +1; 131
   IncOrder example, increment and decrement
      operators; 131
index
   See also array(s)
   array; 114
   indexOf method
      String class; 162
      Vector class; 280
   IndexOutOfBoundsException class; 114, 125,
      162, 233, 235, 447
   Vector use; 279
infinity
   See also numbers and logical operations
   arithmetic, floating-point; 129
   constants, Float and Double class support of; 107
   representation in Float and Double class; 302
inheritance
   See also object-oriented concepts and components
   composition compared with; 91
   controlling, modifiers that manage; **31**
   diamond
      interface use; 95
      term definition; 94
   multiple interface, term definition; 92
   multiple vs single, design issues; 94
   term definition; 18
initialization
   See also assignment; constructors
   blocks; **46**
   ExceptionInInitializerError class; 375
   expressions, = operator use in; 4
   initializers
      array; **117**
      checked exceptions not legal for; 154
      field, checked exceptions not permitted; 117
      static, term definition; 46
      terminating, return use for; 149

throwing checked exceptions not legal for; 154
object values; 10
of objects, with constructors; 33
static fields; 45
of variables; 117
inner classes
   See also classes (concepts and use)
   local; **53**
   term definition; 52
input
   See also file(s); I/O; output; reading; streams
   DataInputStream class; 236
   FileInputStream class; 245
   FileReader class; 238
   InputStream, extended byFileInputStream;
      229
   InputStream class; 227, **227**, 228, 234, 237, 238,
      247, 326
      in type tree for byte streams (*figure*); 227
      loading secondary resources with; 319
   InputStreamReader class; 232, 236, **237**
      in type tree for character streams (*figure*); 232
   InputStreamWriter class; 238
   PipedInputStream class; 236
   PipedReader class; 246
   Reader class; **233**
   SequenceInputStream class; 237, **247**
   streams, term definition; 225
   System.in class, character stream relationship;
      231
inserting
   See also data, structures
   elements in a queue; 189
   insert method (StringBuffer class); 174
   insertElementAt method (Vector class); 278
   into strings; 173, 174
   vector elements; 278
instantiation
   See also object(s); object-oriented concepts and
      components
   instance
      term definition; 1, 29
      variables, constructors invoked after
         initialization of; 33
      variables, term definition; 10
   instanceof keyword
      conditional reference casting use; 125
      explicit casting and; **122**
      reserved word; 106
   InstantiationError class; 376
   InstantiationException class; 312
   of objects, separate from declaration of them; 30
   term definition; 10
instructions
   tracing; 331
integer(s)
   See also arithmetic; numbers and logical
      operations; type(s)
   arithmetic; **128**

integer(s) *(continued)*
  BigInteger class; 370
  Byte class; 301
  casting considerations; 123
  int field type, default value; 117
  int keyword, as Java reserved word; 106
  int type
    as primitive data type, value of; 107
    converting to and from strings; 169
    reading and writing; 255
  intBitsToFloat (Float class); 302
  Integer class; 107, 301
    getInteger; 325
  Integer type, Number class as wrapper for; 300
  IntegerStack example, sharing, problems with; 79
  intValue method (Number class); 300
  intValue (Number class); 300
  literals, characteristics; **108**
  Long class; 301
  longValue (Number class); 300
  parseTypes; 301
  Short class; 301
  shortValue (Number class); 300
  wrapper classes; **301**
interactive programs
  multithreading advantages for; 180
interfaces (concepts and use)
  See also classes (concepts and use); methods
    (concepts and use); object-oriented concepts
    and components
  abstract classes vs; 76, **101**
  (chapter); **91**
  constants, multiple inheritance of; 97
  extending; 22, **95**
  fields, static and final implicit in; 93
  forwarding methods from; 99
  GUI (graphical user interface), threads advantages
    for; *xvi*, 180
  I/O; 225
  identifier name search order; 113
  implementation of; **97**
  implementation use; **99**
  interfaces, term definition; 20
  introduction; **20**
  marker; **100**
  methods, public and abstract implicit in; 92
  multiple inheritance, term definition; 92
  nested
    classes and interfaces in; 93
    hiding in subclasses; 70
  nesting; **50**, 53
  remote interfaces, term definition; 362
  as term for contract, *See* contracts; signature
interfaces (Java and user-defined)
  ActionListener; 360
  BeanInfo; 367
  Changeable; 93
  Cloneable, cloning objects with; 78

  DataInput; 227, 236, 237, 255, 256, 257, 258
  DataOutput; 227, 236, 237, 255, 256, 257, 258
  Enumeration; 293
    implementing; **276**
    SequenceInputStream class use; 247
  Enumeration interface; 54
  EventListener; 360
  Externalizable; 227, **267**
  FilenameFilter; 227, 232
  FilenameFIlter; 270
  interface keyword, as reserved word; 106
  Lookup example; 21
  ObjectInput; 227
  ObjectInputValidation; 227, 264
  ObjectOutput; 227
  Observer; 273, 288
  Runnable; 181, **201**
  Serializable; 227, 236, **260**
    deserialization example; 262
    extended by Externalizable interface; **267**
interleaved execution
  synchronizing threads for; 183
InternalError class; 376
  See also errors (Java and user-defined)
internationalization
  See also country; language; localization; traditions
  (chapter); **335**
  conversion stream use; 238
  java.text package; 353
  Locale class characteristics; 336
  term definition; 335
  text, java.text package; **354**
  TimeZone class; **348**
  Unicode digits *(table)*; 378
  Unicode letters and digits *(table)*; 379
Internet
  See also beans; HTML; networks; RMI; URL
  domain names, package naming convention use;
    26, 210
  InetAddress class; 367
  java.applet package; 353
  java.net package; 367
interrupting
  See also debugging; errors (concepts and use);
    events; exceptions (concepts and use); threads
  InterruptedException class; 182
  InterruptedIOException class; 271
  threads; **195**, **199**
introspection; *See* reflection
inverting
  See also numbers and logical operations
  inversion (!) operator; 132
  number sign; 128
  strings; 175
invocation
  See also constructors; object-oriented concepts and
    components; runtime
  application, main use; 55
  constructor

explicit, this reference use; 34
order dependencies; **65**
InvocationTargetException class; 310, 312
invoke method (Method class); 310
of methods; 36
introduction; **12**
on a buffered output stream; 241
requirements for; 126
superclass, introduction; **19**
is*Xxx* methods
isAbsolute (File class); 268
isArray (Class class); 306, 314
isDaemon (ThreadGroup class); 205
isDefined (Character class); 299
isDigit (Character class); 299
isDirectory (File class); 268
isEmpty
Dictionary class; 284
Vector class; 280
isFile (File class); 268
isInfinite
Double class; 302
Float class; 302
isInterface method (Class class); 306
isInterrupted (Thread class); 196
isJavaIdentifierPart (Character class); 299
isJavaIdentifierStart (Character class);
299
isLeapYear (GregorianCalendar class); 350
isLenient (Calendar class); 347
isLetter (Character class); 299
isLetterOrDigit (Character class); 299
isLowerCase (Character class); 299
isNaN
Double class; 133, 302
Float class; 133, 302
isPrimitive method (Class class); 306
isSet (Calendar class); 346
isSpaceChar (Character class); 299
isTitleCase (Character class); 299
isUnicodeIdentifierPart (Character class);
299
isUnicodeIdentifierStart (Character class);
299
isUpperCase (Character class); 299
isWhitespace (Character class); 234, 299
IsA relationships
HasA relationships contrasted with; 82
ISO
country and language codes, retrieving; 338
Latin-1
as Unicode character set subset; 6
Unicode digits *(table)*; 378
Italian language; 341
iteration
See also control, flow; loops
range, defining; 145
through values in a collection; 276

J

Jackson, Andrew
quotation; **385**
Japanese
date and time; 351
glyphs for the word "kitty"; 106
Java
advantages; *xv*
Beans, *See* beans
concepts and facilities introduction *(chapter)*; **1**
java.applet package; 353
java.awt package; 353
java.beans package; 353
java.io package; 225, 353
java.lang class; 321
java.lang package; 353
java.math package; 354
java.net package; 353
java.rmi package; 353
java.security package; 354
java.sql package; 354
java.text package; 353
java.util package; 353
javadoc tool
documentation comment use by; 5
generating documentation from doc comments
with; 216
platform, introduction; **26**
JDBC
java.sql; **372**
JNI (Java Native Interface)
as C language native method API; 57
Julian calendar
determining when Gregorian change happened;
350

K

keyboard
EventListener interface; 360
keys
See also data, structures; hashtables
getKeys (ResourceBundle class); 343
hashtable, comparing; 285
keys method (Dictionary class); 284
mapping to resource bundles; 340
property list, enumerating; 288
ResourceBundle class use; 338
keywords
abstract; 106
boolean; 106
break; 106, 143, 144, **147**, 149, 158
byte; 106
case; 106, 142, 144
catch; 106
char; 106
class; 30, 107
const; 106

keywords *(continued)*
  `continue`; 106
  `default`; 106
  `do`; 106
  `double`; 106, 107
  `else`; 106, 140
  `extends`; 22, 59, 95, 106
  `false`; 107
  `final`; 5, 40, 42, 67, 71, 86, 92, 106, 110, 111
  `finally`; 106, 150, 155, 157, 158
  `float`; 107
  `for`; 106
  `goto`; 106
  identifiers not permitted to be; 106
  `if`; 106
  `implements`; 106
  `import`; 106
  `instanceof`; 106, 122
  `int`; 106
  `interface`; 106
  keywords; 106
  `long`; 106
  `native`; 106
  `new`; 10, 32, 106, 161
  `null`; 107
  `package`; 106, 209
  `private`; 31, 41, 89, 106, 110
  `protected`; 31, 63, 88, 106, 111
  `public`; 9, 31, 84, 88, 92, 106, 111, 211
  `return`; 106
  `short`; 106
  `static`; 5, 46, 92, 106, 110, 111
  `super`; 68, 70, 81, 106
  `switch`; 106
  `synchronized`; 106, 111, 183, 191
  (table); 106, 377
  `this`; 106
  `throw`; 106
  `throws`; 106
  `transient`; 106
  `true`; 106
  `try`; 106, 155
  `void`; 2, 12, 106
  `volatile`; 106, 203
  `while`; 106
killing
  See also termination
  processes; 327
Kirbati; 340

L

L/l suffix
  See also numbers and logical operations
  as long integer constant indicator; 108
labels
  as AWT component; 360
  statement; **146**

language concepts, *See*
  calling paradigms
  casting
  control, flow
  data, structures
  events
  expressions
  overloading
  packages
  parameters
  streams
  synchronization
  threads
  type(s)
languages
  general purpose, Java features as; *xv*
  ISO codes, retrieving; 338
  natural
    character case issues; 298
    managing with `Locale` class; 336
last
  `lastElement` method (`Vector` class); 280
  `lastIndexOf` method
    `String` class; 162
    `Vector` class; 280
  `lastModified` method (`File` class); 268
Latin-1 character set
  Unicode relationship to; 103
layout manager
  See also AWT (Abstract Window Toolkit)
  `FlowLayoutManager` class; 359
  `GridBagLayoutManager` class; 359
  `LayoutManager` class; 359
  `LayoutManager2` class; 359
  term definition; 359
leak
  See also memory
  memory, avoiding; 48
  open file, avoiding; 49
leap
  seconds *(footnote)*; 349
  year, `isLeapYear` (`GregorianCalendar` class);
    350
left-associative
  See also expressions; operators
  term definition; 119
Lehman, John
  quotation; **333**
length
  See also array(s); strings
  array; 114
  file, obtaining; 259, 269
  `length`
    `File` class; 269
    `RandomAccessFile` class; 259
    `StringBuffer` class; 17
  string
    obtaining with `length`; 161
    setting; 173

lenient
 isLenient (DateFormat class); 352
 setLenient (DateFormat class); 352
 term definition; 347
less than
 See also numbers and logical operations;
  operator(s)
 less than or equal (<=) operator; 132
 less than (<) operator; 132
LETTER_NUMBER constant (Character class)
 as getType return value; 300
lexical scanners
 See also parsing; streams; tokens
 pushback use by; 249
liberty
 weapons in the defense of; 209
libraries
 as defensive weapons; 209
line feed; *See* newline
line numbers
 See also streams
 accessing the current; 255
 lineno (StreamTokenizer class); 255
 LineNumberReader class; 232, 237, **248**
  getLineNumber; 248
  in type tree for character streams *(figure)*; 232
  setLineNumber; 248
 printing; 237
  FindChar example; 238
 tracking; 248˙
  in an input stream; 237
lines
 Canvas class; 360
 LINE_SEPARATOR constant (Character class), as
  getType return value; 300
 reading; 256
Lingala language; 339
linking
 to javadoc documentation; **216**
 LinkageError class; 376
 UnsatisfiedLinkError class; 376
list(ing)
 Enumeration class representation of; 99
 files; 269
 list
  Properties class; 288
  Thread class; 208
 ListResourceBundle class; **340**
 object types, primitive type inclusion with wrapper
  classes; 60
 ordered, creating; 247
 properties in a property list; 288
 property, term definition; 286
listener
 See also events
 ActionListener interface; 360
 EventListener interface; 360
 term definition; 360

literal(s); 107
 See also characters; constants (Java and user-
  defined); numbers and logical operations; and
  type(s)
 character; **109**
 class; **110**
 false, as boolean literal; 108
 floating point; **108**
  characteristics; **108**
 integer, characteristics; 108
 null
  as object reference literal; 108
  as reference to no object; 19
  keyword restrictions apply to; 107
 string; **109**
  comparing; 166
  String object type use; 16
 true, as boolean literal; 108
 type constants represented as; 108
 as unnamed constants; 107
loading
 See also classes (concepts and use); security
 classes; **315**
  Class advantages for; 304
 deserialization requirements; 263
 load, Properties class; 287
 load factor
  fixed nature of; 286
  term definition; 285
 loadClass (ClassLoader class); 316
 property lists; 287
 resources associated with a class; **319**
local variables
 declaration statements; 140
 duplicate identifier restrictions in nested
  constructs; 113
 final keyword use; **111**
 identifier name search order; 113
 initialization of; 117
 search order; 113
localization
 See also Unicode character set
 calendar retrieval; 345
 (chapter); **335**
 classes that implement; 274
 classes that support; 274
 conversion stream use; 238
 displaying dates; 345
 formatting; **355**
 formatting dates and times; **350**
 java.text package; 353
 java.util package; 353
 locale; **336**
  case conversion Strings that specify; 168
  term definition; 335
 Locale class; 274, 336
 locales
  accessing components; 337
  configuring; 337

localization *(continued)*
   locales *(continued)*
      displaying components; 337
      getAvailableLocales (DateFormat class);
        351
     LocalNumber example; 356
     mapping keys to localized objects; 340
     parsing; **355**
     parsing dates and times; **350**
     term definition; 335
     text, java.text package; **354**
     text boundaries; **358**
     TimeZone class; **348**
lock(ing)
   See also file(s); threads
   class-wide, synchronized statement; 187
   classwide, synchronizing class methods with; 185
   lock field
      character stream synchronization use; 231
      Reader class; 233
      Writer class; 235
   objects during multithreading; 183
   term definition; 180
log method (Math class); 332
   See also numbers and logical operations
logical operations
   See also bit operations; numbers and logical
      operations
   BitSet class; 274
   logical XOR, exclusive or (XOR) (∧) use for; 135
   operator precedence; 119
   operators; **132**
   XOR operator; 133
long
   See also numbers and logical operations
   Long class; 106, 301, 325
   long keyword; 106
   long type; 106, 117, 169, 255
   Long type; 300
   longBitsTo Double (Double class); 303
   longValue (Number class); 300
Lookup interface example; 21
loops
   See also control, flow
   do-while statement; 144
   Fibonacci example; 3
   for statement; 145
   variables, declaring in a for statement; 15
   while statement; 144
   while statement use for; 4
lowercase
   See also character(s); Unicode character set
   converting strings to; 168
   LOWERCASE_LETTER constant (Character class),
      as getType return value; 300
   lowerCaseMode method (StreamTokenizer
      class); 254
   Unicode, Character class handling; 298
LSFailedException class; 327

M

main method; **55**
   application use; 2, 56
management
   of resources, finalizes use for; 48
   security manager, term definition; 26
manipulation
   classes, Class advantages for; 304
mapping
   algorithms
      Dictionary class; 273
      Hashtable class; 273
      Properties class; 273
   keys to resource bundles; 340
marker
   interfaces; **100**
math
   See also arithmetic; numbers and logical
      operations; type(s)
   BigDecimal class; 370
   BigInteger class; 370
   java.math package; **370**
   Math class; 13, 14, 291, 321, **332**, 332, 333
   MATH_SYMBOL constant (Character class), as
      getType return value; 300
   Random class; **291**
matrix; *See* arrays, two-dimensional
maximum
   See also arithmetic; numbers and logical
      operations
   max (Math class); 333
   MAX_PRIORITY constant (Thread class); 191, 204
   MAX_RADIX constant (Character class); 297
   MAX_VALUE constant
      Character class; 297
      Number class; 301
   maxThread example, thread group use; 204
measuring
   sorting costs; 86
member(s)
   See also object-oriented concepts and components
   accessing; **125**
   class
      looking up, with reflection methods; 306
      type of, as determinant during access; 125
   Member interface; 308, **309**, **310**
      implemented by Field, Constructor, and
        Method classes; 308
   modifiers for; 110
   public, disadvantages of; 84
   static; **44**
   term definition; 1
memory
   See also garbage collection; runtime; threads
   allocation
   for new objects; 9
   runtime system handling of; 32
   deallocation, *See* garbage collection

leak, avoiding; 48
management; **322**
OutOfMemoryError class; 376
messages
digests, java.security package; 372
MessageFormat class; 356
methods (concepts and use); 36
See also classes (concepts and use); interfaces
(concepts and use); object-oriented concepts
and components
accessor; **41**
class
accessing with null reference; 126
introduction; **14**
overriding not permitted with; 68
synchronizing; 185
declaration compared with implementation; 20
errors, NoSuchMethodError class; 376
examining, Method class use for; **310**
extended arrays restricted from adding; 115
extending, by subclassing; 18
final; **71**
access control use of; 86
forwarding, as interface implementation technique;
99
interface, public and abstract implicit in; 92
introduction; **12**
invocation
from the superclass, introduction; **19**
introduction to; **12**
requirements for; 126
Method class; 308, **310**
MethodBenchmark example; 76
multiple, *See* overloading
multiple class access; 365
native, cautions on use; **57**
overloading; 4, **44**, **67**
access resolution; 126
restrictions on; 127
overriding; **67**
hiding fields compared with; 68
parameters, documenting; **217**
remote method invocation; **362**
replacing, *See* overriding
return values, documenting; **217**
semantics as differentiator; 29
string; 161
superclass, accessing with super; 70
synchronized; **183**
term definition; 1, 9, 12
terminating, return use for; 149
tracing; 331
utility, Java Object class, descriptions; 73
wrapper class common methods; 296
with throws clause, invoker requirements; 154
methods (Java and user-defined)
abs (Math class); 333
accept (FilenameFIlter interface); 270
acceptInput example; 368

acos (Math class); 332
activeCount
Thread class; 207
ThreadGroup class; 206
activeGroupCount (ThreadGroup class); 206
add (Calendar class); 346
addDate example; 174
addElement (Vector class); 278
addObserver (Observable class); 288
after (Date class); 344, 348
and (BitSet class); 275
append (StringBuffer class); 174
arraycopy (System class); 331
arrayToStr; 244
asin (Math class); 332
atan (Math class); 332
available (InputStream class); 228
before (Date class); 344, 348
bytesForClass example; 318
byteValue (Number class); 300
canRead (File class); 268
canWrite (File class); 268
capacity (Vector class); 281
ceil (Math class); 332
checkAccess (ThreadGroup class); 204, 205
clear
BitSet class; 274
Hashtable class; 285
Pixel class; 18
clear (Calendar class); 346
clear example; 12
this reference use; 13
clone
Object class; 73, 77
Vector class; 180
close
OutputStream class; 230
Reader class; 233
Writer class; 235
commentChar (StreamTokenizer class); 253
compare (Collator class); 354
compareTo (String class); 163
concat (String class); 168
contains (Vector class); 280
containsKey (Hashtable class); 285
containsObject (Hashtable class); 285
copyInto (Vector class); 280
copyValueOf (String class); 171
cos (Math class); 332
countBetween example; 162
countObservers (Observable class); 289
countStackFrames (Thread class); 207
countTokens (StringTokenizer class); 294
currentTimeMillis (System class); 331, 343
dataSet example, exception handling; 23
defineClass (ClassLoader class); 318
deleteObserver (Observable class); 288
deleteObservers (Observable class); 289

methods (Java and user-defined) *(continued)*
    destroy
        Process class; 327
        ThreadGroup class; 205
    digit (Character class); 298, 300
    distance example; 13
    dotw example; 347
    doubleToLongBits (Double class); 303
    doubleValue (Number class); 300
    dumpStack (Thread class); 207
    dwim; 105
    elementAt (Vector class); 279
    elements
        Dictionary class; 284
        Hashtable class; 285
        Vector class; 280
    endsWith (String class); 165
    ensureCapacity (Vector class); 281
    enumerate (ThreadGroup class); 206, 207
    eolIsSignificant (StreamTokenizer class);
        254
    equals
        BitSet class; 275
        File class; 269
        Object class; 73
        regionMatches; 163
        String class; 17, 163
        wrapper classes use of; 297
    equalsIgnoreCase (String class); 163
    exec
        Process class; 328
        System class; 325
    exists (File class); 268
    exitValue (Process class); 327
    exp (Math class); 332
    finalize; 48, 49
        invoking; 322, 323
        Object class; 73
    firstElement (Vector class); 280
    floatToIntBits (Float class); 302
    floatValue (Number class); 300
    floor (Math class); 332
    flush
        OutputStream; 230
        Writer class; 235
    forDigit (Character class); 298, 300
    format (DateFormat class); 351
    forName (Class class); 304
    freeMemory (Runtime class); 322
    fullGC example; 322
    gc
        Runtime class; 322
        System class; 322
    get
        BitSet class; 274
        Dictionary class; 284
        Hashtable class; 285
    get (Calendar class); 346
    getAbsolutePath (File class); 268

getAvailableIDs (TimeZone class); 348
getAvailableLocales (DateFormat class); 351
getBoolean (Boolean class); 325
getBundle (ResourceBundle class); 339
getBytes (String class); 171
getCalendar (DateFormat class); 351
getCanonicalPath (File class); 268
getCharacterInstance (BreakIterator class);
    358
getChars
    String class; 171
    StringBuffer class; 175
getClass (Object class); 73, 304
getClassLoader (ClassLoader class); 318
getCollationKey (Collator class); 355
getCountry (Locale class); 337
getCurrentThread (Thread class); 207
getDaemon (Thread class); 201
getDateInstance (DateFormat class); 351
getDateTimeInstance (DateFormat class); 351
getDefault (TimeZone class); 348
getDisplayCountry (Locale class); 337
getDisplayLanguage (Locale class); 337
getDisplayVariant (Locale class); 337
getErrorStream (Process class); 326
getFD (FileDescriptor class); 245
getFilePointer (RandomAccessFile class);
    258
getFirstDayOfWeek (Calendar class); 347
getGreatestMinimum (Calendar class); 346
getGregorianChange (GregorianCalendar
    class); 350
getID (TimeZone class); 348
getInputStream (Process class); 326
getInstance, Calendar class; 337
getInstance (Collator class); 354
getInteger (Integer class); 325
getISO3Country (Locale class); 338
getISO3Language (Locale class); 338
getKeys (ResourceBundle class); 338, 343
getLanguage (Locale class); 337
getLeastMaximum (Calendar class); 346
getLineInstance (BreakIterator class); 358
getLineNumber (LineNumberReader class); 248
getLong (Long class); 325
getMaxPriority (ThreadGroup class); 205
getMinimalDaysInFirstWeek (Calendar class);
    347
getMinimum (Calendar class); 346
getName
    File class; 268
    Thread class; 182
    ThreadGroup class; 205
getNumberFormat (DateFormat class); 351
getNumberInstance (NumberFormat class); 356
getNumericValue (Character class); 298
getObject (ResourceBundle class); 338
getOffset (TimeZone class); 348
getOutputStream (Process class); 326

getParent
File class; 268
ThreadGroup class; 205
getPath (File class); 268
getPercentInstance (NumberFormat class);
356
getPriority, Thread class; 192
getProperty
Properties class; 287
System class; 324
getRawOffset (TimeZone class); 348
getRuntime (Runtime class); 329
getSecurityManager (System class); 332
getSentenceInstance (BreakIterator class);
358
getString (ResourceBundle class); 338
getStringArray (ResourceBundle class); 338
getThreadGroup (ThreadGroup class); 207
getTime (Date class); 344, 345, 347
getTimeInstance (DateFormat class); 351
getTimeZone (DateFormat class); 351
getType (Number class); 300
getVarient (Locale class); 337
getWordInstance (BreakIterator class); 358
handleObject (ResourceBundle class); 343
hashCode; 166
BitSet class; 275
Hashtable class; 285
Object class; 73
wrapper classes use of; 297
hasMoreElements (Enumeration interface); 276,
293
hasMoreElements example; 54
hasMoreTokens (StringTokenizer class); 293
IEEERemainder (Math class); 333
inDaylightTime (TimeZone class); 348
indexOf
String class; 162
Vector class; 280
insert (StringBuffer class); 174
insertElementAt (Vector class); 278
instanceof; 125
intBitsToFloat (Float class); 303
interrupt (Thread class); 196
interrupted (Thread class); 196
intValue (Number class); 300
isAbsolute (File class); 268
isDaemon (ThreadGroup class); 205
isDefined (Character class); 299
isDigit (Character class); 299
isDirectory (File class); 268
isEmpty
Dictionary class; 284
Hashtable class; 285
Vector class; 281
isFile (File class); 268
isInfinite
Double class; 302
Float class; 302

isInterrupted (Thread class); 196
isJavaIdentifierPart (Character class); 299
isJavaIdentifierStart (Character class);
299
isLeapYear (GregorianCalendar class); 350
isLenient (Calendar class); 347
isLenient (DateFormat class); 352
isLetter (Character class); 299
isLetterOrDigit (Character class); 299
isLowerCase (Character class); 299
isNaN; 133
Double class; 133, 302
Float class; 133, 302
isSet (Calendar class); 346
isSpaceChar (Character class); 299
isTitleCase (Character class); 299
isUnicodeIdentifierPart (Character class);
299
isUnicodeIdentifierStart (Character class);
299
isUpperCase (Character class); 299
isWhitespace (Character class); 234, 299
keys
Dictionary class; 284
Hashtable class; 285
lastElement (Vector class); 280
lastIndexOf
String class; 162
Vector class; 280
lastModified (File class); 268
length
File class; 269
RandomAccessFile class; 259, 267
StringBuffer class; 17
lineno (StreamTokenizer class); 255
list
Properties class; 288
Thread class; 208
load, Properties class; 287
loadClass (ClassLoader class); 316
log (Math class); 332
longBitsTo Double (Double class); 303
longValue (Number class); 300
lowerCaseMode (StreamTokenizer class); 254
main; 50, 55
max (Math class); 333
maxThread example; 204
min (Math class); 333
mkdir (File class); 269
mkdirs (File class); 269
move example, this reference use; 13
nextDouble (Random class); 292
nextElement (Enumeration interface); 276, 293
nextFloat (Random class); 292
nextGaussian (Random class); 292
nextInt (Random class); 292
nextLong (Random class); 292
nextToken (StringTokenizer class); 293
notify (Object class); 188, 190

methods (Java and user-defined) *(continued)*
    notifyAll (Object class); 188, 190
    notifyObservers (Observable class); 289
    oneWeek example; 345
    openConnection (URL class); 369
    or (BitSet class); 275
    ordinaryChar (StreamTokenizer class); 253
    parentOf (ThreadGroup class); 205
    parse (DateFormat class); 352
    parseInt (Integer class); 301
    parseLong (Long class); 301
    parseNumbers (StreamTokenizer class); 253
    parseObject (DateFormat class); 352
    peek (Stack class); 282
    personalConfig example; 324
    pow (Math class); 332
    print; 15
    print (Print class); 240
    printField example; 309
    println
        Print class; 240
        PrintStream class; 9
    printType example; 304
    propertyNames (Properties class); 287
    protected, characteristics and use; 63
    push (Stack class); 282
    pushBack (StreamTokenizer class); 255
    put
        Dictionary class; 284
        Hashtable class; 285
    putIn example; 166
    quoteChar (StreamTokenizer class); 253
    quotedString example; 167
    quotedString (String class); 167
    random (Math class), compared with Random class
        methods; 291
    read
        InputStream class; 228
        Reader class; 233
    readArabic; 238
    readArabic example; 238
    readAttrs; 252
    readAttrs example; 252
    readBoolean (DataInput interface); 255
    readByte (DataInput interface); 255
    readChar (DataInput interface); 255
    readDouble (DataInput interface); 255
    readExternal, Externalizable interface; 267
    readFloat (DataInput interface); 255
    readFully (DataInput interface); 256
    reading, readData example; 257
    readInt (DataInput interface); 255
    readLine (DataInput interface); 256
    readLong (DataInput interface); 255
    readObject (ObjectInputStream class); 263
    readShort (DataInput interface); 255
    readUnsignedByte (DataInput interface); 256
    readUnsignedShort (DataInput interface); 256
    readURL example; 369

readUTF (DataInput interface); 255
ready (Reader class); 233
regionMatches (String class); 164
registerValidation (ObjectInputStream
    class); 263
rehash (Hashtable class); 286
remove
    Dictionary class; 284
    Hashtable class; 285
removeAllElements (Vector class); 279
removeElement (Vector class); 279
removeElementAt (Vector class); 279
replace (String class); 168
reset (CharArrayWriter class); 243
resetSyntax (StreamTokenizer class); 254
resume
    Thread class; 200
    ThreadGroup class; 206
reverse (StringBuffer class); 175
rint (Math class); 332
roll (Calendar class); 346
round (Math class); 333
run (Thread class); 181
runFinalization
    Runtime class; 322
    System class; 322
safeExit example; 329
save (Properties class); 287
search (Stack class); 282
searchFor example; 157
seek (RandomAccessFile class); 259, 267
set (BitSet class); 274
set (Calendar class); 346, 347
setCalendar (DateFormat class); 351
setCharAt (StringBuffer class); 173
setDaemon (ThreadGroup class); 201, 205
setDefault (TimeZone class); 348
setElementAt (Vector class); 278
setField example; 309
setFirstDayOfWeek (Calendar class); 347
setGregorianChange (GregorianCalendar
    class); 350
setID (TimeZone class); 348
setLength (StringBuffer class); 173
setLenient (DateFormat class); 352
setLineNumber (LineNumberReader class); 248
setLocale (Locale class); 337
setMaxPriority (ThreadGroup class); 204, 205
setMinimalDaysInFirstWeek (Calendar class);
    347
setNumberFormat (DateFormat class); 351
setPriority, Thread class; 191
setProperties (System class); 324
setRawOffset (TimeZone class); 348
setSecurityManager (System class); 332
setSeed (Random class); 292
setSize (Vector class); 281
setTime (Date class); 344, 347
setTimeZone (DateFormat class); 351

shortValue (Number class); 300
showBreaks example; 358
sin (Math class); 332
size
    BitSet class; 275
    ByteArrayOutputStream class; 242
    CharArrayWriter class; 243
    Dictionary class; 284
    Hashtable class; 285
    Vector class; 280
skip
    InputStream class; 228
    Reader class; 233
skipBytes
    DataInput interface; 256
    RandomAccessFile class; 259
slashSlashComments (StreamTokenizer class); 254
slashStarComments (StreamTokenizer class); 254
sleep (Thread class); 192
sqrt (Math class); 13, 332
sqrtInt example; 174
squeezeOut example; 170
start (Thread class); 181
startsWith (String class); 165
static; 45
stop
    Thread class; 181
    ThreadGroup class; 329
sumStream; 251
sumStream example; 251
suspend
    Thread class; 181, 200
    ThreadGroup class; 206
sync (FileDescriptor class); 245
tan (Math class); 332
ThreadGroup class; 205
toByteArray (ByteArray stream classes); 242
toCharArray
    CharArrayWriter class; 243
    String class; 170
toLowerCase
    Character class; 299
    String class; 168
toString
    ByteArray stream classes; 242
    CharArrayWriter class; 243
    Hashtable class; 286
    Integer class; 301
    Long class; 302
    Number class; 301
    String class; 56, 169
    StringBuffer class; 175
    StringTokenizer class; 255
    Thread class; 207
    ThreadGroup class; 208
    wrapper classes use of; 296
toString, Locale class; 337

toString example; 37
totalMemory (Runtime class); 322
toTitleCase (Character class); 299
toUpperCase
    Character class; 299
    String class; 168
traceInstructions (Runtime class); 331
traceMethodCalls (Runtime class); 331
trim (String class); 168
trimToSize (Vector class); 280
typeValue, wrapper classes use of; 297
uncaughtException (ThreadGroup class); 207
unread (Pushback class); 250
update (Observer interface); 288
useDaylightTime (TimeZone class); 348
userHitCancel example; 199
userProg example; 326
valueOf
    Integer class; 301
    Long class; 302
    Number class; 301
    String class; 169
wait (Thread class); 188, 190
waitFor (Process class); 327
whitespaceChars (StreamTokenizer class); 253
wordChars (StreamTokenizer class); 253
write
    OutputStream class; 229
    Writer class; 235
writeBoolean (DataOutput interface); 255
writeByte (DataOutput interface); 255
writeBytes (DataOutput interface); 256
writeChar (DataOutput interface); 255
writeChars (DataOutput interface); 256
writeDouble (DataOutput interface); 255
writeExternal, Externalizable interface; 267
writeFloat (DataOutput interface); 255
writeInt (DataOutput interface); 255
writeLong (DataOutput interface); 255
writeObject (ObjectOutputStream class); 259, 260, 261, 263, 264
writeObject (ObjectOutputStream class)(ObjectOutputStream class); 264
writeShort (DataOutput interface); 255
writeTo (CharArrayWriter class); 243
writeUTF (DataOutput interface); 255
writing, writeData example; 257
xor (BitSet class); 275
yield (Thread class); 192
millennium crisis
solution for; 331, 343
minimum
min (Math class); 333
MIN_PRIORITY constant (Thread class); 191
MIN_RADIX constant (Character class); 297
MIN_VALUE constant
    Character class; 297
    Number class; 301

minus (–) sign
    decrement (--) operator; **131**
    unary operator; 128
mkdir method (File class); 268
mkdirs method (File class); 268
models
    event
        AWT; 360
        Java Beans same as AWT; 367
    security; 361
    thread
        multiple; 180
        single; 179
modifying
    See also setting
    buffers, of StringBuffer object; **173**
    modification date, retrieving; 268
    modifier declaration
        ordering of; 111
        term definition; 110
    MODIFIER_LETTER constant (Character class), as
        getType return value; 300
    MODIFIER_SYMBOL constant (Character class), as
        getType return value; 300
    strings; **167**
        with StringBuffer class; 172
    time; 344
    vectors; 278, 281
modular arithmetic
    See also arithmetic; numbers and logical
        operations; remainder (%) operator; type(s)
    integer arithmetic as; 128
monitoring
    See also events
    events; 288
Moose example
    this use; 43
More example
    superclass method invocation; 70
mouse
    EventListener interface; 360
move example
    this reference use; 13
multi-tasking
    threads advantages for; *xvi*, 180
multicast
    MulticastSocket class; 367
multiple
    constructors, ColorAttr example; 62
    inheritance, term definition; 94
    interface inheritance, term definition; 92
multiplication
    See also arithmetic; numbers and logical
        operations; operators
    asterisk (*) arithmetic operator; 128
    multiplicative operators, precedence of; 119
multithreading
    See also threads
    multi-tasking advantages; *xvi*, 180

    term definition; 180
music; *See* Zappa, Frank
mutable string(s), *See* StringBuffer class
mutually exclusive
    See also threads
    term definition; 183
MyClass example
    cloning classes; 79

N

name(s)
    See also identifiers; packages; variables
    in attribute pairs, read-only importance; 61
    conflicts
        handling in multiple interface inheritance; **96**
        hierarchical packages as means of preventing;
          25
        packages as mechanism for avoiding; 210
    conventions, packages; 210
    meaning of; **112**
    Name example; 261
        this references; 43
    named constants, creation of; 5
    namespace
        search order relationship; 113
        term definition; 112
    naming
        resource bundle property files; 343
        threads; 182
    Naming class; 366
    naming contexts, term definition; 24
    package; **136**
    packages; **210**
    RMI registry; 366
    threads, obtaining; 182
    type, term definition; 30
NaN (Not-a-Number)
    See also arithmetic; numbers and logical
        operations
    as divide infinity by zero representation; 129
    equality anomalies; 133
    as exception, not supported; 130
    NaN constant
        Double class; 107, 302
        Float class; 107, 302
    ordering anomalies; 133
    representation in Float and Double class; 302
    testing for; 133
narrowing
    term definition; 124
native methods
    See also methods (concepts and use)
    native keyword, as reserved word; 106
    use
        cautions on; **57**
        with RMI; 366
navigating
    type system; 304

negative
See also numbers and logical operations; operators
negation (-) operator; 128
NEGATIVE_INFINITY constant
`Double` class; 302
`Float` and `Double` class support of; 107
`Float` class; 302
infinite arithmetic with; 129
NegativeArraySizeException class; 375
Nepali language; 340
nesting
See also classes (concepts and use); hiding;
    hierarchy; interfaces (concepts and use);
    object-oriented concepts and components
arrays; 116
classes; **67**
    and interfaces; **50**
    hiding in subclasses; 70
    interface declarations; 93
    top-level nested classes term definition
        (*footnote*); 52
comments, not permitted; 104
`if` statements, scoping; 141
interfaces; **50**, 53
    hiding in subclasses; 70
    interface declarations; 93
local variable restrictions; 113
loops, `continue` use to break out of; 148
method invocations, lock handling with; 183
packages; 212
term definition; 50
networks, See
applets
beans
Internet
`java.net` package
RMI (Remote Method Invocation)
sockets
URL (Universal Resource Locator)
new
new keyword
    as reserved word; 106
    creating objects with; 10, 32
    creating strings with; 161
newInstance method
    `Array` class; 314
    `Class` class; 312, 313
newline (\n) escape sequence
    as newline representation in a string; 109
    as white space; 105
    autoflushing control with; 241
    `newLine` (`BufferedOutputStream` class); 241
    `readLine` (`BufferedReader` class)
      acceptance; 241
    Unicode value; 109
next*Xxx* methods
`nextDouble` (Random class); 292
`nextElement` method (`Enumeration` interface);
    276, 293

`nextFloat` (Random class); 292
`nextGaussian` (Random class); 292
`nextInt` (Random class); 291
`nextLong` (Random class); 292
`nextToken` method (`StringTokenizer` class);
    293
no-arg constructors
See also constructors; instantiation
relationship between super and subclass; 64
term definition; 25
NON_SPACING_MARK constant (Character class)
as `getType` return value; 300
non-static fields
class methods restricted from accessing; 110
NORM_PRIORITY constant (Thread class); 191
NoSuchAttributeException example
exception creation; 152
NoSuchElementException class; 276, 293
See also elements
not equal (!=) operator
See also numbers and logical operations; operators
comparing objects; 73
relational operator; 132
Not-a-Number; *See* NaN (Not-a-Number)
notifying
See also events
`notify` (Object class); **188, 190**
`notifyAll` (Object class); **188, 190**
`notifyObservers` (Observable class); 289
`Observer` objects; 289
threads about events; 188
`wait`/`notify` threads mechanism compared with
    Observer/Observable mechanism; 291
null
See also debugging; object-oriented concepts and
    components
arguments, not permitted with `Dictionary`
    subclasses; 284
literal
    as object reference literal; 108
    as reference to no object; 19
    keyword restrictions apply to; 107
`NullPointerException` class; 125, 375
reference
    accessing class methods with; 125
    conversion of other object types to; 122
    `NullPointerException` exception; 125
numbers and logical operations
See also arithmetic; bit operations; expressions;
    floating-point; integer(s); logical operations;
    Math class; operators; primitive types; type(s);
    wrappers
factoring; 244
fields, default value; 11
`java.math` package; 354
Number class; **300**, 301, 302
    doubleValue; 300
    floatValue; 300
    intValue; 300

numbers and logical operations *(continued)*
  Number class *(continued)*
    longValue; 300
    MAX_VALUE constant; 301
    MIN_VALUE constant; 301
  NumberFormat class; 356
  NumberFormatException class; 300, 301, 302,
    375
  parsing; 251, 253
  prime, hashtable load factor use; 285
  pseudo-random
    managing with java.lang.Math.random; 291
    managing with Random; 291
  TT_NUMBER constant (StreamTokenizer class);
    251

O

object(s)
  See also classes (concepts and use); object-
    oriented concepts and components;
    reference(s)
  (chapter); **29**
  cloning; **77**
    clone use; 73
  comparing, == operator and != operator use; 73
  copying, *See* cloning
  creating
    introduction; **10**
    new operator use for; **32**
    reflection methods for; **312**
    separate from declaration; 30
  current, passing references to, this use for; 42
  deserialization, customized; 263
  deserialization of; **259**
  exceptions as; 22, 152
  fields
    initialization of; 117
    See instance variables
  graphs, term definition; 259
  initializing, with constructors; 33
  introduction; **9**
  Object class; 59, **73**, 96, 296
    arrays as implicit extensions of; 115
    getClass; 73, 304
    introduction; **20**
    notify; 188, 190
    notifyAll; 190
  object references vs; 10
  ObjectInput interface, in type tree for byte
    streams *(figure)*; 227
  ObjectInputStream class; **259**
    in type tree for byte streams *(figure)*; 227
  ObjectInputValidation interface, in type tree
    for byte streams *(figure)*; 227
  ObjectOutput interface, in type tree for byte
    streams *(figure)*; 227
  ObjectOutputStream class; **259**
    in type tree for byte streams *(figure)*; 227

  ObjectStreamClass class, in type tree for byte
    streams *(figure)*; 227
  receiving, term definition; 12
  references
    default value; 117
    equality testing; 133
    literals; **108**
    parameters that are; 39
    term definition; 10
  resurrecting, strategies and cautions; 50
  serialization, customized; 263
  serialization of; **259**
  sharing, cautions; 79
  String object type, introduction; **16**
  subclass of abstract class required to create; 77
  term definition; 1
  Thread, obtaining; 182
  types
    explicit casting with; 124
    invoking methods using; 20
    term definition; 9
    vs data types; 4
    vs reference, method invocation vs field access;
      68
  validation, during deserialization; 264
  values, comparing, equals use; 73
  versioning; **265**
  writing; 259, 261
object-oriented concepts and components, *See*
  access
  classes (concepts and use)
  component architecture
  composition
  constructors (concepts and use)
  design patterns
  encapsulation
  fields (concepts and use)
  hierarchy
  inheritance
  instantiation
  interfaces (concepts and use)
  members
  methods (concepts and use)
  object(s)
  references
  state
  variables
Observer design pattern
  See also design patterns
  Observable class; 273, **288**, 289
  Observer interface; 273, **288**
obtaining; *See* access; getting; retrieving
octal
  See also constants (Java and user-defined);
    numbers and logical operations
  literals
    representation and range; 109
    string literal use, precautions; 110
  values, conversion of integer values to; 302

ODBC
JDBC as mapping of; **372**
oneWeek example; 345
operating system
See also runtime
accessing *(chapter)*; **321**
operations
See also methods
locale-sensitive; 335
operator(s)
See also arithmetic; expressions; methods
(concepts and use); numbers and logical
operations; special characters
+=, characteristics; 8
++, characteristics; 8
--, characteristics; 8
%, compared with IEEERemainder (Math class);
333
=, starting values set by; 4
(?:) conditional; **135**
% remainder, characteristics; 9
arithmetic; 128
assignment
=; 4
--; 8
++; 8
+=; **136**
associativity; **118**
bang-equals (!=), comparing objects; 73
binary, assignment use with; 8
bitwise; **134**
(chapter); **103**
conditional, AND (&&); 133
decrement (--); **131**
char variable use; 132
comparison with self assignment +1; 131
dot (.)
accessing members with; 125
method invocation; 2, 12, 36
package vs field and method access use; 26
equality; **132**
greater than or equal (>=); 132
greater than (>); 132
increment (++); **131**
char variable use; 132
comparison with self assignment +1; 131
inversion (!); 132
less than or equal (<=); 132
less than (<); 132
logical; **132**
not equal (!=); 132
postfix
increment and decrement use as; 131
term definition; 8
precedence; **118**
(table); 378
precedence of; 119
prefix
increment and decrement use as; 131

term definition; 8
question-colon (?:); 135
relational; **132**
shift
left (<<); 134
right sign propagate (>>); 134
right zero propagate (>>>); 134
unary, bitwise complement (~); 134
optimization
See also efficiency; performance
final classes and methods advantages; 72
or
See also numbers and logical operations
OR (||) conditional operator; 133
or method (BitSet class); 275
order(ing)
See also expressions
constructor invocation, dependences; **65**
deserialization; **262**
evaluation
conditional operators; 133
operands; **120**
operators; 119
execution, static field initialization; 45
floating-point values; 133
initialization
non-static; 47
static; 46
lists, creating; 247
modifier, in class member declarations; 111
NaN anomalies; 133
not applicable to garbage collection; 49
operation execution, in a multithreading
application; 185
search, identifier name; 113
serialization; **262**
sorting algorithm issues; 84
Unicode, string comparison use; 163
unordered condition, methods for constructing;
130
ordinary characters
See also characters
ordinaryChar (StreamTokenizer class); 253
specifying for tokenizing; 253
organizing
packages; 212
other
as OTHER_LETTER constant (Character class), as
getType return value; 300
OTHER_NUMBER constant (Character class), as
getType return value; 300
OTHER_PUNCTUATION constant (Character class),
as getType return value; 300
OTHER_SYMBOL constant (Character class), as
getType return value; 300
out field (System class); 322
Outer example
inner object synchronization; 186
OutOfMemoryError class; 32

output
  See also I/O; input; reading; writing
  DataOutputStream class; 236
  FileOutputStream class; 245
  FileWriter class; 238
  OutputStream class; **229**, 237, 238, 326
    in type tree for byte streams *(figure)*; 227
  OutputStreamWriter class; 232, 236, **237**, 238
    in type tree for character streams *(figure)*; 232
  PipedOutputStream class; 236
  PipedWriter class; 246
  streams, term definition; 225
  System.out class, character stream relationship;
    231
  Writer class; **235**
ovals
  drawing, Canvas class; 360
overflow
  See also debugging; exceptions (concepts and use);
    numbers and logical operations
  floating-point; 128
overloading
  See also language concepts; object-oriented
    concepts and components
  ColorAttr example; 62
  methods; **44**, **67**
    access resolution; 126
    restrictions on; 127
  term definition; 4, 67
  + operator; 8
overriding
  See also object-oriented concepts and components
  accessing superclass fields, super reference use
    for; 43
  ColorAttr example; 62
  methods; **67**
    hiding fields compared with; 68
  operator precedence; 119
  superclass methods; 19
  term definition; 18, 67
overview, *See*
  data
  language concepts
  numbers and logical operations
  object-oriented concepts and components
  programming
  types
Oxford Union Society
  quotation; **215**

P

packages (concepts and use)
  See also encapsulation; language concepts; names;
    object-oriented concepts and components
  access; **211**
    restriction to; 31
  (chapter); **209**
  contents design guidelines; **212**

  declaring; 26, 209
  I/O *(chapter)*; **225**
  identifier name search order; 113
  importing; 210
  introduction; **24**
  names of; **136**
  naming; **210**
  nesting; 212
  package keyword; 209
    as reserved word; 106
  protected members access; 63
  scope; 212
    in nested packages; 212
  standard *(chapter)*; **353**
  subpackages, access rules; 211
  term definition; 24
  unnamed; 213
packages (Java and user-defined)
  java.applet; 353
  java.awt; 353
  java.awt.datatransfer; 361
  java.beans; 353, **367**
  java.io; 225, 353
    type trees, byte streams *(figure)*; 227
    type trees, character streams *(figure)*; 232
  java.lang; 353
  java.lang.reflect; **303**
  java.math; 354
  java.math package; **370**
  java.net; 353, **367**
  java.rmi; 353, **362**
  java.rmi.server; **362**
  java.security; 354, **372**
  java.sql; 354
  java.sql; **372**
  java.text; 353
    DateFormat class, in calendar abstraction; 344
  java.util; 335, 353
paragraphs
  See also documentation
  doc comments; **216**
  PARAGRAPH_SEPARATOR constant (Character
    class), as getType return value; 300
  tagged, term definition; 216
parameters
  See also language concepts; methods
  in constructor invocation; 35
  fields and, this reference as access differentiator;
    43
  final, modification of by subclasses; 67
  final keyword use; **111**
  fixed number, as requirement; 36
  identifier name search order; 113
  IllegalArgumentException class; 374
  introduction; **12**
  main, program arguments as; 55
  method, documenting; **217**
  multiple return value use; 37
  Object class as, passing interface types to; 96

@param tag; **217**
pass-by-value vs. pass-by-reference; 40
program, main parameters; 55
term definition; 2, 12
values; **38**
parent
See also inheritance; object-oriented concepts and
components; superclass
parentOf method (ThreadGroup class); 205
process, term definition; 325
thread group, methods for handling; 205
parentheses (())
overriding operator precedence with; 120
Park ranger;
quotation; *colophon*
Parker, Dorothy
quotation; **384**
parsing
See also language concepts; programming,
techniques
dates; **350**, 352
finding text boundaries; **358**
input data; 250
locale-sensitive; **355**
parse (DateFormat class); 352
parseLocale example; 357
parseNumbers (StreamTokenizer class); 253
parseObject (DateFormat class); 352
parseType
Byte class; 301
Integer class; 301
Long class; 301
Short class; 301
pushback buffers use for; 237, 249
strings into tokens; 292
time; **350**
passing parameters
See also language concepts
pass-by-value vs. pass-by-reference; 40
PassByValue example; 38
PassRef example; 39
references to the current object with this; 42
pasting
java.awt.datatransfer package; 361
path
See also file(s); filenames; I/O
path field (String class); 269
pathnames
File class abstraction of; 237
manipulating; 267, 324
retrieving; 268
pathSeparator field (File class); 269
pathSeparatorChar field (File class); 269
search, separator character representation; 269
peek method (Stack class); 282
percent sign (%)
remainder (%) operator; 9
performance
collation factor issues; 355

hashtable, efficiency factors; 284, 285
serialization, customized; 263
vector capacity management impact on; 281
Perlis, Alan J.
quotation; **381**
Permissions example; 37
Persian language
glyphs for the word "kitty"; 106
personalConfig example; 324
PI
computing; 364
PI constant (Math class); 332
Picasso, Pablo
quotation; **273**
PingPong example
two-threaded program; 181
pipes
See also streams
creating; 236, 246
Pipe example; 246
Piped class; 236, **246**
PipedInputStream class; 236
in type tree for byte streams *(figure)*; 227
PipedOutputStream class; 236
in type tree for byte streams *(figure)*; 227
PipedReader class; 246
in type tree for character streams *(figure)*; 232
PipedWriter class; 246
in type tree for character streams *(figure)*; 232
Pixel example; 18
place
term definition; 335
placement
absolute, term definition; 359
relative, term definition; 359
player
Player example; 315
PlayerLoader example; 317
plus sign (+)
See also arithmetic; numbers and logical
operations; operators; strings
increment (++) operator; **131**
char variable use; 132
plus (+) operator; 8, 16, 36, 56, 128
string concatenation use; 121, 130
plus-equal (+=) operator; 56
plus-equals (+=) operator; 8, 16, 36
string concatenation use; 130
plus-plus (++) operator; 8
Point example; 9
Polygon example use; 279
pointers
See also file(s); object-oriented concepts and
components; references
file
accessing; 258
setting; 259
NullPointerException; 375

polling
  term definition; 180
Polygon example; 279
  capacity management methods; 281
polymorphism
  See also language concepts
  arrays; 115
  interface inheritance use; 94
  term definition; 19, 59
portability
  Java advantages; *xvi*
position
  pos field (CharArrayReader class); 243
POSITIVE_INFINITY constant
  See also numbers and logical operations
  Double class; 302
  Float and Double class support of; 107
  Float class; 302
  infinite arithmetic with; 129
postfix operators
  See also numbers and logical operations; operators
  increment and decrement use as; 131
  precedence of; 119
  term definition; 8
pound sign (#)
  @see use; 216
pow method (Math class); 332
  See also numbers and logical operations
power
  value of; 333
precedence
  See also expressions; numbers and logical
      operations; operators
  of operators; **118**
    (table); 378
precision
  See also expressions; numbers and logical
      operations; type(s)
  loss of, during implicit conversion; 122
  magnitude, value precision compared with; 122
prefix operators
  See also numbers and logical operations; operators
  increment and decrement use as; 131
  term definition; 8
prime numbers
  See also numbers and logical operations; type(s)
  factors, factors example; 370
  hashtable load factor use; 285
  Primes example, static initializers; 46
primitive types
  See also byte(s); character(s); data, structures;
      double; expressions; floating-point; integer(s);
      long; numbers and logical operations; short;
      type(s)
  access resolution; 127
  decoding system properties into; 324
  getting; 309
  implicit conversion of values; 121
  invoke handling of; 311

(list); 4
names and values; **107**
parameter use; 36
reading and writing; 255
representation as objects, wrapper class use for; 60
setting; 309
string concatenation of; 131
wrappers for *(chapter)*; **295**
printing
  See also I/O; output; streams; writing
  BufferedStream class; 240
  data; 237, 240
  Filter class; 240
  line numbers, FindChar example; 238
  OutputStream class; 240
  Print class; **240**
  print (Print class); 240
  prints, array use; 15
  printField example; 309
  println (Print class); 240
  println (PrintStream class); 9
  PrintStream class; 232, 237, 240, 322
    in type tree for byte streams *(figure)*; 227
    println; 9
  printType example; 304
  PrintWriter class; 237, 240
    in type tree for character streams *(figure)*; 232
  synchronization of; 241
  type hierarchy; 304
  Writer class; 240
priorities
  Dr. Who version; 29
  thread group, methods for handling; 205
  threads
    scheduling impact; 191
    setting; 181
    thread group management; 204
private
  See also access; object-oriented concepts and
      components
  as access modifier, recommended order in class
      member declarations; 110
  extensible class design use and restrictions; 89
  PRIVATE_USE constant (Character class), as
      getType return value; 300
  read-only field access enforcement by; 41
  as reserved word; 106
  term definition; 31
process(es)
  See also programs; runtime; threads
  child
    term definition; 325
    termination status determination; 326
  controlling; 325
  creating; **325**
  killing; 327
  Process class; 321, 325, 326, 327
  ProcessFile example, open file leak avoidance;
      49

querying the state of; 325
threads compared with; 325
programming
  See also debugging; I/O; language concepts
  issues, *See*
    control
    design patterns
    efficiency
    localization
    security
    synchronization
  techniques, *See*
    algorithms
    appending
    counting
    documentation
    hashtables
    parsing
    recursion
    scanning
    search(ing)
    sorting
    threads
programs
  See also classes (concepts and use)
  arguments, term definition; 56
  examples, *See* class(es), examples
  running; 325
  running
    run (Thread class); 181
    runFinalization (Runtime class); 322
    runFinalization (System class); 322
    Runnable interface; 181, **201**
    RunPingPong example; 201
promotion
  type, in expression evaluation; 121
properties
  See also attributes; data, structures; design patterns
  files, for resource bundles; 343
  Properties class; 273, **286**, 287, 323
    getProperty; 287
    save; 287
  .properties files, resource bundle files identified by; 343
  property lists, term definition; 287
  propertyNames method (Properties class); 287
  PropertyResourceBundle class; **342**
  resources represented as; **342**
  system, accessing; **323**
  term definition; 42
protected; **63**
  See also access; object-oriented concepts and components
  as access modifier, recommended order in class member declarations; 111
  extensible class design use and restrictions; 88
  as reserved word; 106
  term definition; 31

providers
  cryptography, java.security package; 372
public
  See also access; object-oriented concepts and components
  as access modifier, recommended order in class member declarations; 111
  contracts, vs protected contracts; 84
  extensible class design use and restrictions; 88
  members, disadvantages of; 84
  methods, implicit in interfaces; 92
  package access use; 211
  as reserved word; 106
  term definition; 9, 31
push method (Stack class); 282
pushback
  See also I/O; parsing
  buffers; 237
    single-character; 249
  Pushback class; 237, **249**
  pushBack (StreamTokenizer class); 255
  PushbackInputStream class; 249, 250
    in type tree for byte streams *(figure)*; 227
  PushbackReader class, in type tree for character streams *(figure)*; 232
  of token into the stream; 255
put
  put method (Dictionary class); 284
  putIn example, intern use by; 166

Q

qualified names; 210
  avoiding name conflict with; 25
quality assurance
  benchmark harness creation; 76
question/colon (?:) operator
  conditional operator (?:) known as; 135
queues
  See also data, structures; list(ing)
  inserting and removing elements from; 189
  Queue example; 189
quotations
  Bach, Johann Sebastian; 103
  Balzac, Honoré de; 294
  Bankhead, Tallulah; 335
  Beal, Louise; 352
  Bombeck, Erma; 89
  Calvin and Hobbes; 27
  Carroll, Lewis; 139
  Chesterton, G.K.; 160
  Cook, Rich; 372
  Davis, Miles; 208
  Dr. Who; 29, 161
  Edison, Thomas; *xix*
  Einstein, Albert; 57
  Emerson, Ralph Waldo; 320
  Estes, James; 213
  Firesign Theater; 179

quotations *(continued)*
  Gilbert and Sullivan; 59
  Goethe, Johann Wolfgang von; 177
  Guaspari, David; 380
  Guthrie, Woody; 295
  Hoare, C.A.R.; 102
  Jackson, Andrew; 385
  Lehman, John; 333
  libraries as weapons; 209
  Oxford Union Society; 215
  Park ranger; *colophon*
  Parker, Dorothy; 384
  Perlis, Alan J.; 381
  Picasso, Pablo; 273
  Rukeyser, Muriel; 224
  Shakespeare, William; 321
  Smith, Logan Pearsall; 442
  transportation commission; 353
  travel agent; 1
  Trillin, Calvin; 137
  U.S. Army's PS magazine; 151
  Williams, H.H.; 150
  Williams, Peter; 225
  Woolf, Virginia; 272, 376
  Wright, Frank Lloyd; *xv*
  Zappa, Frank; 91, 373
  Zinsser, William; *colophon*
quotes
  double (\") escape sequence,; 109
  quoteChar (StreamTokenizer class); 253
  quotedString example, string modification; 167
  quotedString (String class); 167
  single (\') escape sequence; 109

R

race hazard
  See also programming, issues; threads
  term definition; 180
radians
  See also expressions; numbers and logical
      operations
  as Math class representation of angles; 332
radix; 297
random
  access files, RandomAccessFile; 245
  Random class; 274, **291**, 292
  random (Math class); 291
  RandomAccessFile class; 237, **258**
    getFilePointer; 258
    in type tree for byte streams *(figure)*; 227
    length; 259
    seek; 259
    skipBytes; 259
range
  array, checking of; 114
  of values, for statement use; 145
reading
  See also I/O; input; writing

  arrays; 228
  bytes, InputStream; 227
  character data; 321
  characters; 256
  data; 228
  files, testing if possible; 268
  from strings; 242
  InputStreamReader; 236
  InputStreamReader class; 232, **237**
  lines; 256
  objects; 263
  read (Buffered class); 241
  read (InputStream class); 228
  read (Reader class); 233
  read-only
    access, private fields use for; 41
    names in name-value pairs, importance of; 60
    term definition; 17
  readArabic example; 238
  readAttrs example; 252
  readBoolean (DataInput interface); 255
  readByte (DataInput interface); 255
  readChar (DataInput interface); 255
  readData example; 257
  readDouble (DataInput interface); 255
  reader, term definition; 225
  Reader class; **233**, 250
    in type tree for character streams *(figure)*; 232
  readFloat (DataInput interface); 255
  readFully (DataInput interface); 255
  readInt (DataInput interface); 255
  readLine (BufferedReader class); 241
  readLine (DataInput interface); 256
  readLong (DataInput interface); 255
  readShort (DataInput interface); 255
  readUnsignedByte (DataInput interface); 256
  readUnsignedShort (DataInput interface); 256
  readURL example; 369
  readUTF (DataInput interface); 255
  StringReader class; 244
  strings; 256
ready (Reader class); 233
realtime systems
  explicit memory management for; 322
receiver
  term definition; 12
recursion
  See also control, flow; programming, techniques
  explanation of, in toString example; 37
reference(s)
  See also object(s); object-oriented concepts and
      components
  casting; 124
  comparing, with == operator; 165
  conditional casting of; 125
  conversion; 122
  dangling, garbage collection prevention of; 47
  documentation, generating with doc comments
      (chapter); **215**

equality testing; 133
object
    instantiation separate from; 30
    method invocation vs field access; 68
    parameters that are; 39
    term definition; 9
    vs objects; 10
passing, to current object with `this`; 42
RMI handling; 366
superclass, in method invocation; 20
`this`, introduction; **13**
types, parameter use; 36
reflection
  access checking in; 311
  array handling; **313**
  characteristics and uses; **303**
  `Class` as starting point for; 304
  creating
    constructors; **312**
    new objects; **312**
  examining classes; **306**
  sorting algorithm design, reflection use; 312
  use in walking a class hierarchy; 306
regions
  `RegionMatch` example, string region comparison;
    164
  `regionMatches` (`String` class); 164
  string, comparing; 164
rehash method (`Hashtable` class); 286
relational
  See also control, flow; expressions; operators
  databases, `java.sql` package; 354, **372**
  operators; **132**
    precedence of; 119
  predicates, unordered condition, methods for
    constructing; 130
relationships
  See also object-oriented concepts and components
  IsA, HasA relationships contrasted with; 82
relative placement
  term definition; 359
releasing
  I/O resources; 228
remainder
  See also arithmetic; numbers and logical
    operations; type(s)
  comparison of methods; 333
  in floating-point arithmetic
    comparison of `IEERemainder` with % operator;
    333
    results *(table)*; 129
  in integer arithmetic; 128
  percent (%) arithmetic operator; 9, 128
remote
  interface, term definition; 362
  method invocation, term definition; 362
  servers, `java.rmi.server`; 362
removing
  remove (`Dictionary` class); 284

removeAllElements (`Vector` class); 279
removeElement (`Vector` class); 279
removeElementAt (`Vector` class); 279
renaming
  files; 269
replacing
  `replace` (`String` class); 168
  `replaceValue` example; 153
  strings; 168
representation
  See also design patterns
  class, runtime; 73
reserved words; *See* keywords
resetting
  reset (`CharArrayWriter` class); 243
  resetSyntax method (`StreamTokenizer` class);
    254
resizing
  See also size
  arrays, creating with `Vector` class; 278
  hashtables; 286
resource(s)
  bundles; **338**
    listing; **340**
    `MissingBundleException`; 340
    `.properties` as suffix for; 343
    `PropertyResourceBundle` class; **342**
    retrieving resources from; 339
    term definition; 336
  I/O, releasing; 228
  loading; **319**
  managing, `finalizes` use for; 48
  `MissingResourceException`; 375
  releasing, `finally` clause use for; 157
  `ResourceBundle` class; 274, 338
restoring
  property lists; 288
restricting
  superclass methods; 19
resuming
  resume
    `Thread` class; 200
    `ThreadGroup` class; 206
  threads, in a thread group; 206
resurrection
  See also termination
  of objects, strategies and cautions; **50**
retrieving
  See also access; get
  file, modification date; 269
  information about `File` objects; 268
  ISO country and language codes; 338
  locale, components; 337
  locale-sensitive calendars; 345
  package contents; 211
  pathname components; 267
  pathnames; 268
  properties, in a property list; 287
  resources, from resource bundles; 339

retrieving *(continued)*
    substrings; 162
    successive Unicode characters; 132
    system memory information; 322
    system properties; 323
    thread name; 182
    time; 344
    values, value setting differentiation from; 44
    vector elements; 280
return
    See also methods (concepts and use); object-
        oriented concepts and components
    return keyword, as reserved word; 106
    return (\r) escape sequence, Unicode value; 109
    return statement; 149
        finally clause use to clean up for; 158
        switch statement termination use; 144
    @return tag; **217**
    type
        as insufficient for method overloading
            differentiation; 127
        constructors distinguished from methods by
            lack of; 33
        method overriding requirements; 67
        overriding requirements for; 68
    values
        documenting; **217**
        getType; 300
        methods, void use to indicate absence of; 2
        multiple, strategies for handling; 37
        multiple, strategy for; 12
        restrictions on; 38
reuse
    See also object-oriented concepts and components
    code, namespace scoping; 114
    example, namespace scoping; 113
reversing
    reverse (StringBuffer class); 175
    strings; 175
right-associative
    term definition; 119
rint method (Math class); 332
RMI (Remote Method Invocation)
    See also networks
    idempotent, term definition; 363
    java.rmi package; 353, **362**
    partial failure, term definition; 363
    security manager requirements; 365
    UnicastRemoteObject class; 364
robustness
    code, scoping value for; 114
rolling
    roll (Calendar class); 346
romance
    international expressions of *(footnote)*; 298
rounding
    See also arithmetic; numbers and logical
        operations
    BigDecimal class; 371

    differences between IEEE 754-1985 standard and
        Java; 130
    round (Math class); 333
Rukeyser, Muriel
    quotation; **224**
running programs; 325
    See also debugging; errors (concepts and use);
        exceptions (concepts and use); performance;
        security
    run (Thread class); 181
    runFinalization (Runtime class); 322
    runFinalization (System class); 322
    runFinalizersOnExit (System class), forcing
        finalization with; 330
    Runnable interface; 181, **201**
    RunPingPong example; 201
runtime
    See also errors (concepts and use); exceptions
        (concepts and use); performance; security
    errors *(chapter)*; **373**
    exceptions
        (chapter); **373**
        compared with checked exceptions; 154
    loading classes into; **315**
    Runtime class; 321, 322, **329**, 331
    RuntimeException class; 24, 152, 373, **374**
        as unchecked exceptions, reasons for; 154
    system, accessing *(chapter)*; **321**
    term definition; 26
    termination; 329
    type conversions, casts as; 121
Russian
    comparing strings; 354
    glyphs for the word "kitty"; 106

S

safeExit example; 329
saving
    property lists; 287
    save, Properties class; 287
ScaleVector example
    arrays; 115
scanning
    See also parsing; programming, techniques;
        search(ing)
    input data; 250
    pushback buffers use for; 237, 249
scheduling
    threads; **191**
scope
    See also encapsulation; name(s); object-oriented
        concepts and components; packages
    of classes; 113
    code reuse value of; 114
    of identifiers; 110
    nested if statements, else clauses in; 141
    package; 211
        in nested packages; 212

variable initialization determined by; 117
scroll bars
as AWT component; 360
search(ing)
See also programming, techniques
binary, ordering issues and algorithm; 163
order, identifier name; 113
path, separator character representation; 269
search method (Stack class); 282
searchFor example; 157
string; 162
vectors; 280
seconds
leap *(footnote)*; 349
security
See also programming, issues; runtime; type(s)
access control considerations in extensible class design; 88
applet downloading issues; 361
extensible class design issues; 86
final classes and methods advantages; 71
getSecurityManager (System class); 332
java.security package; 354
manager
RMI requirements; 365
term definition; 27
models; 361
reflection constraints resulting from; 303
remote execution, as Java advantage; *xv*, 365
SecurityException class; 204, 205, 375
SecurityManager class; **331**
setSecurityManager (System class); 332
System class methods; **331**
thread; **203**
tools for handling, java.security; **372**
@see tag; **216**
seed
setting for random number generation use; 291
seeking
seek method (RandomAccessFile class); 259
self reference; *See* this reference
semantics
operator, impact on expression type; 121
term definition; 29
semicolon (;)
expression statements terminated by; 139
separator
readLine (BufferedReader class) acceptance; 241
terminator compared with *(footnote)*; 139
sequences
See also data, structures
escape, special character representation *(table)*; 109
numbering elements of; 7
SequenceCount example; 249
SequenceInputStream class; 237, **247**
in type tree for byte streams *(figure)*; 227

try-catch-finally, as exception handling paradigm; 23
Serbo-Croatian language
glyphs for the word "kitty"; 106
serialization
customized; **263**
BetterName example; 264
Externalizable interface; **267**
default; 261
Externalizable interface; **267**
graph integrity preservation by; 260
of hashtables; 259
Name example; 261
NotSerializableException; 262, 264
object; **259**
order considerations; **262**
requirements for classes; **260**
RMI use; 366
serial version UID
serialVersionUID field; 265
term definition; 264
Serializable interface; 236, **260**
extended by Externalizable interface; **267**
in type tree for byte streams *(figure)*; 227
term definition; 259
servers
acceptInput example; 368
multiple class access; 365
remote, java.rmi.server; 362
term definition; 363
setting
See also getting
file pointer; 259
set (BitSet class); 274
set (Calendar class); 346, 347
set method (Field class); 309
setType methods (Array class); 314
setCalendar (DateFormat class); 351
setCharAt (StringBuffer class); 173
setDaemon (ThreadGroup class); 200, 205
setDefault (Calendar class); 348
setElementAt (Vector class); 278
setField example; 309
setFirstDayOfWeek (Calendar class); 347
setGregorianChange (GregorianCalendar class); 350
setID (Calendar class); 348
setLength (StringBuffer class); 173
setLineNumber (LineNumberReader class); 248
setLocale (Locale class); 337
setMaxPriority (ThreadGroup class); 204, 205
setMinimalDaysInFirstWeek (Calendar class); 348
setNumberFormat (DateFormat class); 351
setPriority, Thread class; 191
setProperties (System class); 324
setRawOffset (Calendar class); 348
setSecurityManager (System class); 332
setSeed (Random class); 291

setting *(continued)*
  setSize (Vector class); 281
  setTime (Date class); 344, 347
  setTimeZone (DateFormat class); 351
  thread priorities; 181, 191
  values, value access differentiation from; 44
shadowing; *See* hiding
Shakespeare, William
  quotation; **321**
sharing
  See also encapsulation; hiding; object-oriented
      concepts and components
  access
      among threads; 180
      volatile marking for; **202**
  objects, cautions; 79
  variables, *See* class variables
shift operators
  See also numbers and logical operations; operators
  left (<<); 134
  precedence of; 119
  right sign propagate (>>); 134
  right zero propagate (>>>); 134
Shimmer example; 95
short
  See also numbers and logical operations; primitive
      types; type(s)
  keyword, as reserved word; 106
  Short class; 301
  type
      as primitive data type, value of; 106
      default value; 117
      reading and writing; 255
  values, conversion of, vs. char conversion; 121
side effects
  See also language concepts
  evaluation order importance; 120
sign
  inverting; 128
signaling
  See also events; exceptions (concepts and use)
  errors, through exception mechanism *(chapter)*;
      151
signatures
  See also methods (concepts and use)
  constructor, relationship between super- and
      subclass; 64
  digital, java.security package; 372
  java.security package; 354
  method, invocation use of; 126
  method overriding requirements; 67
  overloading compared with overriding; 68
  semantics relationship with; 29
  term definition; 12, 44
silicon
  virtual machine implementation; 26
simple
  SimpleClass example; 36
  SimpleDateFormat class; 352

SimpleSortDouble example; 87
  SimpleTimeZone class; 274
SimpleTimeZone class; 348
sin method (Math class); 332
  See also numbers and logical operations
@since tag; 219
  See also documentation
single
  inheritance, term definition; 94
  quote (\') escape sequence, Unicode value; 109
  threaded, term definition; 179
sink; *See* destination
size
  array, applicable to object not reference; 114
  buffers
      obtaining; 242
      specifying; 241
  dimension, creating arrays with different; 116
  size
      BitSet class; 275
      ByteArrayOutputStream class; 242
      CharArrayWriter class; 242
      Dictionary class; 284
      Vector class; 280
  string, length return of; 17
  StringBuffer object, managing; **176**
  vectors, setting; 281
skipping
  bytes while reading; 256
  input data; 228
  skip (InputStream class); 228
  skip (Reader class); 233
  skipBytes (DataInput interface); 256
  skipBytes method (RandomAccessFile class);
      259
slash (/)
  See also operators
  arithmetic operator; 128
  doc comments use; 215
  slashSlashComments (StreamTokenizer class);
      254
  slashStarComments (StreamTokenizer class);
      254
sleep
  See also events; threads
  putting threads to; 192
  sleep (Thread class); 192
Smith, Logan Pearsall
  quotation; **442**
snapshots
  Dictionary concerns; 284
  ensuring in
      dictionary loops; 285
      enumeration loops; 276
  methods for obtaining, with Enumeration; 276
  property list, obtaining; 287
  StringTokenizer enumeration; 293
sockets
  See also networks

acceptInput example; 368
DatagramSocket class; 367
InetAddress class; 367
java.net package; 353, 367
MulticastSocket class; 367
SecurityManager class control of; 331
ServerSocket class; 367
Socket class; 367
sorting
  See also collation; programming, techniques
  algorithms
    comparing, class design for; 84
    user class specification; 312
  arrays; 84
  SortDouble example, extensible class design; 84
  SortMetrics example, measuring costs; 86
  Unicode order issues; 163
sounds
  loading; 319
source
  term definition; 225
spaces
  See also character(s)
  SPACE_SEPARATOR constant (Character class), as getType return value; 300
  testing characters for; 299
  as white space; 105
spawning
  See also threads
  threads; 181
special characters
  See also Special Characters section at end of index
  StreamTokenizer class handling; 251
  using backslash (\) *(table)*; 380
specifications
  reference documentation differences; 216
SQL
  java.sql package; 354
square root
  See also arithmetic; numbers and logical operations; operators
  sqrt (Math class); 13, 332
    as static method; 14
  sqrtInt example, appending strings with; 174
squeezing
  characters from a string; 170
  squeezeOut example; 170
stacks
  See also data, structures
  accessing number of frames in a thread; 207
  Stack class; 273, **282**
  StackOverflowError class; 376
  tracing; 207
standard
  I/O
    character stream relationship; **231**
    streams for handling; 321
  packages *(chapter)*; **353**

start
  start method (Thread class); 181
  START_PUNCTUATION constant (Character class), as getType return value; 300
  startsWith method (String class); 165
state
  See also object-oriented concepts and components; variables
  ambiguous, as multiple inheritance problem; 94
  of cloned objects; 78
  evaluation order importance; 121
  handling cleanup, finally clause use for; 157
  initial
    constructor role in setting up; 33
    establishing with constructors; 35
  manipulation of by methods; 36
  object, embodied in fields; 31
  process, querying; 325
  reclaiming resources with; 48
  runtime, Runtime class representation of; 329
  setting in an object; 34
  setting up, static initializer use; 46
  term definition; 1
  thread group, tracking; 208
statements
  See also language concepts
  blocks and; **139**
  blocks as compound; 140
  break, switch statement, case use; 143
  continue; **148**
  declaration; 140
  do-while; 7, **144**
  expressions that can be converted into; 139
  for; 145
    control variable declaration in; 15
  goto
    finally as replacement for; 150
    labeled break contrasted with; 148
  if; **140**
    conditional operator compared with; 135
    if-else in ImprovedFibonacci example; 7
    nested, scoping issues; 141
  import; 210
  labels; **146**
  return; 149
    finally clause use to clean up for; 158
  switch; 7, **142**
  synchronized; **185**
  term definition; 1
  throw; **153**
    finally clause; **157**
  while; **144**
static
  See also classes (concepts and use); fields (concepts and use); methods (concepts and use)
  fields
    implicit in interfaces; 92
    See class(es), variables

`static` *(continued)*
  initialization blocks, term definition; 46
  as Java reserved word; 106
  members; **44**
  methods
    introduction; **14**
    See class(es), methods
  named constant declaration; 5
  recommended order in class member declarations;
    111
  in variable declarations; 110
stopping
  See also termination
  `stop`
    `Thread` class; 181, **198**
    `ThreadGroup` class; 206, 329
  threads; 181
    in a thread group; 206
storage management; *See* garbage collection
strategy; *See* programming, issues; programming,
    techniques
streams
  See also I/O; language concepts
  abstract classes for; 225
  buffered; 241
  `Buffered` class; **240**
  byte; **226**
    array; **242**
    term definition; 225
    type tree *(figure)*; 227
  chaining together; 237
  character; **231**
    array; **242**
    reading, `Reader` class; **233**
    standard stream relationship; **231**
    `String` character streams; **244**
    term definition; 225
    type tree *(figure)*; 232
    writing, `Writer` class; **235**
  closing; 228, 230
  composite, creating; 237
  concatenating; 236
  connecting; 326
  conversion, between Unicode and bytes; **237**
  data; **255**
    classes; **257**
  `Data`, corresponding to `DataInput` and
    `DataOutput` interfaces; 256
  `DataInputStream` class; 236
  `DataOutputStream` class; 236
  filters, `Filter` class; **238**
  flushing; 230
  I/O
    accessing in a child process; 325
    standard; **321**
  input
    `FileInputStream` class; 245
    `InputStream` class; 227, 238
      `InputStream` class extended
        by`FileInputStream`; 229
      `InputStreamReader` class; 232, 236, **237**
      `InputStreamWriter` class; 238
      `PipedReader` class; 246
      `SequenceInputStream` class; **247**
      term definition; 225
  `Object` class; **259**
  output
    `FileOutputStream` class; 245
    `FileWriter` class; 245
    `OutputStream` class; **229**, 238
    `OutputStreamWriter` class; 232, 236, **237**,
      238
    `PipedWriter` class; 246
    term definition; 225
  piped
    `Piped` class; **246**
    `PipedInputStream` class; 236
    `PipedOutputStream` class; 236
  pushback
    `Pushback` class; **249**
    `PushbackInputStream`; 250
  random access; 237
  reading from; 228
  `SequenceInputStream` class; 237
  standard, character stream relationship; **231**
  `streamFor` (`FileInputStream` class); 318, 320
  `StreamTokenizer` class; 237, **250**, 253, 254, 255
    in type tree for character streams *(figure)*; 232
    `sumStream`; 251
  synchronization, character vs. byte streams; 231
  term definition; 225
  token type constants; 251
string(s)
  See also array(s); character(s); data, structures;
    type(s)
  appending; 173, 174
  breaking into tokens; 274, 292
  buffers
    as input streams; 237
    managing the size of; **176**
  byte array conversion; **171**
  case-related issues; 163
  `char` arrays and; **170**
  comparing; **163**
    locale-sensitive; 354
    regions of; 164
  comparison, `equals`; 17
  concatenation; **130**
    during expression evaluation; 121
    + operator use; 16
  conversions; **125**, **169**
    `toString`; 56
  copying; 161
  creating; 161
  deleting characters from; 170
  equality testing; 133
    with `intern`; 166

extending; 174
extracting characters from, with `charAt`; 161
extracting data from a `StringBuffer`; **175**
facilities and operations *(chapter)*; **161**
I/O using byte arrays; 242
immutability of `String` objects; 17
inserting into; 173, 174
introduction; **16**
`java.lang` package; 353
`java.text` package; 353
length
    obtaining with `length`; 161
    setting; 173
literals, comparing; 166
mapping, `Properties` class; 273
modifying; **167**
    with `StringBuffer` class; 172, 173
mutable, *See* `StringBuffer` class
reading from; 242
replacing; 168
representation; **109**
reversing; 175
searching; 162
`String` character streams; **244**
`String` class; **56**, 110, **161**, 162, 163, 164, 165,
    167, 168, 170, 171, 236, 269
    `hashCode` overriding; 285
`StringBuffer` class; 17, **172**, 173, 174, 175, 176
    `StringWriter` use; 245
`StringBufferInputStream` class; 237
`StringReader`, use with `StreamTokenizer`; 293
`StringReader` class; 244
    in type tree for character streams *(figure)*; 232
`StringsDemo` example; 16
`StringTokenizer` class; 274, 292, 293
`StringWriter` class; 244
    in type tree for character streams *(figure)*; 232
substrings
    extracting; 167
    locating; 162
testing, beginning and end; 165
`toString`; 36
    `Byte` class; 301
    `ByteArray` stream classes; 242
    `CharArrayWriter` class; 243
    `Hashtable`; 286
    `Integer` class; 301
    `Long` class; 301, 302
    `Member` interface; 308
    `Number` class; 301
    `Short` class; 301
    `String` class; **56**, 169
    `StringBuffer` class; 175
    `StringTokenizer` class; 255
    `Thread` class; 207
    `ThreadGroup` class; 208
    `Vector` class; 282
    wrapper classes use of; 296
truncating; 174

Unicode, sorting order issues; 163
utility functions; **166**
writing; 243, 256
subclass(es)
    See also classes (concepts and use); fields
        (concepts and use); inheritance; interfaces
        (concepts and use); methods (concepts and
        use); object-oriented concepts and
        components
    appropriate use of, compared with inappropriate
        use of; 82
    creation by extending classes *(chapter)*; **59**
    `final` classes not permitted to have; 71
    `ResourceBundle` class; **343**
    superclass change impact, field hiding advantage;
        70
    term definition; 18, 59
`SubException` example
    `catch` clause design; 157
subpackages
    See also packages
    access rules; 211
subtraction
    See also arithmetic; numbers and logical
        operations
    minus (–) arithmetic operator; 128
subtype
    See also type(s)
    term definition; 94
summing
    See also arithmetic
    `sumStream` example; 251
super
    See also classes (concepts and use); inheritance;
        interfaces (concepts and use); object-oriented
        concepts and components
    `super` keyword
        accessing hidden fields with; 68
        casting use in object cloning; 81
        invoking superclass constructors with; 64
        Java reserved word; 106
        reference, accessing superclass fields; 43
        reference, `this` reference compared with; 19
        reference type control of method selection with;
        70
    superclass
        accessing overridden fields, `super` reference
        use for; 43
        constructors; 64
        term definition; 18, 59
    `SuperException` example, `catch` clause design;
        157
    `SuperShow` example, method overriding vs field
        hiding; 68
    supertype
        implicit conversion to; 122
        term definition; 22, 94
SURROGATE constant (`Character` class)
    as `getType` return value; 300

suspension
See also debugging; events; threads
suspend
Thread class; 181, 200
ThreadGroup class; 206
of threads; 181
in a thread group; 206
term definition; **199**
swapping
in array sorting (example); 85
switch
See also control, flow
keyword, as reserved word; 106
statement; **142**
as flow of control statement; 7
synchronization
See also language concepts; programming, issues;
threads
of byte array stream methods; 242
character streams vs. byte streams; 231
class extension; 185
next use for pseudo-random number generation;
292
of print methods; 241
queue manipulation; 190
SyncFailedException; 245
synchronized; 242
synchronized keyword; **183**
as reserved word; 106
recommended order in class member
declarations; 111
required for wait and notify; 191
synchronized statement; **185**
term definition; 183
thread; **183**
syntax
See also expressions
braces; 2
braces ({}), methods delimited by; 12
brackets; 15
cast conversion; 123
dot (.); 2
method invocation use; 12
table, resetting; 254
system
See also runtime; security
concepts, See
garbage collection
I/O
runtime
security
programming (chapter); **321**
properties, accessing; **323**
realtime, explicit memory management for; 322
resources, loading; 319
System class; 321, 330, 331, 332, 343
err field; 322
gc; 322
getProperty; 324

in field; 321
out field; 322
runFinalization; 322
setProperties; 324
System.err class; 237
character stream relationship; **231**
System.in class; 234
character stream relationship; **231**
System.out class; 237
character stream relationship; **231**

T

tab (\t) escape sequence
See also escape sequences
Unicode value; 109
as white space; 105
tables
documentation comment tags; 380
operator precedence; 378
special characters using backslash (\); 380
Unicode digits; 378
Unicode letters and digits (table); 379
useful (chapter); **377**
tagged paragraphs
term definition; 216
tags
documentation comments (table); 380
Tamil language
glyphs for the word "kitty"; 106
tan method (Math class); 332
See also arithmetic; numbers and logical
operations
Task example; 362
tenPower example; 146
term definitions
absolute placement; 359
abstract class; 75
accessor methods; 41
applets; xv
arrays; 14, 114
bounds; 15
atomic; 188
blank finals; 111
blocked; 191
blocks, initialization; 46
bounds, array; 15
byte, streams; 225
bytecodes; 2, 26
calendar fields; 346
casting
down; 124
safe; 124
unsafe; 124
up; 124
catching, exceptions; 22, 151
character, streams; 225
checked exceptions; 22, 152
child process; 325

class(es); 1, 29
    abstract; 75
    concrete; 75
    methods; 14, 47
    variables; 11
client; 363
comments; 5
    documentation; 5
    skew; 223
concrete class; 75
constants; 5
constructors; 33
    no-arg; 25
contexts, naming; 25
contract; 29, 59
control, flow; 139
daemon, threads; 201
datagrams; 367
deadlock; 194
deadly embrace; 194
declaration; 110
    statements; 139
deserialization; 259
destination; 225
diamond inheritance; 94
documentation, comments; 5
encapsulation; 12
enclosing
    class; 50
    type; 50
environment variables; 328
epoch; 343
exceptions; 22, 151
    catching; 22, 151
    checked; 22, 152
    throwing; 22, 151
    unchecked; 24, 152
expressions, statements; 139
extensibility; 59
fields; 1, 9, 30
forwarding; 99
garbage collector; 11
hashtables; 284
heap; 10
hiding; 13
idempotent; 363
identifiers; 106
    in declarations; 110
immutable; 17
implicit conversion; 121
inheritance; 18
    multiple; 94
    multiple interface; 92
    single; 94
initialization blocks; 46
initializers, `static`; 46
inner classes, local; 53
input, streams; 225
instance; 1, 29

variables; 10
instantiation; 10
interface; 20
    multiple inheritance; 92
internationalization; 335
invocation, method; 12
layout manager; 359
left-associative; 119
lenient; 347
listener; 360
load factor; 285
local inner classes; 53
localization; 335
lock; 180
members; 1
methods; 1, 9, 11, 36
    accessor; 41
    class; 14
modifiers, declaration; 110
multiple, inheritance; 94
multiple interface inheritance; 92
multithreading; 180
mutually exclusive; 183
names
    namespace; 113
    naming contexts; 24
    type; 30
namespace; 112
narrowing; 124
nesting; 50
no-arg constructors; 25
object; 1, 29
    graphs; 259
    receiving; 12
    references; 10
    types; 9
output, streams; 225
overloading; 4, 67
overriding; 18, 67
packages; 24
parameters; 2, 12
parent, process; 325
partial failure; 363
place; 335
placement
    absolute; 359
    relative; 359
polling; 180
polymorphism; 19, 59
postfix operators; 8
prefix operators; 8
`private` keyword; 31
program arguments
property; 42
    lists; 286
`protected` keyword; 31
`public` keyword; 9, 31
race hazard; 180
read-only; 17

term definitions *(continued)*
reader; 225
receiver; 12
reference
object; 10
this; 13
remote
method invocation; 362
server; 362
resource, bundles; 336
right-associative; 119
runtime; 26
security, model; 26
semantics; 29
serial version UID; 265
serialization; 259
servers; 363
signatures; 12, 44
single inheritance; 94
single-threaded; 179
source; 225
state; 1
statements; 1
declaration; 139
expression; 139
static keyword, initialization blocks; 46
streams; 225
byte; 225
character; 225
input; 225
output; 225
subclass; 18, 59
subtype; 94
superclass; 18, 59
supertype; 22, 94
suspension; 199
synchronization; 183
tagged paragraphs; 216
this reference; 13
threads; 179
thread groups; 203
throwing, exceptions; 22, 151
tokens; 105
top-level nested classes; 52
type; 3
declaration; 110
name; 30
object; 9
unchecked exceptions; 24, 152
Unicode character set; 103
user threads; 201
variables; 3
blank final; 111
class
environment; 328
instance; 10
virtual machine; 26
widening; 124
writer; 225

termination
See also deleting
of method execution, return use for; 149
separator compared with *(footnote)*; 139
status, child process, determining; 326
thread; **195**, **199**
ternary operator
See also control, flow; operators
conditional operator (?:) known as; 135
precedence of; 119
testing
See also comparison; conditional; control, flow
characters for their properties; 299
File objects; 268
methods that implement; 84
strings, beginning and end; 165
TestSort example; 87, 312
vectors, for emptiness; 281
text; 241
See also character(s); string(s)
boundaries; **358**
date and time formatting issues; 350
fields, as AWT component; 360
java.text, DateFormat class as part of calendar abstraction; 344
java.text package; 353
loading; 319
localization and internationalization, java.text package; **354**
regions, as AWT component; 360
TextGenerator class; 246
That example
superclass method invocation; 70
this reference
See also object(s); object-oriented concepts and components
introduction; **13**
keyword, as reserved word; 106
multiple constructor invocation use; 34
nested class use; 53
passing references to the current object with; **42**
prohibited in statics; 45
subclass constructor use; 64
super reference compared with; 19
threads
See also language concepts; programming, techniques
aborting; 329
(chapter); **179**
communication between; **188**
configuring; 181
creating; **181**
daemon, user threads compared with; 200
deadlock avoidance; **194**
debugging applications use; **207**
as differentiator of Java from C and C++; *xvi*
IllegalThreadStateException class; 375
interrupting; **195**
interrupts; **199**

I/O exceptions; 271
`java.lang` package; 353
multi-tasking advantages; *xvi,* 180
name, obtaining; 182
`Piped` stream safety; 246
priorities
 setting; 181, 191
 thread group management; 204
processes compared with; 325
putting to sleep; 192
`Runnable` interface, implementing; 201
scheduling; **191**
security; 203
spawning; 181
stopping; 181
 cautions against; **198**
suspending; 181, **199**
synchronization; **183**
 of `ByteArray` methods; 242
term definition; 179
terminating execution of; **195**
`Thread` class; 181, 182, 188, 190, 191, 192, 201,
 202, 204, 207
thread groups
 class methods; 207
 counting; 206, 207
 encapsulation of; 203
 resuming; 206
 state, tracking; 208
 stopping; 206
 suspending; 206
 term definition; 203
`ThreadDeath` class; 329, 376
`ThreadGroup` class; 201, **203**, 204–206, 207, 329
user, daemon threads compared with; 201
`wait` and `notify` details; 190
`wait`, `notify`, and `notifyAll` methods; **188**
`wait`/`notify` mechanism compared with
 Observer/Observable mechanism; 291
waiting for completion of; **197**
yielding execution; 192
throwing exceptions
 See also debugging; errors (concepts and use);
 exceptions (concepts and use)
 term definition; 22, 151
 `throw` keyword, as reserved word; 106
 `throw` statement; **153**
 in a `switch` statement, termination use; 144
 `Throwable` class; 23, 73, 152
 `throws` clause; **153**
 in method overriding; 68
 `throws` keyword, as reserved word; 106
Tibetan language
 glyphs for the word "rose"; 260
time
 benchmark timing, abstract class example; 77
 calendar fields representing; 346
 `currentTimeMillis` (`System` class); 331, 343
 `Date` class functions related to; 343

daylight saving; 348
formatting; **350**
`getDateTimeInstance` (`DateFormat` class); 351
`getTime` (`Date` class); 344, 348
`getTimeInstance` (`DateFormat` class); 351
operations related to; **343**
parsing; **350**
retrieving; 344
`setTime` (`Date` class); 344, 347
`SimpleTimeZone` class; **348**, 350
time zone, `SimpleTimeZone` class; 344
time zones, `TimeZone` class; **348**
`TimeZone` class; 274, 344, 350
UTC compared with UT *(footnote)*; 349
titlecase
 See also character(s); string(s); tokens
 TITLECASE_LETTER constant (`Character` class),
 as `getType` return value; 300
 Unicode, `Character` class handling; 298
to*Xxx* methods
 `toBinaryString`
 `Integer` class; 302
 `Long` class; 302
 `toByteArray` (`ByteArray` stream classes); 242
 `toCharArray` (`String` class); 170
 `toHexString`
 `Integer` class; 302
 `Long` class; 302
 `toLowerCase`
 `Character` class; 299
 `String` class; 168
 `toOctalString`
 `Integer` class; 302
 `Long` class; 302
 `toString`; 36
 `Byte` class; 301
 `ByteArray` stream classes; 242
 `Integer` class; 301
 `Long` class; 301, 302
 `Member` interface; 308
 `Number` class; 301
 `Short` class; 301
 `String` class; **56**, 169
 `StringBuffer` class; 175
 `StringTokenizer` class; 255
 `Thread` class; 207
 `ThreadGroup` class; 208
 wrapper classes use of; 296
 `toString`, `Locale` class; 337
 `toTitleCase` (`Character` class); 299
 `toUpperCase`
 `Character` class; 299
 `String` class; 168
tokens; **105**
 See also parsing; streams; string(s)
 breaking
 a stream into; 249
 input data into; **250**
 strings into; 274, 292

tokens *(continued)*
    (chapter); **103**
    counting, those remaining in a string; 293
    countTokens (StringTokenizer class); 294
    finding text boundaries; 358
    StreamTokenizer class; 237
    term definition; **105**
    tokenizer handling; 105
    types of; 251
top-level nested classes
    term definition *(footnote)*; 52
totalMemory method (Runtime class); 322
tracing
    See also debugging
    Runtimes; 331
    stacks; 207
    traceInstructions method (Runtime class);
       331
    traceMethodCalls method (Runtime class); 331
tracking
    line numbers; 248
    thread group state; 208
traditions
    differences, managing with Locale class; 336
transient keyword
    as reserved word; 106
translating
    See also character(s); conversion; parsing
    characters; 298
    TranslateByte example; 230
transportation commission
    quotation; **353**
travel agent
    quotation; **1**
tree
    See also data, structures
    type
        for byte streams *(figure)*; 227
        for character streams *(figure)*; 232
Trillin, Calvin
    quotation; **137**
trimming
    See also string(s)
    trim (String class); 168
    trimToSize (Vector class); 280
    vectors; 280
    white space; 168
true literal
    See also constants (Java and user-defined);
       numbers and logical operations
    as boolean literal; 108
    keyword restrictions apply to; 106
truncation
    in integer arithmetic; 128
    of strings; 174
try-catch-finally sequence
    See also errors (concepts and use); events;
       exceptions (concepts and use)
    as exception handling paradigm; 23

try keyword
    as reserved word; 106
    block; **155**
try-catch, finalize use; 49
TT (Token Type) constants (StreamTokenizer class)
    TT_EOF constant; 251
    TT_EOL constant; 251
    TT_NUMBER constant; 251
    TT_WORD constant; 251
type(s)
    See also data, structures; expressions; language
       concepts; numbers and logical operations
    abstract, interface declaration of; 91
    assignment operators requirements; 136
    (chapter); **103**
    char, Character class representation of; 297
    character, testing methods; 299
    checking, final class impact on; 72
    class, class literal use of; 110
    classes
       as Java feature; 27
       member as determinant during access; 125
    conversions; **121**
       characteristics; 123
       during expression evaluation; 121
       run time, casts as; 121
    converting and inserting or appending into strings;
       174
    data types vs object types; 4
    declaration, term definition; 110
    enclosing, term definition; 50
    examining
       reflect package use; **303**
       reflection use for; **306**
    exception, creating; **152**
    expression, determination of; **121**
    hierarchy
       for primitive type wrapper classes; 295
       walking; 304
    I/O classes that handle; **236**
    imported, identifier name search order; 113
    interface, multiple inheritance provided through;
       94
    java.lang package; 353
    name, term definition; 30
    object
       explicit casting with; 124
       invoking methods using; 20
       term definition; 9
       vs reference, method invocation vs field access;
       68
    parameter, method declaration of; 36
    primitive
       See also bytes; character(s); data, structures;
        double; expressions; floating-point; integer(s);
        long; numbers and logical operations; short
       access resolution; 127
       decoding system properties into; 324

getting; 309
implicit conversion of values; 121
`invoke` handling of; 311
(list); 4
names and values; **107**
parameter use; 36
reading and writing; 255
setting; 309
string concatenation of; 131
wrapper class use; 60
wrapper class use *(chapter)*; **295**
return
method declaration of; 36
overriding requirements for; 68
rules, difference between shift operators and other
binary operators; 134
safety of, as robust code facilitator; *xvi*
stream; 225
system, navigating; 304
term definition; 3
tree
for byte streams *(figure)*; 227
for character streams *(figure)*; 232
TypeDesc example; 304
typeValue, wrapper classes use of; 296

U

U.S. Army's PS magazine
quotation; **151**
UID (Unique Identifier)
serial version, term definition; 265
unary operators
See also numbers and logical operations; operators
bitwise complement (~); 134
minus (–); 128
plus (+); 128
precedence of; 119
UNASSIGNED constant (Character class)
as getType return value; 300
uncaughtException method (ThreadGroup class);
207
unchecked exceptions
See also errors (concepts and use); exceptions
(concepts and use)
precautions against creating; 374
term definition; 24, 152
undefined variables
See also language concepts; variables
impact of; 4
underflow
floating-point; 129
unicast
UnicastRemoteObject class; 364
Unicode character set
See also ASCII character set; character(s);
internationalization; locale(s)
accessing successive members of; 132
case issues; 163

character case issues; 298
converting to bytes; 238
digits *(table)*; 378
exceptions; 271
identifier use; 106
identifiers, requirements for; 299
as internationalization/localization tool; 335
introduction; **6**
letters and digits *(table)*; 379
sorting order issues; 163
streams, conversion between byte streams and; **237**
term definition; 103
testing characters for; 299
UTF
reading and writing; 256
UTFDataFormatException; 271
unit-testing
See also debugging
of classes, multiple main advantages; 56
United Kingdom
parsing; 357
UNIX operating system
cat utility, Concat version; 247
unloading; classes, *See* garbage collection
unnamed package; 213
unordered; *See* order(ing)
updating
update method (Observer interface); 288
uppercase
See also case (character); character(s)
converting strings to; 168
Unicode, Character class handling; 298
UPPERCASE_LETTER constant (Character class),
as getType return value; 300
URL (Universal Resource Locator)
accessing; 320
APPLET tag use; 361
java.net package; 353, 367
readURL example; 369
resource bundle handling; 340
URLConnection class; 367
URLEncoder class; 367
URLInput class, deserialization example; 262
user(s)
logged-in, displaying; 290
threads, term definition; 201
userHitCancel example, suspending threads; 199
userProg example; 326
Users example; 289
UTC
UT compared with *(footnote)*; 349
UTF (Unicode Transmission Format)
reading and writing; 256
UTFDataFormatException class; 272
utilities
methods, Java Object class, descriptions; 73
standard *(chapter)*; **273**

V

validation
   object, during deserialization; 264
values
   See also variables
   access, value setting differentiation from; 44
   default
      fields *(table)*; 117
      local variables, not assigned; 117
      numeric fields; 11
   Gaussian-distributed, as seed for random number
      generation use; 292
   object, comparing, `equals` use; 73
   parameters; **38**
   return
      documenting; **217**
      `getType`; 300
      multiple, strategy for; 13
      restrictions on; 38
   setting, value access differentiation from; 44
   synchronizing; 185
   `Value` example, class variables; 45
   `valueOf`
      `Long` class; 302
      `String` class; 169
   `valueOf`s, integer wrapper classes; 301
   of variables, initializing; **117**
variables
   See also language concepts; object-oriented
      concepts and components; values
   array; **114**
   blank finals, term definition and use; 111
   class
      characteristics and use; 44
      declaring; 31
      initialization of; 117
      introduction; **11**
      term definition
   control, declaring in a `for` statement; 15
   declarations; **110**
      separate from object creation; 30
   environment, term definition; 328
   `final`, named constants creation using; 5
   initializing; **117**
   instance
      constructors invoked after initialization of; 33
      term definition; 10
   introduction; **3**
   local
      declaration statements; 140
      duplicate identifier restrictions in nested
         constructs; 113
   scope of; 113
   shared, *See* class variables
   `static`, named constants creation using; 5
   term definition; 3
   of variables; 113

vectors
   bit, `BitSet` class; 274
   `BitSet` class; 273
   capacity, managing; 281
   changing the contents of; 278
   copying into arrays; 280
   modifying; 281
   obtaining elements of; 280
   searching; 280
   trimming; 280
   `Vector` class; 180, 273, **278**, 278, 279, 280, 281
      extended by `Stack`; 282
verifier
   class, as security model component; 27
versioning
   documenting version specification; **218**
   object; **265**
   objects; **265**
   serial version UID, term definition; 265
   `@since` tag; **219**
   `@version` tag; **218**
virtual machine
   term definition; 26
   `VirtualMachineError` class; 376
visibility
   levels of, for members of a class; 9
Void class
   as wrapper class; **297**
void keyword
   meaning in method declarations; 2
   as reserved word; 106
   return value absence indicated by; 12
volatile keyword
   as reserved word; 106
   thread management with; **202**

W

waiting
   See also events; threads
   on events; 188
   for thread completion; **197**
   `wait` (Thread class); **188**, 188, **190**
   `wait/notify` threads mechanism compared with
      Observer/Observable; 291
   `waitFor` (Process class); 327
waking
   threads that have been waiting on an event; 189
walking
   type hierarchy; 304
weeks
   configuring; 347, 348
   `getMinimalDaysInFirstWeek` (Calendar class);
      348
   `oneWeek` example; 345
   `setMinimalDaysInFirstWeek` (Calendar class);
      348
Welsh language
   parsing; 357

WhichChars example; 275, 276, 277
while keyword
    as reserved word; 106
while statement; **144**
    See also control, flow
    do-while compared with; 144
    as loop construction; 4
whitespace characters
    See also character(s); string(s)
    components and handling; 105
    counting; 234
    isWhitespace (Character class); 234
    specifying for tokenizing; 253
    StreamTokenizer class handling; 251
    testing characters for; 299
    whitespaceChars (StreamTokenizer class);
        253
widening
    term definition; 124
Williams, H.H.
    quotation; **150**
Williams, Peter
    quotation; **225**
window
    EventListener interface; 360
windows
    as AWT component; 360
Woolf, Virginia
    quotations; **272, 376**
words
    See also character(s); parsing; string(s); tokens
    breaking strings into; 292
    tokenizing
        specifying for; 253
        TT_WORD constant; 251
    wordChars (StreamTokenizer class); 253
wrappers; **301**
    See also numbers and logical operations; primitive
        types; type(s)
    classes; 60
    integer; **301**
    floating point; **302**
    overview; **296**
        advantages of; **296**
        (chapter); **295**
    use with Observer design pattern; 291
Wright, Frank Lloyd
    quotation; *xv*
writing
    See also I/O; reading
    arrays; 230
    buffered data to a file; 241
    characters; 256, 322
    data; 229
    files, testing if possible to; 268
    from strings; 243
    newLine (BufferedOutputStream class); 241
    objects; 259, 261, 263, 265
    OutputStreamWriter class; 232, 236, **237**

    strings; 256
    StringWriter class; 244
    write
        Buffered class; 241
        OutputStream; 229
        Writer class; 235
    writeBoolean (DataOutput interface); 255
    writeByte (DataOutput interface); 255
    writeBytes (DataOutput interface); 256
    writeChar (DataOutput interface); 255
    writeChars (DataOutput interface); 256
    writeData example; 257
    writeDouble (DataOutput interface); 255
    writeFloat (DataOutput interface); 255
    writeInt (DataOutput interface); 255
    writeLong (DataOutput interface); 255
    writeObject
        BetterName class; 264
        ObjectInputStream class; 263
        ObjectOutputStream class; 259
    writeObject, ObjectOutputStream class; 261
    writer, term definition; 225
    Writer class; **235**
        in type tree for character streams *(figure)*; 232
    writeShort (DataOutput interface); 255
    writeTo (CharArrayWriter class); 243
    writeUTF (DataOutput interface); 255
WWW (World Wide Web)
    Applet class; 361
    URL accessing; 320

X

xor method (BitSet class); 275

Y

yield method (Thread class); 192

Z

Zappa, Frank
    quotations; **91, 373**
zero
    division by, ArithmeticException thrown by;
        128
    remainder by, ArithmeticException thrown by;
        128
Zinsser, William
    quotation; **385**

Special Characters
(sorted in ASCII order)

! (inversion) operator; 132
!= (not equal) operator
    comparing objects; 73
    relational operator; 132
 # (pound sign)
    @see use; 216

$ (dollar sign)
  in identifiers; 106
% (remainder) operator; 9, 128
  compared with IEEERemainder (Math class); 333
& (bitwise AND) operator; *See* bit operations
&& (logical AND) operator; 133
\' (single quote) escape sequence
  Unicode value; 109
() (parentheses)
  overriding operator precedence with; 120
* (asterisk)
  doc comments use; 215
* (multiply) operator; 128
+ (add) operator; 128
  assignment use; 8
  string concatenation use; 16, 121, 130
++ (increment) operator; **131**, 132
  assignment use; 8
+= (plus equals) operator
  assignment use; 8
  operators, +=; **136**
  string concatenation use; 16, 130
- (minus) operator; 128
-- (decrement) operator; **131**, 132
. (dot) operator
  accessing members with; 125
  method invocation; 2, 12, 36
  package vs field and method access use; 26
/ (divide) operator; 128
/** */ comment
  characteristics; 104
// comment
  characteristics; 104
/* */ comment
  characteristics; 104
: defining labels
  case labels; **142**
  default labels; **143**
  statement labels; **146**
; statement terminator; 139
< (less than) operator; 132
<= (less than or equal) operator; 132
<< (left shift) operator; 134
= (equals); 132
  initialization expression use; 4
  initialization, of variables with; 117
  assignment; **136**
  operators, op=; 136
== (equality) operator
  comparing references with; 165
> (greater than) operator; 132
>= (greater than or equals) operator; 132
>> (right shift, sign propagate) operator; 134

>>> (right shift, zero propagate) operator; 134
?: (conditional) operator; **135**, 136
@author tag; **218**
@deprecated tag; **217**
@exception tag; **217**
@param tag; **217**
@return tag; **217**
@see tag; **216**
@since tag; **219**
@version tag; **218**
[] brackets
  arrays
    declared using; 114
    positioning of; 116
\ (backslash) character
  special characters using *(table)*; 380
\\ (backslash backslash) escape sequence
  Unicode value; 109
ddd (octal value) escape sequence
  Unicode value; 109
\" (double quote) escape sequence
  Unicode value; 109
\b (backspace) escape sequence
  Unicode value; 109
\f (form feed) escape sequence
  Unicode value; 109
\n line terminator
  comment styles that ignore; 104
\n (newline) escape sequence
  autoflushing control with; 241
  newLine (BufferedOutputStream class); 241
  readLine (BufferedReader class) acceptance; 241
  Unicode value; 109
  as white space; 105
\r line terminator
  comment styles that ignore; 104
\r (return) escape sequence
  Unicode value; 109
\t (tab) escape sequence
  Unicode value; 109
\u*dddd* escape sequence
  Unicode encoding with; 103
\uu*dddd* escape sequence
  reason for *(footnote)*; 104
^ (exclusive or) operator; 134
{} (braces)
  blocks delimited by; 140
  class member identification by, in Java program; 2
  flow of control blocks delimited by; 7
  methods delimited by; 12
| (inclusive or) operator; 134
|| (logical OR) operator; 133

Colophon

The most basic rule of survival in any situation is "Never look like food."
—Park Ranger

THIS book is printed primarily in 11-point Times. Code text is in Lucida Sans Typewriter at 85% of the size of the surrounding text. A few decorations are in Zapf Dingbats.

The text was written in FrameMaker on several Sun Solaris systems, several Macintosh computers, including laptops, and, for a mercifully brief while, on a 486i laptop computer running Windows 3.1.

The non-ISO Latin-1 text on pages 90, 106, and 260 was created on Macintosh computers using Adobe Illustrator to create encapsulated PostScript drawings of the letters included as pictures in the text. The fonts used are Kourier for Cyrillic, ParsZiba for Persian, Palladam for Tamil, Sambhota for Tibetan, and Ryumin for Kanji.

Code examples were written and compiled on the Sparc systems and then broken into fragments by a Perl script looking for specially formatted comments. Source fragments and generated output were inserted in the book by another Perl script.

NOTE TO TRANSLATORS

The fonts in this book have been chosen carefully. The font for code, when mixed with body text, has the same "x" height and roughly the same weight and "color." Code in text looks even—if you read quickly it can seem like body text, but it is nonetheless easy to tell that code text *is* different. Please use the fonts that we have used (we would be happy to help you locate any that you do not have) or choose other code and body fonts that are balanced in the same way.

There's not much to be said about the period
except that most writers don't reach it soon enough.
—William Zinsser

"Mail Myself to You," (page 295) words and music by Woody Guthrie.
TRO 1962 (renewed), 1963 (renewed) by Ludlow Music, Inc. New York, NY. Used by permission.

The Addison-Wesley Java™ Series

Ken Arnold · James Gosling
The Java™ Programming Language Second Edition
The Java Series
ISBN 0-201-31006-6

Mary Campione · Kathy Walrath
The Java™ Tutorial Second Edition
Object-Oriented Programming for the Internet
The Java Series OFFICIAL
...from the Source
ISBN 0-201-31007-4

Campione · Walrath · Huml · Tutorial Team
The Java™ Tutorial Continued
The Rest of the JDK™
The Java Series
...from the Source
ISBN 0-201-48558-3

Patrick Chan
The Java™ Developers ALMANAC 1999
The Java Series
...from the Source
ISBN 0-201-43298-6

Patrick Chan · Rosanna Lee
The Java™ Class Libraries Second Edition, Volume 2
java.applet java.awt java.beans
The Java Series
...from the Source
ISBN 0-201-31003-1

Patrick Chan · Rosanna Lee · Douglas Kramer
The Java™ Class Libraries Second Edition, Volume 1
java.io java.lang java.math
java.net java.text java.util
The Java Series OFFICIAL
...from the Source
ISBN 0-201-31002-3

Patrick Chan · Rosanna Lee · Douglas Kramer
The Java™ Class Libraries Second Edition, Volume 1
Supplement for the Java 2 Platform Standard Edition, v1.2
The Java Series
...from the Source
ISBN 0-201-48552-4

James Gosling · Bill Joy · Guy Steele
The Java™ Language Specification
The Java Series
...from the Source
ISBN 0-201-63451-1

James Gosling · Frank Yellin · The Java Team
The Java™ Application Programming Interface, Volume 1
Core Packages
The Java Series
...from the Source
ISBN 0-201-63453-8

James Gosling · Frank Yellin · The Java Team
The Java™ Application Programming Interface, Volume 2
Window Toolkit and Applets
The Java Series
...from the Source
ISBN 0-201-63459-7

Li Gong
Inside Java™ 2 Platform Security
Architecture, API Design, and Implementation
The Java Series
...from the Source
ISBN 0-201-31000-7

Jonni Kanerva
The Java™ FAQ
The Java Series
...from the Source
ISBN 0-201-63456-2

Doug Lea
Concurrent Programming in Java™ Second Edition
Design Principles and Patterns
The Java Series
...from the Source
ISBN 0-201-31009-0

Sheng Liang
The Java™ Native Interface
Programmer's Guide and Specification
The Java Series
...from the Source
ISBN 0-201-32577-2

Tim Lindholm · Frank Yellin
The Java™ Virtual Machine Specification Second Edition
The Java Series
...from the Source
ISBN 0-201-43294-3

Henry Sowizral · Kevin Rushforth · Michael Deering
The Java™ 3D API Specification
The Java Series
...from the Source
ISBN 0-201-32576-4

Kathy Walrath · Mary Campione
The JFC Swing Tutorial
A Guide to Constructing GUIs
The Java Series
...from the Source
ISBN 0-201-43321-4

White · Fisher · Cattell · Hamilton · Hapner
JDBC™ API Tutorial and Reference, Second Edition
Universal Data Access for the Java™ 2 Platform
The Java Series
...from the Source
ISBN 0-201-43328-1

Please see our web site (http://www.awl.com/cseng/javaseries)
for more information on these titles.